D1555580

A SPLURCH IN THE KISSER

Wesleyan Film

A series from Wesleyan University Press
Edited by Jeanine Basinger

The WESLEYAN FILM series takes
a back-to-basics approach to the art
of cinema. Books in the series deal
with the formal, the historical, and
the cultural—putting a premium on
visual analysis, close readings, and
an understanding of the history of
Hollywood and international cinema,
both artistically and industrially. The
volumes are rigorous, critical, and
accessible both to academics and to lay
readers with a serious interest in film.

Series editor Jeanine Basinger,
Corwin-Fuller Professor of Film Studies
at Wesleyan University and Founder/
Curator of the Wesleyan Cinema
Archives, is the author of such landmark
books as *The World War II Combat Film:
Anatomy of a Genre, A Woman's View: How
Hollywood Spoke to Women, 1930–1960,
Silent Stars,* and *The Star Machine.*

Anthony Mann
New and Expanded Edition
by Jeanine Basinger

It's the Pictures That Got Small
Hollywood Film Stars on 1950s Television
Christine Becker

The Films of Samuel Fuller
If You Die, I'll Kill You!
by Lisa Dombrowski

Physical Evidence
Selected Film Criticism
by Kent Jones

Action Speaks Louder
Violence, Spectacle, and the
American Action Movie
Revised and Expanded Edition
by Eric Lichtenfeld

Hollywood Ambitions
Celebrity in the Movie Age
by Marsha Orgeron

A Splurch in the Kisser
The Movies of Blake Edwards
by Sam Wasson

SAM WASSON

A Splurch in the Kisser

THE MOVIES OF BLAKE EDWARDS

WESLEYAN UNIVERSITY PRESS Middletown, Connecticut

Published by
Wesleyan University Press,
Middletown, CT 06459
www.wesleyan.edu/wespress

Library of Congress
Cataloging-in-Publication Data
Wasson, Sam.
A splurch in the kisser:
    the movies of Blake Edwards / by Sam Wasson.
    p. cm. — (Wesleyan film)
Includes filmography.
Includes bibliographical references and index.
ISBN 978-0-8195-6915-8 (cloth : alk. paper)
1. Edwards, Blake, 1922–   Criticism and
interpretation. I. Title.
PN1998.3.E33W37 2009
791.4302'33092—dc22   2009026514

To

(in order of appearance)

JEANINE BASINGER

and

DAVID FREEMAN

The struggle is less to hold onto our fantasies then to let go of them, to see the world truly and crazily, and master ourselves by surmounting it. Out of this struggle, Edwards has fashioned some of the funniest and truest work to emerge from the declining years of Hollywood artistry.
—Myron Meisel

In 1993, the combined decision of the Directors' and the Writers' Guilds gave the Preston Sturges Award to Edwards. There was something so macabre, inappropriate, and inevitable in that decision—somehow the decline of Hollywood had been encapsulated.
—David Thomson

CONTENTS

ACKNOWLEDGMENTS

Loneliness, anxiety, doubt, financial crises, lower back pain, and marked sexual depreciation aside, writing a book can be a joyous experience. Those who know what I'm talking about know what I'm talking about because they've heard me talk about it so much, and what's more, when I would get nutty with apologies the morning after, they even convinced me that they had enjoyed my company throughout. Whether by movies, humor, or saintly patience, these Capraesque crusaders have plied me from depths, filled me up with gin, and cheered me back to life with the resolve of Jefferson Smith in the great filibuster scene of *Mr. Smith Goes to Washington*. For all that (and more) I would shower them with hyacinths and prostrate my naked body at their feet, but not everyone loves hyacinths. Instead, I will list them here and hope they know I mean it when I write: I am lucky to have you. They are: Mom, Dad (parents); Sophie (sister); Jack (for everyday); Jake (for a long time); Max (for brilliance); the Hoffmans: Lisa, Dustin, Becky, Max, Ali, Jenna, Seamus, and James and Phyllis Chanes (for making things a little more *Fanny and Alexander*); Andrea Martin (he chose you); Bob Dolman (who knows what a carcass is for); Ann and Mark Goldblatt (for their love, cuisine, and their Synagogue du Cinema); Sarah Shepard (with whom it is always midnight in Manhattan on a Saturday in 1927); Steve and Lynn Shepard (*Portnoy's Complaint* et al.); Alex Horwitz ("Bernaise?"); Jocelyn Medawar (who reminds me of everything good); Marquart (finding alternatives to Zoloft since 1998); Lynne Littman (sorry about *Barry Lyndon*); Judy Gingold (Nora Charles lives!); Lisa Petrazzolo (Zolo); Robin Swicord (George Sanders, the office on Main St.); Travers Huff (who plays "The Good Life," and who plays "Invitation"); Ed Sikov (this book's father); Sara Rutenberg (this book's mother); SCBWI (banquet); Amalia Ellison (that old thing); Kate Eickmeyer (bang); Parker Smathers (who kept it alive); Lisa Dombrowski (who showed me how); naturally David Halpern (folks, I have an agent who loves William Powell); and in a big, big way, Eric Levy (editor/mensch, for his unending confidence, intellect, and tenacity).

And then there are those in the field who gave an opinion, or looked over my shoulder, or offered a point of view on Blake Edwards and/or the process of making a book about him. For the assistance of Sandra Archer,

William Peter Blatty, David and Julia Chasman, Gary Copeland, Stephanie Elliot, Nina Foch, Barbara Hall, Molly Haskell, Leah Ketcham-Antonio, Dale Launer, Eric Lichtenfeld, Linda Lichter, Howard and Buddy Mandelbaum, Paul Mazursky, Brian Meecham, Joanna Ney, Michael Ovitz, Jonathan Reynolds, Kathy Robbins, Andrew Sarris, Leslie Starr, Suzanna Tamminen, Faye Thompson, Angela Turnbull, Helen Wheeler, and Patrick Williams, I offer a happy and grateful thank you.

And for their knowledge of my subject, I am much obliged to Carmen Garcia, Jennifer Edwards, Blake Edwards, and Julie Andrews. I had many thrills.

And finally, I bend a knee to the ground for Jeanine Basinger and David Freeman, to whom this book is dedicated. Without Jeanine, I would not have written it, and without David, I would not have wanted to.

A SPLURCH IN THE KISSER

MATTERS OF INTRODUCTION

Before we get to Blake Edwards, let's agree that if only they had met, James Agee and Norma Desmond would have enjoyed the hell out of each other. Just think of them, blinds drawn, monkey dead, sharing their third pitcher of vodka-something and talking about how it used to be.

"You *are* big, Miss Desmond. It's the pictures that got small."

"You took the words right out of my mouth."

"They're dead. They're finished," he says, filling their glasses. "There was a time in this business when they had the eyes of the whole wide world."

"Yes, I completely—"

"But that wasn't good enough for them. Oh, no! They had to have the ears of the world, too. So they opened up their big mouths and out came talk, talk, talk!"

"Are you married?"

"Look at them in the front offices, the masterminds! They took the idols and smashed them! The Chaplins, the Keatons, the Lloyds! And who have we got now? Some nobodies!"

Luckily, the meeting never occurred. If it had, James might have ended up face down in her swimming pool without ever having written this:

The best of comedies these days hand out plenty of titters and once in a while it is possible to achieve a yowl without overstraining. Even those who have never seen anything better must occasionally have the feeling, as they watch the current run or, rather, trickle of screen comedy, that they are having to make a little cause for laughter go an awfully long way. And anyone who has watched screen comedy of the past ten or fifteen years is bound to realize that it has quietly but steadily deteriorated. As for those happy atavists who remember silent comedy in its heyday and the bellylaughs and boffos that went with it, they have something close to an absolutely standard by which to measure the deterioration.

He's not finished.

To put it unkindly, the only thing wrong with screen comedy today is that it takes place on a screen which talks. Because it talks, the only comedians who ever mastered the screen cannot work, for they cannot combine their comic styles with talk.[1]

This excerpt from the article "Comedy's Greatest Era" was printed in *Life* magazine on September 3, 1949. By that time, certain comedies of Lubitsch, Hawks, Cukor, Capra, and Sturges—films today's lamenters of comedy ache for—had already been released. Screwball skid marks were everywhere; *Baby* had been brought up, and Preston Sturges, his great moment long since past, was having serious trouble with *The Beautiful Blonde from Bashful Bend*. The second golden age was dying before his eyes, but Agee was too busy grieving for the death of slapstick to sit shivah for anything else.

"Preston Sturges," he wrote, "has made brilliant, satirical comedies, but his pictures are smart, nervous comedies merely italicized with slapstick." Today, the observation is tantamount to sacrilege (Sturges *imperfect?*), but Agee's point shouldn't go dishonored: though he populated his world with rubber bodies, Preston was first and foremost a dialogue artist, and used slapstick primarily as garnish for the meat. There are, of course, exceptions; think of Veronica Lake crashing into the backyard pool (*Sullivan's Travels*), Henry Fonda by way of Barbara Stanwyck's chokehold (*The Lady Eve*), or the spastic combustibility of Betty Hutton and Eddie Bracken (*The Miracle of Morgan's Creek*).

But let us be clear: my intention is not to denigrate dialogue. Talk is wonderful, brilliant even, and indeed most of the greatest comedies Hollywood has ever produced have been spoken ones, but, as Agee reminds us, there is too often a casualty. He calls it slapstick, but it also goes by the name visual comedy. It consists, quite simply, of jokes we can *see*. These are gags. And as pictures of motion they do what motion pictures do best.

FECAL MATTERS

Gag. The word itself is dumb. It *sounds* dumb. *Gag*. Like the sound a baby makes. It's also ugly. The dorsal consonant G, first at the beginning and then at end, comes up like mud in the throat, and that A in between is just plain flat. Speaking it feels like talking with a mouthful of tuna fish. What's more, as "a thing, typically a piece of cloth, put in or over a person's mouth to prevent speaking or crying out," a gag isn't especially endearing, nor is it in its more figurative incarnation, "a restriction on freedom of speech or the dissemination of information" (these from the Oxford American Dictionary). And let's not forget the intransitive, "to suffer a throat spasm that makes swallowing or breathing difficult," and its etymological grandparent "gaggen," the Middle English verb "to strangle" (those from Merriam-Webster). So yes, any way you cut it, "gag" hurts.

Whether it's by unforeseen staircase, slamming door, pothole, collision, thin ice, or frying pan, the gag is likely to inflict damage. If we find ourselves cringing before the laugh it's because we can anticipate the moment of horrible impact as that rogue flowerpot edges out the window, slips, and lands on an unsuspecting pedestrian. *Ouch*. Even the term "slapstick" is painful. When an actual slap stick—a clublike device composed of twin wooden slates—is whacked (on someone), it produces a loud slapping noise that makes the smack seem a lot harder (and funnier) than it actually was. And this is what James Agee, a high-minded literary man, wanted to see Preston Sturges, a high-minded literary man, do more of? Didn't he realize that broad comedy was for teenagers and idiots?

When sound came to motion pictures at the end of the 1920s, talk became commercially viable—more than that, it became fashionable. Silence was on its way out, and that meant the days of gag-based humor were yesterday's news. Now Hollywood required a new kind of writer, urbane scenarists who specialized in words, not vaudevilles. East Coast literati were exported by the trainload; Faulkner, Fitzgerald, Dorothy Parker, Odets—those with an established intellectual cachet—helped theater and literature make their way onto the screen, turning what was regularly considered lowbrow entertainment into legitimate, cosmopolitan art. And because physical comedy was no longer essential to convey humor (hence Agee's lament), corporeal comedians became living relics of *autres temps*. No matter how hilarious, Stan and Ollie would be less suitable to the new "sophisticated" comedy than Noel and Cole. Now the articulate elite—Sturges, Samson Raphaelson, Ben Hecht—trumped the clowns, and wit became synonymous with intelligence.

Slapstick, meanwhile, assumed cruder connotations: if verbal ability is an indicator of intellectual capacity, then clowns are the domain of infantile minds. One need only think of the term "dumb show" to be reminded of why apologies must follow the thrill of the custard flung. And the stigma still exists. Even today, slapstick remains a low-minded word. But why? Is there something inherently second class in physical comedy? Can the pratfall, by virtue of its unrefined implications, ever be grown up?

According to anthropologist Ernest Becker, this persistent distinction between mind and body—between "highbrow" and "lowbrow"—has its origins not in the transition to sound, but in the most basic dilemma of all mankind. In his book *The Denial of Death*, Becker argues that the central project of the human being is to deny, as the title suggests, all evidence of his impending decay. To do this, he will try literally everything, and even risk his own sanity if it will grant him the ignorant illusion of, as he calls it, "individuality within finitude." Man's denial says that he has a mind that allows him to transcend his animal limitations. Of course, this is the greatest insanity of all, and try as we might to disprove it, the fact of death, the fate that links all animals, is irrevocable. So what do we do? We banish it. And we begin with the eradication of carnality.

The body, which cannot be trumped by man's capacity for self-consciousness (his individuality in nature), is buried away in humiliation. Becker writes,

> Nature's values are bodily values, human values are mental values, and though they take the loftiest flights they are built upon excrement, impossible without it, always brought back to it. As Montaigne puts it, on the highest throne in the world man sits on his ass.[2]

Within this conceptual framework, we can better understand the tendency towards the division of humor. The cerebral joke, the witty and gorgeous fantasy of human ingenuity, is Becker's denial. (Verbal comedy by its very definition falls into this category. After all, which other animals can talk?) Even if we're joking about feces, it's our singularly human capacity for speech that makes the crack possible.

When it comes to Ernst Lubitsch or Woody Allen or any of the cinema's great dialogicians, the aforementioned "mental values" and "loftiest flights" are combined to create a superhuman dream world of nonstop verbal brilliance. Though both enjoy diversions into the strata of silent-era physical antics (don't forget *Ninotchka* and *Sleeper*), Lubitsch and Allen (like Sturges) are first and foremost masters of a dialogue-driven cinema. In Becker's terms, they are death-deniers at their most sublime. Their comedy presents a vision of humanity independent of nature, and though they may even address mortality head on (think *To Be or Not to Be* or *Hannah and Her Sisters)*, they do so in the most antideterministic way possible: through speech. On the flipside is physical comedy, a universal predicament with a frightening mandate: we humans are flesh and bones, humiliating shitters and fuckers who, despite what we'd like to believe, are existentially susceptible to the frying pan, flying brick, or gangplank that whacks Oliver Hardy in the face. It's brutal, unrefined, even (at times) disgusting, but it is as accurate a depiction of mankind's bodily crisis as Woody's neuroses are of mankind's intellectual one. Taken together, they describe the sometimes tragedy/sometimes comedy of human dualism.

What I'm saying is this: if we intend to fully examine the challenges to our existence, we must accept a world in which physical comedy and verbal comedy are equally viable. This requires us to unite bodily "lowbrow" and mental "highbrow" in a fusion of silent-era slapstick and shimmering wit. From this union an advanced comic vision of the existential paradox will emerge, inciting a distinctly twentieth-century vaudeville that, in restoring our dumb-show roots (both cinematic and developmental), will deliver us to a comic consciousness free of denial. Along the way, we must remember that beneath our civilizing veneer, we're nothing but morons, susceptible not only to physical calamity, but to laughter of that particular kind—unconscious laughter—the one that comes not from the brain, but straight out of the gut. Agee called it the boffo, and by 1949, he was desperate for a good one. To him, I would say this: if silent comedy has disappeared from the movies it's not because Sturges missed an opportunity, or because Billy Wilder was preoccupied with his best-ever dialogue, but because the gag—that dumb-sounding word—was never at ease with the problems of modern-day consciousness. Never, that is, until Blake Edwards. Unfortunately for Agee, physical determinism got the better of him in 1955, a month before Blake's first comedy was released.

CRITICAL MATTERS

"I think a lot of my comedy can be compared to blind-siding, which is a football term," Blake Edwards says.

> A quarterback will be looking to throw a pass downfield when all of a sudden, he'll get nailed by a tackler he hasn't seen. Suddenly, he's wiped out, and I think that's my job—to sort of blind-side people in order to shake them up and make them think. I prefer to do it in the comedic arena, because it makes it more palatable and easier to digest.

When you deliver a message very heavily, it becomes preachy and too many people just lock up. I much prefer to deliver a sermon through laughter."[3]

The football analogy is a good one: it identifies the physical ingredient in the comic transformation, and also the ideological one. For in Blake's world, we never see it coming, usually because we never see it *properly*. What things appear to be in his films is rarely, if ever, what they really are. Masks are everywhere, deceit is rampant, and pretense abounds. In fact, the whole notion of blindsiding is so pervasive in Edwards' work, it informs his movies inside and out, in both form and content, doing to story and character what it does to genre and style. Take the gag, for instance, which works like the tackler, nailing the quarterback who thinks the truth is manifest in what he sees. As a result, the idea of visual perception becomes the primary Edwardian fascination. Time and again, voyeurs of all kinds are walloped for trusting the veracity of what appears before them onscreen. Audiences and performers are also subject to the crises of appearance, as are the creative artists that devote their lives to presentation, because what is presentation after all, but a mask that disguises authenticity? Or are they one and the same? In Blake Edwards' films, it is difficult to say.

The appearance/reality dialectic is conducive to the director's comic mechanism, in which slapstick does the blindsiding, but what of his non-comedies, pictures like *Days of Wine and Roses*, *Experiment in Terror*, *Wild Rovers*, and *The Tamarind Seed* (even *Breakfast at Tiffany's*)? Watching these films we must remember that Edwards' cinema, indeed his vision of the world, is not confined to slapstick, which means that we must expand the Edwardian lexicon to include more than gags alone. Thus, in discussing these films, it is not my intention to name and date the rainbows of gags in the Edwards arsenal, or to dutifully Dewey Decimal them, or to catalogue them alphabetically by subject, or trace them back to Chaplin and Co., who can be traced back to vaudeville, which can be traced back to Shakespeare, and to the Greeks, and little amoebae doing pratfalls in the big black. No, no, not here. This is not a book about slapstick. It's a book about Blake Edwards' movies, and slapstick is only one piece of that custard pie.

The other pieces, all involved with the phenomena of false perception, surface in even his weakest and lesser-known films, some rightfully neglected (*A Fine Mess*), some criminally so (*What Did You Do in the War*,

1. *The Party* (1968) A hard day at work for Blake Edwards.
(Courtesy of the Academy of Motion Picture Arts and Sciences)

Daddy?). In these works, problems of identity—the true aspects of anything —become the director's chief concern. Gender is malleable, reality is changeable, and the very idea of the filmed image is thrown into question. That question, "What is this *really*?" applies to Edwards' recurring use of shallow depth of field, his perpetually self-reforming banter in dialogue, the presentation of his musical numbers, and his challenges to conformist approaches to stereotypes, sex, love, and marriage. As we will see, even the Hollywood cinema itself is deconstructed by Blake's unrelenting refusal to accept the dominion of any single reality.

Much of the criticism Edwards has received over the years—and there's been a lot of it—can be traced back to this investment in morphology. As a director of comedy, drama, comedy-drama, musical, musical-drama, drama-slapstick, spy films, live-action cartoons, combat pictures, and any combination thereof, Blake Edwards' career posed and poses difficulties to those out for quick and easy labels. (Not surprisingly, this is an idea at the moral heart of so many of his movies.) If we are to consider Edwards, as so many have, as a director of comedies, then the other films, the ones that can't be categorized along those lines, become difficult to deal with. Those out to find comedy in these pictures will dismiss them as failures, and those committed to cinematic regularity will have no choice but to exempt them from what they believe to be the director's auteurist impulses. Of course, the opposite is true. Any artist obsessed with the universal changeability of all things, will not excuse himself from scrutiny, and so Blake Edwards, as such an artist, will undergo a lifelong process of reinvention, in both form and philosophy.

And in defense of the skeptics, the results are mixed.

If Edwards has not achieved the place he deserves in the American film pantheon, it is in part because his fifty-film career has had more than its share of commercial and critical disasters. "I don't know who I really am in terms of my work," Blake wrote, "and probably never will totally."

> I keep discovering [he says], I keep making mistakes and doing a flop here and a flop there and all of a sudden a hit comes along and I say let's take a look at that, and let's take a look at the flop and all of the pain and the anguish that go along with the real highs of success. It's all a big kind of experiment for me.[4]

Sometimes the experiments don't pay off. The reasons why vary from film to film, but quite often it's because one is apt to confuse financial with artistic failure. Again and again, with good reason and bad, Blake has bombed—and bombed hard. But what makes these bombs fascinating, both in terms of their relationship to changes in Hollywood commerce and Blake's own artistic growing pains, is that they are evidence of a director in a unique place in the history of American film, that is, one caught in the transition from the classical studio days to the present horrors of conglomerate supremacy. Blake was a guinea pig at a threshold, struggling not only with the major paradigm shift of the New Hollywood and all of the cultural, aesthetic, and fiscal revolutions therein, but with the par-for-the-course predicaments of personal filmmaking that every commercial director faces.

Yes, Hollywood has been bad to Blake, but fair's fair: with a career encompassing more than forty feature films and countless hours of TV and radio, Blake Edwards has made his own share of mistakes. Often redundant, often unfunny, often painfully unfunny, certain moments in these films are unquestionably awkward (and that's putting it mildly). Even Janet Maslin, one of Blake's steadfast proponents, concedes the point. On the occasion of Blind Date's (perhaps undeserved) commercial success, she wrote,

> With a career that spans 30 years and is surely one of the most check-ered in Hollywood history, Mr. Edwards has yet to establish anything like a loyal following. And for good reason: no Edwards film, however entertaining, has ever failed to make its audience wince here and there, with the wrong actor, the wrong song, the too-garish setting or the too-dumb gag.

In her wisdom, Maslin concludes, "Comedy like this, never really fashionable in the first place, can't even go out of style."[5] But is this praise or an admission of defeat?

Pauline Kael opted for the latter. S.O.B., she said, was "snide in a square, unfunny way"; The Party was "too long for its one-note jokes, and often too obvious to be really funny," and she saw in Victor/Victoria "the crudest setups and the moldiest, most cynical dumb jokes."[6] And she was not alone: The critic David Thomson, quoted in this book's epigraph, was none too pleased with the combined decision of the Directors' and Writers' Guilds to honor Edwards with the prestigious Preston Sturges Award.[7] (Needless to say, both Guilds disagreed.) George Morris, a longtime Edwardian, specu-lated that perhaps the dissenters thought the movies just plain shallow. In a collection of soundbites called "Lost in Gloss or Cineaste Maudit," he wrote, "Edwards' detractors acknowledge his formal skill but deplore the absence of profundity in his movies. They are too slick, too glossy. And how can any director be taken seriously whose admirers point to a film like Darling Lili—a Julie Andrews musical—as his masterpiece?"[8] Morris brings up a good point. Has Camp Edwards rallied behind the wrong neglected masterpieces? Have they rallied behind any masterpieces? Is Breakfast at

Tiffany's a masterpiece?* Is *The Pink Panther*? And who belongs to Camp Edwards, anyway?

Andrew Sarris, for one. Well, kind of. As of 1963, Sarris deemed Blake worthy only of cult recognition: "Despite occasional lapses in taste and increasingly frequent bursts of visual flamboyance, Edwards confirms on a minor scale what Lubitsch established on a major scale, and that is the correlation between buoyancy and conviction." There is optimism here, but also a heavy strain of ambivalence. Had Sarris waited a year longer to publish his legendary survey of American cinema, he would have seen *The Pink Panther*, Blake's watershed film, and the picture that drew Edwards, as Sarris would write in 1968, "from the ranks of commissioned directors" to a maker of personal works "who has got some of his biggest laughs out of jokes that are too gruesome for most horror films." He continues,

> For a time Edwards seemed to be following in the footsteps of Billy Wilder, with somewhat more visual style and somewhat less verbal crackle. But their paths have diverged. Wilder is a curdled Lubitsch, romanticism gone sour, 78 rpm played at 45, an old wordling from Vienna perpetually sneering at Hollywood as it engulfs him. Edwards is more a new breed, post-Hitler, post-Freud, post-sick-joke, with all the sticky sentimentality of electronic music. The world he celebrates is cold, heartless, and inhuman, but the people in it manage a marginal integrity and individuality.[9]

This entry from *The American Cinema* appears in the section "The Far Side of Paradise" with Sarris' other silver medal awardees, those who "fall just short of the Pantheon either because of a fragmentation of their personal vision or because of disruptive career problems." Considering the debacle over *Darling Lili* had not yet occurred (it was only months away), Sarris' placement of Edwards must have been in response to a body of work that seemed promising, but was ultimately inconsistent. Having only just begun his mature period of work, Blake had not yet produced enough film to give Sarris the firm footing he needed to make any definitive claim. Nonetheless—and here is where Sarris demonstrates his true affection—Blake was categorized alongside those whose pictures had already withstood the test of time. Other "Far Siders" included Capra, Cukor, Minnelli, Preminger, Ray, Sirk and Sturges, fellows among whom Blake Edwards was the least

* No.

experienced by far. As early as 1968, Chaplin, Keaton, and Lubitsch were the only comedy directors Sarris placed above him.

Today, Edwards is the highest ranked living director in Sarris' book, though whether he owes this distinction to good filmmaking or good doctoring must be determined on a critic-by-critic bias—I mean basis. With no hard feelings for those physicians, Peter Lehman and William Luhr have devoted two whole volumes to the director's filmography. *Blake Edwards* and *Blake Edwards Volume 2: Returning to the Scene*, published in 1980 and 1989, are pioneering attempts to bring Edwards-study to the forefront of film criticism. Their work—crucial, unprecedented, and informative— spanned the length of Edwards' career from his earliest pictures all the way through *Sunset*, the film he was shooting at the time of their final chapter. Until now, the double-volume was the only major text devoted to the director, and included comprehensive and semi-comprehensive analyses of many of his most remarkable movies. Lehman and Luhr are any artist's ideal audience; they are intelligent fans, devoted critics, and have illuminated a personal body of work that, in the dark days before them, was virtually unlit. If ever members of an ambivalent audience of *Gunn* sought to consider refreshing their interpretation, they might turn to these co-authors, the first colonists to arrive on Planet Edwards.

But that was over fifteen years ago. Since then, Edwards has produced several new films, some of which cast new light on the films preceding them, and invite us to consider revising our analyses of his work and career up to that point. *Skin Deep*, for instance, a film that was at the time of its release glossed over as more of the same, can be viewed retrospectively as a guidepost through Blake's entire career. As a melancholy testament of lifelong fascinations both cinematic and emotional, the movie reminds us of what we might have forgotten after reviewing an *oeuvre* consisting of over forty films, that is, Blake Edwards, above all else, is a man for whom slapstick is not only the central expression of his medium, but also the metaphysical terms of his reality (see Ernest Becker). Lehman and Luhr laid noble groundwork with other intentions in mind, and, perhaps due to the importance of their subject, were generous when they might have been hesitant.

However, if Blake Edwards is to be delivered to his rightful status as one of Hollywood's greatest directors of comedy, then our examinations must be critically forthright in every aspect. That necessitates a harmony of doubt *and* the benefit of it. For in giving the benefit of the doubt, we open ourselves to greater understanding, and therefore, greater benefit—that is the benefit of the benefit of the doubt. There is also much to be gained from doubt alone, which is why challenging even the most commonly accepted truths will sharpen our sensibilities and, in turn, deepen our appreciation of Edwards' achievements. In this way, skepticism and charity are for the critic equal parts of love. This book is intended to be a balance of both.

LAUGHING MATTERS

In 1944, Blake Edwards went to a matinee revival of one of Larry Semon's old silent comedies.* It changed his life.

> I not only found myself in complete, utter hysterics, but I looked around me and there was an audience as one screaming with laughter. . . And I thought, "These people are laughing harder at this than anything turned out in Hollywood by today's standards. They're screaming. Look at them."[10]

Finding the proper modern idiom for an old mode of comedy is arguably the central challenge of Edwards' career—call it his auteurist destination. There are others, of course, but his greatest, most enduring achievements owe their success to the articulation of this goal, to answering the question, "How does one make slapstick relevant today?" Suffice to say, most of this book is devoted to explaining exactly how this is accomplished, which means fully explicating it here would be a bit premature. However, there are some underlying principles of Edwardian slapstick that ought to be outlined before they are explored in any great detail.

Let's begin with the bedrock of physical comedy: the gag.

The gag is a unit of slapstick. It takes many different forms, ranging from physical stunts to visual punch lines (often called sight gags), and, as we have seen, dates back to the earliest days of film comedy when the medium's very definition (silent) required humor be received optically. On their own, gags are vaudevilles in miniature: self-sustained routines committed to entertainment, with no obligation to context. When they are

---

* It's a shame not many remember Larry Semon. He may have been a little-faced man in a little derby hat, but he was truly gargantuan in slapstick. His style, full of chases, mud, goo, and toppling cans of paint, harkens back to his early days as a cartoonist, when nothing was impossible and bigger was most definitely better.

placed within the context of a narrative, however, they acquire relationships to character, theme, and story that demand more of them than pure comic value alone. Certain lesser Marx Brothers films, for instance, are often criticized for their failure to make the transition from vaudeville. What this means is that the gags in question, no matter how brilliant in conception, lack narrative purpose. And it's true: how often have we stood by as Groucho, Chico, or Harpo performed fabulous and intricate spectaculars that serve no cinematic or narrative function? We may find ourselves on the floor, gasping in hysteria, clutching at our friends for support, but on our way out of the theater, certain questions arise, namely, "What did that [insert slapstick routine] have to do with *anything*?" If we are content to apply the term "zany" as praise enough, then we are depriving serious gag work of the attention it deserves. But what is "serious" gag work? Does it exist? Could it? Should it?

There is a danger in trying to "redeem" low comedy by recommending it to existentialists (as I have done), feminists, Marxists, or other ists on whom the gag builds its philosophical supports. It should be said right off that gags are funny for many reasons, and though they may meddle with death and socialism (these discussions still to come), they get their bang from just plain fun. Attempting to elevate them is, in a sense, apologizing for an inherent flaw—this I do not want to do. As popular comic devices, gags are worthy of scholarly regard whether or not they embrace ontological content. That said, truly great slapstick gags, the ones that have bang *and* brains—those exemplary of Blake Edwards' best work—take apparent silliness and add to it something that makes pies and banana peels not just hilarious, but hilarious plus x. To accomplish this Beckerian blending of high and low, the gag must be dramatized; it must carry consistent expositional heft. Only then will it take on ideological consequence. So how does it do it? What is x?

To find out, let's take a brief tour of Edwards' career, from "Blake Begins" to "Blake Bows."

The first x is bound to theme. Edwards' earliest experiments in physical/visual comedy, those discussed in (although not confined to) the chapter "Blake Begins," are consistently paired with an idea shared by each film, which amounts to a kind of social equilibrium demanding, through slapstick, that pride and arrogance be subordinated. Whether it's a humiliating situation designed to embarrass a blustering tyrant (He Laughed Last), pretentious snob (Mister Cory), aging lothario (This Happy Feeling), or uptight prude (*The Perfect Furlough*), some of Edwards' most effective (and renowned) gags draw strength from these power reversals. In such instances, when false authority is undone by physical comedy, slapstick and justice join forces to right the wrong. We laugh not simply at the gag, but because the gag has come at the expense of the right person, the person who deserves the humiliation (gag + x). A kind of narrative responsibility—in this case, thematic consistency—has enhanced the effects of the comedy.

Splurch, the word I will use to describe this phenomenon, refers to the gag's ability to violate its subject's dignity, to cut him down to size. Quite often, in fact *always*, those in Blake Edwards' movies who ascend by way of socially or philosophically unethical means are wide open to a good splurching. As in the examples listed above, these can include gangsters, snooty headwaiters, and the sexually repressed. In fact, anyone who has committed an Edwardian crime will receive a pie in the face. And that's what a splurch is—the sound a dessert makes when it lands. A little footnote in Mack Sennett's autobiography, *The King of Comedy*, reveals the word's etymology: "Splurch: a technical and onomatopoeic word coined by Mack Sennett; applies only to the effect of sudden custard in the puss."[11] Sennett, father of the Keystone Cops and genuine slapstick aficionado, saw the rise of many a silent clown, and pioneered, as he put it, this "wish-fulfilling, universal idea" that "exasperated dignity and the discombombulation of authority "[12] deserve a kick in the pants. And so, when we speak of the splurch, it is with respect to a certain thematic tendency—the opposition to false social/political/intellectual/sexual authority that begins in Edwards' first films and continues on through his last.

Let's take it one step further: if a splurch is diegetically effective it will result in a change in character. When the proverbial pie in the face becomes instructive to the subject, either instantly or over time, we might say that the gag's narrative responsibility has extended to include character development. In these cases of lessons learned, outbursts of physical comedy are visual externalizations of internal processes. In "Blake Blossoms" we will see Edwards' involvement in character-based slapstick deepen to include this type of splurch, which makes emotional and intellectual epiphany (other xs) a matter of pies and pratfalls. (In fact, the splurch becomes so psychologically loaded, that in *The Party*, one of Edwards' most successfully mannered films, it outmodes dialogue almost entirely.)

The chapter "Blake Booms" adds drama to the previous xs, theme and character. In these films, Blake's best, slapstick becomes essential not only to Edwardian ideology and individual psyches, but to the very fabric of the story. Remove a gag from 10 or S.O.B., for instance, and the film's events become unmotivated and incomprehensible (unlike certain Marx Brothers' pictures). What results is an inimitable equation between physical derangement and narrative gesticulation, such that gag + x = story. In these films, slapstick attains the highest degree of dramaturgical muscle in American film since Chaplin, and is presented with the greatest of stylistic sophistication. Edwards speaks to this point in an article for *Cahiers du Cinéma* entitled "Sophisticated Naturalism," revealing the central device of his picture making. Let it be a guide:

> To think that slapstick and sophistication are insoluble is not true at all. I think that there's a wonderful kind of thing that happens with the two. It takes slapstick a step up and it takes sophistication a step down and they kind of meet. There's a great element of humor that takes place. . . When presented in a sophisticated way the sort of onus is taken off.[13]

This brings us to the fourth x. It is a cinematic technique—a trademark style—that heightens comic effect. The specifics of Edwardian style will be discussed in detail throughout the book, but for the purposes of this introduction it should be stated that when mastered, the elements of Edwards' cinema—angle, cutting, lighting, composition, etc.—weave story and comedy into a strand so constant, the enhancement of one is identical to the enhancement of the other.

The four other aggressively alliterative chapters of this book—"Blake Builds," "Blake Burns," "Blake Breaks," "Blake Bows"—represent, for the most part, experimental phases in Edwards' career, transitions from one x to the next. These risky deviations from the main line of his cine-comic development are alternately far off the mark and spot on the bullseye. One of the exciting (and tidy) qualities of this filmography is that it describes a series of hills and valleys of artistic change, dramatic enough in its own right to make an engaging three-act screenplay teeming with conflict and resolution. That the valleys ("Blake Burns") are always followed by hills ("Blake Booms") is one of the glorious aspects of Edwards' career, and goes far in explaining a great deal not just about why these films were made when they were, but also the director's personal philosophy of artistic (and emotional) survival. Most importantly, though, the nearly forty-year rollercoaster from "Blake Begins" to "Blake Bows" is evidence of Edwards' commitment to—for better *and* worse—continued cinematic experimentation.

But it wasn't all art.

Some of it was money. In this book, Edwards' career chronology has only been broken a handful of times, and, in each case, it has been to keep the *Panthers* in their gilded cages. With the exception of *The Pink Panther* and *A Shot in the Dark*, the first two Clouseau movies, the *Panther* franchise did little to enhance anything but Edwards' bank account, and, that being so, it has been confined to twin sections at the dead center of the book. The first, "Sellers Lives," discusses *Panthers* three, four, and five, made in slam-bang succession between 1975 and 1978, and the second, "Sellers Lives On," takes a look at the Pink Empire after Sellers left it, surveying *Trail of the Pink Panther*, *Curse of the Pink Panther*, and 1993's *Son of the Pink Panther*, Blake's last film to date. There are eight films in all, and as they multiply, it becomes clearer that they would do better to be considered as an independent trajectory than as part of Blake's main body of work.

Those *Panthers* aside, by the end of Edwards' career, slapstick will encapsulate, as Becker wrote, "the tragedy of man's dualism, his ludicrous situation," by responding directly to man's hubristic inability to overcome death and decay. In Sisyphean cycles of slapstick, characters will try to climb out of the world of shit only to be violently returned to it. These pictures use physical pain to explicate emotional pain, making splurches into metaphors for crises of consciousness. And here we find what we might have seen coming: the introduction of the fifth and final kind of gag, the splurch of enlightenment. Where we once laughed at Clouseau suffering a relentless succession of humiliations, we observe George Webber, Felix Farmer, and Zach Hutton *literally fall* into despair and grief. (One of *Skin Deep*'s promotional taglines was "there's a fine line between falling in love and falling on your face.") To Blake Edwards, these misfortunes must be assuaged by humor. He said,

> I would not be able to get through life had I not been able to view its painfulness in a comedic way. So when I put life up there on the screen, quite often it resembles things that happen to me or at least comic metaphors for those things. Leo McCarey used to talk about breaking the pain barrier, where you're faced with so much pain it compounds itself and you can't take it anymore. So you laugh.[14]

Breaking the pain barrier of the heart is not only a comic device of Edwards' later masterpieces; it's his personal therapy. It teaches that the only difference between comedy and tragedy is the time it takes the former to realize it is actually the latter—yet another trick of perception. Consider the following episode from Edwards' own life:

> Throughout my life, I've had serious spells of depression, monstrous. Churchill called it his "black dog." And it got so bad that I could hardly get out of bed. I became seriously suicidal. I could not go on. And so I went through a process of trying to be as practical about suicide as possible. I didn't want to leave too much of a mess around for Julie and the people that I love.
>
> I didn't know if I would be able to drown myself, because at the last moment, I would probably have to take a breath. A gun? That's a mess. And I've known too many people who tried it and ended up vegetables. I thought about filling the bathtub with rose petals so they'd mingle with my blood—I was being very creative. But that's not where I wanted to be found.

Ultimately, after a bit more of this, Edwards decided upon wrist-slitting ("by process of elimination"), outdoors, on Malibu beach, "looking out at the ocean, alone on a bluff." Blake readied all the props—his razor, his chair, his wardrobe—and was about to throw in the final towel when his Great Dane appeared at his side. His other dog, a retriever, came next, carrying a ball in its mouth ("I think he sensed something," Blake said). Edwards took the slobbery ball, cocked it back his arm in preparation for a long throw, dislocated his shoulder, and fell backward. It was then that he decided to call the whole thing off. He picked up his chair, turned to go, and stepped on the razor hidden in the sand. Blood everywhere, Blake hobbled to the phone and eventually got himself to the ER. "I was afraid I was going to bleed to death, but I had been trying to kill myself. I just started to laugh."[15]

And that brings us to the end. As we will see in Skin Deep, Edwards' ultimate statement on the nature of pain and humor, sanity is dependent upon Zach's acceptance of life's hilarious afflictions. If he is right and God is a gag writer, then missing the tragic joke isn't just shortsighted, it's a sin. And since fecal matters are laughing matters, and laughing matters are spiritual matters, then by the transitive property, *fecal matters are spiritual matters*. We are nothing, but isn't that hilarious? And isn't hilarity a god-

2. *Gunn* (1967) The splurch, taken to its logical extreme, pushes the feeling of comfortable danger right into death. Blink and you'll miss the changeover. (Author's collection)

send? It's Blake's eureka after fifty years of making movies. And it's all in the splurch.

WHAT MATTERS

Since Billy Wilder, Blake Edwards remains the last Hollywood writer/director to make major studio comedies of personal and formal distinction. Others have made major studio comedies, and countless others have gone on to make funny movies of personal and formal distinction (Woody Allen, Paul Mazursky, Robert Altman, the Coen Brothers), but in postclassical Hollywood, Edwards is the only filmmaker to do both—and regularly.

That makes him more than just a unique talent, it makes him an auteur of the highest order, one who lays claim, like Chaplin, Lubitsch, Sturges, and Wilder before him, to the moniker great comedic artist of Hollywood.

Sadly, Edwards has stopped making films just when we need him—or someone like him—most. Today, during Hollywood comedy's darkest age, in which funny movies are synonymous with feature-length sitcoms, it falls to those of us in want of a consequential cinema to look behind us and wonder at what went wrong, and where, and how, with the hope that retracing our steps will restore us our lost heritage. I suggest we begin with Blake Edwards.

PROLOGUE
BREAKING IN, 1922–1955

William Blake Crump was born to Donald and Lillian Crump on July 22, 1922, in Tulsa, Oklahoma. Three years later, after the dissolution of his parents' marriage, the boy and his mother were brought out to Los Angeles by her new husband, Jack McEdward (no *s*), whose own father, silent film director J. Gordon Edwards (yes *s*, no *Mc*), had made his name directing Theda Bara in her vampiest films at Fox. The success of the Bara pictures brought J. Gordon studio renown and paved the way for Jack's own work as an in-house production manager and assistant director. Naturally, when the time came for Blake to take a career, he chose the most convenient. The family business held no magic for him, but nepotism was simple, and for a high school kid, that was good enough.

Young Edwards became a script courier on the Fox lot earning a few teenage bucks delivering pages to and from people and buildings he had known since childhood. That turned into some work as an extra (he was always around, after all) and then, in 1942, his acting debut came by way of his stepfather. Jack got him a small part in Henry Hathaway's period drama *Ten Gentlemen from West Point*, and from there Edwards took a series of minor roles in nearly thirty features. He worked for Victor Fleming, Mervyn LeRoy, William Wellman, and Budd Boetticher; Otto Preminger kicked him off the set of *In the Meantime, Darling*, and he received a John Fordian roughing up on *They Were Expendable*. "Ford got so mad at me," he remembers, "that he made me climb up this palm tree on this island where we were shooting. I thought it was for a scene, but when I looked down I saw the entire company sailing away for the next location, leaving me stranded up a tree!"[1]

Blake's little big break came in 1946, when he landed the lead in *Strangler of the Swamp*, a B horror film about a foggy marshland, a ferry service, and an uncooperative ghost. It's a reasonable picture, and Blake is reasonable in it. He plays Christian Sanders, the heroine's love interest, and has the good looks to bring it off without too much trouble. At twenty-four, he cuts a sturdy physique—all American, you could say—but with the kind of sharp facial contours and wide, white grin that belied Christian's own

3. Blake Edwards (center) flanked by his mother, Lillian, and his stepfather, veteran Hollywood production manager Jack McEdward. The family is on location for *Darling Lili*. (Courtesy of Jennifer Edwards)

naiveté.* The combination of aw-gee-shucks and devilish charm aren't quite right here, but they amount to a screen presence puzzling enough to keep our interest.

After *Strangler*, Blake appeared in only a few other pictures, most notably for a moment in Wyler's *The Best Years of Our Lives*, but it was only a matter of time before he realized acting wasn't for him. He remembers,

---

* Henry Mancini, whose collaboration with Blake was ten years away, described him as "about five foot ten. [There was] some Indian blood apparent in his chiseled features, with strong cheekbones and jawline. He watches his weight, and he has always been lean. He is deliberate in his movements and always very direct, not circumspect, always knowing where he is going. He wore his hair on the short side . . . He has a bizarre sense of black humor."[2]

I went to see a Western with Gary Cooper, with a friend of mine [John Champion]. When we left we played a game of miniature golf and talked about it. And I kept saying, "I could do better." Somehow we decided that we'd collaborate and write a Western. To raise money we painted his mother's house, and to have a kind of bible to go by, we took one of my father's scripts and practically copied it. If you took the Western we wrote, I'm sure it had the same scene numbers and everything practically the same. And we ended up producing it—it was called *Panhandle*.[3]

"I've always loved the West and that part of our culture," Edwards said, adding, "I think that it particularly inspires the younger mind in terms of dramatics."[4] He was right about that: inspiration came again the following year, when Edwards and Champion collaborated on *Stampede*, another Western, which did moderately well for Allied Artists, a "B-plus" subsidiary of Monogram Pictures on the outskirts on Poverty Row.

Then Edwards and Champion split, Edwards kept writing, and after a challenge from his then girlfriend, he wrote a radio script, sent it to a producer, and suddenly he was in radio. A few weeks later, he was asked if he had written anything in the style of a Dick Powell detective drama series called *Rogue's Gallery*. Blake answered in the affirmative, lying, and agreed to deliver his script at ten o'clock the following morning. That night, he went home and wrote what would become *Richard Diamond, Private Detective*:

My name's Diamond, and like a lot of working people at five o'clock in the afternoon, I get pretty anxious for six o'clock to roll around, especially if I haven't had a client for the last three days. But even if I don't expect anyone to drop in before six, I can't take a chance, so I stare out of my office window on 53rd street just to kill time. I see the night starting to bustle in on the Broadway bright lights and I wonder just how many prospective clients are out in the city, who's getting in trouble, what kind of trouble, and will they come to Richard Diamond for guidance?

The show was a hit, running from 1949 to 1952. Blake directed a few episodes, bought himself a Cadillac, and began to build momentum.

Meanwhile, Blake's old friend, director Richard Quine (who had cast him as a boxer in *Leather Gloves*), invited him to co-author a film script at Columbia, and Edwards jumped at the opportunity. As a filmmaker, Quine

4. *Strangler of the Swamp* (1946) The young actor Blake Edwards, not a day over twenty-four, with Rosemary La Planche. It's tough to see from this angle, but Blake's outward-pointed ears have been taped down. (PRC/Photofest)

may have been a kind of second (or third) tier Cukor, but as a mentor, he was ideal. "For the first time," Blake recalls, "I began to see that I had more stake in writing than just making money—there was some sort of passion involved."[5] In the period between 1952 and 1955, Blake co-wrote seven films with Quine, starting with *Sound Off*, starring Mickey Rooney. *Rainbow 'Round My Shoulder* came next, followed by *All Ashore, Cruisin' Down the River, Drive a Crooked Road*, and the musical *My Sister Eileen*, starring Jack Lemmon in his second film role. These were middleweight, workmanlike gigs, but they allowed Blake room to flex his chameleonic genre muscle (not to mention practice the delicate art of letting someone else direct his work). But most important in these years was Blake's relationship with Lemmon, whose style he would later match to his own.

Throughout the Quine apprenticeship, Blake used his leverage as screenwriter, as well as his association with Dick Powell, to get him directing work on the TV anthology series *Four Star Playhouse*. As one of the show's producers, it was Powell's idea to use each of one of four stars—David Niven, Ida Lupino, Charles Boyer, and himself—in weekly episodes. The continual rotation of stars (and genres) produced a great variety of programs, ranging from Westerns to mysteries to comedies, as well as the spin-offs *The Dick Powell Show* and *Zane Grey Theater*, and offered Blake Edwards his first forays into writing-directing. His 1954 episodes, "Detective's Holiday," "The Bomb," and "The Indian Taker," featured Powell, Niven, and Lupino respectively, and earned Blake enough credibility to sell himself as a feature director back at Columbia, which is how, in 1955, when Richard Quine was promoted to the A list, Edwards was perfectly positioned to fill his shoes.

1

BLAKE BEGINS

1955–1959

BRING YOUR SMILE ALONG (1955)

Jerry: You'll get further with a smile than you will with a frown.

HE LAUGHED LAST (1956)

Doctor: He laughed himself to death.

MISTER CORY (1957)

Mr. Earnshaw: Manners, Mister Cory. I find them a prerequisite in any circle.

THIS HAPPY FEELING (1958)

Mitch: When a man retires he doesn't give up women. Not entirely anyway. When a man does that he's not retired, he's dead.

THE PERFECT FURLOUGH (1959)

Colonel Leland: He's loose in Paris?
Liz: Everybody's loose in Paris.

Edwards gets off to an Edwardian start in Bring Your Smile Along, a B musical he conceived and directed under the mentorship of Richard Quine, and the first of his two Frankie Laine pictures for Columbia. Looking back on it he said,

> I recognized very early on that [directing was] where the control was. And it was more fun for me, too. I get great rewards from writing—the best rewards—but then I have my joy and my fun and my laughs on the stage because it becomes for me a kind of extended family. And I always work best that way. I need that family.[1]

Out of his crew came a family—a stock company of favorite actors and technicians—and later, out of his own family would come a crew—a posse of actual relations (son, daughter, and, of course, wife) plucked from the Edwards dinner table to star, write, and even co-direct alongside the patriarch. "My life has always been a struggle to create a family around me," Blake said, "I needed it, I didn't have it, and I wanted it desperately."[2] And on Bring Your Smile Along he got it.

The film offers several key, though rudimentary, glimpses into the auteur-to-be. Chief among them is an interest in the true nature of idenity, a fascination that will nourish Edwards' comic and dramatic technique for the next forty years of filmmaking. The identity question is introduced early in the film when unemployed songwriters Jerry Dennis (Frankie Laine) and Marty Adams (Keefe Brasselle) discover a sheet of mystery lyrics slipped under their studio door. At first, Jerry and Marty refer to the unknown author as "he," though, as the audience knows, it is actually their new neighbor, Nancy Willows (Constance Towers), a she. It is an innocent enough confusion, but it gains significance as one that looks ahead to the gender plays that will dominate Edwards' later farces. Farce, as we will see, is a form perfectly suited to identities revealed and concealed, and in Bring Your Smile Along, Edwards makes a few notable gestures in that direction, some of which result in the kind of antic physicality, both on and off camera, that will, in time, blossom into pitch-perfect splurching. But those are all nascent components. Bring Your Smile Along's most prominent feature is its musicality, presented here in a style borrowed from Quine's own singing pictures, but it isn't until He Laughed Last, made the following year, that Edwards' uniquely Edwardian realization of performance spaces truly begins to come into focus.

He Laughed Last, Blake's second Frankie Laine vehicle, is a Runyonesque tale about a mob boss and the empire he bequeaths to his gun moll, Rosemary (Lucy Marlow). She's really big-hearted underneath it all and isn't cut out for the back-alley lifestyle like Max Lassiter (Jesse White), the former second-in-command, who plans to marry the girl and regain control of the organization. Rosemary likes a cop, though, who's concerned about her family ties and getting her out safely, which puts the dame in a tough spot, especially with respect to the ermine and pearls. Lucky for her, she's in a Blake Edwards comedy, which means she'll show the fellas what's what ("you gonna take orders from a dame?"), and turn masculinity on its head. She also does a few numbers at the Happy Club, directed with a sense of spatial awareness that rehearses Edwards' musical presentation of Darling Lili. Performance space is ideal for Blake's split characters, especially female figures who struggle with conflicting allegiances, inner crises, and ultimately the most Edwardian tension of all—how they appear to be versus who they really are. A couple of gags look ahead to The Pink Panther's use of off-screen sound and space; architectural framing predicts the proscenium frame; bright, saturated colors abound; and the occasional outburst of knockabout physicality proves that Blake's interest in rubber bodies was with him from the start. It is only 1956, and the director has shown signs of the artist he will come to be.

Auteurist gesticulations are also evident in the picture's thematic components. We've got reversals of gender and power structures, nostalgic yearning for "the good ol' days" (the story is told in flashback), and even gruesome readings into the perils of humor. Originally titled *He Died Laughing, He Laughed Last* makes our acquaintance in the form of a title sequence that begins with bullet-hole lettering shot out of a machine gun. It's cute, but it hurts. After mob boss Big Dan (Alan Reed)'s hospital scene, the commingling of laughs and death is reinstated quite literally when the doctor, hunched and bespectacled, declares the boss "laughed himself to death." The absolute high point of dying/laughing occurs late in the film in the "mix the cement" routine, which plays out more like a vaudeville insert than mafia murder. Edwards has infused a torture scene with emotional unreality, somewhere between pantomime and cartoon, and all with a theatrical, self-conscious ear for rhythm that removes the naturalistic threats of danger.

In fact, there is never any anxiety in *He Laughed Last*. Like the gangsters we will see in *Breakfast at Tiffany's*, *Revenge of the Pink Panther*, and *Victor/Victoria*, these wiseguys all lack that Corleone something. They are teddy bears dressed up in pinstripes, failures when it comes to *real* authority, and, consequentially, first-rate splurching material. Observe the cigar gag: played twice, it splurches at the expense of Max Lassiter, king of the phonies. Both times it begins with the off-screen sound of what is best described as gunfire. Edwards then cuts to the reaction shot of an uninvolved participant, and then to the source of the sound, Lassiter's exploded cigar. The choice of sight gag and its visual construction answer to Blake's enthusiasm for busted masculinity (the cigar, which is not *just* a cigar) and the jumble of perception and actuality; that is, when we hear the sound we *think* gunshot, but when Edwards cuts to the smoking butt we *know* we've been intentionally confused. Lassiter's reaction to the reading of the will works in exactly the same way: the off-camera crash (audio only), followed by a reaction shot of an observer, and then the reveal—the splurched victim writhing on the carpet. Even Jimmy (Dick Long), the cop, a genuine authoritarian, is at risk of suffering a weensy pratfall, composed of the off-camera audio punch line, the befuddlement of perception (a closed door refutes what's actually behind it), and, quite naturally, a face-first spill designed to deflate him at the peak of his arrogance. The comic mechanism is admittedly crude, and without the elegance of later Blake, but it is effective nonetheless.

Enter the crane shot, a recurring character in Edwards' musicals. In *He Laughed Last*, the camera movement romances those of director Vincente Minnelli gliding in from on high, drifting over the audience's heads and on up to the stage. More than just an establishing technique, the crane draws us through space in a manner that carefully alters our understanding of key expositional elements. Gino's (Frankie Laine) performance of "Danny Boy" for instance, begins with his close-up and pulls back ever so slowly to reveal a crowd of spellbound listeners, and continues back until the entire screen is filled with audience. As in (*Darling*) Lili's rendition of "Whistling Away in the Dark" (still to come), Edwards changes personal space into public space with a swift movement that helps him play the game of peek-a-boo he loves so much. He uses cranes, like gags, to reveal, to take a point of view and then, in a flourish, revise it. Minnelli's glide may help an aria take flight, reinforcing it, but Edwards suggests otherwise. By delaying our awareness of an audience, and thereby "tricking" us into thinking the performer is alone, it represents the inherent duplicity in performance. No, Blake's saying, this isn't a confession, this is an *act*.

The film received good enough notices to earn Edwards another shot behind the camera. "An amusing spoof," went *Variety*, "The pacing is good and the laugh handling productive."[3] Most papers responded in the same fashion. They saw in it the stuff of competent comedy, and in Lucy Marlow, an up-and-coming Judy Holliday. (Frankie Laine, for reasons it is difficult to comprehend, was regarded as having an auteurist's influence over the picture). The *Hollywood Reporter*'s piece on *He Laughed Last*, although unfavorable, is noteworthy for having singled out, as early as 1956, a soon-to-be trademark of Edwards' work. "More deadly than devastating," they said, the film was "mostly frantic without being funny," adding, "The chief flaw in the production is that the gangsters seem to often to be not amusing but deadly and unpleasant. With all the credits going to Blake Edwards, he will have to take the blame for the production's general failure as well."[4] Ah, yes: the bad taste, the sick jokes, and the death fixation. Thus commences the great critical kvetch that will trail Blake for his next forty years.

And here is *Mister Cory* to the rescue. Blake's 1957 film, which he called his "first film of any consequence,"[5] allowed him a bigger budget, gave him a bigger star in Tony Curtis, and was his first film out from under the shadow of Quine. Although *Cory* was adapted from a story by Leo Rosten, Edwards was given sole screenwriting credit. From script to screen, he imbued the picture with the kind of formal, thematic, and comic inclinations that would make his best work work. Among them we see a solid (though rudimentary) engagement with topping the topper, a gag structure passed down to Blake from director Leo McCarey (discussed at length in the section on *The Great Race*), and gestations of what will become Edwards' visual style, rooted in the notion of exteriority.

In the film, Tony Curtis plays Cory, a gruff kid from the windy streets of Chicago, who in the brisk opening moments of *Mister Cory* makes it clear that he's going to get the hell out and make something of his life. His transformation comes not in the form of physical abuse (as we will see in the films to come), but in his realization that style—the seductive appearance of things—isn't really as wonderful as the window of Tiffany's makes it out to be. Indeed, the film's love triangle, a not-so-equilateral exchange between Cory and two sisters (one beautiful, one fun), elucidates Blake's investment in the perils of book covers and the illusions by which they are judged.

The casting of Tony Curtis is perfectly in keeping with the Tiffany dialectic. As a Bronx boy turned Cary Grant, Curtis represents the ideal combination of gruff and glamour, a persona that, as the film demonstrates, is equally at home with a carburetor as it is in a tuxedo. Curtis' voice, too, is town and country; baritone tough, but *Spartacus* smooth. In fact, Curtis was so well suited to the Edwardian agenda that Blake cast him in three more of his pictures, a distinction that earns the actor a place beside Jack Lemmon and Peter Sellers as one of the director's principal appointees. However, as we will see in *The Perfect Furlough*, *Operation Petticoat*, and *The Great Race*, Curtis was not recalled to play one of Blake's men in crisis (like Lemmon) or splurch-worthy pretenders (like Sellers), but to embody a natural inner duplicity that is to Blake Edwards inherent in the human condition. Over the course of these four films, Curtis makes the same arc he does in *Mister Cory*. From street kid (*Cory*), to rake (*The Perfect Furlough*), to smoothie (*Operation Petticoat*), to a fancy-man hero (*The Great Race*), both sides of Tony Curtis find expression throughout his nearly ten-year collaboration with Edwards. By the time he reaches the Great Leslie, his character in *The Great Race*, Tony won't be the one throwing the splurches in the kisser of authority (as he does in *Cory*), he will be the one receiving them.

A large part of Blake's aesthetic is determined by this interest in the risks of self-stylization. If truths are never what they seem, then "in [Edwards'] comedies, the widescreen space becomes a vortex fraught with perils—hidden traps, aggressive objects, spaces that abruptly open onto other, unexpected spaces." Critic Dave Kehr is terrific on this point. The idea here is to place a man at odds with his environment, something Kehr relates to the visual composition of Edwards' thrillers, in which "the threat comes not from empty space, but from the crowding of objects, colors, surfaces—the hard, cold *thingness* of things."[5] Space in *Mister Cory*, neither thriller nor comedy, works in the exact opposite manner. Rather than make his frame frighteningly claustrophobic for a thriller or hilariously cluttered for a comedy, Blake opens it up. Thus, dramas like *Cory* are free from spatial restriction. Instead, Edwards offers an aesthetic of exteriority.

To do so, he employs one of his favorite angles—introduced in *Mister Cory*—a two shot, wide, generally shared between a man and a woman facing one another. They are far enough apart to make a close-up difficult, but squarely within slapping distance. The shot will play out in a master take, often lasting for minutes on end without so much as a pan, tilt, or dolly. Theoretically, an arrangement such as this—one unimpeded by cuts or movement—keeps us at an objective distance. It emphasizes the actual space between its subjects, doesn't play favorites by manipulating our gaze, and ultimately holds us outside character subjectivity. In other words, it is a shot about surface exteriority. We are meant to *regard* the scene with an eye on its physical properties, not for the psychological complexity of its people. In a world where style gets in the way of authenticity, this kind of shot is no less than totally precise. *Mister Cory* has it in spades.

For reasons we will see, these master shots do wonders for the sight gag (and vice versa), but in the meantime, before slapstick becomes Blake Edwards' primary carrier of narrative, character, thought, and theme, they will do well to service dialogue. For Myron Meisel this is at the auteur's heart. "The most immediately recognizable quality in a Blake Edwards film," he writes, "is a wise-guy verbal facility keyed to visual fluidity across a lateral field," adding, "Edwards charges his surfaces with significance by using the appearance of objects to suggest their essence. The same principle applies to the behavior of his characters."[6] Or rather, *can* apply. The character of Cory is most certainly stricken with the malady of appearance, but he is punished for it. In Edwards' films, those who overcome it (as Cory in fact does), or, better still, those who know how to really use it (generally artists) are the ones that transcend pretense, evade the harshness of the gag, and earn their director's deserved admiration.

And the critics were pleased. "Robert Arthur's production wears a slick polish, enhanced by the use of Eastman Color and CinemaScope, and the physical values do a first rate job of backing the dramatic action, even when the latter shows some thinness here and there. Blake Edwards' direction gets good performances from the cast and gives the storytelling a well-paced unfoldment."[7] ("Unfoldment"?) "The achievement of *Mister Cory* is primarily that of Blake Edwards, its writer-director, who steers an improbable raft of story situations past the shoals of disbelief and disaster. Despite having what the censors would describe as low moral content, the movie depicts high life in a manner constantly intriguing to those who are not quite able to afford it."[8] And there they are again: "slick polish" and "low moral content." Blake was on his way.

Up next was *This Happy Feeling*, a gawky, mirthless movie brought down by Curt Jurgens, a man who did for comedy what Joseph Goebbels did for watercolors. If it's worth discussing, it's because of what it means to Edwards' great pictures, those that share *This Happy Feeling*'s feeling for the middle-aged man of dubious sexual mores. Jurgens' Preston Mitchell is the first in a line of Edwards' menopausal lotharios, but for screenwriter F. Hugh Herbert, who had made his name writing roués, Mitchell was one of many. In fact, Herbert was known as something of a sexual iconoclast even before he adapted his own Broadway play, *For Love or Money*, into *This Happy Feeling*. His frank and pleasant take on the subject hearkened back to the days when they made pictures with titles like *The Waning Sex* and *On Ze Boulevard*, but it wasn't until Otto Preminger brought his hit play *The Moon is Blue* to the big screen that Herbert's career was given its ribald boost. The film is often credited for dealing the Production Code its final blow, and giving writers the latitude to use words like "virgin" and "seduce" without breaking too hot a sweat. Preminger is rightfully remembered for such *scandales du cinéma*, but at the time Herbert was also credited for the accomplishment, and, as a result, his post-*Moon* scripts conveyed money-making potential of the two-feet-off-the-floor variety. Universal attached Debbie Reynolds, hot off her successes in the *Tammy and the Bachelor* phenoms, and reteamed her with producer Ross Hunter and cameraman Arthur E. Arling. On the heels of their Oscar-nominated song "Tammy," Jay Livingston and Ray Evans were brought in for music and lyrics, and Blake Edwards—who was at that time not known for sex comedy—was recruited to tie it all together. It was a prestige package on the scale that Blake had never encountered, indicating a certain rise in studio esteem.

Like George Webber in 10, Preston Mitchell (Jurgens) is a celebrity of foreign origin with a crush on a younger woman (Janet, played by Debbie Reynolds), and is taken to task by the gag for straying beyond his designated demographic. Running beside her train as it leaves the station, Mitch, straining to keep up, calls after his young amourette and promptly falls below screen. We cut to a slightly high-angle answer-shot that shows Mitch climbing out of a construction worker's hole by the side of the track. By forcing us to imagine the moment of impact on our own (we are given only before and after the fall), Edwards has minimized audience anxiety, and maximized the comic irony. If Edwards were to actually show Mitch's fall, whatever irony was incurred by the sudden disruption would itself be disrupted by the depiction of physical pain.

The ability to laugh at someone else's misfortune without feeling guilty is absolutely essential to a funny pratfall. But the onus isn't on the actor here; it's on the filmmaker. "It's not to the guy who is doing it [the actor]," Edwards said, "to give the audience the ability not to feel guilty about laughing at somebody taking a pratfall. Or about some situation that they would not normally laugh at. You've got to give them that escape clause. You've got to somehow provide it for them so they can laugh and not feel guilty."[9] Offscreen sound and action is one way to accomplish this. Used one way, they make the scene about the fall (the laugh) and not about the impact (the hurt); used another, as they are throughout the rest of the film, a treacherous reversal can result, one that favors the pain over the pleasure. The remark Sarris made about Edwardian humor, that Blake is a "writer-director who has got some of his biggest laughs out of jokes that are too gruesome for most horror films,"[10] undoubtedly refers to precisely this delicate tension.

What is unusual (and unsuccessful) about This Happy Feeling is that Blake's ordinarily impeccable sense of the pain/pleasure equilibrium has been tipped too far to one side. The train gag notwithstanding, Edwards generally fails to provide us with this necessary "escape clause." He continually foregrounds Mitch's intense physical back pain,* forcing his audience to endure, almost sadistically, the insufferable groans of Curt Jur-

---

* Edwards: "I used to have the worst back in the world . . . things like that would show up in lieu of having to perform either artistically or sexually . . . so, obviously the best way to overcome that, the best way to be able to live with it and not make it too painful was to laugh at it."[11]

gens. Bedridden philanderers will recur through these films, but the ones who elicit laughter will act with an emphasis on cartoon physicality, or a bit of clowning intended to add a reprieve of ridiculousness to the torture.

This Happy Feeling's comedy may not work, but the back gag is given thematic justification, one that warns of decrepitude and failing masculinity. Also present is the theme of fathers and sons essential to many Edwardian narratives. In an interview with Stuart Byron, Blake said,

> Sure, [Wild] Rovers is a "love story" between two men, an older, William Holden, and a younger, Ryan O'Neal. There have been relationships like that since at least [Mister] Cory in 1957, when Charles Bickford took Curtis under his wing and taught him the gambling trade. Something like that happens in This Happy Feeling, Operation Petticoat, High Time, Panther, and also Soldier in the Rain, which I produced but didn't direct. Is it a search for a father? I won't dispute that. I always felt alienated, estranged from my own father. . . .[12]

In the case of This Happy Feeling, it is the Mitch/Bill relationship that Blake is referring to. As Blake noted, the father/son paradigm has its roots in the director's biographical past, but it also serves a highly functional role, thematically speaking. The conflict between youth and age—fundamental to Edwards' greatest works—is addressed in This Happy Feeling, though it is less involved with the Oedipal crisis (both men do pursue the same girl), than it is with questions of masculinity and mortality. The idea of Mitch-as-paterfamilias serves what is essentially a classic Edwardian decay narrative, and not, as we will see in Wild Rovers and Sunset, a tale of fathers and sons. There is a prominent relation, however, and Byron was right to point it out.

Following This Happy Feeling, the Los Angeles Times called Edwards a "writer and director of unfailing discrimination and knowledgeable screen sense,"[13] to which the Reporter added "expert."[14] For the first time, he was pegged a bankable and inventive director of comedy. If ever Blake was wrongly accused of being solely a slapstician, he had this picture to blame— it was the one that typecast him. And so, as his reputation mounted ("there's nothing wrong at Universal City that a few pictures like this can't cure"),[15] Blake, in a major milestone move, followed a comedy with a comedy.

The gag takes a hefty step up in 1958 with the service comedy The Perfect Furlough. In it, Tony Curtis reteams with Edwards to play Paul Hodges, a

5. *This Happy Feeling* (1958) Preston Mitchell (Curt Jurgens), the first of Edwards' middle-aged rakes, suffers the painful consequences of running alongside trains carrying attractive younger women. (Author's collection)

corporal who is given a break from his all-male Arctic base in the form of a trip to Paris with Sandra Roca, the Argentine Bombshell (Linda Cristal). Because the whole world is watching, the Pentagon sends along Lieutenant Vicki Loren (Janet Leigh) to keep Hodges and Roca out of bed. A setup such as this, in which pleasure and authority are placed in comic opposition, lends itself quite nicely to the kind of slapstick Edwards loves to film. The splurch then is aimed to pie *Furlough* smack in the kisser, signifying Edwards' first major involvement with what will become the central ideological mechanism of his work. Already we can track the sprouting of a gag tree that began with standard sight gags (*He Laughed Last*) and simple falls (*This Happy Feeling*) and is now continued with challenging acrobatics, enhanced visual ambition, and richer thematic relevance.

The pointer gag, something we will see perfected by Sellers in *A Shot in the Dark*, comes to *Furlough* by way of *He Laughed Last*, but the exploding cigar is now a long, indubitably phallic, stick. In each case, the splurch is a dig at false authority (with sexual undertones) and upends the recipient's hollow demonstrations of control. It should be said, though, that not all of the gags in *The Perfect Furlough* splurch or edify (the bodycast and man-in-ice sequences are purely comic decoration), but the ones that do—the pointer gag in particular—expose the methodology behind thematic splurching. Here's the setup: the same officer who, earlier, broke his pointer, arrogantly addresses a room of his subordinates. What he needs— what Blake needs for him—is a bit of physical humiliation to bring him back to earth. Thus, the punch line: he trips on his way out the door. That's poetic justice, Edwards-style. (Later, he is discovered behind closed doors, stealing a drink, alone, and in his underwear. Splurched again!)

Where Edwards' previous films were involved mostly with the mechanics of visual humor, *The Perfect Furlough* takes a sizable interest in expanding the lines of thought that accompany it. For instance, in addition to the standard splurch—the diminishment of pomposity—the gag becomes a vehicle for sexual perception. We are by now familiar with the phallus breakers and the pratfalls, the reactive gags that lack dramatic muscularity, and *The Perfect Furlough* is in large part composed of such stunts, but there is one significant exception: an *active* gag that doesn't just splurch ideology but is indepensable to the story. And it happens in a wine vat. We are witness to two slips into the grape, the first of which looks like a splurch but in fact is just the opposite. When Sandra Roca falls into the vat, she is not humiliated, she is titillated—she laughs. Later, when she is spotted covered in grape, it is believed that a sexual escapade was to blame for it. On the other hand, when Lieutenant Vicki Loren is thrown in is when the real splurch occurs. Sexual abandon is, after all, adverse to her authority.

The ensuing juxtaposition of military order and pleasure is representative of what Myron Meisel calls "the central conflict to all of Edwards' films." He continues:

This opposition forms the central action to his early comedy-dramas for Universal, each of which shows the basic Edwardian themes in gestation. The dramatic situations in these films are remarkably similar: in each, a character with a strongly developed sense of how he ought to lead his life finds this confidence/complacency challenged by an opposing lifestyle. Sometimes the protagonist is loosened up and made more responsive to life by the graded acceptance of degrees of chaos; conversely, a "wild" character realizes the private, internal value of social conventions, manners, morals, or values.[16]

In this way, Edwards' Universal pictures are not unique. These conventions are evidenced in romantic comedy as early as Shakespeare (and before), and though accurate, do little to distinguish Blake's work from the rest. What does distinguish them—and this comes in *Furlough* and develops in *Operation Petticoat*—is the director's use of the gag to indicate these changes, which brings us back to the vat. After Vicki emerges from the wine, she becomes more accepting of her Dionysian side, even going so far as to wear a toga-looking sheet to dinner. She has been changed, and it's the physical shift (not intellectual!) that does the changing. And that's more than slapstick—that's slapstick storytelling.

There are other Edwardian touches: the womanizer in need of domestification; the interest in public relations (image versus identity); and even twinkles of the director's later association with the patient/therapist relationship, but what *Furlough* lacks is the director's characteristic camera style. *Furlough* is a dialogue film (written by Stanley Shapiro, who will go on to write *Operation Petticoat*), and Edwards concedes to (Shapiro's) language. Whereas the later Blake will favor long takes, shot wide, the principal grammar of his cinema, Blake the rookie feels more comfortable cutting between speakers. And yet there is one moment of bravura movement—choreography is more like it—syncopated in rhythm, and timed with an eye on entrances and exits. We see it in the news of Sandra's pregnancy scene as word spreads around the hotel lobby from one bellhop to the next. The camera glides with one foreground figure, who is then replaced by another from the background, who in turn guides the camera to the next replacement. This kind of blocking, more musical than farcical, will be absolutely perfected in *S.O.B.*, where comings and goings achieve (dare I say it?) a spatial complexity that verges on *Rules of the Game* (I said it).

"It was a kind of milestone for me," Edwards said about *Furlough* in 1966. "I got the feeling of comedy. Everything seemed to work. It didn't have any great screenplay, we shot it in thirty days, and I look at it now and

I say, 'How could I have done some of those things?' But, all in all, in its own strange way, it is one of my favorite films. . . . "[17] If Edwards remembers it fondly it is because *The Perfect Furlough* was actually a Blake Edwards movie, and arguably the very first. Certainly, one could see that the others had Blake in them, but the glimpses were intermittent; in *Furlough* he came the closest yet to a sustained expression of his sensibility. And *Variety* agreed: "Blake Edwards' direction is responsible for getting as much fun as there is in the picture. He not only points up the lines but backs them with sight gags. Edwards also uses the CinemaScope camera ingeniously for comedy."[18] Having made his mark with camera and dialogue, the director could finally claim responsibility for elevating the film above its middling material. *Time*, after running off a list of ten clichés* that keep *The Perfect Furlough* from being perfect, wrote, "The beauty of Blake Edwards' direction is that it restores to these familiar jokes something of their first time fervor and surprise."[19]

The picture made its way to France where it caught the eye of a twenty-eight-year-old Jean-Luc Godard, just before he began production on *Breathless*. He wrote,

> Of Blake Edwards, one excellent and one unpleasant memory. The excellent one was *Mister Cory*, in which Tony Curtis played a character morally similar to Stendahl's Lamiel. The unpleasant one was a nasty little film with Curt Jurgens. Now here comes *The Perfect Furlough* to make one regret that Blake Edwards did not write the script himself, as he did for *Mister Cory*. Given a Tony Curtis in good form, Edwards could surely have made something more out of this banal comedy concerning the Parisian misadventures of a NATO soldier. That said, the direction still manages an idea per shot, often charming (Tony Curtis behind a curtain as Janet Leigh takes a bath), sometimes funny (Tony Curtis worrying about the meaning of the word *ampoule*) and occasionally remarkable (Janet Leigh falling into a wine vat under the gaze of a sublimely eccentric Dalio).[20]

Godard goes on to call the wine vat episode "a gag worthy of Buster Keaton," and concludes that *Furlough* is all in all, "A very small film . . . but it leaves one with one's confidence in Blake Edwards intact." Those with

---

* The magazine devised a formula for money-making farce: $(G.I. + id^n) \times (WAC + Sex) =$ Box Office TNT.

6. *The Perfect Furlough* (1958) Behind the scenes with Edwards, Janet Leigh, and her husband/co-star, Tony Curtis. The film was the second of four Edwards–Curtis collaborations. (Universal Pictures/Photofest)

the fine-tooth combs had taken notice, but that wouldn't get Edwards his next picture. That, as it always has been, is about box office, and box office, to the great chagrin of Godard and Co., has little to do with Stendahl's Lamiel; and thankfully, neither had *Furlough*. The picture did do business, Blake stayed at Universal, and another service comedy came his way. And to everyone's surprise, so did Cary Grant.

2

BLAKE BUILDS
1959–1962

OPERATION PETTICOAT (1959)

Lieutenant Commander Sherman: Please assemble the crew.
You will instruct them that they're to completely ignore the fact
that our passengers are women.

When Cary Grant signed on to *Operation Petticoat* the film's budget shot up from about one million dollars to three ("a lot in those days").[1] The studio was so excited about landing the actor that they elected not only to shoot the picture in color, but to give Mr. Grant, under the banner of his Granart Company, the unprecedented amount of 75 pecent of the net profits or 10 percent of the film's gross (whichever was higher), and offered him sole ownership of the film's rights. All Cary Grant had to do was agree to make his next four pictures at Universal* and he would be a very wealthy man. (Naturally, he did, and he was.) Tony Curtis, meanwhile, was thrilled to be acting alongside the man he impersonated only months earlier on *Some Like It Hot*, and the two got on beautifully. But for thirty-seven-year-old Blake Edwards, who had never had to direct a star of Grant's magnitude, *Operation Petticoat* would be a challenging shoot. Blake remembers,

> I nearly got in a fight with him. He would come up with things that were just. . . And there was one thing that I tried to get him to do—the writers and I got down on our knees and said, "Look Cary, do it anyway. You own the film; you can get rid of the scene if you don't think it's any good, but let us show you what we're talking about!" No good. Missed one of the great comedy moments. To this day I'm sorry about it. It's one of the few things I regret in my career.[2]

The joke had to do with the stealing of a pig. In the film, Tony Curtis has the idea to dress up the animal in human clothing and smuggle it past the shore patrol, but Blake thought that it would be funnier (and more endearing) if Grant did it instead. Unfortunately, Cary refused, insisting that it made no sense to associate *him* with a *pig*. Of course, he was right, which was why Blake was right. The joke remained, but not with Cary Grant.

In the film, Grant, as Lieutenant Commander Matt Sherman, is more than a little put off by Lieutenant Nick Holden (Curtis), the fancy-pants

---

* *The Grass is Greener, That Touch of Mink, Charade,* and *Father Goose.*

7. *Operation Petticoat* (1959) A moment of uncharacteristically low tension for Edwards and Cary Grant, on location in Key West. Their relationship was fraught, but it paid off for both; the picture made Grant the highest paid actor in Hollywood, and Edwards a director of serious box-office value. (Courtesy of the Academy of Motion Picture Arts and Sciences)

sailor who has been ordered to board his submarine, the USS *Sea Tiger*. After Holden discovers a group of stranded female soldiers and brings them abroad, Sherman's frustrations build, and for good reason: his men get distracted from the war. The lieutenant commander does his best to keep them in line, but when the lovely Dolores accidentally releases a torpedo, things go from sexy to serious: the sub's position is revealed to the Japanese. But because the crew has since painted the sub pink, the

Americans cannot identify it as their own. How will the crew defend themselves now? (With a gag, of course.)

Over the course of the picture, the crew aboard the USS *Sea Tiger* will have the man's war splurched out of them. Masculine veneers will be assaulted, women will prove themselves capable seamen, and, with a coat of pink paint, the graying bifurcation of identities will be overcome. To be a successful submariner, the film suggests that individuals of one sex must adopt certain qualities of the other, a notion reinforced by the incongruity of its title. Lieutenant Commander Matt Sherman (Cary Grant) begins the film a crusty old sea dog, intolerant of play, sexuality, or anything he deems contrary to the American war effort. But every Felix must have his Oscar, and so Matt Sherman has Nicholas Holden (Tony Curtis), a spotless model of Beau Brummellish splendor and a self-proclaimed "idea man" with a made-to-order uniform from Sachs. When the scowling Sherman warns Mr. Holden that a certain amount of physical effort would ruin his manicure, we might wonder if the term "idea man" is meant euphemistically. "Man" indeed! What kind of a marine counts cruise ship director amongst his nautical accomplishments?

The film is not ambiguous on this point. It gives us a diptych of maleness; one side represents normative masculinity and the other feminine. The first wears utilitarian khakis, and the second, impractical whites.* ("He looks like the Good Humor man," chuckles one of the shipmates.) When we are introduced to Holden in the crosshairs of the periscope's viewfinder, he is presented in a wide shot which shrinks (emasculates) him in the frame. He appears here as Sherman sees him—a puny weakling. When Sherman goes outside to greet Holden, he passes through his crew of shirtless men's men working aboard the ship and descends onto the dock with the camera following him from a position high above ground down to Holden's level. Once again, Nicholas Holden is diminished. Even in their two-shot, Sherman looms over Holden. Cary Grant's innate physical dominance (he was over six feet tall) is the subject of many compositions throughout *Operation Petticoat*, and is used in crosscut over-the-shoulder shots in contrast to the weakness of Holden's effeminacy.

The use of crosscutting is rare for Edwards. Generally, he will use the

---

* The Great Leslie, Curtis' role in *The Great Race*, is dressed similarly, and like Lieutenant Holden, is emblematic of dandyish macho.

two-shot to illustrate character contrast, but the tension created in the crosscut is perhaps more appropriate to this moment of high interpersonal disparity. Both the scene on the dock and the following scene in the barracks are notable for this reason. In the latter, Edwards returns to the wide shot directly after Sherman officially hires Holden. "I might regret this," he says, "but you've just been made my supply officer." The shot that follows places Sherman and Holden on the same spatial plane, and offers an equanimity of foreground prominence. (Compare this to the film's first shot of Holden, and we see it is a small victory for his character both dramatically and visually.)

Nicholas Holden's relationship to Matt Sherman is changing, and it's Edwards' use of color contrast, cutting, and blocking that tells us so. Further indication of this can be found in the breakfast-in-bed scene, when Sherman delivers a pitcher of orange juice to Holden's bunk. Once again, the scene is told through crosscut over-the-shoulder shots, but this time with a significant change. These shots are wider, and the cuts are less frequent. This pairing gives way to a friendlier, more leisurely pace, one that tells of a developing congruity between the men. Developing, maybe, but not fully developed. Crucial differences still exist. Like, for instance, Holden's embracing attitude towards sexuality. Strangely enough, Sherman actually seems to be *opposed* to sex—or at least, heter-sex. When he says, "a woman just shouldn't mess around with a man's machinery," it begs the question, Who should? Another man? If so, is Sherman still the proponent of normative masculinity aboard the USS *Sea Tiger*? Or has the libidinous fancy-boy ushered in a new virility? This conflict, as represented by Edwards' comic commingling of the woman's world and the man's world, launches the gag into *Operation Petticoat*.

With the exception of the "I want my wall back!" sequence, these gags are built upon the incompatibility Sherman perceives between the sexes. As the film's masculine extremist, and as the highest authority figure aboard the USS *Sea Tiger*, he is, from the splurch's point of view, a sitting duck. The especially narrow spaces of the USS *Sea Tiger*, for instance, are conducive to hindering progress. Thrust into impossibly tight passageways, the seamen and women of *Operation Petticoat* can't pass each other without touching. "The submarine was not designed to be co-educational," one of the crewmen explains, and neither, for that matter, is Lieutenant Commander Sherman, who is continually forced into intimate proximity with Dolores Crandall (Joan O'Brien), whose massive breasts make bodily contact an inevitability.* Splurched! Into this, Blake adds outward-opening doors, creating an environment as physically treacherous as it is sexually permissive.

> Those passageways are four inches narrower than they should be [he said to an on-set journalist]. And that lever there that fires a torpedo is a half-foot higher up the bulkhead than regulation. And I'll admit the collision button has been moved out and a bit lower, and the steps on those hatch ladders are three inches farther apart than they should be. Let's just say we've used a sort of poetic license.[3]

That poetic license has made abstinence an impossible ideal for Matt Sherman. Bearing witness to the gag—a woman reaching too high, bending too low, or stepping too far—is too much, even for him.

Most of the gags in *Operation Petticoat* are standard issue stuff, but interesting insofar as they demonstrate Edwards' early efforts at thematically organized visual comedy. The highlights reel: a woman gets her shoe stuck in the sub's deck; Lieutenant Dolores Crandall turns the shower on in Sherman's face; the *Sea Tiger* gets painted pink; and, of course, when the sub expels its on-board lingerie to save itself (Blake Edwards makes a cameo here—he is the first marine to rescue an undergarment). This last gag is notable for several reasons. First, Edwards understood its timing: the placement of this joke at the end of the film marks the culmination of *Operation Petticoat*'s splurch development. Up to this point, Edwards' visual comedy has built *gradually* up from minor sight gags, working itself up to a comic climax of extraordinary visual invention. But invention is only part of the picture; the lingerie explosion is also thematically relevant. Using bras and ladies underwear to defend themselves, the seamen have synthesized the previously discrepant gender worlds of sex and combat. Furthermore, the gag is indicative of major character change (*Sherman* orders it), and, as a result, it is integral to the drama. Remove this gag from the film and the story collapses. In short, this is a muscular gag—Blake's best thus far—sophisticated in the manner of the director's mature technique.

Operation Petticoat brought Universal $6.8 million, the strongest box office in the studio's fifty-year history. It was also the biggest hit of

---

* From the Production Code files: "It seems to us that the business of the sailors brushing by the girl with the large breasts in the narrow passageway of the submarine is greatly overdone."[4]

Grant's sixty-seven-picture career and earned him no less than $3 million, the highest fee an actor had ever earned for a single film. If Cary Grant thought he was hallucinating, he most likely was, though it probably had less to do with the wealth than the LSD. For 1959, the year the film was released, was also the year the world found out about the actor's adventures in acid, a fact that may have offended many, but, as the numbers show, did little to beset the picture's Christmas box office.

Blake was on the map.

HIGH TIME (1960)

Harvey: I'm a freshman!

In *High Time* widower Harvey Howard (Bing Crosby) decides to return to college, moves into a dorm with a handful of other students and engages in the day-to-day of fraternity events, football games, dances, and student rallies, falls for Helene Gauthier, a French professor (Nicole Maurey), encourages a love affair, and by junior year finds himself enmeshed in scandal (student-faculty relations are prohibited at Pinehurst College), only to be undone by student protest and then graduate with honors. The story of *High Time*—indeed just about everything about it—is incidental, but Edwards leaves a few fingerprints worth examining. His interest in movement tops the list. Whether they're dancing, ice-skating, or bustling through a coeducational congregation, these actors are in a constant state of motion. With very few exceptions (certain uninspiring classroom settings and romantic close-ups), the entirety of *High Time* is conveyed through a vigorous physicality of performance that will come to characterize the movies of Blake Edwards. The difference between those films and this film is that here, Edwards' interest in gesticulation is related not to the expression of character or narrative, but to its potential for graphic dynamism.

High Time is awash in a kinetic aesthetic of color and action. From the title animations to the slick, evenly lit foreground arrangements, to the not-a-hair-out-of-place compositions of his anamorphic work, Blake Edwards is undoubtedly a director in love with surface and gloss. At one point during *High Time*'s many transitional effects, the image literally becomes a canvas as four figures interrupt a freeze-frame and paint (yes, paint) over the scene we were just watching. After the screen is covered in blue, they paint the word " Freshman" in bold white lettering and the next sequence begins. This interest in the illustrational quality of imagery is typical of *High Time* and Edwards' later tendency towards artifice. For a director intent on skin-deep shallowness it is an indispensable technique.

Edwards' experiments in framing continue with his treatment of movement. When we are first introduced to Howard's roommates, Gil Sparrow (Fabian), Joy Elder (Tuesday Weld), and Bob Bannerman (Richard Beymer), they are dancing. They even dance through their dialogue. Later, in the bonfire sequence, students burst over the frame in all directions, an ice-skating scene follows along with a gym dance, a formal ball, a basketball game, and countless other instances of continuous on-screen motion. Even a stationary exchange between two people, as in Howard's discussion with his gym teacher, is backgrounded by a melee of jittery basketball players. To Edwards, this is college: a youthful setting distinguished by constant physical activity. By contrast, the world of age is utterly static. Case in point: brittle old Judge Carter (Douglass Dumbrille) has a broken foot. Until Harvey lifts him up and onto the dance floor, Carter's cast forces him to stay put. According to the visual logic of *High Time*, the judge represents a nightmare of elderly incapacitation—Harvey's *actual* nightmare says as much. In his dream, Harvey is roped up and tied to a slab, unable to move. Even the Howard children, who drop Harvey off at school every year (as though they were his parents), are confined to their seats in the car. Never once are they seen descending from their vehicle, though they are given ample opportunity to do so.

The clash between physical freedom and restraint is summarized in the film's closing scene. Harvey Howard, valedictorian, faces the kind of lifeless student congregation we have seen many times before. As he delivers his speech, it seems he has now adopted aged professorial inertia. (After all, he is now older *and* learned.) Will he become the kind of stiff the film has carefully pitted him against? The answer comes a moment later when Harvey throws up his arms, flies into the air, and soars over the crowd. It is the epitome of freedom-through-motion, and the final image of the film.

In Edwards' later films, physical freedom and the forces that inhibit it become indispensable components of gag logic. When he commits an adulterous act (or even an adulterous gesture), George Webber (10) will suffer *physical* consequences. It's a punishment: emotional or sexual violations beget injury. For Inspector Clouseau, it is his pompous pretension that triggers the splurch. But in *High Time*, a film that is unsophisticated in its gagging, this logic does not apply. Here the gags are motiveless. Aside for a few intimations of Edwards' contempt for Clouseau-like authoritarians (which we see in the few calamities that befall Professor Thayer and the maitre d' at Harvey Howard's), the visual humor in the film is composed of ideologically unjustified and dramatically irrelevant non sequiturs. These may be gags, but they are certainly not splurches. When Harvey slips after his final pull-up, for instance, we wonder why. We know that

8. *High Time* (1960) Ladies and Gentlemen, the lovely Bing Crosby.
(Courtesy of the Academy of Motion Picture Arts and Sciences)

he's physically capable, so the joke can't be an indication of weakness, and he has committed no splurch-worthy transgression.

With its glossy surfaces and bold physicality, *High Time* provided Blake Edwards an opportunity to rehearse a few auteurist gestures, but none receives as much attention as his beloved proscenium staging. Though actual stages and curtains appear only sporadically, Edwards goes to great lengths to remind us that we are never far from theatricality. For instance, crowd scenes are everywhere; gathered around a speaker or spectacle the hordes of students are transformed into an audience. This notion is evidenced in the bonfire, phys. ed., and faculty auction sequences, all of which feature a man who, raised above the group, changes a crowd into an audience. Also, spectatorship is naturally explicit in the ice-skating, basketball, and dance scenes. If the simple addition of an on-screen observer makes these activities performances, then we might consider High Time to be something of a talent show with timid musical aspirations. Think of the many auditorium scenes and speechmakers, perfect fodder for Blake's proscenium compositions. And musical numbers abound: "Nobody's Perfect," "It Came upon A Midnight Clear," and the Oscar-nominated "The Second Time Around" are all sung to an informal crowd—an audience.

Though, how a film conceived by Garson Kanin, produced by Charles Brackett, and directed by Blake Edwards could have such a lousy script will remain a great mystery to film lovers the world over. Even the near-psychedelic bliss of watching Bing Crosby la-di-da through a dance hall in hoop skirt can't reverse the damage of Frank and Tom Waldman's screenwriting, which bears a stronger resemblance to brother Frank's Esther Williams pictures than it does to Kanin's for Cukor or Brackett's for Wilder. And yet, when it was released in September of 1960 (just in time for back-to-school box office), High Time was met with a warm critical response. Most reviewers praised Edwards' pleasant visual gimmickry, those transitional special effects for which Fox paid $250,000. This "new montage"—the studio's phrase for it—was, for the minimal screentime involved, the picture's costliest quirk.[5] But considering the critical attention it received, it was money well spent.

Citing the director's "usual astringency," the Hollywood Reporter saw in Edwards a leader of the next generation, naming him amongst "one of two or three younger directors who seems aware that the screen is a separate medium, and is willing to chance using its unique properties. Edwards uses split screen and half a dozen other cinema tricks to set his mood, forward his story and provide spot jokes along the way."[6] Others were less supportive: "Blake Edwards," wrote the Los Angeles Times, "reverts shamelessly to the sight gags of the old silents."[7] The old silents, yes, but shamelessly? A reversion? It's a different song, but the same tune. For these critics, the gag is more than just obsolete—it is dishonorable.

BREAKFAST AT TIFFANY'S (1961)

*O. J.: She's a real phony. You know why? Because she
honestly believes all this phony junk she believes in.*

Truman Capote wanted Marilyn Monroe. "Holly had to have
something touching about her," he said, "unfinished. Marilyn had that."[8]
But Paula Strasberg wouldn't hear of it. As soon as Marilyn's acting coach
discovered her client was under consideration for the part, Strasberg dis-
qualified her, asserting that a "woman of the night" was an unsuitable part
for the bombshell. But it was a moot point: Monroe was under contract at
Twentieth Century Fox and would be too expensive to bring over to Paramount. And so, Richard Shepherd and Martin Jurow, the film's producers,
went straight to Audrey Hepburn with the script. It was perfect: not only
was Hepburn in the midst of a three-picture deal at Paramount, but she
was in eerie accord with Capote's description of Holly Golightly. As he
described her, the character had "a flat little bottom, chic thinness, her
mouth was large, her nose upturned. It was a face beyond childhood, yet
this side of belonging to a woman."[9] Who better than Audrey?

Impressed with the spirited pace of *Operation Petticoat*, Martin Jurow
brought Blake Edwards aboard to direct, but how responsible is Edwards
for the holy eminence the film has today? Devout *Breakfasters* kneel at the
altar of Audrey (and rightfully so), but where does that leave us, the Blake
Edwardians? In their trailblazing double volume on Blake, Lehman and
Luhr go to great lengths to point out the picture's auteurist components,
citing certain moments of genre bending and the recurrence of particular
themes as indication of the director's influence. Though these elements
are most certainly present, they are not prominent, and their attendance
adds little to the *Breakfast at Tiffany's* experience. There are a handful of
noteworthy exceptions, but most are upstaged by the hallowed triumvirate
of Hepburn, her style, and her song. Perhaps this is why the picture
unfolds in mostly innocuous medium shots, as if the auteur, in his good
judgment, knew when *not* to auteur.

Not according to Andrew Sarris. Back in 1961, the year of the picture's
release, he called *Breakfast at Tiffany's* the directorial surprise of the year. It
is not easy to understand why, but, before we attempt to, a refresher: Holly
Golightly, nutty and chic, makes her living in the powder room, takes

9. *Breakfast at Tiffany's* (1961) Audrey loathed Danish pastries.
(Paramount Pictures/Photofest)

money for her visits to Sing Sing, and has had a longstanding engagement
to do some photos for Mr. Yunioshi, which she keeps putting off. Her new
friendship with the writer Paul Varjak (George Peppard), who she soon
discovers is being "kept" by a married woman (Patricia Neal), begins to
get strange when Holly's long lost husband, Doc, comes looking for her.
After explaining to Paul that their marriage had been annulled years ago,
Holly sends poor Doc away, and soon, quite expectedly, Paul begins to fall
for her. (And who wouldn't?) Unfortunately for the both of them, Holly
wants to be free, and that means resisting the love she feels for Paul in
favor of heading to South America with a Latin millionaire named José.
But her plans are thwarted when the feds discover that she has been
(unknowingly) carrying criminal information to Sally Tomato, her client at
Sing Sing. José dumps her, and Holly, devastated, decides to leave Manhattan. Luckily, Paul stops her on her way out, and convinces her that people
do indeed belong together. They kiss in the rain.

Where is the director's hand in there? Holly's cocktail party, realized in
a series of anecdotal asides, may be the only scene that has "Edwards"

written all over it ("the general party was only indicated [in the screen-play]," he remembers, "and I had to improvise it on the set"[10]). The scene is built on a foundation of minor sight gags—visual one-liners—running past like pictures on a conveyor belt. Curiously, the director links these jokes in a montage form uncharacteristic of his mature style (in the future, long takes will be favored). At this party, the first significant gag show of Edwards' career, and, to Pauline Kael, one of "the best screen parties of the era,"[11] Holly inadvertently sets a woman's hat aflame, another woman is seen laughing at herself in the mirror (later she's crying at the same spot), a conversation between two women continues unchanged after one of the women rises up into the air (we see she's been sitting on someone's shoulders), and a man removes his eye-patch to reveal a perfectly intact eye beneath. Turn down the volume and you're watching a silent comedy.

What makes the gags Edwardian is that a strong majority of them are predicated on the notion of duplicitous identity. These fakes, we see, match O. J. Berman's (Martin Balsam's) description of Holly as "a real phony." In fact, phonies of all kinds play havoc throughout the movie. From Doc Golightly's (Buddy Ebsen's) pursuit of Paul to the Huckleberry Hound masks of the shoplifting scene, falsity is the name of the game. Names themselves are constantly being renounced and revised, as if changing one's label might have some effect on character ("Mind if I call you Fred?" Holly asks Paul). With this in mind, the film's very first scene assumes new meaning. Standing outside of Tiffany's, Holly can only look. Edwards makes much of the glass separating her from what's inside, cutting from over her shoulder to behind the window display (looking out at her) and back again. As she says to Paul, she loves "the proud look" of Tiffany's. Looking is, after all, what she's all about. Why? Because facades—and here's a directorial concern—keep her free from the perma-nence of self.

Holly's dream of freedom finds its visual correlate in Edwards' use of open and closed spaces. In what seems to be a direct engagement with the aesthetic arc of *Experiment in Terror*, Blake's next film, Holly's crisis of containment is dramatized first through spatial privilege and then, as she acquiesces, through spatial restriction (Paul: "You're afraid somebody's gonna put you in a cage!"). It is the opposite of *Experiment in Terror*, and for a very good reason: Holly must join a man, Kelly Sherwood (Lee Remick) must escape from one. Think of *Breakfast at Tiffany's* very opening shot: a long, limitless stretch of Fifth Avenue, with a deep-space vanishing point way downtown. And no one is around. This is Holly's dream of independence. Her reality, by contrast, is presented in pictures of limitation. She may have been shot in low angle as she approached Tiffany's, but inside her apartment she's imaged from above. The overhead shot, often taken from Mr. Yunioshi's (Mickey Rooney's) landing, compresses the space, and thereby restricts her physical freedom. Similarly, if his apartment is cluttered with Orientalia (he hits his head on a paper lantern), it's because Holly's is almost object free. Thus, those in Breakfast at Tiffany's who love things—like Patricia Neal's character, an interior decorator—are, as Holly states, held back by them. Consequently, the film's miserable characters are continually photographed in cramped spaces, practically engulfed in décor. (When Holly consents to marry José, her apartment shows signs of tacky collecting).

Even physical proximity to another person is a kind of containment. As the film draws to a (feminist?) close, Edwards' visual concept takes a turn for the restrictive. Consider the famous cab ride in the rain. In one long two-shot Paul and Holly are squeezed together, and the camera does not move or cut. This, as seen through Holly's eyes, is a picture of incarceration. Under these circumstances, Breakfast at Tiffany's memorable last shot —Holly and Paul kissing in the rain—is problematic. One the one hand, their embrace is set outside in the rain, presented in a wide shot that seems to be all about unlimited space (as was the interior of Tiffany's). On the other hand, they are in a dirty alley, enclosed on all sides by sky-high buildings of brick. So what is Edwards saying here? Is this containment or liberty? It's a strangely insecure conclusion, and, unlike most of the film, indicative of strong directorial influence.

But is that what makes it a classic? No. Then what does?

A star. A style. A song. After we remove the myth from the moviemaking, this is what remains of Breakfast at Tiffany's. After we have separated the picture's cultural impact from the picture itself, we are left not with an auteurist masterwork, but the product of fortuitous collaborations. Edwards remembers it this way:

I was sort of inadvertently thrown in with some of the truly great fashion people in the world, and suddenly I was looking at wardrobe to be approved by Audrey Hepburn. And, of course, I'm not stupid, I'm not going to say "Well, gee, fellas, I don't really know about those kinds of things." It gave me an education. How wrong can you go?[12]

With Audrey and couturier Hubert de Givenchy, you can't; their little black dress, modern and sporty, left the poodle skirt in the dust. It did away with the voluptuous Jane Russell/Marilyn Monroe model of the fifties in favor of the clean lines and simple colors of the Golightly plan, and as gentlemen's preferences veered from blondes, Audrey Hepburn became the new it girl à la mode.

Like all great stars, Audrey was a volatile mix of contradictions. Half princess, half beatnik, part girl, and part woman, she combined European grace with the American dream of self-reliance. For as we see in *Roman Holiday*, she's a twentieth-century Cinderella in reverse, the royal who tries to make it out there on her own. Unlike Grace Kelly, for whom a life without diamonds is unthinkable, Audrey's touch of earthliness grants her complexity, which is precisely why Holly Golightly was the perfect role; it allowed her to contrast (not quarantine) the warring aspects of her screen persona. As a hooker-cum-ingénue, she could be both *at once*. From the studio's point of view, it was just the mixture they were looking for, making Hepburn's evocation of Holly a triumph of finagling just sugary enough to turn hustling commercial. With the help of screenwriter George Axelrod's strategic adaptation, the character became a vision of studio innuendo—as if Mae West birthed her in the Hays Office.

As a result, she was ready for the transitional early sixties, and no doubt the picture's success was contingent upon good timing. Hepburn's performance aptly dramatized the tension in the American *zeitgeist*, between a life of domesticity (with Paul) and the dream of independence. Like many women of the postwar generation, Holly seeks for herself an identity distinct from her relation to couplehood. As she says to Cat, her cat, "we belong to nobody, and nobody belongs to us." But by the end of the film—and here's where it gets tricky—Holly has revised her dream. Paul Varjak begs her to, pleading,

> people *do* fall in love, people *do* belong to each other, because that's the only chance anybody's got for real happiness. You call yourself a free spirit, a "wild thing," and you're terrified somebody's gonna stick you in a cage. Well baby, you're already in that cage. You built it yourself.

Apparently, liberty (sexual or otherwise) lost out to the "Moon River" girl. All she needed was the right man to point it out to her. Or is she still free? Such ambivalence has existed in Audrey Hepburn since *Roman Holiday*, her first starring role (will she stay at home or see the world?), and unlike Katherine Hepburn or Barbara Stanwyck, her persona is too much at odds

10. *Breakfast at Tiffany's* (1961) Blake, Audrey, and George Peppard rehearsing at the northeast corner of Fifty-second Street and Park Avenue. Earlier that morning—the first day of filming—they shot the famous scene outside Tiffany's. Because it was early enough on a Sunday, there were no crowds on Fifth Avenue, and the scene came off in perfect serenity. Now, after lunch, the throngs had gathered for a look. (Paramount Pictures / Photofest)

with its convictions to render her fully matured. And yet, it is precisely this inner irreconcilability that is at the heart of her uniqueness. That's movie star stuff.

But without the genius of Givenchy, it's safe to say that none of it would exist. Beginning with "décolletée Sabrina" in 1954, Givenchy's designs, somewhere between formal and casual, and seemingly rendered in a single brushstroke, were perfectly tailored to Hepburn in form and sensibility. Like Audrey herself, the clothing was lean and slender, representing a new glamour of simplicity and restraint. Eloquence trumped opulence, color and fabric went the way of the fifties, and together designer and muse popularized a revised femininity predicated not on forthright sexuality, but gamine chic. The actress may have found considerable success on her own, but it was the couturier that turned her into an icon. The new era was fast approaching, and the new woman was right behind it.

Then there's "Moon River," the instant standard that became an Oscar-winning song. Its sweet prairie melody is poised in firm contrast to the rest of the film's jazz/pop score, and, taken together, they capture the disparity and union of Holly's alter ego, Texan Lula Mae, and uptown Holly. The song's extraordinary success was due not only to its exquisite melody and rich lyric—staples of Henry Mancini and Johnny Mercer—but to the authenticity of Audrey's singing voice. In impact, the song is the musical equivalent to the little black dress, though in content, it's its worthy opposition. "It took me a month to think it through," Mancini recalls. "I built the melody in a range of an octave and one. It was simple and completely diatonic: in the key of C, you can play it entirely on the white keys."[13] What results is a fortuitous unity of star, style, and song, braided together in brilliant consonance.

Grossing $4 million domestically, *Breakfast at Tiffany's* was a modest hit and would go on to receive significant Oscar attention (Hepburn was nominated, as were the art directors and George Axelrod, but it was Mancini who took home the statuettes—two of them—one for Best Score and one for Best Song, which he shared with Mercer). It was Blake's first prestige picture and as such an important step in the advancement of his reputation as a serious director of mainstream cinema. Upon its release, Eric Rohmer wrote *Cahiers du Cinéma*'s first full-length piece on a Blake Edwards movie, and *Variety* was satiated, though its review is more concerned with the film's achievements in acting and photography than in direction. But the last word on the matter ought to go to the *New York Times* critic A. H. Weiler. "In the person of Miss Hepburn," he wrote, "[Holly] is a genuinely charming, elfin waif who will be believed and adored when seen."[14] More than that, to nascent feminists with few to lead them, Audrey's Holly presented an affront to the status quo, an autonomous young woman bristling with dissent. No one could have predicted it, but she had broken exciting new ground."

EXPERIMENT IN TERROR (1962)

Man at bar: Are you looking for someone? Kelly: Yes.
Man at bar: I could be that someone.

If it wasn't for his inchoate fear of genre, the popular reception of *Breakfast at Tiffany's* might have compelled Blake Edwards to make
another romantic comedy. Instead, he decided upon *Experiment in Terror*, a
suspense film of unprecedented moodiness in the Edwards *oeuvre*. This
one was set in the foggy undertow of San Francisco, far, far away from the
fabulousness of Manhattan society. In it, a heavy-breathing psychopath
(Ross Martin) abducts bank teller Kelly Sherwood (Lee Remick) and orders her to steal him $100,000 from her bank. FBI agent John Ripley
(Glenn Ford) advises her to play along, which she does really quite well,
buying the bureau enough time to get information on the faceless assailant. On the day of the crime though, Kelly dutifully follows her tormen-
ter's instructions and heads to Candlestick Park, where Ripley is positioned to interrupt the handoff. At the right moment, he sacks the villain
and salvages the money. There is no love scene.

The price Columbia Pictures paid for the rights to *Operation Terror* was at
the time the highest figure ever paid to film a suspense novel.[15] The book's
co-authors, Mildred Gordon and her husband, Gordon Gordon (the film
credits them as simply "The Gordons"), received a staggering $112,500 for
the rights, a sum telling of the studio's high regard for the adaptation. At
roughly $590 a page, *Operation Terror* was an unquestionably valuable prop-
erty, and with a sequel in the works even before production began, Blake
Edwards was selected to direct. After a string of light comedies—*Operation
Petticoat*, *High Time*, and *Breakfast at Tiffany's*—Blake was ready to turn his
attention to something different, something darker. But a thriller? Did he
have it in him? "That period of my life was a constant testing," he remembers. "I really didn't know where I was going."[16] *Experiment* was one of many
experiments. "I wanted to try something that was . . . away from the things
that I was suddenly finding myself involved with."[17] And yet there are
certain harmonious resonances between the *Experiment*'s interest in mas-
culine/feminine queries and the mystery of true identity, and Edwards'
auteurist concern for what is really real underneath it all. The film is also

indicative of Blake Edwards' skeptical outlook on the state of coupledom, sharing with *Breakfast at Tiffany's* and *Days of Wine and Roses* (among others) challenges to the values of committed monogamy. Like Holly Golightly, Kelly Sherwood (Lee Remick) will go it alone. Both are women for whom men pose a considerable threat, but while Holly's story ends in romantic acquiescence (she'll marry Paul), Kelly might continue into a stronger life of independence, free from conjugal obligation. The San Franciscan is freed, and the New Yorker is bound.

The freedom/bondage dialectic finds visual expression in Edwards' organization of screen space, and his clever use of camera and light. Quite often, the frame literally imprisons Kelly. Consider this scene from the beginning of the film: as the garage door closes behind her, Kelly is attacked by an unidentified assailant. Here, the camera is complicit in Kelly's containment. For one, her face is surrounded by total darkness, which gives our eye no place to escape. Blake, like her assailant, will not let us look anywhere else in the shot; rather, he enhances our/her claustrophobia through the unyielding pressure of his camera; it does not move, it does not cut. Instead, it is held in place, and, like the attacker, will not release Kelly from its control. Right away, the elements of camera, light, and mise-en-scène have introduced us to one of *Experiment in Terror*'s thematic and visual tendencies: psychological and cinematic containment.

With containment comes the threat of sexual submission. We can tell by his heavy breathing and innuendo ("No, no, no, I don't want to hurt you") that Kelly's assailant is after more than just money: he wants to control Kelly, perhaps even to rape her. Though it is rarely made explicit, the dominant male/submissive female dynamic recurs visually throughout *Experiment in Terror*, generally in the form of crushing, claustrophobic compositions, which place the woman at a distinct disadvantage. In this way, Edwards' framing technique prefigures his work in *Days of Wine and Roses*, a film that is founded upon a similar aesthetic of visual containment. A clever wide shot of the interior of the bank where Kelly Sherwood works reinforces this ideology. The bank tellers, all female, are shown working in their cubicles. Placed side by side and photographed in a single shot, these cubicles assume cagelike connotations, and with the added element of surveillance—the (male) manager watching his women—the image takes on a sexual perversity. Objectively, the shot is a benign description of bank life: *this is Kelly's place of work and this is what she does*, it says, but within

©CPC-8626-37

11. *Experiment in Terror* (1962) Kelly Sherwood (Lee Remick) begins the film contained, as shown here, and ends the film released. Edwards' aesthetic follows suit, shifting gradually from an emphasis on closed spaces to open spaces, and culminating finally in a climax set in Candlestick Park. (Author's collection)

the context of *Experiment in Terror*'s concern with sexual domination, the image is an exemplary recapitulation of the theme. And Kelly is not the only woman contained—so too is every woman in the shot.

Edwards' use of the high angle works the same way. The shot that takes Kelly into the bank, for instance, makes her appear shrunken and helpless. The same applies to the shot of her in the Orange Grove bathroom (before she is attacked). Looking down upon Kelly is itself an act of containment: the space appears to be crushing her. Conversely, her captor is shot in extreme close-ups. Before his identity is revealed and his control over Kelly is at its most terrifying height, Red Lynch is broken down metonymically and then exaggerated to gigantic size. One shot in particular is so close, only Red's mouth fits into frame. By contrast, Kelly appears even smaller. Edwards' contrapuntal treatment of the Red/Kelly relationship only aggravates the movie's male/female tension. But female subservience doesn't end there. It even persists between "positive" characters, good guys like Kelly and agent John Ripley, who do not seek to control one another. Though their alliance is, unlike Red and Kelly's, morally justified, the imbalance of power between the sexes is still present. For example, when Kelly is called into the back office of the bank to have a private conference with Ripley, she is, once again, shut in by framing. As she enters the room, Edwards places Kelly far enough away from the camera that she seems almost to disappear in the space under Ripley's arm. Like Red Lynch, the exaggeration of one of John Ripley's features—in this case his arm—is presented in harsh contrast to the graphic insignificance of Kelly Sherwood. She a woman enclosed in masculine space.

The subject of female submission is clearly reaffirmed in the playfully creepy mannequin sequence. Faceless female bodies are hung everywhere; some without limbs, others without heads. They dangle from the ceiling and reach out from the floor like teeth in the jaws of a room ready to crunch the seductive Nancy Ashton (Patricia Huston) who, with an hour before her male rescuer (Ripley) comes to save her, must survive in the house on her own. When she goes upstairs to undress, we know it's official: she can't have much longer. Stripped down to her lingerie, Nancy is now just as vulnerable as her mannequins. Into this room comes Lynch. He's hidden from view, and watches (surveillance again) his prey. Later, the cops find Nancy's body hung amongst the mannequins. (As if the analogy wasn't clear enough: subjugation has turned to objectification.) In less capable hands, the film could have easily devolved into pedantic repetitions of theme, reinstating and self-plagiarizing ad nauseam. But not so of Edwards. Instead, he turns the camera on us. Cut to an old silent movie house: the upstairs office is decorated with head shots; on every wall there is a face, and every face is a woman's. These are nameless figures, and like the mannequins, they are indistinguishable. But by setting this sequence in a cinema, Edwards is explicitly playing with his own movie's investigation of watching women. Now the film's notion of female submission has been expanded to implicate moviegoers in the crime of voyeurism.

Experiment in Terror tells a story of a woman's attempt to live free of men. Whereas Nancy and Lisa (Lynch's current girlfriend) need male protection (one physical, the other financial), Kelly has learned, as the saying goes, to take matters into her own hands, and subsequently she can overcome male subjugation. To illustrate this arc, Edwards reverses the containment aesthetic by delivering Kelly into large open spaces. Consider the Candlestick Park climax. Could there be a more appropriate location to stage the captive woman's release from the world of male containment? With these final images, the film's problematic gender delineations are dismantled, and in their place, a recurring trope of the Blake Edwards movie is established: concurrence of gender. It suggests that in a world of amorphous identity, no man or woman can survive on "masculinity" or "femininity" alone. To achieve his or her goal, he and she must each be he/she, Victor and Victoria. Perhaps this is why married life, which offers a solution through the collaborative fusion of male and female, receives the cold shoulder in Edwards' films, which favor the union of yin and yang within a single individual—not the couple. Thus, if they are to survive, the successful figures of Planet Edwards must face and reverse the cultural restrictions placed upon their sex.

The film's final shot is interrupted by a single credit—Ross Martin's—and then fades to black. To contemporary audiences, the credit answered a riddle they were probably puzzling out since the picture began, and perhaps even well before. The game began when Columbia's publicity department made a very big deal of keeping the identity of the actor playing Red Lynch a secret. A fuss was made for the benefit of the press as the actor in question, masked and gagged, was escorted through a series of "Who is he?" interviews. (Studio mandate decreed he was only to be referred to as "Mr. Blank."[18]) Moviegoer curiosity was spiked, but audiences had to wait until the very end of Experiment in Terror to be relieved. It was silly bit of buzz making, but the boys in publicity were onto something: the game of peek-a-boo is a critical pivot of Edwards' story apparatus. "I think audiences go to suspense films for escape and enjoyment," Edwards said on the set of *Experiment in Terror*. "That's why you won't see a lot of obvious violence in *Experiment*. And Lee [Remick], of course, is perfect for the part. Can you think of a more apple-pie normal heroine to tie to the railroad tracks?"[19] In this statement, the director's use of silent film imagery very tellingly addresses his propensity toward the fusion of comedy and suspense. For others, the genres are mutually exclusive, but for Edwards, each enhances the other. The scream is nothing more than a perverted punch line, a laugh turned inside out. Both are contingent upon setup and payoff, tension and release. What they have in common—Edwards' idea of "escape and enjoyment"—is inseparable from the feeling of anxiety. After all, what is Inspector Clouseau but a Mabel Normand tied to the tracks?

DAYS OF WINE AND ROSES (1962)

Kirsten: You see, the world looks so dirty to me when I'm not drinking.
Joe: Remember Fisherman's Wharf, the water when you look too close?
That's the way the world looks to me when I'm not drinking.

Days of Wine and Roses doesn't look like a Blake Edwards movie. It's bleak, it's dark, and there isn't a car crash in sight. But then again, the Blake Edwards brand didn't always signify what it does today. Back in the early sixties, before he had his name above the title, Blake was a director for hire, changing genres like a cinematic chameleon. After all, this was 1962 B.C. (Before Clouseau), and Blake's comedies only punctuated his repertoire. In fact, his first two screenplays, *Panhandle* (1948) and *Stampede* (1949), were Westerns, and were followed by the detective radio shows *Richard Diamond, Private Detective* and *Yours Truly, Johnny Dollar*, and then his first directorial effort: a musical. And there was *Experiment in Terror*. In this company, we might view *Days of Wine and Roses* as atypical of Edwards, but it is typical of this, his journeyman period.

It begins as Joe Clay (Jack Lemmon) and Kirsten Arnesen (Lee Remick) meet cute and, against her better judgment, he convinces her to try a chocolate cocktail. Soon, she's an alcoholic. They're alcoholics together. Drinking becomes the only thing they do because it's the only thing they can do, and realizing this, they decide to sober up. But it doesn't work. Joe breaks into a rural liquor store and wakes up the next morning in a straightjacket. There in the hospital he meets Jim Hungerford, a one-time addict who sponsors him through AA. A few meetings later, Joe gets his act together, but Kirsten remains a hopeless case. Without her, Joe moves with their child into a modest apartment and begins to put his life in order. One night, Kirsten comes to the door, begging him to give her another chance, but Joe refuses. The last shot sees Joe at the window, watching Kirsten, alone, headed on to the next bar.

Indeed, *Days of Wine and Roses* is bleak, but contains many Edwards trademarks that will be perfected in subsequent films; that is to say, his preference for wide shots, an interplay of comedy and drama, a robust physicality to the performances, and early experimentations with precision framing. Conversely, *Days of Wine and Roses* includes certain stylistic gestures that seem out of step with most of the director's work. For instance, like *Experiment in Terror*, it's shot in black and white. To Edwards, this lent the picture "a documentary feel,"[20] a quality we typically don't associate with his films. Also unusual for Blake (but appropriate to the material), *Days of Wine and Roses* is presented in the 1.85:1 aperture, a smaller frame that forces the characters into intimate proximity with one another. In an era of ever-widening aspect ratios,* selecting the 1.85:1 format might have been a touch anachronistic, but Blake was never one to worry about trends.

The casting of Jack Lemmon continues a decades-long collaboration between the filmmaker and his alter ego. "They asked Jack Lemmon and Lee Remick who they'd like to direct it," Edwards remembers. "Lemmon asked for me because he felt that it was such a bleak script that it needed a director who had the ability to inject humor into the piece."[21] After two successful projects with Edwards on Richard Quine's *My Sister Eileen* (1955) and *Operation Mad Ball* (1957), Lemmon recognized the value in harnessing Edwards' penchant for crossbreeding comedy and drama. Side by side, the actor and the director drew from each other a bittersweetness that would endure, together and apart, throughout their final films. But for Lemmon, it was a turning point in an already startling career.

In 1955, six years before he got the script of *Days of Wine and Roses*, Lemmon was already an Oscar winner. His Best Supporting Actor win for *Mister Roberts* was followed by a handful of appearances in forgettable movies, but it was his trio with Quine—*Operation Mad Ball* (1957), *Bell, Book and Candle* (1958), and *It Happened to Jane* (1959)—that solidified his screen image and delivered him to the curmudgeonly genius of Billy Wilder. The rest is American film history. *Some Like It Hot* and *The Apartment* won Jack two more nominations, further encouraging his aptitude for easy-going neurotics and edging him to the precipice of typecasting's black vortex. He realized he had become a Hollywood commodity, and that it was time to begin the search for a role that would redefine him. Enter *Days of Wine and Roses*: the perfect opportunity. "Nothing has been closer to me, ever," he said,[22] and it remains one of the greatest performances of his career.

It's a testament to Blake's sensitivity and restraint that the comic outbursts in the film do not break tone, but, as Lemmon planned, provide temporary relief. "There is often a bizarre, comedic side to tragedy," Lemmon said, though "there are some who have an aversion to films that are

---

* *How the West Was Won*, shot in Cinerama, was released the same year.

comedy-drama. They want comedy or drama, but not both, as in real life."[23] No doubt Edwards agreed. We can see evidence of this throughout the film, but it is in the early moments of Joe and Kirsten's courtship that Edwards' incomparable personality is most prominent. Their office scene, for instance, places us squarely in romantic comedy. It begins with a meet-cute and develops into an elevator episode that's baked with all the old screwball ingredients; the boy's misdirected pursuit of the girl (the couple is clearly mismatched), and she holds all the cards (Joe sticks his tongue out at Kirsten behind her back), while he is pleasantly (if a bit violently) discombobulated. On his way up to her apartment, Joe knocks right into the staircase, shakes himself off, and continues upward. The moment is so vigorously disorienting, it's inconceivable that it didn't spring from Blake's imagination. And the cockroach scene that follows is all laughs.

Days of Wine and Roses has its share of funny moments, but its real power comes from Edwards' uncanny facility with the darker side of slapstick. Remove the laugh from a gag and what you've got is a humiliated man—that's the premise behind many of the film's finest sequences. It's the difference between a drunken fool and a plain drunk, and as we see in Joe Clay, the line between them is, like the window he's about to smack into, almost invisible. The business of pulling up flowers from the dirt—equal parts touching and disruptive—sets the tone for Joe's drunken collision. It is endearing, but there is altogether too much soil displacement for us to be at ease. We have to feel safe to laugh, and this brief act of civil obedience sets the audience on edge. One tulip is cute, even Chaplinesque, but four tulips is three too many. Heading to his apartment, Joe swaggers over from the flowerbed and slams into a window he mistakes for an open space. It's definitely a splurch (based on the premise of WYS isn't WYG), but our laugh is tempered by concern.

To achieve the balance, Edwards infuses the moment with quiet tension. Because he shoots the scene through the glass, we see what Joe doesn't—that there's a window there—and cannot share in his surprise upon meeting it. If this were a moment out of *10* or *Skin Deep*, the drunk's response to the impact would be greatly exaggerated. Dudley Moore might shriek and throw his hands in the air, John Ritter would explode into a spastic fit, but Lemmon's reaction is quite the opposite: he plays the physical pain, *not* the absurdity of the situation.

The scene ends when the flowers are decapitated in the elevator door. We might smile at the strangeness of the image—flower heads jutting out of an elevator are pleasantly surreal—but the implication is one of pure violence, typical of Lemmon's characterization. Unlike Ray Milland's brooding interiority in The Lost Weekend, Joe Clay is drawn with almost vaudevillian extroversion. He stumbles, falls, crashes, and, in the hospital scene, endures shocking convulsions. He is tied down and straightjacketed. He jumps on the bed, climbs down a tree, and crawls through the dirt. Lemmon's hyperphysicalization of his character's psychological conflict is unmistakably Edwards, a performance concept that runs throughout his films, and, though it is generally exploited for comedic effect, it is in Days of Wine and Roses no less than harrowing.

For precisely this reason, the greenhouse sequence is the most memorable in the film. It is also the most physically demanding scene in the picture, perhaps even of Lemmon's career, and Edwards doesn't let his camera get in the way. "I intentionally in this film decided not to be a clever photographer," he says, "unlike Experiment in Terror where I used my camera a lot with spooky, moody set-ups. I tried to be as straightforward and unaware of the camera as I could be. Even in the severely drunk scenes I didn't exaggerate my set-ups to make it more dramatic."[24] It's true. In the greenhouse scene, the will of the camera is subordinated to the whim of the actor. As is evidenced in the slight disparity between the actor and the frame (often the camera is a beat off), it is the lens that follows Lemmon, not the other way around. Building the four-minute sequence with only four shots allows Edwards to minimize his presence even further, and almost to disappear. In fact, the camera is so compliant, it allows Lemmon to drop out of focus and, at one point, even fall out of the frame entirely. This "antistyle" appears throughout the movie, and perhaps most notably during Remick's Shore Motel monologue. Shot in a single take, these nearly two minutes of film share with the greenhouse scene certain documentary-influenced, almost neorealist gestures.

But there is another side to coin. For a film of realist ambition, Days of Wine and Roses contains a great number of highly stylized images. The two showpieces mentioned are remarkable as much for their directorial restraint as for their graphic hyperstylization. For one, the greenhouse atmosphere borders on the expressionistic. With the thunder and lightning, the angular infrastructure of the set, and the occasional strobe-light effect (to simulate lightning), the scene is closer to Dr. Frankenstein's laboratory than to Rossellini's Rome, Open City. Similarly, inside the Shore Motel bungalow, Lee Remick's face is cast in high-contrast light—a shadow slices

12. *Days of Wine and Roses* (1962) Jack Lemmon and Lee Remick, ensconced in shadow, earn their Oscar nominations with a little help from chiaroscuro. Their performances—and Edwards' camerawork—fuse in perfect harmony, containing equal parts realism and expressionism. (Warner Bros./Photofest)

down the center of her face. It's an elegant device, and nicely accents her dual personae, but it's unmistakably contrived, almost theatrical. Does this mean the director has failed to achieve his "documentary feel"? Or was his naturalist aesthetic just a stylistic point of entry? The confluence of styles yield what amounts to an operatic naturalism, reminiscent of Visconti's late neorealist masterpiece *Rocco and his Brothers*, released only two years earlier. In both films, hard-edged grit is met with sporadic lyricism, but do they contradict? To answer that question, another question: what happens when you mix love and addiction? The opposition runs throughout.

When alcohol is present in the narrative, Edwards clogs the composition with conflicting lines of all kinds; squares in squares, crisscrossing perpendiculars, and geometric light patterns scream out to the audience that the screen world is descending into psychedelic rubble. And the deeper the drunkenness, the more cluttered the frame. At Joe and Kirsten's emotional low points (the greenhouse and motel scenes, respectively) compositional clarity—the visual order with which the film began—is obliterated. These images are structured architecturally, and are built with bold intersecting surfaces that at times appear even to imprison the actors. (It's an ideal metaphor for alcoholism: their world is literally closing in on them.) Nowhere is the claustrophobia more pronounced than in Joe and Kirsten's home. Here in the apartment, the picture chokes on graphic complication. Even the Braque poster on the wall (which serves as visual obstruction during an argument) is a neurotic mess of knotted lines. From foreground to background, the elements in the frame block clear eye-lines, amounting to a kind of pictorial equivalent to *coitus interruptus*. Edwards grants us no satisfaction here, continually frustrating our desire for compositional clarity. And so, when the end of the film comes and Kirsten, defeated, says, "I can't get over how dirty everything looks," we know exactly what she means. Things are no longer what they were. As the title song says, the door marked "nevermore" has shut.

The movie's lighting scheme describes the same downward trajectory. The transition from light to dark articulates the descent from clarity, or emotional security, into chaos. On her first date with Joe, Kirsten hasn't had a drink in her life. She's pure as can be, and accordingly, is blasted with soft white light, which in conjunction with her all-white outfit turns her into a gleaming angel of sobriety. Joe, by contrast, is dark. He wears a black suit—half of his face is muted in gentle shadow. As the film unfolds, they drink (and drink), and white seems to drain from Edwards' palette. It returns for a moment when the Clays dry out at Ellis Arnesen's (Charles Bickford's) farm. The picture is telling us that there is hope ahead, and the bath of white light is so warm that for this brief moment even we begin to feel better. But they are not long, the days of wine and roses. Soon, the images are enveloped in grays. And then the grays turn black. Kirsten's white nightgowns lose their sheen, and every shot of her is drenched in shadow. Finally, at the Shore Motel, deep darkness covers her face. If we have to strain to see her, it's because she isn't really there anymore.

Joe, on the other hand, begins to come back. As he pulls himself together, emerging from the pitch-blackness of his hospital cell, white is reintroduced. Not the kind of sublime white assigned to sober Kirsten on their first date, but a just light, without judgment, consistent, and evenly distributed about his face. The final scene, set in Joe's new apartment, summarizes and concludes this visual narrative, what began with the Clays' first date so long ago. In it, Edwards fades Remick from the picture: the actress is shot in a light so drab she nearly disappears into the walls behind her. "I want things to look prettier than they are," she says, but her lifeless overcoat betrays the dream. Conversely, Lemmon is given a stronger back-light, a faint halo that distinguishes him from the dreariness of his sur-roundings, as if to suggest his departure from a troubled past. He has changed—his clean white shirt confirms it—and his home has changed, too. No longer is the space infested with warring bric-a-brac and eerie geometries. All that is left are the bare essentials—a chair, a bureau, a lamp—clear indication that Joe Clay has cleaned up, and this time for good ... or hasn't he? The final image of the film throws all this into question.

Joe approaches the window overlooking an abandoned street. The neon lights of the sign "BAR" pulse in the glass beside him. The camera pushes into a close-up as if to preempt an epiphany or decisive action. But nothing happens. He just looks out. A horn on the score sounds a minor note; it hangs in the air, and we fade to black. Blake has set us up for a major event, and we wonder, "What will Joe do now?" but no answer is given. Maybe he will go back to the bar, and maybe he won't. We don't know. We've watched a man trying to change, we've even seen him change, but will it be perma-nent? Can it ever be? It's a question that will haunt Blake Edwards for the rest of his career.

Days of Wine and Roses earned its two leads Oscar nominations, and overwhelming critical support for Lemmon and Edwards. The *New Yorker's* Brendan Gill wrote the film marked "the point in [Lemmon's] career where he feels, and is right to feel, that there's nothing he can't bring off"[25] and the *Hollywood Reporter* called it "one of the year's most moving and rewarding films."[26] Edwards said, "If I were restricted to only one actor that I could work with for the rest of my career, without a doubt it would be Jack Lemmon."[27] As for team Mancini and Mercer, their theme song for *Days of Wine and Roses* won them their second consecutive Oscar.

Mancini's melody is typically simple and sincere, written with customary grace, economy, and speed: It only took him half an hour to write.[28] As for Mercer, the muse was just as efficient. "I completed [the lyrics] in nine minutes," he said. "I had it all in my mind and couldn't get the words down fast enough."[29] The ease of writing is bred into the lyric's grammatical structure. Only two sentences long, the solitary verse does not allow for pause, but rather, like "the passing breeze," it rushes away from us, ending almost as soon as it is begun. Mercer said he believed it was God who wrote the song, but today's experts wholeheartedly disagree.[30]

3

BLAKE BLOSSOMS
1963–1968

THE PINK PANTHER (1964)

Inspector Clouseau: It has been a night of surprises. Madame Clouseau: You can say that again. Inspector Clouseau: It has been a—oh.

Maurice Richlin, one of the co-writers of *Operation Petticoat*, came to Blake with an idea he had about "a French inspector of police who was determined to catch this notorious jewel thief and who didn't know that his own wife was sleeping with this jewel thief."[1] Blake liked the story, it had some of his favorite subjects—crime, duplicity, and sex—and so he brought it to the Mirisch Company, an independent production team with a multipicture deal at United Artists. "Our philosophy was to create a family," said Walter Mirisch years later. "We felt that Blake Edwards was a spiritual heir to Billy Wilder."[2] That's high praise, and in 1963 somewhat contestable, but in the coming years they would prove themselves correct.

The Pink Panther, the first of four films Blake was to make for the Mirisches, was in the good company of *Some Like It Hot*, *West Side Story*, and *The Apartment*, the company's recent string of Oscar-winning power pictures. But it wasn't just prestige that brought Edwards to the Mirisches, it was the promise of creative autonomy. According to David Chasman, then director of marketing and advertising for United Artists, the organization was renowned for it. "Executives did not look at dailies unless they were specifically invited," he said. "You made a deal with a filmmaker. You approve a script, you approve certain creative elements, you approved a budget, and you had your guy there to make sure the money was spent the way it was supposed to be spent, but we never saw a film until the filmmaker was ready to show it to us. We were midwives, not parents."[3] It was a felicitous arrangement; Blake had the suits where he wanted them, and the suits had what looked like a surefire hit. With David Niven, Ava Gardner, and Peter Ustinov leading the cast, there was very little to fear. Mirisch money was in good hands.

Things started to go south when Gardner arrived in Rome. From the moment she got off the plane, her outrageous demands sent Martin Jurow, one of the film's producers, into a tailspin. Ava required a private villa, her own full-time chauffeur, and a personal chef. And she was foul tempered, too. "She cursed the photographers," Jurow remembers, "she cursed me prolifically, [and] she cursed the driver and the luggage carriers."[4] She even insisted that production be relocated to her beloved vacation spot in Madrid. It was one of many "excessive demands"⁵ Jurow refused to grant, and with only two weeks until principal photography was set to begin, the producer was forced to discharge her from the film.

Who would inherit the role of Madame Clouseau? It was offered to Janet Leigh, but she was newly married and didn't take to the idea of a location shoot away from her husband. Audrey Hepburn suggested Capucine, a melancholic model/actress she'd befriended in her Paris days, and after brief consideration Blake approved. All were satisfied and it looked like production could finally begin, but Mrs. Peter Ustinov wasn't having it. "With a nobody playing Ustinov's wife," Jurow recalls, "she [Suzanne Cloutier] felt that the film was reduced to a routine comedy of no artistic merit."⁶ Soon thereafter, Ustinov broke his contract (the Mirisch Company sued for damages), and fled the production. Now with only three days before his picture was set to shoot, Edwards had to recast, and fast. Luckily, the English actor Peter Sellers was available for a few weeks before he had to begin work on a picture called *Dr. Strangelove: Or How I Learned to Stop Worrying and Love the Bomb*.

Edwards was incredulous. He didn't know a great deal about Sellers' work—he had only seen him in the British comedy *I'm All Right Jack*—but he was too desperate to say no, so Sellers hopped on a plane for Rome. Without a moment to lose, Blake drove out to the airport to meet him with the hope that they could begin rehearsing right there in the car. By the time they reached the hotel, a whole new Clouseau was born. Edwards tells it like this:

> From the Rome airport into the city Peter and I got to know each other and found out we were soul mates as far as silent comedy was concerned. Our heroes and favorites were Laurel and Hardy and Buster Keaton and people like that. We decided to try and make Clouseau a real clumsy, accident-prone, well-intentioned, but idiotic character. We decided that the one thing about Clouseau that could make him succeed was that he embodied what I considered to be the eleventh commandment, which is "Thou Shalt not Give up." He never figured he could lose, never figured that he could fail.⁷

That car ride would change the careers of both men—and film comedy—forever. Without time to rewrite the script for the new Clouseau, Sellers and Edwards had to improvise their way through the shoot. Suddenly, to

David Niven's utter shock, The Pink Panther was no longer just about a debonair jewel thief.

Now it was also about Inspector Jacques Clouseau, who, in pursuit of said jewel thief, heads to a posh resort with a wife he can never get into bed, who is herself in amorous cahoots with the very thief he's trying to catch. After days of sexual and professional humiliation, the inspector finally nabs the crook and lands him in court, where in an eleventh-hour twist, he is framed by his wife, convicted of stealing the jewel in question, and is carted off by the police as she drives away with the villain. That's The Pink Panther, and if it weren't so funny, it would be tragic. So why do we laugh?

Edwards says,

> In the case of Inspector Clouseau, slapstick, like any other form of comedy, is born of character. . . . If the character exemplifies some kind of authority that you or I would like to laugh at, and if we can present it in the kind of violent, physical action of slipping on a banana or falling into a manhole, the better the character is defined, the funnier it will be.[8]

Big men will fall hard, and the bigger the ego, the funnier the fall. Cutting arrogance down to size—laughing at it—is in its own way an act of justice; it exposes fallibility in false authorities and promotes the audience to a position of security. In this way, the splurch represents a reversal of power in favor of the viewer, and our laughter is an expression of it. When Madame Clouseau (Capucine) opens the door to her bedroom, she finds her cuckolded husband (Peter Sellers) fuming in the hallway. With great confidence he declares, "That phone call was a ruse!" and promptly trips over a potted plant. We laugh not just because Sellers takes a good fall (and does he ever), but because Edwards has found the perfect place for the plant. Timing the splurch to coincide with an authoritative outburst allows the director to contrast Clouseau's self-assuredness with deserved physical humiliation. But Blake isn't just trying to shame the inspector here, he's trying to elicit a buried truth. In this case it's the inspector's ineptitude.

When successfully enacted, The Pink Panther's formula for justice (hubris + slapstick-violence = authenticity), tears down the masks its characters hide behind. Take a close look at the film and one discovers a proliferation of masks so pervasive that even the structural composition of its narrative is subjected to abrupt changes in tone, genre, story, and location.

Quite regularly, we are positioned to expect one thing, but we are given something else. In this way, the story itself becomes a kind of Clouseau, bumbling and fumbling and perpetually undermined throughout. First it's a travelogue, then it's a slapstick detective story, then *wham!* it's a Feydeau cartoon (there is even a conspicuously out-of-place musical interlude). Consider *The Pink Panther*'s introductory sequence; "once upon a time" in a far-off kingdom is invaded by the iconic Panther cartoon, which breaks into a sequence in Rome, then Paris, another in Hollywood, and a "meanwhile" in Cortina d'Ampezzo. Right away, we are acquainted with the disjointed structural scheme that will continually destabilize the *The Pink Panther*'s identity. As Sir Charles Lytton (David Niven) says, "Reality could use a swift belt every now and then." Edwards does it with genre.

Perhaps unsurprisingly, the notion of surprise is of tremendous importance to the film. Think of the splurch: it's necessary that Clouseau does not see what's ahead of him in order for the gag to work (for instance, the plant in his bedroom). That he is an inspector, a man of reason, doubles the deliciousness. After all, nothing should surprise a man whose job requires him to be a master of logic, but *The Pink Panther* contradicts that assumption—it contradicts *every* assumption. Duplicity and illusion are everywhere, things are never what they seem, and the man brought in to expose it all is, well, Clouseau. But there's a twist. Clouseau may be the source of great chaos, but it is a chaos that inadvertently uncovers lies. Though they are never apparent to him, when the liars meet with his reckless stupidity, their pretensions are momentarily shed, and for a nanosecond we are offered a glimpse of justice. Thus, Clouseau is both destabilized, and destabilizer. He is the source *and* the recipient of the splurch. It may be accidental, but with him out of the picture there's no justice. In this way, Clouseau is actually (ironically) good as his job. For instance, in the dazzling bedroom scene, Clouseau's persistent idiocy brings the adulterers to humiliation. Sir Charles Lytton is left outside to freeze, his nephew George (Robert Wagner), is submerged in a bath of suds, and Madame Clouseau runs around like a mad fool trying to maintain the lie. Although the criminals succeed in keeping the cuckold in the dark, they've been stripped of their cool know-how. For once, they appear as goofy and susceptible as the inspector himself. But this is an exception; Clouseau spends most of the picture in conflict with the world around him.

Stylistically, Clouseau clashes. While the other characters are vividly rendered in high-fashion apparel, the inspector is strictly middle-class. His trench coat is the sole streak of gray in a rainbow of voluptuous bodies, exotic locations, and expensive tastes. Edwards culls *The Pink Panther* aesthetic from precisely this comic contrast, creating a James Bond world only to put a schlimazel behind the wheel. The movie's visual agenda, dominated by hearty formal compositions, is suited perfectly to its roster of debonair personages (save for one). Each frame of film is ordered with a keen eye to strong architectural authority, and the sets are compulsively dressed in crisp, vibrant colors. Not a single hair is out of place in this perfect dream of *haute* cinema, and the camera itself is just as reserved; it hardly moves or cuts, but rather, stands still, watching passively, apathetically, and, like Mancini's famous theme, is cool, cool, cool. Rarely do we get a close-up or glide in for a dramatic crescendo. Obviously, this is no place for a man as ridiculous as Inspector Clouseau—but that's why Blake puts him in: his presence happily splurches the movie's formal veneer. Without his crash and burn incompetence, *The Pink Panther* would be, like Hitchcock's *To Catch a Thief*, a cloying trifle of pretty places and faces.

The very moment Jacques Clouseau is introduced, the clash between Edwards' rigid formalism and Sellers' silliness takes hold of the film's comic mechanism. Rising from his desk (authority), he crosses to a globe (knowledge), spins it purposelessly (pretension) and, leaning upon it, loses his balance and crashes to the floor. One might expect the camera to pan down with his fall or to cut in for his reaction, but Edwards does neither. Instead, the lens remains constant, frozen stiff like a stubborn mother waiting on her child. Apathetically, Edwards allows Sellers to fall entirely out of the frame and then holds, undisturbed, as he rises back into it. Placing the moment of impact off screen (we only *hear* it) allows Edwards to create the illusion that Clouseau has fallen farther than he actually has. Because it breaks the frame lines, Sellers' pratfall is contingent upon the illusion of having achieved greater physical distance, which, enhancing the absurdity of the error, makes for a much better gag. But there is also a very practical purpose to keeping us from the moment of impact. By protecting us from the violence, Edwards has kept us from Clouseau's pain. Whatever injury he may have incurred is abstract, and we can laugh without guilt—but only for now. As we grow comfortable with the character, subsequent *Panthers* will see Blake mischievously provoking Clouseau's/our pain threshold. But that's later.

Sometimes, one gets the feeling that the camera is bored with Clouseau. Unlike Sir Charles, who is shot in exquisitely lit close-ups, Clouseau is, cinematically speaking, practically ignored. His big love scenes, for instance (in which he tries to seduce his own wife) are played almost entirely off camera. A large open window dominates the shot, whereas the bed, crucial to the seduction, is predominately out of frame. The subject of the scene, in other words, is not the subject of the shot: Les Clouseaux have been literally relegated to the margins. What's more, the scene is very long, and by not moving the camera Blake has slowed its tempo to an absolute halt. Denying the dramatic potentials of space and time, Edwards is doing his best to kill the moment—and it will be a slow death. We grow restless, we are getting bored, and like Madame Clouseau we are unimpressed. Though contrary to what we might expect, this technique does not detract from the scene, precisely because monotony, rather than being monotonous, is the subject of the drama, not the effect of it (see the Boléro scene in 10). What results is a slight air of condescension, which heightens the absurdity of Clouseau's travails, and enriches the punch line. Juxtaposing clownishness and restraint, Edwards has proven, is funnier than clownishness alone.

Another advantage of the long-take/wide-shot proscenium venue is that it forces Clouseau to contest with more physical space. Maximizing the size of the frame, Edwards has placed his character at a hilariously uncharitable disadvantage. In this space, Clouseau must run for longer, fall harder, and slide further than he would in a close-up. But it is in the long take that Edwards' sadism is at its worst. In these prolonged stretches of film, there is no cut to rescue Clouseau from misfortune; rather, we are forced to watch and wait as the gag plays itself out. Once again, we see that time and space are essential to Edwards' comic presentation. Not only do they contribute to the stately, often beautiful aesthetic, they undermine it, and make for a funnier scene. It's an idea Edwards states quite succinctly in an interview mentioned in this book's introduction, entitled "Sophisticated Naturalism."

> To think that slapstick and sophistication are insoluble is not true at all [he says]. I think that there's a wonderful kind of thing that happens with the two. It takes slapstick a step up and it takes sophistication a step down and they kind of meet. There's a great element of humor that takes place.[9]

As is the case with so many of Edwards' male characters, Inspector Clouseau is systematically faced with the problem of his own impotence,

13. *The Pink Panther* (1964) Edwards, Sellers, Capucine, and David Niven (upper left, under the bed) designing the finale to a gorgeous piece of farce. The entire sequence, from "A quick shower, my love, and I'll be right with you" to the exploding champagne bottle, spans a total of fifteen continuous minutes, accomplishing in drama what the splurch achieves in comedy. (Courtesy of the Academy of Motion Picture Arts and Sciences)

paving the way for midlife crisis sufferers like George Webber (10), Felix Farmer (S.O.B.), Zach Hutton (Skin Deep), and Harvey Fairchild (That's Life!) for whom degeneration, sexual or otherwise, is an unending (and for us, hilarious) terror. The Pink Panther is quite significant in this respect, for it represents Edwards' first sustained exploration into the subject. There was This Happy Feeling back in 1958, but Blake had not yet embraced the splurch. But in The Pink Panther, whether he is struggling with the quilt, or the temperature, or he is obeying one of Madame's odd requests, Jacques Clouseau finds no physical security in the bedroom. Space is never as challenging to him as it is here, in the very large room (longer to get to his wife), with too many doors (easier to hide her lovers), and where obstacles spring up like booby traps. No wonder he can't even land a kiss! Even at the home of Princess Dala (Claudia Cardinale), his lips are detoured on their way to her hand. With his wife it's more of the same. He pounces on her, but they fall into the closet. He leans in for a smooch, but his hat falls in front of his face. He calls out, "Just a quick shower, my love, and I will be right with you," but he never is.

As we have seen, Inspector Jacques Clouseau is sexually, professionally, and physically condemned to humiliation, as much by the people around him as by the world he inhabits and the way it is filmed. Everyone and everything involved in the production of The Pink Panther is united in the task, and Peter Sellers the comic actor is no exception. While the surrounding actors play the masks their characters wear—like performers playing performers—Sellers plays fiercely against his role. Niven's technique is debonair and no deeper (a choice appropriate to his part), but Sellers' style is full of complexity, further alienating Clouseau from his environment. As "low" and "high" comedy rolled into one, it's the performative counterpart to Edwardian sophisticated naturalism. (Collaborators take note: both actor and director have found in each other a synchronous expression of their life's art.)

Let's examine the Clouseau splurch to see how it's done. Upon recovering from humiliation, Clouseau will do his ridiculous best to assure everyone around him that he still is, and always was, in control of the situation. This, not the slapstick, is Clouseau's emotional struggle, and it permits Sellers to impress a bit of naturalistic acting into the absurd (a bit of "high" in the "low"), and, in turn, achieves multidimensionality where his fellow players have self-stylized to opacity. They are gloss—and that too is Edwardian—but Peter Sellers is not. His intepretation may be nonsensically stubborn, his falls may be impossible to survive, but in these pictures he is the sole representative of humanity. Off screen, however, the extreme opposite was true. Blake said,

> When the picture was finished, I got the first sense of these unpredictable crazy kind of actions when Sellers—after we had this wonderful time and the picture was run—went crazy and sent word to the Mirisches that it was a disaster, which was very typical of him on the films he would do.[10]

To focus himself on post-production, Blake disengaged from Sellers' madness. "I just heard about it and I thought, shit, who wants to get involved with that? I'm never going to see him again, so what's the difference?"[11] Thus began one of the most tumultuous love affairs in film history.

A SHOT IN THE DARK (1964)

Dominique Ballon: You fell off the sofa, you stupid . . .
Inspector Clouseau: I know I fell off the sofa, there's no need to tell me.
Everything I do is carefully planned, Madame.

Clouseau may have been conceived in *The Pink Panther*, but he wasn't born until *A Shot in the Dark*. As we will see, Edwards' and Sellers' approach to Clouseauiana has changed drastically in the few months between pictures (both were released in 1964). Their stylistic and thematic familiars are present, as is the iconography of the *Panther* world, but what's different here is Edwards' treatment of slapstick. The gag has been purposefully reorganized in *A Shot in the Dark*, the splurch has narrowed its aim, and the intentions of Edwardian physical comedy are realized anew with unprecedented perspicuity. But finally it's the reinvention of Clouseau, with his baroque combinations of sight gag and pratfall—the binary strands of Edwards' comic DNA—that is articulated here for the first time. As proof, Plas Johnson's saxophone is conspicuously absent from *A Shot in the Dark*. "That music was designed as the phantom-thief music," Mancini writes, "not to be *The Pink Panther* theme."[12] Charles Lytton's tune went out with the iconic DePatie-Freleng rendering of the *Panther* titles, and was replaced in *A Shot in the Dark* by "the inspector" animation and the accompanying baseline twang of an electric guitar. Two themes, two cartoons, and two different films. *A Shot in the Dark* officially belonged to Clouseau.

And to think that it almost didn't happen.

In 1961, the Mirisch brothers bought the film rights to the Harry Kurnitz play *A Shot in the Dark*, an English-language version of Marcel Achard's *L'Idiote*. At the time of its purchase, the play was enjoying a successful run at Broadway's Booth Theater, starring Julie Harris and Walter Matthau in what would be a Tony Award winning performance. To direct the film adaptation, the Mirisches brought on Anatole Litvak, a competent filmmaker, though one of limited comic gifts, and cast Sophia Loren in the part that ultimately went to Elke Sommer. When Loren's husband, producer Carlo Ponti, read Alec Coppel's script, he advised Loren to drop out, and the Mirisches, equally disappointed with the adaptation, sent it to Norman Krasna for rewrites. When the new pages came back, it was still

14. *A Shot in the Dark* (1964) The "whodunit" scene, a staple of the detective genre, is seen here at a moment of calm, before it is overturned—like the coffee table between Sellers and George Sanders (far left)—by Inspector Clouseau. (Author's collection)

flat. With the picture uncast, Litvak withdrew from the project (he claimed a mysterious illness),[13] and left the Mirisches in a hole.

That's when Edwards' phone rang. The situation, Walter Mirisch told him, was dire. They had no script, production was at a standstill, and the studio was losing more money every second. Would Blake please take a look? Yes, he would. And so, after reading the script (which he also found deplorable), Blake agreed to take over the film on one condition: that he could undertake major rewrites. "You must give me carte blanche on this one," he told them.[14] The Mirisches had no choice but to comply, and, with the entire film up in the air, Blake prepared to save it the only way he knew how—he turned the character of Detective Paul Sevigne into Inspector Jacques Clouseau. Edwards and Mirisch flew to New York and pitched the idea to Sellers, who agreed, and then Blake boarded an ocean liner to London, where the picture was to shoot, and, along with co-writer William Peter Blatty, spent the five-day transatlantic cruise reworking the script into the first full-fledged Clouseau comedy. Blatty remembers their eleventh hour rewrite "depended upon two things:"

> (1) The plot would involve a series of murders of people all connected to the same household, so that obviously murders were interconnected and would be made to look as if each victim had been offed to cover up the initial crime; which would turn out to be wrong: each murder would turn out to be separately motivated and totally independent of all the others. (2) Inspector Clouseau [would be] the main character.[15]

The production began well for Blake and Peter. Sellers was his usual brilliant self and the entire cast, even the caddishly depressed George Sanders, enjoyed him immensely. Due to recurring outbursts of character-breaking laughter, Sanders suggested that every actor who broke up during the shot had to pay a penalty of five pounds to the production.[16] Two hundred pounds later they finally had a useable take. "Things were fine for the first half of filming," Edwards remembers, "but then the shit hit the fan. Sellers became a monster. He just got bored with the part and became angry, sullen, and unprofessional. He wouldn't show up for work and began looking for anyone and everyone to blame."[17] Sellers' biographer Ed Sikov reports that by the end of the shoot star and director had stopped speaking entirely:

> Their communication consisted of little notes slipped underneath each other's door. Each man was experienced; each knew comedy; each had precise ideas; each was neurotic and disturbed. After all, Edwards's nickname is "Blackie"—not a diminutive of Blake, but a reference to one his most frequent moods. In retrospect, it seems inevitable that because Sellers and Edwards shared a kind of communal personality, at a certain point they would necessarily cease to communicate.[18]

It was a case of doppelgangers. Edwards and Sellers were two halves of the same whole, unable to coexist, but drawn together by mutual respect, and even, at times, affection. David Chasman calls it "a horrible marriage that produced beautiful babies."[19] Blake calls it the enigma of his life.[20]

Unlike The Pink Panther, which is ostensibly a film about a thief, A Shot in the Dark is about a detective. The story begins as Maria Gambrelli (Elke Sommer) is accused of killing her Spanish lover and Inspector Jacques Clouseau de la Sûreté is assigned to the case. All the facts point to her guilt, but the inspector is in love and refuses to believe it. Chief Inspector Dreyfus (Herbert Lom), who loathes Clouseau, is outraged at his incompetence and takes him off the case, and then, under pressure from greater powers, puts him back on again. Clouseau, meanwhile, is determined to defend Maria's innocence, releases her from prison, and trails her to a dead body. Still, he's sure she isn't the killer. And then it happens again: Maria is imprisoned, released, trailed, and then discovered at the scene of another crime. This goes on until Clouseau finally gets all the suspects together in a single room and is helplessly sidelined as pandemonium breaks out amongst them. The film ends as the accused flee in his car which explodes offscreen (Dreyfus, the real killer, planted the bomb.)

Unlike The Pink Panther, the villain in A Shot in the Dark is marginalized, making Clouseau officially its star, though he is still very much a passive protagonist. In neither film does he move the events of the story forward (the events move him forward), and, as a result, Edwards matches dramatic ineptitude to explicate his professional ineptitude. But there is one important distinction: in A Shot in the Dark, Edwards turns Clouseau's incompetence into indirect narrative agency, and dramatic futility into the film's chief structural determinant. It is a film, in other words, driven by a passenger: how many times is Clouseau taken off the case, put back on it, and then taken off of it again? How many times does he disguise himself outside of Maria Gambrelli's jail, only to be busted by a gendarme, and then sent off in a police car? Several. So why does he keep doing it? Why doesn't he see his failures as failures? For the same reason that anyone, real or fictional, refuses to acknowledge their failings: pride. Arrogance is the defense (in Edwards' terms, the disguise) Clouseau uses to cover his ineptitude.

As we have seen in The Pink Panther, it's precisely this assertion of unearned authority that incurs the gag and disrupts the alignment of assumed persona and true self, but in A Shot in the Dark, the discrepancy between the two is even greater (and therefore funnier). Early in the film, Clouseau inspects Maria Gambrelli's bedroom, the scene of the crime, while reciting trite aphorisms to Maurice (Martin Benson), butler to Parisian plutocrat Benjamin Ballon (George Sanders). To emphasize a point, the inspector shakes his pen at him and ink splats over the butler's white shirt. Splurch: Clouseau's assumed persona has been undone by his true, inept self, and suddenly, for a split second, the *real* fool emerges. Pacing now, Clouseau crosses to Maria Gambrelli's vanity table, examines a tin of face powder, turns to Maurice, and proudly declares, "I suspect everyone and no one." Removing the tin from his face, we see his nose is covered in white powder. Splurched again.

This use of sight gag comprises half of A Shot in the Dark's slapstick repertoire. The pratfall makes up the other half. "Prat," an informal term for buttocks, means the word "pratfall" literally refers to a fall on one's backside. The anatomical specificity of the word is significant; falling on your face sounds shocking, falling on your back sounds serious, but falling on your backside—that's funny. Why? Because where the others are painful, the pratfall is just humiliating. And humility, not pain, is exactly what Inspector Clouseau needs. Our introduction to Clouseau comes as one such pratfall. After his car stops in front of Monsieur Ballon's estate, Clouseau steps out of the vehicle and into a fountain. (Once again, the ingredients of the splurch are present; that is, the car drove with such authority we do not expect it to be followed by flummoxed ineptitude.) Later in Ballon's garden, Clouseau trips over his assistant, Hercule (Graham Stark), and cries, "You fool!" adding, "Just for that you are off the case!" But the joke's on him— arrogance has met its match in the splurch.

Though this mechanism was introduced in The Pink Panther, it has gained increased relevance in A Shot in the Dark. The former is really a story about masks, lying, and betrayal (still relevant to the comic tenets of false authority), but because the latter addresses hierarchical malfeasance head-on, there is more splurching to be done. It's the difference between tricksters and snobs, a discrepancy clearly delineated by each film's thematic basis for the splurch: Panther climaxes in a masquerade ball, and Shot in a gathering of the demimonde. "Now then," Clouseau announces to the suspects at Ballon's mansion, "I will tell you why I've called you here tonight. One of you is the murderer." A delicious pause. "I will explain to you the facts that led me to discover his—or her—identity." He falls through an open door. Brushing himself off, he continues with the facts of the case, and is interrupted by Monsieur Ballon. Clouseau then charges at him from across the room and steps on Madame Ballon's toe. She screams ("I am very sorry, Madame"), he bends over to examine her, throws over a coffee table, and knocks heads with Monsieur Ballon. The rhythm of the gag is perfect, almost musical, and here's why: Edwards and Sellers have timed the progression of misfortunes (foot, table, head) in accordance with audience laughter, which gives us enough time to recover, but not so much time that we lose the momentum of the sequence. Rather than simply extending the gag, they have built upon it. And placing this outburst at the moment of Clouseau's confrontation with Monsieur Ballon allows Edwards to counter A Shot in the Dark's most dramatic moment of authoritarian disruption with its most intricate succession of slapstick.

Splurches, as we have seen, do not obey the chain of social command. Ballon and Dreyfus, because of their high station, are perfect targets for Clouseau, just as Kato and Hercule, Clouseau's underlings, continually undermine his own authority, whether by Kato's surprise attacks or Hercule's poise. Edwards' addition of these characters complicates the film's hierarchy and represents another significant departure from The Pink Panther. In that film, Clouseau was the sole symbol of false order, and therefore the antagonist (who pays for his "crime" in jail time). Now that Clouseau has a superior, the roles are reversed; Dreyfus is the new villain and Clouseau, as phony as he may be, has gained our sympathy by contrast. Thus, A Shot in the Dark, like many of Blake's pictures to follow, becomes, in the director's words, "skeptical of institutions and the establishment."[21]

You could also say that A Shot in the Dark is skeptical of masculinity. In Clouseau's hands, phallic objects such as pool cues, cigarettes, pens, and sticks, will undoubtedly break in two. Maria Gambrelli has the same effect. When she is present, Clouseau's desire is translated into a bogus suaveness that incurs the film's gag reflex and sends his physical possession (sometimes literally) right out the window. After lighting his and her cigarettes, Clouseau returns the flame (still burning) to his inside jacket pocket, and a moment later, he's on fire. Later, to set the mood for a seduction, Clouseau lowers the window shade behind his desk and the room goes dark (too dark). That he trips over a chair indicates that the inspector's masculinity is as false as his authority and must be splurched away. To keep the splurches flying, the A Shot in the Dark engages in a cyclical pattern of coitus interruptus that continually foils our Don Juan. Throughout the film, Clouseau insists that Maria be released from prison with the expectation that she will lead him to the killer (and later to bed), but every time she is set free, a body turns up and she returns to jail, leaving Clouseau professionally *and* sexually frustrated. In this way, an equation is drawn between Maria's innocence and Clouseau's dream of sexual satisfaction, but because Clouseau is inept, he'll never acquit her, and never go to bed with her.

He'll also never solve the case. When Clouseau arrives at Château Ballon with the intention of exposing the killer, he brings even more chaos, incurring a frenzy that complicates the story beyond all recognition. As Lehman and Luhr observe, this finale is in ironic violation of the mystery genre's conventions. Traditionally, when the detective gathers the suspects in a room, we expect him to reveal the secrets and expose the criminals. We crave a solution, and in a film typical of the genre we get our satisfaction. But not in *A Shot in the Dark*. Edwards not only denies us the resolution we crave, he violates the central convention of mystery with one big splurch to genre itself. It's another pleasure thwarted, another expectation falsified.

The film's attention to doors and windows dovetails nicely with this notion of concealment and surprise. Looking through a window or opening a door, we don't always believe what we see, or find what we expect (in fact, in the farces of Blake Edwards, we find the exact opposite). The film's first scene, for instance, is presented exclusively through windows, and takes as its subject the perils of voyeurism. Looking in, we see a long hallway lined with doors leading off to other rooms, which we can see into, but can't hear into. With doors it's the exact opposite: we can hear through them, but we can't see what's actually going on inside. Edwards gets a lot of mileage out of this: concealing certain aural and visual cues facilitates both his interrogations into identity and his comedy of concealment and surprise. What's behind the door/window is (a) never what we thought, and (b) always funnier than what we expected. Upon closer inspection, the first appearance of Kato is based on this concept. It begins with Clouseau asleep in bed. Behind him a door rattles. His eyes open. Someone is trying to get in—*but who?* Is it a villain? No, it's Kato. Surprise!

To summarize, Edwards' increased interest in voyeurism, antiauthoritarianism, and Clouseau as an agent of indirect narrative motion represent the bulk of *A Shot in the Dark*'s improvements on its predecessor, but the film's single greatest contribution to the *Panther* legacy is in the alterations Edwards and Sellers make to Clouseau himself. The addition of a messy

French accent, the omission of Madame Clouseau, and the augmentation of his arrogance are all substantial enhancements of the character precisely because they combine in sadistic synergy to make life harder on Clouseau than it has ever been before. Consider the meuths:

Ballon: I've often been in that closet.
Clouseau: For what reason?
Ballon: Last time was moths.
Clouseau: *Meuths?*
Ballon: Moths!
Clouseau: Yes, *meuths.*
Ballon: Maria was complaining of *murths.*
Clouseau: *Meurths?* Is that right, Maria, that—that you were complaining about these *meurths?*
Maria: Yes, I did complain about moths.
Clouseau: Oh, you mean *meuths!*

Clouseau's pratfalls through the English language are detrimental to his poise, but with his wife out of the picture (Madame Clouseau isn't even referenced in the film), his struggle for sexual satisfaction in *A Shot in the Dark* is amplified considerably. To achieve satisfaction, the new Clouseau must free Maria from prison, woo her, bring her to his apartment, carry her into bed (difficult, when he keeps knocking her head against the wall), and then he's in the clear. Or is he? Just as they are about to begin lovemaking, Kato interrupts with a sneak attack. (The pairing begs the question, What kind of couplehood exists between two men who live together in a womanless house? When that couplehood expresses itself in constant play fighting—often in or around the bed—that inhibits Clouseau's heterosexual exploits, we might wonder if Kato represents more than just a manservant. The matter may go unresolved, but its presence is undeniable.)

Giving Clouseau a troublesome accent and cutting his wife from the picture further humiliates him, but it is the great increase in his arrogance that gives the splurch in *A Shot in the Dark* its comedic power. Late in *The Pink Panther*, a triumphant Clouseau steps into Charles and George Lytton's prison cell. At a moment of high confidence, Clouseau, grinning, sets his fists into two bowls of porridge, looks up in distress, and we fade out of the scene. Significantly, Clouseau does not try to cover up his embarrassment (as he does in *A Shot in the Dark*), but is instead humiliated by it. The theme of the splurch is blindness, not arrogance, but that has changed. Sellers said, "Because of his dignity, Blake wanted [Clouseau] to be, shall we say, accident prone."[22] In *The Pink Panther* he was accident prone; in *A Shot in the Dark* he is accident prone and arrogant.

Of course, there are stylistic elements that carry over from the first film, but certain additions, namely Edwards' introduction of camera movement, go a long way in distinguishing *Shot* from *Panther*. Consider the following sequence: Discoursing on the "facts" of the case, Clouseau paces his office for the benefit of Hercule, who remains still. If this were *The Pink Panther*, the camera would hold on Hercule and let the inspector wander out of frame, but instead the camera *follows* Clouseau, panning left and right to keep him within the shot. Now he is the subject; before, in *The Pink Panther*, the subject was his subjugation. And with more close-ups than ever before, Clouseau is promoted to the level of protagonist. But take note: that doesn't mean the camera is always his ally. Edwards' manipulation of background staging, for instance, underlines Clouseau's impotence in a manner that harks back to *The Pink Panther*. However, when viewed in comparison to the marked flatness of that film (it is a film of foreground surfaces), these deep space contrasts signify a dramatic stylistic development in the world of Clouseau. From the nudist colony to Château Ballon, settings that defy Clouseau's expertise (mainly exteriors) become wild with spatial variation. Here, Clouseau is marginalized by his physical environment, significantly reduced in size and stature, and at times completely upstaged by mise-en-scène. It is as if the shot doesn't need him, and, like the gag, dramatizes the plight of his subjugation.

Edwards' explorations into spatial depth, though timid, are relevant to genre. As a mystery (or a film that masquerades as a mystery), *A Shot in the Dark* relies heavily upon the concealment and disclosure of information, which Edwards manipulates with clever and decisive camera movement. In one such circumstance, Clouseau follows Maria Gambrelli deeper into the shot on her way to the greenhouse. To evoke the sensation of discovery, Edwards' camera pans with him to reveal new, previously hidden pieces information. The director opts for the pan here because the space–time continuum, so crucial to the simulation of discovery, would be disrupted by a cut. For related reasons, increasing depth of field (which forces our eye to move instead of the camera) is also conducive to the mystery genre, and is essential to *A Shot in the Dark*, whereas *The Pink Panther*, which we might call a comedy caper (it follows the exploits of the criminal, not the detective) is not concerned with solving a crime, and consequently can accommodate a static frame more readily. Although there is a relationship between the filmic tendencies of both films (after all, they were made consecutively, and by the same man, or men), it is in their separateness that Edwards' artistic development is most apparent.

A legend was born instantly. The film's enormous box office had the Mirisches talking sequels, and, with a cartoon serial well underway, the Pink Panther franchise was set in irrevocable motion. A Clouseau craze ensused, due in large part to the films' unconventional back-to-back release strategy. In a coup of clever publicity, United Artists opened The Pink Panther and A Shot in the Dark only a few months apart, an idea Harold Mirisch was particularly in love with. He said, "critics discussed [Clouseau] while Panther was in neighborhoods, causing patrons to see that picture after they had seen Shot or adding impetus to their going to see Shot after Panther."[23] Rare is the sequel that plays in Cinema 1 as its predecessor screens in Cinema 2. Rare and exciting, too—even the films' detractors were in agreement about that. For Stephen Watts of the New York Times, the film was "a modern screen comedy in a style which has not been seen much in recent years."[24]

Watts is referring to the movie's hip refashioning of cinema's slapstick heritage, a contemporary riff on the silent masters that Edwards infused with the ethos of the new sexuality. If Clouseau is an old stuffed shirt of the fifties—traditional in his approach to male/female relations—then the nudists of Camp Sunshine are the first of many hippies to run (naked) through Edwards' sixties' cinema. They are, like George Webber's neighbors (10) and Felix Farmer's live-in partyers (S.O.B.), indicative of Blake's burgeoning interest in the appealing and appalling aspects of cultural sea change. But revolution aside, A Shot in the Dark was a great personal success for the director. With his style solidified and his sensibility validated, Edwards was no longer relegated to mendicant craftsmanship—he was now a filmmaker with a marketable signature. "[A Shot in the Dark] proved something to me," he said, "if the gag is well-designed you can pull it off."[25] And for his next feature, Blake would pull if off on a scale the world had never seen.

THE GREAT RACE (1965)

The Great Leslie: Greatness is a lighthearted title for
theatrical amusements. Or a definition endowed on men too long
dead to know that it's been awarded.

In 1964, Blake Edwards was a prince of Hollywood. *Operation Petticoat* made him a hit, *Breakfast at Tiffany's* and *Days of Wine and Roses* solidified his reputation, and the smash successes he had in *The Pink Panther* and *A Shot in the Dark* delivered him into the company of America's most important filmmakers. With a body of work this diverse, it seemed he could ace anything and make money in the process. A lot of money. (Really a lot of money.) No wonder Jack Warner felt secure in lavishing $6 million on *The Great Race*, Blake's explosive, anarchic, round 'em up, line 'em up, shoot 'em up, no-holds-barred, take-no-prisoners, all-stops-pulled, pie-in-the-face, eight cylinder, slapstick smorgasbord. True, it was quite a sum to spend on a comedy, especially one that, unlike *My Fair Lady*, Warner's other big-budget baby, wasn't based on proven source material. But the name Blake Edwards was enough for Mr. Warner, and for a time it seemed "no" wasn't in his vocabulary. If Blake asked for an authentic full-size train for the Hannibal 8 railroad gag, his uncle Jack bought it for him. (It cost the production a working week and $100,000.) When Blake needed 4,000 pies for what the script called "the pie fight of the century," Jack picked up the $18,000 pastry bill. (They shot the scene for five days at an estimated $200,000. It bought the studio just four minutes and twenty seconds of screen time.)[26]

Soon the budget doubled. *The Great Race*, at $12 million, became the most expensive film comedy ever made. Naturally, with money comes stakes, and with stakes came tension. At one point, budgetary disagreements between director and studio chief got so fierce, Blake walked off the set with the intention never to return. An anxious gloom settled over the production, but it troubled no one more than Natalie Wood. The twenty-seven-year-old actress simply didn't want to be there; but she was after the title part in Gavin Lambert's *Inside Daisy Clover*. But Jack Warner had other plans for her. He wanted her for Blake's picture, a goof-ball chase movie she thought unworthy of her talent, and she agreed reluctantly on the condition that Warner would give her *Daisy* in exchange. What followed was one of the hardest shooting experiences of her life, made worse by her recent split with Robert Wagner (they remarried ten years later) and her history with depression, pills, and alcohol. The last thing Natalie wanted was a pie in the face. She wanted order. "Everything about her was very organized," Tony Curtis remembers, "the way she presented herself, the way she worked, her social life. I never felt much spontaneity."[27] She didn't have the right temperament for the practical joke battleground that was the Blake Edwards set, and alienated herself from the company. At one point, Blake offered five dollars to anyone who could land a pie at her crotch. Natalie found none of it funny. "Natalie had a sense of humor," her sister Lana remembers, "but she didn't like jokes."[28]

For Edwards and his collaborators, play is the lingua franca of the movie set. On *The Great Race*, cast and crew would game and gamble in between takes, whether at Jack Lemmon's pool table (where he always seemed to lose to Peter Falk) or in one of the many mini-casinos set up in traveling tents. Indeed the best way to ensure a funny movie is to keep your actors laughing—and eating. The mighty Nina Foch saw precisely this on the set of *Skin Deep*. "We had enormous fun," she said, "that's the only way Blake knows how to make a comedy," and then, after a great sigh, she murmured, "best craft table in town."[29] To drum up publicity, Jack Warner, in a feat of PR inspired by P. T. Barnum, opened the gates of his Burbank Studio to welcome crowds (free of charge) into "*The Great Race* Exhibit and Studio Tour." For an afternoon, folks could dine out on the Warner Brothers in big tops put up between soundstages courtesy of "the greatest laugh show of all time." The festival included a memorabilia exhibit, a costume display, a behind-the-scenes two-reeler, and even cameo appearances by the Leslie Special and Hannibal 8, which slowed for photo ops with ticket buyers-to-be.

Meanwhile, Warner's publicity chief, Marty Weiser, was planning a "REAL race of vintage cars in relays from New York City to Warner Brothers Studios ending with a Carnival for the newsman from all over the world,"[30] while Trans World Airlines, which transported the film's two vehicles from place to place, ran ads showing flight attendants treating the cars like Hollywood stars.* But Warner's coup de grâce was still to come. For The Great Race Jubilee, over three hundred and fifty members of the

---

* An interoffice memo from Weiser's desk: "water fed into the radiator from a pitcher by two gorgeous hostesses. Gas fed into tank by spoon etc."

press were shipped in from all corners of the earth to (his words) "not only arouse enthusiasm for the picture itself, but . . . to bring to global attention the dynamic quality that exists here [in Hollywood], today more than ever before."[31] More than just hype for a film, The Great Race Jubilee was an ad for an industry, an opportunity to fortify Hollywood's position in the international market. Warner saw it as the height of big studio filmmaking, and there was Blake at the center of it all.

It may not sound like it, but The Great Race was actually a personal film for Edwards, in fact it was his most personal yet. As a textbook compendium of silent film's greatest hits, a nostalgic tumble down memory lane, and mad tribute to Edwards' cinematic heritage, the film is crammed with wall-to-wall gagsmanship and practically bursts at the seams with goofy good cheer. The story follows the Great Leslie (Tony Curtis) and the evil Professor Fate (Jack Lemmon) as they set off on a transatlantic road race from New York to Paris. When she gets news of it, suffragette Maggie Dubois (Natalie Wood) climbs aboard and begins to fall for Leslie. Along the way, they encounter a number of slapstick showpieces and end up at Carpania, a tiny kingdom ruled by the drunken Prince Hapnick (Jack Lemmon again). Noticing his likeness to Fate, the sinister Baron von Stuppe pulls a Prisoner of Zenda-like switcheroo with the hopes of starting a revolution, but fails when Fate escapes after the greatest pie fight of all time, and the great race resumes its course to the finish line.

Edwards starts with an overture, preparing us for something grand, something epic. But is that the kind of film this is going to be? We don't think twice when we encounter an overture in films about "important" subjects by "serious" directors, but Blake Edwards? What's it doing here? The answer: subverting genre. As in the first sequence of A Shot in the Dark, a supposed comedy that starts as a mystery, the opening of The Great Race initiates the first of countless genre collusions to come. This one evokes comedy and epic in the same beat and thus produces a conflict that takes as its subtext the reconciliation of low comedy with high art. It is a noble and controversial undertaking, and no doubt certain viewers will be put off by it, but in case there was any doubt, Blake wastes no time in cutting to the chase: he plainly dedicates the film to "Mr. Laurel and Mr. Hardy." This reverent tip of the hat intimates what will in many ways be a film about reverence; reverence for slapstick, for spectacle, and for silent cinema— the anachronistic items of Edwards' comic pedigree. The film's title sequence follows suit, and asks us to revel in spectacle and spectatorship.

15. *The Great Race* (1965) "MAAAAAAAAAAAAAAAAAAAAAAX!" The evil Professor Fate (Jack Lemmon)—one of the picture's many silent film archetypes—as the titular race is about to begin. (Author's collection)

A simulated flicker from the projector takes us from the overture's wide 2:2.35 frame (a contemporary aspect ratio) to the old 1:1.33 box (the nostalgic aperture of yesteryear) and in an instant the time travel begins. Suddenly, we're in a silent movie house. An animated title card slides onto the screen, bearing the request "Ladies Kindly Remove Your Hats," and a honky-tonk piano pops onto the sound track. But what we're hearing isn't score, it's "live" accompaniment. When Jack Lemmon's name appears, boos and hisses are heard from an invisible audience. And then Tony

Curtis' card sails onto the screen, followed by raucous cheers and applause. Right away, Blake has (re)introduced his pet theme, the confusion of perception. We are an audience watching a film in which we hear an audience watching a film. In a sense, Edwards has fused movie and reality, and, like he did in The Pink Panther, is asking us to consider the relationship between assumed personae and actual personae.

After the credits, a dissolve takes us from an illustration of a hot-air balloon to its filmed double. The story that we're about to see, like the picture it's drawn from, is just a representation; not real, but another Edwardian façade. When the Great Leslie, dressed head-to-toe in gleaming white, steps up to the hot air balloon and smiles into the camera, we aren't surprised when an animated twinkle shines on his teeth. He is, like everything else in this world, a spectacle. So too is the dastardly Professor Fate, whose funereal blacks and skull and crossbones signify an archetypical evil that exists only in fiction, and, specifically, silent film comedy. Lemmon, Curtis, and Wood aren't playing people here; they're playing caricatures. Maggie points in the air when she's lecturing, Fate twirls his black moustache, and the Great Leslie holds up a pinky when sipping champagne. Rarely, if ever, do these gestures occur in reality. If we recognize them, it's only because we've seen them in films. Apparently, Edwards has asked his actors (as he has asked us) to embrace the artificiality that will become not only the chief stylistic component of the film, but its central thematic preoccupation.

Even slapstick is, at its core, rooted in illusion. To accept that Professor Fate can fall out of the sky and land unharmed requires a certain suspension of disbelief, and that he will get up and try again is, frankly, absurd. And yet, these are the principles of slapstick, parts of an unspoken agreement between audience and gag maker, one that demands, as the credit sequence suggests, our complicity with spectacle. With these terms well established, Edwards has licensed himself to take the gag—to take everything, really—and celebrate its unreality. Unlike films like 10 and Skin Deep, pictures with a splurch structure firmly rooted in ideological, emotional, and dramatic logic, the gag mechanism of The Great Race appears to activate indiscriminately. Consider the saloon scuffle in Boracho or the pie fight in Potzdorf. What sets them off? Practically nothing. Fate steps into a bakery, falls into a cake, and starts launching pastries. Soon the whole room is covered in custard. The same goes for Boracho. What begins as a tiff between two people snowballs into a lawless orgy of slapstick.

To understand the significance of these apparently unmotivated gags, we must go back to the King of Comedy, Mack Sennett himself. In the chapter of his autobiography entitled "How to Throw a Pie," the King states, "The introduction of pie-throwing was no stumbling block at all to our scenario writers. They simply inserted a restaurant or bakery into the scene whenever it seemed like a good idea to fling a pie."[32] Evidently, motivation wasn't Sennett's top priority and, wearing its influences on its sleeve, it isn't on *The Great Race*'s agenda either. The frivolous gag, therefore, is a direct allusion to the silent cinema's pioneers, not, as it may seem, a lapse in Edwards' good judgment. In these terms, the pie fight in *The Great Race* isn't simply the pie fight to end all pie fights, it's a pie fight *about* pie fights. It is thinly motivated, highly improbable, crazily long, and makes no attempts at utilitarian splurching. If the scene feels frivolous, that's because we're not in the realm of the splurch, but fifty years earlier, in the realm of the gag. That's Mack Sennett working; Blake Edwards is merely taking dictation.

Despite all this, *The Great Race* is not a step back for the splurch. What Edwards did to it in *The Pink Panther*, and improved upon in *A Shot in the Dark*, he methodizes here. From a developmental standpoint, *The Great Race* is a laboratory that allows Edwards to examine the gag in a vacuum, free from the demands of story and character. From it emerges a gag structure: a method of building, embellishing, and then paying off the visual joke that is explicitly descendant from Leo McCarey.* For McCarey, one of Blake's heroes, beautiful slapstick comes by way of an organizing concept he called "topping the topper." From the very beginning of his career, Edwards' explication of this principle (which he cites in countless interviews) prompts him to recount the same story about a streetcar, the canonical illustration of the subject passed down to Blake from McCarey himself. At the time of Edwards' promotional tour for *The Great Race*, the streetcar story went like this: McCarey says to Blake, "In the old days we used to dream up a gag and it wouldn't stop at that. We'd get the gag and we'd say, 'Alright now, how do we top that?' And we wouldn't stop at that. We'd top the topper. It's an art that's been lost." Blake continues,

---

* McCarey, director of the comic treasures *Duck Soup*, *Ruggles of Red Gap*, and *The Awful Truth*, was a major influence on the artistic and professional development of *The Great Race*'s dedicatees, Laurel and Hardy.

He gave me an example. We were shooting a film in downtown Los Angeles when they had the streetcars with the stationary steps. And it was a scene with a boy saying goodbye to his girl and making a date for the evening. The streetcar began to move and the boy began to run and continued the conversation with the girl. At one point, the streetcar was going too fast for him and the stationary steps clipped him and he did a one-eighty in the street. Now by today's standards, he'd usually get out with that joke. Dissolve and go to something else. But no. Now what they've got to do is they've got to pick the boy up in the middle of traffic, which obviously is fraught with all kinds of possibilities. He has hurt himself. He is limping a little. In picking himself up, all the things are falling out of his pocket. And he's trying to put the things back in his pocket, avoid the traffic, and pick up his hat. And each time he leans over again to pick up something else everything falls out. And finally, in desperation, he tries to figure: "What will I do?" He takes his hat, takes all of these things, puts them in the hat, and limps over the curb and sits down. Now, will it get off there? No. So while he's sitting there with his hat, we bring an old lady by who looks at him and feels sorry for him. He looks like such a mess. She drops fifty cents in his hat and takes his best pen and goes off. And that was doing the joke, topping the joke, and topping the topper.[33]

McCarey's gag construction appears throughout *The Great Race*, and in many forms. It makes its first appearance in the prologue in a sequence involving Fate, his henchman Max, and their efforts at defeating the Great Leslie. The A gag comes as the parachute they shot down lands on their aircraft; the B gag, which tops A, ends in their airborne collision in a barn; the C gag, which tops B, sees the dastardly duo explode in a burst of flames; and the D gag, the topper—the final variant on the theme—returns them to the barn, but this time to the muddy trough outside of it.

But there's more to it than that. Even within the gag's individual parts, McCarey's principle of escalation and embellishment is apparent. For instance, if we look closely at the topper—by definition the most elaborate riff on the premise—we see a subset of A, B, and C gags built into it. The D gag begins as Fate and Max board their black rocket, light the fuse, and speed off down the track. This is the set up: it delivers the expositional information required for the payoff by upping the ante on the preparatory events that have preceded it. (It looks like the bad guys are actually going to pull this one off.) After they discover their rocket doesn't have enough juice to stay airborne, they begin to fall (D gag, subset A). Blake cuts to the barn from the B gag and we hear an off-screen collision (D gag, subset B: first topper), and then we cut to the barnyard to see the rocket sticking out of a brown, gurgling trough (D gag, subset C: second topper), from which Fate and Max emerge, covered in mud (D gag, subset D: the topper is topped). At any point along the way, Edwards might have ended the gag—after falling from the sky, or after crashing offscreen, or after cutting to the crash—but he doesn't. Instead, he pushes the joke as far as he can, topping and re topping the topper to milk it for all it's worth.

McCarey's principle, when combined with Edwards' concern with illusion, is in sync with The Great Race's attitude toward genre. As soon as we've grown comfortable with a backdrop, Edwards pulls it out from under us. He alternates between the Western, the musical, the costume drama, the swashbuckler, the epic, and the screwball, invoking the wisdom of Del Lord, director of many a Stooges short, and one of Sennett's favorites at Keystone. "The wisest technique," Lord said, "is to con your victim into a sense of security and then slip it to him."[34] As in The Pink Panther, genre is a running joke in the film, and changes about as often and indiscriminately as Maggie's gowns (tastefully realized, as always, by Edith Head). This vision of changeability is locked to Edwards' theory of duplicity, that nothing is ever any one thing, only many things. Topping the topper, a concept that will appear through Blake Edwards' final film, sensationalizes this state through visual comedy.

The Great Race, as we have established, is a spectacle about spectatorship. "Laaaaaaaaadies and Geeeentlemen!" the film begins, "You are about to witness the most spectacular feat ever attempted by the greatest daredevil in the world, the Great Leslie!" But which audience is being addressed here, the on- or off-screen? Both, naturally. We are the first of many spectators to shuffle through the film, and are followed by the impromptu crowds that form around the Great Leslie, the assortment of wallflowers at Hapnik's ball, and the drunken riff-raff at Lily Olay's feet. We're even asked to follow the bouncing ball in "The Sweetheart Tree" sing-along (another indication of the complicity between spectatorship and spectacle). To accommodate the great size of these crowds, Edwards uses the most spectacular spectacle of all: the 2.35 frame, an aspect ratio wide enough to photograph an entire crowd in one shot. The imagery delights in audiences, but there is also dark side to spectatorship. As will be explicated in *Darling Lili*, *10*, and *Victor/Victoria*, the notion of spectacle brings with it the implication of illusion. Voyeurs submit themselves to the perils of misinterpretation, often forcing both the spectator and the spectacle into cataclysmic misunderstandings.

There are illusions in *The Great Race*—conspicuously false sets, a proliferation of blue-screen techniques, and Fate's/Lemmon's duplicitous double roles—but what makes this picture different, and a kind of dress rehearsal for the larger statements to come, is that its attitude toward mis/representation, duplicity, performance, and all the other things that will actually end lives in *Darling Lili*, is mostly positive, making the film a uniquely buoyant entry in an *oeuvre* of extraordinary cynicism. However, *The Great Race* isn't just fun and games. In its curiosity about gender, one of Blake's most combustible illusions, it is a watershed film for the director. Throughout, men behave effeminately, women are macho, relationships that appear to be heterosexual are a little more complicated, and those that aren't, on further examination, might require further examination.

In the Blake Edwards movie, gender is as unpredictable as a pie in the face, and the line between masculinity and femininity is always tested, but never set. The Great Leslie, for instance, with his genderless name, is equal parts masculine and feminine. His fastidious whites appear utterly asexual, and the kiss he gives a worshipful woman in the film's first scene is about as *froid* as *sang* can get. And what of his car, the wistfully androgynous Leslie Special? It seems better suited to Liberace's poolside than a transatlantic road trip.

Add to this the presence of Leslie's valet Hezekiah (Keenan Wynn), and a near-complete portrait of a homosexual comes into focus. Why else would there be such competitiveness between Hezekiah and Maggie? Are they both vying for the same spot in the passenger's seat? As a self-described "emancipated woman," Maggie herself straddles both men's and women's worlds. To join Leslie, she's even willing to play "damsel in distress," a role that completely contradicts her ideals of progressive femininity. But what kind of suffragette prescribes trickery as a means of achieving their goals? (No doubt, one for whom the title "emancipated" is as illusory as "damsel in distress.") With this twist on Maggie, Edwards has cited a silent film archetype yet again. This time, it's Mack Sennett's star actress, Mabel Normand, who film historian Jeanine Basinger describes as "a figure of delicious liberation who made a joke out of the idea of damsel in distress. When Mabel showed up, it was everyone else who was potentially in distress."[35] Beneath so many layers of identity, it's difficult to locate the real Maggie, if there even is one.*

Hezekiah will not reappear until the end of the film. Dramatically speaking (and perhaps sexually speaking as well), he has been replaced by that "double-crossing female," Maggie Dubois. True, Maggie could have just joined the duo in progress—there is more room in the back seat, and more than enough screen time for her and Hezekiah to work out their differences—but the fact that a one-for-one exchange occurs between them connotes a change in Leslie's homo-exclusivity. From here on out, a heterosexual love story takes shape, one that forces both man and woman to confront their gender stereotypes, thereby allowing them to evolve beyond their ideological illusions.

Professor Fate and Max are up next. Everything about them reeks of competition and violence, in short, masculine aggression. Their car, the Hannibal 8, is arguably the most phallic automobile ever devised, containing pointed rockets of all kinds, and expansion mechanisms that swell the machine to a black beast many times it size. And yet, they share a hidden intimacy. Actually, they live together. Max serves Fate dinner, and at one point he even offers to feed him. In fact, he is even a bit naive when it comes to heterosexuality. Consider the following exchange:

Max: I'm hungry.
Fate: She's getting it.
Max: How long does it take to open a can of beans?
Fate: The eternal struggle takes time, Max.
Max: What struggle? She's got a can opener.
Fate: You cork brain, I'm talking about man-woman sex. Conquest!

This is typical Edwards' dialogue. In it, meaning is both doubled and obscured by comic misreading; that is, doubled for the audience, and obscured for the characters. But in the end, whether or not Fate and Max are actually homosexual is immaterial. What is significant is that in *The Great Race*, sexual identity—like genre and the very spectacle of moviemaking—is illusory and eminently duplicitous.

The Great Race did pretty good business, but not enough to make up for the $12 million spent. Who to blame? How about Blake for raising the

---

* That a character with the name of Dubois (meaning "of the wood") is played by an actress with the name of Wood suggests deeper levels of illusion and identity play.

budget and Warner for letting him? Or the mid-sixties for changing the people's taste in movies? At this point Edwards had been working in Hollywood for nearly twenty years, but now, as the studio system began its decline, his lifelong training in classical moviemaking started to show its age, and the relevance of the Blake Edwards picture was suddenly called into question. True, *The Great Race* was behind the times well before it was even shot, but did that mean it was Edwards or his technique that was out of style? To find the answer, Blake had to get his head out of Mack Sennett and into the problems of modern times. Slapstick had to be updated, but exactly how that was going to happen was anybody's guess.

WHAT DID YOU DO IN THE WAR, DADDY? (1966)

Lieutenant Christian: This is supposed to resemble a real battle!

One of the greatest tragedies of Blake Edwards' career (and there are many) is that *What Did You Do in the War, Daddy?* has fallen into obscurity. Many of the director's flops have since made happy homes on video shelves, and, like *The Party* and *Darling Lili*, have been favorably reappraised by critics and have even gone on to achieve "masterpiece" status, but for the picture in question (Julie Andrews' favorite amongst her husband's films) there has been a paltry afterlife. Peter Lehman and William Luhr let it slip away, as did Stuart Byron,[36] while the eight-page survey of Blake in *World Film Directors* devotes only one sentence to the picture[37] and even goes so far as to call it wearisome. But Myron Meisel, in his analysis of Edwards' work up to 1982, ranks *What Did You Do in the War, Daddy?* with the director's most complex and profound works. "It was also his finest, most resonant achievement to date," he continues, "a near masterpiece in which every comic conception contributed to a profound elucidation of Edwards' most fundamental concerns."[38] And *New York Times* critic Dave Kehr, on the occasion of the film's 2008 DVD release, appraised it "one of the most ingeniously constructed American comedies."[39] (Not to mention Sarris' appreciation of Dick Shawn's brilliant drag routine, which as late as 1987, twenty years after the film's release, was still the funniest he "had ever seen in a narrative context."[40])

That the film was not a box-office or critical success is only unsurprisingly surprising, but how this irrefutably auteurist work could go on uncelebrated by so many latter-day Edwardians is tougher to grasp. How could they have missed the picture's eloquent inquiry into the false/reality interchange or the tension between appearance and actuality that has been a crucial part of the filmmaker's cinematic personality since his very first films? To find it, they wouldn't have to look past the film's title. According to studio publicity, the idea for *What Did You Do in the War, Daddy?* came to Edwards when his son Geoffrey asked him the very same question. (The logo on the film's press kit shows a little boy with toy gun standing before a cross-legged man in an oversized armchair.) Although there are no

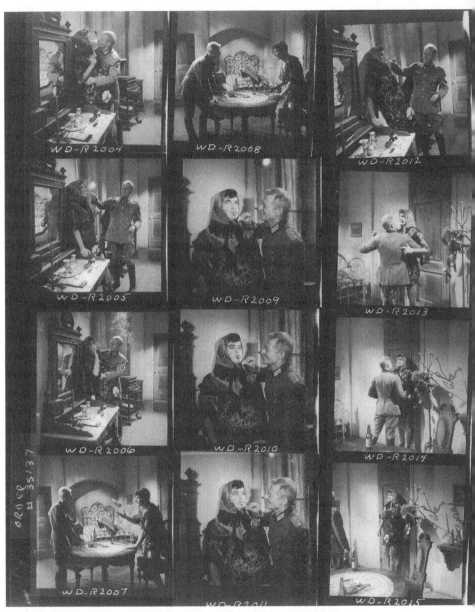

16. *What Did You Do in the War, Daddy?* (1966) Dick Shawn, seen here with Kurt Kreuger, in a drag sequence. Disguises in Edwards' films are a matter of personal and national security, which means that the flimsy ideological constructs of gender and allegiance are defenestrated at a moment's notice. (Courtesy of the Academy of Motion Picture Arts and Sciences)

fathers or sons in the film, its title evokes Edwards' recurring theme of patrimony, just as it imbues the narrative with an uncertainty that throws the whole film into question. Does daddy's response to junior's question match the film we see, or does he tell the boy something else and keep what's up there on the screen to himself? Or does *What Did You Do in the War, Daddy?* have nothing at all to do with what daddy actually did in the war? Of course, it's not the answers that are relevant to Edwards, but the questions. Wondering at what's really true is just what he wants us to do, and in this film that's exactly what he gets.

With this idea in mind, Blake composed a scenario with his sometime collaborator Maurice Richlin, and then sent it to William Peter Blatty (of *A Shot in the Dark*) who had a crack at the script. The Mirisches were ready to make it the first of six planned pictures under their new $20 million contract as Mirisch-Geoffrey Productions, but Blake was hesitant. After his financial troubles on *The Great Race*, he wasn't yet ready to do a big-budget war film. Instead he thought about doing something smaller, more intimate. *Toy Soldier*, a dramatic father-son vehicle he wanted to shoot with Lemmon, had immediate appeal to him, but Walter Mirisch didn't like it. He saw his new partner as a comedy director and, in Blake's words, "didn't want [him] to get involved with anything heavy." Blake says,

> Also, I myself was having serious domestic, personal problems; my marriage was heading for the rocks and I was about to get a divorce. I told Mirisch that I couldn't leave the county because I didn't want to leave my kids behind. So it meant that I would have to do *War, Daddy* here. It wouldn't have the documentary look that it needed; in order for the film to work it had to look real and that meant shooting in Italy.[41]

Instead, they built Valerno at Lake Sherwood Ranch, some thirty-five miles away from Hollywood in the San Fernando Valley. It cost around $800,000 of the film's $5 million—not a small amount for a movie without stars, but the Mirisches didn't think twice. They were so hot on the Edwards/war combo they were already talking about doing *The Battle of Gettysburg* next.

When *Variety* columnist Army Archerd drove out to the valley to see Italy, Blake was trying his best to salvage the documentary look he wanted. "This is one picture in which (we hope) the audience will not be conscious of camera—just actors and the dialogue." In his column, Army noted that Blake would use "color colorlessly at the outset of the film for 'documentary' effect, [and] segue into bright hues as [the] humor mounts."[42] (And so he did.) Blake wore to the set a baseball cap with five stars on it—one for each million the film was costing—and if he went over, he told everyone he'd add another. The hat was a cute way of reminding everyone of what was at stake, but underneath it was a mind in turmoil: the financial pressure was getting to him. To maintain his balance, Edwards began to think about his next picture, an adaptation of *Sweet November* with Jack Lemmon and perhaps even Audrey Hepburn.[43] But like *Gettysburg* and *Toy Soldier* it was never made.

What Did You Do in the War, Daddy? follows a ragtag group of American soldiers who, rather than fight their Sicilian enemies, strike a deal with them. Why not just pretend to battle? Why not join forces and stage a fake battle to fool the American commanding officers? It seems a good idea at first. The Americans get their instant surrender and the Italians get their party, but when the Germans arrive World War II starts to resemble an actual war, forcing the American and Italian soldiers into real life-and-death situations. From this premise, an elaborate chain reaction of farce and disguise occurs, all arranged by Lieutenant Christian (James Coburn). As Meisel observes, "Christian slyly mimics Edwards' own physical gestures and movements, which accentuate his slight resemblance to the filmmaker."[44] Indeed Christian, like Edwards, is a filmmaker. The soldier performs all the tasks of a director from dressing the extras (putting pants on naked legs), handling the casting (commanding Gina to play the nurse), scripting the dialogue (feeding Rizzo his lines during Major Pott's stickup), and even directing the cameraman to where he should point his lens.

The marriage of theatricality and warfare looks ahead to *Darling Lili* (also co-written by Edwards and Blatty). In both these films, performing literally saves lives. Whether it's Lili's musical numbers or Christian's battle scenes, pretending serves the dual function of keeping up patriotic appearances while allowing creative artists to lead alternate, even subversive lives. To do so, they must undermine the chain of command. They must, in slapstick terms, splurch authority. And it begins at the top: *What Did You Do in the War, Daddy?* opens as General Bolt (Carroll O'Connor), a big drinker (and therefore prone to misconceptions), hands Captain Cash (Dick Shawn) the responsibility of overseeing the American takeover of Valerno. Later, when things gets sticky for Cash (after *he* gets drunk), Lieutenant Christian assumes control of C Company, but when Major Pott (Harry Morgan) arrives at what he believes to be the site of an American triumph, he is held up by a low-ranking American officer (posing as an

Italian) and taken to jail. Meanwhile, General Bolt, the highest-ranking officer in the film, sits atop a hill looking down on what he believes to be the site of C Company's victorious battle. All this is to say that military hierarchy has been reversed in a splurch of epic proportions. The general is deluded and the privates have real authority. Rizzo does to Pott what the spinning globe does to Clouseau.

Quite naturally, *What Did You Do in the War, Daddy?* uses the gag to disrupt military authority, but it has a similar effect on genre. Consider the very first gag, a soccer ball that seems to fly out of nowhere and lands on a bayonet. It comes well after the film has established itself from within combat film conventions. Jeanine Basinger writes,

> As the film opens, it first presents traditional combat in straightfor-
> ward terms. Then it moves into a scene inside a tent between Dick
> Shawn and Carroll O'Connor that does not tip its hand. At first, it could
> be a typical scene from a combat film that we have seen many, many
> times before. But as it plays itself out, it slowly begins to come apart at
> the seams—it descends into comedy.[45]

As is customary of Blake Edwards, the film begins in a way that defies what it will become. *What Did You Do in the War, Daddy?* starts with a real, "serious" battle, a signifier that respects genre convention, and proceeds to gradually integrate slapstick such that, by the end of the film, combat and comedy will have actually fused. Edwards' shrewd manipulation of these narrative styles speaks to the picture's larger investment in what might be called the realities of battle. War may be hell, but if you shift your focus, you'll see it's also a farce.

If combat is comedy, then comedy is also combat. Edwards presents the morning after the Valerno street festival in pans across the piazza, revealing a succession of lifeless bodies wrung with streamers. Are they dead? Partying, we see, does to partygoers what fighting does to soldiers. The analogy is confirmed by Captain Oppo (Sergio Fantoni)'s jest that war is "the survival of the loudest." In these terms, it's no wonder that the sound design of the festival sequence is more elaborate and indeed louder than any of the combat scenes, real or staged. Crackling fireworks (like gunshots) bring us into the festival and a whirling burning firewall, the first image of the sequence, evokes the explosive danger of the combat scene that opened the film. So is Edwards saying there's no difference between the battlefield and the dance floor? No: he's saying that, like everything else, it's so much about how it looks and who's doing the looking, which is why, throughout the street festival, we see American soldiers monitoring the party from second-floor balconies, just as we will see Italian prostitutes cheering on the fake battle from their windows. But it is only when the generals are seen misinterpreting the "documentary" photographs that spectatorship becomes a means of winning the war.

And the real general is the director. When Captain Cash compares Christian to C. B. DeMille, an epic analogy for the American motion picture industry fades into place, and contextualizes the picture's seemingly trivial references to Greta Garbo and "Giovanni Wayne." This concept assumes biographical nuance when placed within the context of Blake's own career. Looking back to the troubles he faced on *The Great Race* and ahead to his troubles on *Darling Lili*, we understand that film production often requires the same degree of antiauthoritarian contempt we see in Lieutenant Christian. Films about fights can be a fight to make, but in the case of these pictures, the real farce is the one that occurs behind the scenes. Between the real and the created exists this confusing enterprise of making art. Is it a façade or a survival? Decoration or deceit? It's a problem that the midlife crisis artists of of 10, S.O.B., and *Victor/Victoria* will face, and in all cases, the gag—bridging the two worlds of perception and actuality— does the teaching. And in *What Did You Do in the War, Daddy?* Captain Lionel Cash is its star pupil.

Cash is an ideal target. So consumed is he with hierarchical military procedure, he refuses to stand at ease even when General Bolt explicitly commands him to do so. He can't even call Bolt by his first name; his lips literally struggle to make their way around "Max." Cash, in short, is the model soldier and as a result, most of the gags in *What Did You Do in the War, Daddy?* splurch at his expense. The first, the soccer ball that impales itself on the bayonet, carries a bulk of the film's thematic load. Not only does it effectively undermine the authority with which C Company, led by Cash, has infiltrated Valerno, it introduces the genre-bending conflict of combat versus comedy, which it posits instantly in the form of a visual metaphor. In the same gesture, the gag draws an ideological parallel between battle and gaming. Just after the soccer ball deflates on the weapon, a referee blows his whistle and halts the game, giving precedent to the moment when Lieutenant Christian, a referee in the filmed game of fake fighting, blows his whistle to stop the staged action of "war." And because the gag is set in an arena filled with Italian spectators, it conveys theatricality—a relationship between perceived and actual—that bears Edwards' preoccupation with the duplicitous absurdity of the farce that masquerades as battle (the Italians see pleasure, the Americans see war). Even the phallic nature of the bayonet cashes in on meaning: it splurches the masculinity of battle-hungry Americans with the feminine values of Italian pleasure.

Each of these tensions is embodied in Captain Cash, who as a middle-level authoritarian is caught in a dialectical conflict between duty and desire, making him both the gag target *and* gag reflex of *What Did You Do in the War, Daddy?* It begins for Cash at the Valerno street party, where all manner of party gags run down his efforts at decorum. His protest of "I am the commanding officer!" cannot be heard over the revelry (he loses the battle of the loudest), wine is poured into his hat before he puts it on, a bottle is smashed on him, and he faces the problem of endless strands of streamers getting in his mouth and around his neck. Now *that* sounds like war. His pretensions to authority are nearly undermined by some serious drinking—alcohol being the elixir of the splurch—but it isn't until he is led upstairs by the lovely Gina (Giovanna Ralli) that they manage to slip away (though not for good). The business of the flag gag, a pole that continually keeps Cash from the bedroom, further represents the clash of duty and desire (in this case, the pole is both phallic and patriotic), suggesting that though he thinks he is leading with one pole, he is actually leading with the other. Each instance of physical derangement that befalls Cash wears him down one step further until he can be worn down no more. Ultimately, his body goes the way of his resolve, and the gag—heretofore an exclusively thematic device for Edwards—assumes substantial psychological value.

Unlike Clouseau, whose relationship to slapstick is fixed (the character never receives the gag's information—*that's* the joke), Captain Cash is *changed* by the physical recriminations of calamity. His morning-after pratfall off the balcony and into a pool of water preempts the next beat in his character and informs his behavior for the following sequence of film. It should be noted, though, that these gags, while thematically and psychologically relevant, do not carry the dramatic weight of the slapstick in Edwards' mature masterpieces, films with narratives that cannot be sustained without their splurches. Therefore, we might consider *What Did You Do in the War, Daddy?* a transitional work, one that bridges the gap between the thematic unity of Clouseau's knockabout and the narrative structure of *The Party*, a drama built entirely of visual humor. That said, the film does feature the odd dramatically indispensible splurch. The extended drag sequence, a pivotal moment for both Cash and the gag, is unique in the film because of its narrative muscularity (without it, the story would have a hole), and because it effectively splurches both Cash and the German officer who fancies him. Now Cash is both the source *and* subject of authoritarian contempt; we laugh at him for trying to act like a woman, and we laugh with him because he is doing his patriotic duty of distracting the German officer, who is splurched accordingly. Theme, character, and drama all contained within a single hilarious moment of transvestism. That's Blake at his best.

Edwards doesn't have the full picture yet, but he has taken great pains to update what in *The Great Race* he memorialized. Using the splurch to describe Cash's transformation from soldier to lover, Edwards has slyly integrated slapstick into a very political predicament. How did he do it? He used the mask of genre to bait us with combat and hook us into comedy. Myron Meisel said it well: "Edwards' slapstick is laid like a grid over the social satire, deepening not the drama so much as the expression of his own viewpoint of the world in which he and his characters operate."[46] In this film, that viewpoint concerns the ritualistic theatrics of war. Basinger again:

> War by its nature is a kind of theatrical event. We even refer to the theater of war. World War II had the ETO and the PTO—European and Pacific theaters of operation. People have roles to play with titles and appropriate costumes, insignias, and prescribed behavior. There are "leads" (generals) and "bit players" (privates), and when it is all over, there are the inevitable reviews—by historians. *What Did You Do in the War, Daddy?* uses this idea of theater to the hilt.[47]

No wonder Cash can change into a hooker as easily as he can become a Nazi. Like the other successful soldiers, his victory turns upon his ability to transform, or, in theatrical terms, to act. The metaphor is recapitulated in Edwards' use of a ubiquitous sewer hole that essentially acts as a trapdoor, dropping soldiers into the safety of the catacombs beneath. It's ironic that these men find safety in the presence of death, but it's also classic Edwards. Using a stone coffin as a footstool, C Company can step down into the solace of darkness, as if a life of death would be preferable to a life of war. (Is this the suicidal impulse that will recur throughout Blake's life?)

Time and again, as if on loop, people are seen falling through the trapdoor or popping out of it. As in the film's battle sequences (real or staged), which replay throughout, repetition is a structural device that gains in meaning through its recurrence. As in the plays of Beckett, with recurrence—even the recurrence of trauma—comes absurdity, and perhaps even levity. (Note for a possible dissertation: Clouseau as Vladimir/Estragon.) Consider the film's ending, which suggests that its narrative will begin again. These repetitions bring home the point that even something as devastating as war becomes funny on repeat, what director Leo McCarey referred to as "breaking the pain barrier." One tragedy is tragic, but when tragedy is compounded, when the pain barrier is broken, is when it becomes funny. But it is a funny tinged with existential fear. The armies of *What Did You Do in the War, Daddy?* face the bleak absurdity of repetition which, like the myth of Sisyphus, suggests an infinitude liable to drive anyone insane (or is it insane with laughter?). One need only think of Major Pott, lost in his endless underground, to sense the fine line between hysterical and hysteria.

This structural concept finds visual articulation in compositional repetition. Over and over, Edwards will frame a two-person argument in a single-take shot that laterally foregrounds the combatants in a face-to-face stand-off, and has the effect of emphasizing the sameness of the disputants. In these arrangements, neither character is privileged or condemned, but rather, they are seen as equalized interchangeables, mirror reflections of one another with only wardrobes to help us tell them apart (hence the effectiveness of changing uniform in the film). So what is the point of arguing if it gets them nowhere? It's a tragic-comic question that can be seen, as demonstrated, within the shots, but also from shot to shot (Edwards repeats this image of repetition). Likewise, the precise foregrounding of actors, often cheated out to the camera like actors to their audience, evokes the theatricality of proscenium framing. By not cutting or moving, the single long take honors the fourth-wall effect and as a result, reinforces the film's stance on war as farce. This is not merely an effective theme-related device in *What Did You Do in the War, Daddy?*, it's a technique that corresponds to Edwards' larger stylistic stratagem. He says, "Although these days we are able to tell very good stories and make some wonderful films without much dialogue, we're forgetting that there are theatrics involved in what we do. I enjoy the theatrics. But with such an emphasis on naturalism—and there's nothing wrong with that—somehow the theatricality is lost."[48] Restoring theatrics to the cinema is one of the projects of Edwards' career and farce is the primary tool of that restoration.

Within the context of a combat narrative, theatricality assumes satirical resonance, but, to its credit, in *What Did You Do in the War, Daddy?* it never spills over into agitprop. No one gets on his high horse for a lecture on amnesty, nor is there dogmatic debate or Strangeloving nuclear extremes. There is only farce. In this picture, satire comes through form—through comedy. Save for a single image of a dove on a gun and a flower in its barrel, Edwards keeps his moralizing to himself. His contempt for battle is clear, but political right and wrong are irrelevant; moreover, they are dangerous. If the Nazis are bad guys it's because their politics is more important than their pleasure. The Italians and Americans have no political orientation, except to save their skins and have a good time while they're doing it. Likewise, the eponymous defector of *Darling Lili* will discover that blood in heart is better than blood on sand, and, like Captain Cash, her realization is carried out through theatricality.

Although the film impressed many critics, most thought it too long. *Variety* wrote, as only that publication can, that the picture had "lots of laughs but goes overboard in pitching for yocks and is sorely in need of trimming and snap."[49] Brendan Gill disagreed: "One keeps hearing—and one keeps having more and more reason to fear—that Hollywood just doesn't know how to make those good old-fashioned slapstick farces anymore; Mr. Edwards has struck several sharp blows against this notion in the past, and with "WDYDITWD?" he knocks it into a cocked hat."[50] Perhaps the most rewarding appraisal came from the *Hollywood Reporter*, which printed, quite simply, that Blake Edwards "thinks and creates in film terms."[51] What better indication of success? Well, for one, there's the box office.

Satire was for too light a dish for emergent Vietnam War audiences of 1966. They wanted their antiwar served without metaphor and covered in blood, or not at all. If comedy and combat were to mix, as they did in *The Russians Are Coming, the Russians Are Coming*, another Mirisch war farce released the same year, they had better do it with wall-to-wall stars. (Walter Mirisch later wrote of *War, Daddy*, "I think its casting certainly affected its grossing potential."[52])

The public reception of *What Did You Do in the War, Daddy?* was symptomatic of a greater change: the sixties were coming to Hollywood. *Dr. Strangelove*, *The Graduate*, and *Bonnie and Clyde* were only a few years off, but the old-guard auteurs could already hear them approach, and perhaps none better than Blake Edwards. With a cinematic sensibility that was conceived in anachronism, he had every reason to fear the revolution. Like *The Great Race*, *What Did You Do in the War, Daddy?* represents the growing schism between Edwardian slapstick revival and the rising commercial interest in a new, postclassical American cinema that would make M*A*S*H of Blake's nostalgia. There was no denying it: Edwards was about to embark on a difficult journey. Only now is it clear that he suffered in this period not from overambitious artistry (as contemporary critics believed), but from something in the moment it was harder to see: a change in the national zeitgeist. If he were to go on, he would have to do one of two things. Either he would have to abandon his silent film sensibility for something with contemporary versimilitude, or he would have to integrate them. With *Gunn* and *The Party*, he would do both, and in that order.

GUNN (1967)

Peter Gunn: Something about a new grave makes me want to
run a four-minute mile, get drunk, and shack-up with a redhead.
Not necessarily in that order.

Because *Gunn* has touches of film noir, let's open with a flashback: it's 1957, MCA has purchased Universal, and Henry Mancini is let go. The Supreme Court decision to divest the studios of their distribution and exhibition monopolies had after ten years of slow bloodletting finally destabilized the Hollywood factories, and the composer, along with many other studio musicians, had found himself with an expired contract. In those days, there was a barbershop on the Universal lot, and, lucky for Mancini, his studio pass hadn't yet been revoked. After what he called the haircut of his life, Henry ran into his old friend, Blake Edwards. (By that time, Edwards and Mancini had worked together on three films—*Mister Cory, This Happy Feeling,* and *The Perfect Furlough*—none of which were complete Mancini scores.) Quite fortuitously, Blake offered him some work on the new detective series he was developing, called *Peter Gunn.* This one was about a different kind of detective, Blake told him, boiled somewhere between soft and hard, where the existential fog of forties' noir didn't get too thick. As was true of many of Blake's scripts to follow, music was built into the story: Gunn's girl sings with a five-piece ensemble at little jazz joint called Mother's. "In the pilot," Mancini wrote, "five or six minutes took place in Mother's. That's a long time, so it was obvious that jazz had to be used." He continues,

> It was the time of so-called cool West Coast jazz, with Shelly Manne, the Candoli brothers, and Shorty Rogers among others. And that was the sound that came to me, the walking bass and drums. The 'Peter Gunn' title theme actually derives more from rock and roll than from jazz. I used guitar and piano in unison, playing what is known in music as an *ostinato*, which means obstinate. It was sustained throughout the piece, giving it a sinister effect, with some frightened saxophone sounds and some shouting brass.

To all this, Mancini added what was to become a part of his signature sound: a quartet of bass flutes. They were used, he said, "for a dark effect, sometimes writing a fall—a descending figure—at the end of the note, which gave a kind of paranoid effect."[53]

Mancini built his theme upon a unique blend of dance band and orchestra, drawing the intimacy of a small combo into a symphonic evocation of blues. Until then, jazz on television was used mostly as source music, something that originated from on-screen, like a radio or dark alley. But Mancini did away with all that. He made jazz—or in this case, a jazz-rock fusion—the show's primary musical ingredient. *The Music from Peter Gunn* was a number one hit on the *Billboard* chart, selling more than a million copies, and earned him an Emmy and two Grammys. It was quite an achievement for a jazz release (let alone one that began as a television score) and from that point on, the Blake Edwards movie would be almost inseparable from its Henry Mancini score. Their mutually enriching sense of chic would produce some of the most iconic image-sound relationships of the twentieth century, and it all began here, with *Peter Gunn*.

Swayed by the commercial success of the television series, Paramount offered Blake the opportunity to make *Gunn* the first in an exclusive four-picture deal between them. At the time, 1966, Edwards' second of the four pictures was to be a James Coburn vehicle called *Waterhole No. 3*, which the trades described as "a wildly comic Western involving the robbery of tons of gold bullion, frontier fighters and practically the entire U.S. Cavalry."[54] The final two pictures would be a screen version of *Mr. Lucky*—Blake's television hit from 1959—and "another comedy with music now in stages of development."[55] Of course, it didn't quite turn out that way. After *Gunn*, *Waterhole No. 3* went to director William Graham, and *Mr. Lucky* never came through. Only the fourth planned project stayed with Blake. It was called *Darling Lili, or Where Were You the Night You Said You Shot Down Baron von Richtofen?*, and known to its enemies simply as The Film that Almost Sunk Paramount. More on that later.

In the meantime, Daisy Jane (Marion Marshall), owner of a prominent bordello, has offered Peter Gunn (Craig Stevens) the sum of $10,000 to investigate Nick Fusco (Albert Paulsen), who she believes murdered the mobster Julio Scarlotti (Lincoln Demyan). Gunn begins to suspect a fellow by the name of Grethers, and after breaking into his apartment is tommy-gunned by a mystery assailant. Moments later, Gunn catches up with the gunman and learns that Grethers is none other than Daisy Jane (a transvestite), who wanted only to frame Fusco. Case closed.

If that story sounds ridiculous it's because, for Edwards, suspense and comedy are intertwined. From *This Happy Feeling* to Clouseau (and beyond), one never seems to be that far from the other. "My entire life," Blake once said, "has been a search for the funny side to that very tough life out there. I developed a kind of eye for scenes that made me laugh to take the pain away."[56] In his work, we observe a constant interchange between danger and laughter, its antidote. The feeling of anxiety rarely goes unbroken by irony, and the most hilarious gags are regularly precipitated by fear. Tension begets comedy and comedy begets tension, but luckily there is catharsis in the punchline. With laughter, uneasiness is obliterated, and the previously vulnerable moment is converted to into a new security (of course, only to be disrupted again).

This manic-depressive cycle, pessimistic and yet hopeful, is founded upon the principle of information concealed (Cato is hidden before a sneak attack), a fact that suggests the gag and suspense aren't opposed in Edwards, but are rather two sides of the same nervous coin. When partnered and blended in various combinations, they can produce a wide array of genres ranging from *The Great Race* at one extreme to *Experiment in Terror* at the other. Naturally, Edwards' most personal films occur somewhere in between, far from the limitations of generic convention. In the comedies, films like *The Pink Panther* and *What Did You Do in the War, Daddy?*, the presence of fear is expressed through farce ("Who's in there?" Nervous response: "Here? Uh, no one!"), while in the dramas, stories of characters afflicted by betrayal and falsity, the presense of farce is charged with fear. For instance, the longest sustained comic passage in *Darling Lili*—a rainstorm seduction between Lili and Larrabee—is pure farce, complete with interrupting servants (in disguise, *naturellement*) and nosy detectives peeping in from the roof. Of course, in these circumstances, polarizing "comedy" and "drama" becomes quite problematic, for each contains so much of the other that the originally assumed label becomes practically meaningless. As we have seen, Edwards' best work is characterized by this breakdown of genre. His narratives, which are tonally consistent in their commitment to inconsistency, undermine whatever security we would draw from impeachable genre boundaries. In this environment, the potential for all manner of treachery is fearfully high. Enter one of Blake Edwards' mottoes: nothing is what it appears to be. So how do we know what's real?

Luckily, Edwards arms his films with gags and detectives, two truth-wielding weapons that can bring justice and order to the anarchy. The gag

17. *Gunn* (1967) The duplicitous world of Blake Edwards, as seen here through visual infinitude (and, of course, a wig), belies authenticity, but beautifies comedy and suspense. *Gunn*, like many of Edwards' films, excels at both. (Author's collection)

splurches reason into a dissident, and the detective, a kind of walking splurch-maker, deposes tyrants who have made a mess of their authority. Because of their overlap, any single Blake Edwards film does not require both at once. If it does, as in the Clouseau movies, the notable exception, it is because the detective in question necessitates it. (Clouseau is gagged for his pretentious arrogance and embarrassing efforts at masculinity. Because the gag nails the detective, splurcher and splurched are one, rendering justice indistinguishable from anarchy.) In films like *Gunn*, in which the detective (or detective figure in the case of *The Carey Treatment* and

Sunset) is a capable arbiter of justice, slapstick is extraneous. The result? Where there is no figure of justice there is the splurch (and therefore comedy), and where there is justice, there is no gag (and therefore drama).

What places Edwards' successful detectives beyond the gag? What do they have that Clouseau lacks? The answer: a sense of humor that gives them authority over their superiors. Wyatt, Carey, and Gunn may not be professional detectives, but in their mastery of the riposte they have professional effectiveness. Instead of gags, these gentlemen sleuths use wit to supplant the real feds—think of M. Emmett Walsh (in *Sunset*), Dan O'Herlihy (in *Carey*), and Ed Asner (in *Gunn*)—using ridicule, like the splurch, to exact justice. Funny *happens* to Clouseau and derives *from* Gunn. The "pro" suffers by it, but the "amateur" gains by it.

When we are first introduced to him, the only thing we know about Peter Gunn is that he is a man of tremendous verbal facility—though it's not what he says that gives Gunn credibility, it's how he says it. Of course, the content of his speech is essential, but it's the style—a rhythm imparted on Craig Stevens by his director—that carries his authority. Here's that first scene, set in a graveyard:

> Jacoby: You in mourning?
> Gunn: No, I'm a funeral buff. What about you?
> Jacoby: Just bringing my "Who's Who in the Mafia" up to date.
> Gunn: I'm relieved.
> Jacoby: Really?
> Gunn: I thought you might be making your first communion.
> Jacoby: This isn't a temple.
> Gunn: It isn't?
> Jacoby: That man speaking Latin is a Priest.
> Gunn: You're not serious.
> Jacoby: What did you think he was?
> Gunn: A terribly avant garde rabbi?

Retorts come quickly. Rhythm is unbroken. Beyond authority, his manner of speaking lends him, like many movie detectives before and since, a cynicism that guards him from pain. Like Edwards, Gunn has the ability to laugh away difficult situations, death in particular, with an irony that gives him the upper hand on heartache. In this pain-filled world, only those who can laugh off shock and violence (the gag, in other words) will maintain their poise, but none more readily than Gunn, who, as the pinnacle of

Blake's formula for comfort (craziness turned funny) is not just the film's leading figure of authority, but the most enlightened character in all of Edwards' cinema. Others will reach this point of enlightment, but Gunn's pain barrier was broken long ago.

Blake's formal presentation of the graveyard brings its dialogue to the fore. The camera, like Gunn, is distant to the point of nonexistence and unfolds in one long master take unbroken by movement or disruption of any kind. Every possible visual activity has been denied and distractions have been banished. Blocking is mute, costumes are mute, the image is mute, even the expressions on the actors' faces are mute. The only action here is speech, and it is conveyed with an antinaturalistic betrayal of emotion and psychology that borders on the robotic. What emerges is a kind of ascetic aesthetic that deprives the speakers of their humanity. Their infallible patter, emphasized by the infallibility of their visual representation, drains all spontaneity from their personae and reduces them to mise-en-scène: Gunn and Jacoby are no more than objects in the frame, stylized to a hard-boiled pulp. The air of artificiality Edwards has imposed upon their behavior, both in speech and stillness, is used throughout Gunn to create an effect absolute control.

Gunn is all about the constructed image. And image, like identity, often has nothing to do with authenticity. Changeability, therefore, is a threat not just to the film's formal elements, but to the whole enterprise of logic that is the detective's principal means of perception. Samantha wants to be called "Sam," Ernestine wants to be called "Ernie," and of course "Daisy Jane" is actually a man. Gender is quite literally assumed in this world, and so, for that matter, is Gunn's own persona. On the job, he is tough as nails; he's steely in movement, sturdy in composition, and responds without so much as a thought. He's practically a James Bond fantasy of masculine aptitude. But Craig Stevens is no Sean Connery. This is, after all, Blake Edwards we're talking about, a man who would let no "man" really be as "manly" as he would have us believe. To illustrate this other side of Gunn (okay, the feminine side), Blake has given him the kind of bachelor pad that would send a noir detective into fits of laughter. Just take a look at the zebra rug. No, Sam Spade just doesn't have Gunn's flair for fabric.

We see a different Gunn when he's is at home. No longer does he dominate composition, now composition dominates him. This visual reversal evidences a man without mastery of his private environment: like Lili Schmidt, Captain Cash, and so many other Edwardians, he is publicly forceful, but privately inept. And of course, it is the tension between image and authenticity that Blake adores. In this case, it's the exterior of masculine detective, but the interior of an interior designer. When, for instance, Jacoby interrupts him in the middle of the night, Gunn is seen (quite slender) in his silken night robe. Too tired to manage the coffee, Gunn bumps into a kitchen cabinet and spills a bit of java. Wait—Gunn bumps? What's happened to manly unflappability? What kind of man can't make himself a cup of coffee? The splurch has stepped in to negotiate Gunn's previously concealed gender-image crisis as the dames infiltrate his home and Gunn goes from ladies man to lady's man. And there's more to come: it begins when Sam (Sherry Jackson) lets herself in (how?), gets undressed, and slips into bed, and soon gets worse: there's a knock downstairs—it's Edie (his girl). (Good luck, Gunn!) As he is wont to do, Edwards has made a farce of the womanizer, punishing the man who loves women for his excess of females by an excess of females. It's a theme Lehman and Luhr have observed many times over:

> Edwards repeatedly develops scenes in which someone invades another person's private and deceptively secure space, often causing an instantaneous and horrifying reorganization of power within the scene. Moments later, however, the invader finds himself/herself at the mercy of another invader.[57]

In the above example, the reorganization of power is horrifying, but when it is applied to the Sam/Edie farce, it's comical. Whether it's suspense or comedy, the fright and the laugh emerge from the same stylistic pattern—spatial invasion.

That gags and attacks are both predicated on surprise demonstrates how closely the genres are related in the Blake Edwards' movie. Late in *Gunn*, they're practically one: when Gunn begs Edie to believe that he never slept with Sam, he exclaims, "May God strike me dead if it isn't the gospel truth!"* *KABOOM!* The room explodes into rubble. Power has shifted to the woman, the compulsive aesthetic of manly control is violated, and surprise has lent the splurch its horrific comedy. Restated, sexual incapacity does damage both to Gunn's physical poise and to Blake's formal agenda. With Gunn flaccid, the film has a visual identity crisis of its own, variations of which recur through the end of the picture. The climactic shoot-out scene,

---

* The gag looks ahead to the religious invocation in *Skin Deep*.

for instance, begins in absolute compositional order—the kind of graphic approach that defines the early parts of *Gunn*—and ends in a violent exchange that makes chaos of the façade. As in *The Lady from Shanghai*, the infinite mirror reflections crescendo to the point of self-destruction, suggesting that Grethers (in drag as Daisy Jane) has multiplied to impossible lengths. But then his mask is ripped off and the illusion is broken. Gunfire is exchanged, the glass comes crashing down (Gunn will later throw Grethers/Daisy Jane through a pane of glass), and the phony multiplicity of image(s), of order through appearance, is turned to rubble. And that's just how Blake wants it.

It follows that a film about the illusion of images/personae would have a significant interest in the interplay between perception and its opponent, obscurity. Like so many Blake Edwards movies, be they comedy or drama (whatever those mean), *Gunn* begins in the dark. The detective picture often favors unlit spaces—they help to conceal information—but for Blake, the black is useful when it comes to conveying these tricks of visual and informational cognizance. The boat scene that opens the film is a perfect example. Here, the picture is so fractured by darkness (not to mention cutting and spatial disorientation) that we must struggle even to make narrative sense of the images placed before us. The mystery is not simply a question of whodunit, but of whoisit, and Blake's playful use of zoom adds another one to the mix: whatisit. Quite often, scenes in *Gunn* begin with a close-up so extreme that what we're looking at is abstracted beyond recognition. From this close, there's no way of knowing that the red line running across the frame is—zoom out here—actually the painted net in an indoor racketball court. It's a technique that has come to *Gunn* by way of its TV predecessor *Peter Gunn*, with the major difference that Blake's television cameras couldn't zoom, only track. Although the effect is slightly different, the ideological basis is similar: Blake pulls away to fill in the missing information. His lens deliberately conceals, and then in a snap, reveals.

The idea was that *Gunn* would kick off a James Bond-type franchise, but after the picture's less-than-satisfactory performance at the box office, there was no hope for a sequel. And it was too bad, too. Blake brought the picture in early and under budget, he even reshot some risqué scenes to get the kinder Production Code Seal, but the dollars were against him. The news might have disappointed fans like Charles Champlin ("*Gunn* is an expert entertainment"[58]) and John Mahoney ("Edwards [is] in the top of his form"[59]), but for Pauline Kael, it was probably for the best. "For the past couple of years," she wrote, "whenever someone says, 'I've just seen the worst movie ever made,' I ask, 'Is it really worse than *The Satan Bug*?' I guess I shouldn't have walked out on Blake Edwards' *Gunn*, because I think it might have provided a new low base, but it would be cheating to use a film one didn't see all the way through."[60] Oh, well. Maybe she'd like Blake's next one.*

* She didn't.

THE PARTY (1968)

Hrundi: In India we don't think who we are, we know who we are.

Blake had fallen on hard times. *The Great Race, Gunn,* and *What Did You Do in the War, Daddy?* were more ambitious than lucrative, and challenged the marketability of Edwards' personal cinema. Thinking back on his last hit, *A Shot in the Dark,* raised the question, if audiences were hungry for Clouseau, should he feed them another *Panther?* Or would that be a regression, an artistic default tantamount to surrender? It was unclear. On one hand, he had resolved never to work with Sellers again (*A Shot,* he vowed, would be their last), and on the other, he yearned to return to the box office's good graces. Such was Blake Edwards' predicament in 1967.

"One thing [Peter and I] had talked about during the good times," Edwards remembers, "was wouldn't it be great to take a structure, just that, and mostly improvise a whole film? I had this notion which didn't have anything to do with Sellers to begin with—it was a comedy notion— but the more I developed it along those lines, the more it seemed impossible to do with anyone else."[61] In other words, some of the Clouseau ingredients, but an entirely different dish. But would Sellers bite? Fortunately for Edwards (and posterity), the actor was nearly broke and in the midst of his own losing streak (*What's New Pussycat?, Casino Royale*). And so, holding his breath, Sellers returned to Los Angeles to re-team with his darling nemesis Blake Edwards. The film, then titled R.S.V.P, was to be Sellers' first in Hollywood.*

The ready-to-shoot script was only sixty-eight pages long—about half the length of a typical feature film script. The screen time that wasn't accounted for on the page was intended to offer the filmmakers improvisational latitude; it was a story that was to be written in the telling. If it seems a far-out concept, it's because it was, conducive more to the inexpensive digital video techniques of today's filmmakers than the costly studio processes of the late sixties. In fact, Blake Edwards, along with Jerry

---

* In 1964, Peter began shooting Billy Wilder's *Kiss Me, Stupid,* which would have been his first Hollywood film, but had a heart attack and dropped out. He was replaced by Ray Walston. "Heart attack?" Wilder once said about Sellers. "You have to have a heart before you can have an attack."

Lewis, the father of the technique, was one of the pioneers of video-assist filmmaking. Attaching a videotape camera to his film camera allowed Edwards to review a scene as soon as it was shot, a shortcut that saved him a considerable amount of time and money. Ordinarily, he would have had to wait for the rushes to see his progress, but with instantaneous video playback, Edwards could correct errors on the spot. It was an ideal arrangement for improvisation and essential in honing the complexity of The Party's intricate physical choreography. How else was Blake to trace the half-dozen concurrent storylines?

Those who look upon The Party with distain (and there are many) generally cite a reputedly underdeveloped story. They'll say it's little more than a series of slapshtick goofs, loosely related, and devoid of meaning. (They're wrong.) In it, Hrundi V. Bakshi (Peter Sellers), accidental invitee, wreaks havoc upon a posh Hollywood party, inadvertently turns it into a wonderful evening, and leaves with a pretty girl. The film, it should be noted, is one hour and forty minutes long; plot is not one of its virtues. On the other hand, that one hour and forty minutes is comprised of the finest gag-based storytelling Blake Edwards—or anyone—has ever put on film. In The Party, the splurches are not asides hung on the periphery of the narrative thread; they are the narrative thread, and act as the sole structural force of the drama. Whether or not this experiment is successful is for each individual to decide, but what is incontrovertible is the brazen inventiveness with which the filmmaker has fashioned it.

Lehman and Luhr put it best: "Shocking as it may seem, The Party may very well be one of the most radically experimental films in Hollywood history; in fact, it may be the single most radical film made in Hollywood since D. W. Griffith's style came to dominate the American cinema." Citing its perpetual avoidance of traditional compositional techniques, they argue that Edwards' film represents a significant departure from the Griffith manner in which "the narrative action became centered—that is, literally centered in the frame." In these films, "important narrative events were foregrounded so that they could not be missed."[62] The drama, in other words, plays out downstage center. The authors maintain that this tendency, the ruling Hollywood aesthetic, is undermined in The Party by Edwards' compositional subjugation technique; that is, the film's major dramatic events unfold on the edges or background of the frame. In this manner, Hrundi Bakshi, like many Edwards klutzes, is condemned to incessant visual neglect. What makes The Party unique is Edwards' unflag-

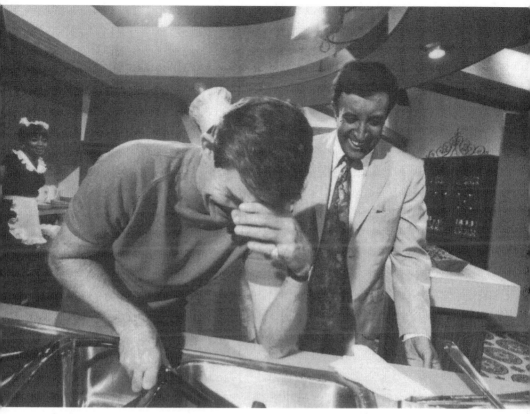

18. *The Party* (1968) Thankfully, Edwards and Sellers loved comedy more than they hated each other, but not by much. *The Party* pushed them to the brink. (Courtesy of the Academy of Motion Picture Arts and Sciences)

ging commitment to this technique, one that doesn't just brand the film, but defines it in its entirety.*

It is fitting that a film about Hollywood pretension is constructed with such anti-Hollywood methodology. But *The Party* posits more than stylistic counterpoint to the American cinema, it is deeply antagonistic to the people who make it. Like S.O.B., Edwards' other tribute to Hollywood misanthropy, *The Party* takes aim at phonies and phoniness and splurches

---

* Edwards' film owes a debt of gratitude to Jacques Tati's *Playtime*, which predates *The Party*'s innovative use of space, innocuous ambience, and sight gagging. Also, Sellers' Hrundi Bakshi bears a striking, almost explicit resemblance to Monsieur Hulot in both physicality and temperament. They are fraternal films, released only months apart.

at will. It begins on the set of a film, the kind of *Gunga Dinish* desert epic we expect of big-budget studio filmmaking. With its exotic locations, cast of thousands, and "important" historical setting, Edwards gives us a taste of the Hollywood paradigm. But it's a trick. Before we know we're watching a film in production, we assume that these events are actually happening. It isn't until the man who will later be identified as Hrundi messes up the shot that we cut to a film crew and realize that what we have just seen was only a scene. This illusion, typical of Edwards' genre-bending prologues, is not only a contradiction of the Peter Sellers/Blake Edwards comedy we have expected to see, but in its artificiality (we're on location), an indictment of Hollywood superficiality. It's a fake movie; the "real" one will begin just after the opening credits.

This epic movie is a mask *The Party* wears, and it is as phony as the people who are making it, people like C. S. Divot (Gavin MacLeod), the film's producer. Between takes, Divot snaps at a sunbathing bombshell—her cue to accompany him into his trailer (Edwards doesn't need to cut inside, we get the picture)—and when he arrives at the eponymous party, he's with a different girl altogether. Clearly, this is a man for whom intimacy and filmmaking are equally fraudulent. As the embodiment of Hollywood duplicity, he is the film's villain. Hrundi Bakshi, by contrast, is a man of great sincerity (at least, at first, when he's alone).

The establishing shot of his home, an Edenic enclave apart from the world, gently cranes up in a soothing and subtle movement that contrasts with the aggressive visual rigidity of the party, a space that will be characterized by a static and spiritless camera. (When camera movement does occur at the party, it will be laterally grounded to the x-axis, and unlike this establishing shot, without the ethereal grace implied by vertical ascension.) We cut inside to a close-up of Hrundi's sitar. The camera floats around him in a dreamy circumferential glide that seems to underscore his serenity of heart. Whereas most of the partygoers will be shot head-on, at an angle that emphasizes their flatness, Hrundi is given the three-dimensional treatment here, an indication of his inner sanctity. The moment's calm is interrupted by mail dropping through his door, and suddenly, the music hardens. It's party music, and it is the first of many threats to Hrundi's authenticity.

The other threats come in the form of splurches, each a product of Hrundi's ill-conceived attempts at "fitting in." These gags have more dramatic weight than the comic embellishments of *The Pink Panther* or *A*

Shot in the Dark, both of which achieve thematic unity (authoritarian contempt/masculine ineptitude), but do not describe Clouseau's change in attitude (Clouseau, after all, doesn't change in attitude). By contrast, Hrundi Bakshi *does* have a character arc, and his transformation is told not through dialogue (as is typical of Hollywood sound films), but through his relationship to physical and visual comedy; more specifically, what springs the splurch, the splurch itself, and Hrundi's response to it.

To understand this change, we must examine the party's tripartite gag structure. Phase one, the gag reflex, is initiated by Hrundi's incompetence. Like Clouseau, he is naturally clumsy and prone to the most embarrassing situations. Hrundi's cover-ups, his attempts at self-preservation, kick off phase two. To survive in a world as pretentious as Hollywood, he must mask his follies, and if he wants to gain acceptance, deny his authentic incompetence. As the film's prologue has demonstrated, Hrundi is accident-prone on the epic scale, and any effort to overcome his errors will be met with—phase three—the splurch's recriminations. Thus, when it occurs, his transformation will require Hrundi to embrace his folly and submit to the anarchy of slapstick, the antidote to human pretense, such that, by the end of the film, the tripartite pattern of incompetence-euphemism-calamity will become intended anarchy-exposure-celebration.

From the moment he walks into the Clutterbuck home, we know that Hrundi Bakshi doesn't belong. He is, as we have seen, Hollywood poison, a detriment to film production and a threat to the pretensions of movie people everywhere. The first shot inside the party house follows a pair of glamorous legs (black tights, high heels) up to the front door. The person belonging to the legs opens it, and a pair of white shoes (one covered in brown muck) steps inside. The contrast of footwear (fashionable versus ordinary) perfectly describes the imminent conflict, and the dirt on the white shoes, a sign of Hrundi's incompetence, enters him into phase one of the splurch.

A cut takes us to the woman's face. Now we discover that the legs belong not to the hostess, but to the Clutterbuck maid—it's an Edwardian identity trick—we expected someone of higher rank, but the ruse of chic has led us astray. The maid takes one look at his shoes and knows that Hrundi doesn't belong. To prove himself, he presents his invitation. When she walks away, Hrundi slips his glasses out of his pocket, examines the muck, and hides his glasses once again. It is significant that he will not let himself be seen in his glasses, which, as we have observed, he wears to play his sitar in the privacy of his own home. Now that he has entered the world of Hollywood falsehood, he must dress himself accordingly, and that means no glasses. It is an attempt at self-perfection, and in the same spirit he hops (walking would dirty the floor) to the indoor pool to rinse his foot. This is phase two, the euphemism. Carefully, so carefully, Hrundi cleans his foot, making sure there's no one around to see him. Having taken his attention away from his foot (he is wrongly focused on public judgment), the shoe slips off and drifts away. Now, shoeless, he is in phase three, the calamity. In these three steps, without any dialogue, Edwards has painted a vivid psychological portrait of failed assimilation.

Meanwhile, the topper is about to be topped: Hrundi lunges after his floating shoe and misses. He looks up, and Edwards cuts to the party guests' reaction shot, instilling a fear of judgement in Hrundi. He clasps his hand in grateful prayer, hides his wet tie in his jacket, and turns to the door. Suddenly, the jazz combo walks in towards him, forcing Hrundi to turn back in the other direction. He conforms to their path and follows them into the party. (A visual metaphor: the conspicuous Indian is trying to blend in.) Once inside, he finds his lost shoe caught in the pool's stepping-stones. How should he get it back? At this point, Hrundi has two options. In an act of humiliating authenticity, he could unabashedly leap into the water and rescue his shoe, or he could maintain the decorum necessary to the Hollywood guise and pretend everything is fine. One decision will end the gag, and the other will top it. He opts for the latter.

Hrundi covers his naked foot in his invitation (a literal covering-up) and hobbles across the floor. Edwards' cut to the wide shot serves several functions here. First, it accents Hrundi's vulnerability by contrasting him with the ongoing party around him. (We see the poor man overwhelmed by the world of ordered luxury he can't fit into.) Second, it forces Hrundi to walk greater lengths of floor, thereby making his task of covering up more of a challenge. (The stakes are higher in the wide shot: he has more to lose and farther to travel.) Now where does Hrundi go? He crosses the floor and hides behind a bamboo plant, his fourth effort to conceal his authenticity (after the glasses, tie, and foot). Edwards cuts to another wide shot through the back window, creating the kind of anti-Hollywood composition Lehman and Luhr have so cogently observed. In this shot, a window frame is larger than he is. A window frame! The dramatic incongruity marginalizes Hrundi one step further.

After he looks around to make sure no one can see him, Hrundi crosses the stone path and his "cover" (the invitation) slips off. Once again, his assimilation compulsion incurs the incompetence (phase one) that yields the euphemism (phase two) that carries the splurch (phase three). To recover, he leaps back, and, using a bamboo stalk, lifts the shoe out of the water. A disruption from Levinson (Steve Franken), the waiter, sends the bamboo into ricochet and the shoe goes flying backwards through the open door and into the kitchen. Up until now, Hrundi has been isolated. Forcing him into contact with another character, Edwards has raised the dramatic tension of the gag, and by topping the topper (the flying shoe), Blake isn't merely throwing in another laugh, he's raising the emotional stakes. Hrundi must now face a greater challenge—socialization.

The next time we see the shoe it's being carried out on an hors d'oeuvre tray by Harry, the head waiter (James Lanphier, whom Blake loves to cast as a servant). In the meantime, Levinson has stolen a drink from his own tray, a violation of party pretense that links him to authenticity, Hrundi, and most importantly, the gag. Back to Harry, and he's still too busy being pompous to notice the shoe *right in front of his eyes*, and as he offers the tray to various guests, we see that they don't notice it either. When the tray comes to Hrundi, he hesitates, and then goes for it: "Well, I'm on a diet, but to hell with it!" He lifts his loafer off the platter and walks away. The shoe gag, topped, topped, and topped again, has at long last come to its delicious end. With the status quo restored, Hrundi has gained enough confidence to enter the party, though unfortunately he has forfeited his authenticity in the process.

With the security of feigned assimilation attained, Hrundi is poised to mingle. He emerges from behind a wall, and in perfect syncopation the jazz combo starts to play. Their song is timed to Hrundi's re-entrance—his first step and their first note are simultaneous—indicating that the musical cue represents not only the change in party atmosphere, but a change in our protagonist's improved confidence. But alas, Hrundi's attempts at socialization will all fail. Each effort is marred by visual discrepancy; the first couple Hrundi approaches stands when he sits, the second group is gathered on a raised platform up above him, and the third is framed by a large brown column that visually quarantines poor Bakshi. Whatever the circumstances, the camera is telling us that despite Hrundi's enthusiasm, genuine human connection is impossible. The shoe splurch, though useful in building his self-possession, failed to imbue him with the qualities he needs for a successful interaction.

The sequence ends when Divot and Michele (Claudine Longet) enter the party. Hrundi's desire ignites (his point of view shot indicates as much), and as we fade out into the next sequence, a new musical atmosphere is established. The combo's brassy twang underlines the new, sexually curious Hrundi. He moves into the billiard room, which is lit, of course, by a seductive fireplace, and after some useless small talk with a drunken blonde, Hrundi is goosed by a billiard cue. The man who does the goosing is a true "man's man," a hulking cowboy in the midst of his own seduction. If we accept the billiard cue as a phallic device, their exchange becomes irrefutably homosexual, and an affront to Hrundi's heterosexual dignity. (He says, "Pay no attention to me, sir, I'm merely spectating.") Through a series of thinly veiled erotic metaphors, the outsider learns how to play pool, and gradually Hrundi's gaze shifts from the woman to the man. The cowboy is none other than film star Wyoming Bill Kelso, one of Hrundi's favorites, and the little man gushes. The lesson in heterosexuality has become a celebration of male bonding, and the pool cue gag predicted the whole thing. Edwards has now established the two challenges Hrundi must overcome in order to be a successful party guest. He must accept (a) the true nature of his clumsiness and (b) the true nature of his masculinity. If he does not, and continues to feign (a) dexterity and (b) masculinity, he will suffer the same interpersonal estrangement as the Hollywood phonies that engulf him.

The control-panel gag set that follows, like the shoe blunder, obeys the tripartite formula Hrundi must resolve. After accidentally setting off the fire pit and the peeing cupid, he scrambles to undo the error by recklessly fiddling with the panel switches. But, of course, instead of turning them off, he activates the movable bar. The wooden slab retracts, glasses break, and Hrundi rushes to save the telephone from meeting the same fate. Catching it, he hands the receiver to Clutterbuck and inadvertently tangles him in the cord. Again, phase two yields phase three and back to one: the cover-up (switch fiddling), calamity (bar disruption), and incompetence (phone gag). Because the splurch is cyclical (three engages one) Edwards can build upon them with the intricacy of a Rube Goldberg machine. A gag gains momentum, and picking up steam, can disrupt more phonies, which establishes Hrundi as an affront to the party guests as well as it covers up his own social and sexual inadequacies. In this way, Edwards has increased the depth (functionality) and breadth (size) of the gag, and topping the topper, has upgraded the dramatic consequences of Hrundi's inadequacy from merely funny to a little tense.

Hrundi's desire for Michele and the air of suave he fabricates for her benefit set the stage for the following gag sequence. Beginning with her entrance into the film, which framed Michele in the background and Hrundi in the foreground, Edwards will insist upon placing spatial restrictions between the soon-to-be lovers, and this case is no exception: Hrundi must now cross the entire length of the house to be by her side. Unfortunately, after heading to Michele, Hrundi is once again distracted by Wyoming Bill. They shake hands, and Wyoming crushes his fingers, and to ease the pain, Hrundi sticks his hand in a tower of ice. When he removes it, it's covered in caviar. This is another example of the cover-up gag, a device of self-concealment appropriate to Hrundi's fractured masculinity. Of course, euphemizing the pain makes it worse (that's the Edwards equation), and now that his hand is drenched in syrupy black Hrundi heads to the bathroom to wash it off. This would be an ideal moment for Michele's reaction shot, but Blake abstains. Instead, he pans with Hrundi to the bathroom (the moving camera accenting the urgency of the maneuver) and leaves Michele behind, subordinating her to Hrundi's attention to self-perfection. Meanwhile, Hrundi throws open the bathroom door to find C. S. Divot adjusting his toupee in what is yet another cover-up, but with no cover himself, Hrundi is exposed. What will he do?

Just then, Michele crosses the room to greet him, and for the first time in The Party, they are both shot on the same plane and not in the back of the shot but the foreground. It's a visual match and intimacy looks likely, but unfortunately Hrundi's still trying to be suave. With his right hand hidden behind his back, he must shake her hand with his left (it's a cover-up on a par with Divot's toupee). At that moment, Divot comes in, shakes (soiled) hands with Hrundi, and steals Michele from the conversation. Divot is later seen smelling his smelly hand and hiding it behind his back just like Hrundi did, and when Hrundi emerges from the bathroom, he crosses paths with Divot and the two shake hands again. As the gag is perpetuated, it becomes apparent that Michele's suitors are equally deceptive when it comes to cleanliness. Consequently, if Hrundi is to triumph, he must learn the value of a gag disclosed. He must embrace messiness. But for now, he'll remain Divot's equal in insincerity.

At dinner, Hrundi's true authenticity begins to publicly emerge for the first time. Seated upon a stool that puts him well below the other guests, Hrundi appears vulnerable in a way that appeals to Michele. Moreover, when he is knocked off his stool by the swinging door, she smiles at him. Crosscutting between the splurch and Michele's reaction to it, Edwards indicates that Hrundi's displays of inadequacy are actually attractive to the ingénue. Simultaneously, in a compositional arrangement typical of Edwards' anti-Hollywood framing technique (the main action is backgrounded), Levinson and Harry are spotted in the midst of a vaudevillian dumb show. The conflict is over salad: Levinson, drunk, is serving it with his hands, and Harry, as pompous as Clouseau, is trying his best to pull it away. There's a slip, heads knock, and lettuce takes to the air. We see authenticity pitted against pretension in an upheaval of authority that sets the stage for Hrundi's own transformation. The cake incident, the final sight gag of the dinner sequence, also points ahead to the changing atmosphere; though contrary to expectations, the guests delight in the infraction that occurs (only Mrs. Clutterbuck is scandalized), a fact that suggests at the partygoer's latent lust for authentic human foible.

Could the gag be a positive force? Not as far as Hrundi is concerned—he slips away before he can be implicated in the anarchy. And as his apologies to Mr. and Mrs. Clutterbuck indicate, he's still trying to assimilate (an act punishable by the ensuing tie gag). Levinson, on the other hand, has embraced his true drunken self, and we know it because he proudly walks through the pool on his way to serve drinks (Hrundi still uses the stone path). The following splurch, Edwards' biggest threat yet to Hrundi's civilized veneer, is initiated by Hrundi's point-of-view shot of the urinating cherub. Once again, Edwards uses point-of-view shots (not dialogue!) to create a dramatic context for the gag. These images are externalizations of desire, and in this case, that desire is Hrundi's urgent need to pee. Up to this point, the gags have been motivated by increasingly dire circumstances, beginning with Hrundi's efforts at assimilation (shoe, billiards, control panel) and culminating here with his attempt to overcome his bodily functions. Sublimating his authenticity is harder now than it's ever been.

Throughout his search for a free toilet, Hrundi opens several wrong doors, and each time he uncovers people in the midst of covering up or hiding. From the women making up, to the waiters getting high, to Harry flexing in the mirror (a feeble attempt at masculinity—the script describes him as "an old queen")[63] we discover that Hrundi isn't the only one who must deny his true self.

This is a party of hypocrites. In the meantime, Edwards is using water imagery in visual crescendo to illustrate Hrundi's mounting bladder pain: first it's the peeing cupid, then the sink, and then the water cooler, the swimming pool, and finally the sprinklers. When, after all this, Hrundi finally comes inside, he is wet from the sprinklers (phase one) and more uncomfortable than ever. Too bad his sprint to the bathroom (an attempt at phase two) is interrupted by a musical performance—Michele is singing to a rapt audience—placing him in a conflict that represents a culmination of the film's gags up to this point. He wants to hide his physical pain and humiliation *and* he wants to watch her. Can he do it all? Sexual desire is pitted against pretense in the biggest challenge yet to Hrundi's politesse. But rather than rush to the toilet where he could clean himself up, he decides to stay and watch the performance. It is a significant moment: for the first time in *The Party*, Hrundi has actually chosen humiliating but authentic self-disclosure. The partyers may be offended by his vulgarity, but Michele, as we see, is charmed. (Perhaps pretense isn't the way to get the girl after all.)

The song ends and Hrundi runs to yet another bathroom (phase two). Locked. Edwards then takes us to one of his favorite locations, a door-lined hallway. In the wide shot, the door motif that has been topped throughout the gag reaches its inevitable climax. At last Hrundi picks the right door and steps into a vacant bathroom, where he finds himself face to face with a gurgling toilet. Fixing it (phase two) only makes it worse (phase three), and the damage intensifies—a painting falls, toilet paper rolls out, paint is smeared—to the point of serious calamity. The toilet's heavy lid drops to the floor and knocks a piece off the first story ceiling (and onto a drum below). Edwards' camerawork here is notable for its conspicuous restraint: he does not cut to close-up inserts of either Hrundi's reaction to the gag or to his (mis)handling of mise-en-scène. Instead, Blake holds back in a seemingly endless wide shot, which in its monotony enhances the viewer's feeling of exasperation and helplessness.

The overflowing toilet marks the next stage in the development of the water motif that Edwards began with the urinating cherub. As we will see, the imminent flood gag, which stands in harsh contrast to the desert setting of *The Party*'s opening, "cleans" Hollywood and Hrundi of their pretensions. For the time being, Hrundi has escaped to the roof to avoid the fallout from the toilet disaster. A wide shot of fierce geometric partitions now describes Hrundi in relation to the party. The elaborate parallel and bisecting lines throughout the interior of the house are recapitulated ad infinitum here on the exterior in a visual excess which speaks to the current state of Hrundi's mounting dilemma. (Edwards has escalated the graphic intensity to match the gag narrative's build.) As we might expect, Hrundi slides off the roof and into the pool. To his surprise, Michele is the first to jump in after him. And now a shift in slapstick ideology occurs: her *willing participation* in the gag is evidence that the splurch, initially perceived to be a social inhibitor, is actually a social lubricant. All at once, the gag is love.

It sounds far-fetched, but the ideological transformation from the incompetence-euphemism-calamity gag model to the anarchy-exposure-celebration template reflects the changing ethos of late-sixties America. If authenticity and love are synonymous with the gag and the film ends with a barrage of slapstick, it would appear that *The Party* chronicles the triumph of the countercultural youth revolution over the 1950's middle-class conservatives. After all, in 1968, the year of the film's release, the Vietnam War was at its horrific height and the Woodstock music festival was only months away. In this context, we might consider *The Party*'s splurch as a social-political force, emblematic not just of love, but the evolving American temperament. Likewise, Hrundi's change of clothes (he has left his wet suit for a bright red terrycloth jumpsuit), and the flower he delivers to Michele, point to the kind of hippie facelift that the Sellers character sees in *I Love You, Alice B. Toklas*, released the same year.

Stepping into an upstairs bedroom, Hrundi finds Michele, wrapped in a towel, and crying.

Hrundi: Hello.
Michele: Hello.
Hrundi: Are you having some difficulty?
Michele: No.
Hrundi: You sure?
Michele: Yes.
Hrundi: Excuse me.
He leaves. He returns.
Hrundi: You know that I don't think you are being entirely honest with me.

At last, pretensions are shed. And so are visual obstructions. Edwards has rid the frame of the sort of geometric partitioning that defined the film up to this point. Graphic barriers, the objects that helped Hrundi to hide from the party (and himself), have finally been eliminated, and in their place Blake has introduced the blank open space of the bedroom. Hrundi's close-up, for instance, is shot against a totally white wall, an image that breathes fresh air into a world flormerly clogged with complicated compositions. (Michele: "I feel better, thank you very much.")

Now, when Hrundi defends Michele against Divot, it is without the deference he would ordinarily pay to such a "masculine" type. "If Miss Monet wishes to remain, that is her right," he says, pronouncing the name in a way that sounds more like "money" than the great Impressionist. (Hrundi's mangling of her name addresses Edwards' view of Hollywood as a place where money has more value than art and men like Divot, whose own name is particularly telling, peddle dreams of stardom in exchange for sex.) Returning downstairs, Hrundi and Michele find the party in full swing. Indeed the house is so full that its architectural skeleton is completely hidden from the camera's eye. Happy dancing partygoers have upstaged the prisonlike bars of the luxurious interior, and as the Russian performers take the spotlight, it appears cultural integration may be possible after all. The Indian and Frenchwoman have been assimilated into the Hollywood party, but has Hollywood been assimilated into the gag?—it's coming.

Hrundi goes to the control panel and *intentionally* flips a switch. The floor opens beneath the house, exposing a massive subterranean swimming pool à la *It's A Wonderful Life*. It is the first intended gag of the film and it is met with overwhelming celebration. That Michele is standing beside Hrundi at the control panel is additional proof that Edwards has resolved the gag problem by wedding it to love. What's more, washing the psychedelic colors off the elephant (Bakshi: "If you desire a love symbol, I would advise you to love the elephant the way she was created"), a communal act that upgrades the love gag to the pinnacle of Hindu spiritualism, gives way to a flood of soapsuds that washes through the entire house and bears the connotation of complete and sacred purity. Taking the pachyderm to the pool evokes the Festivals of Lord Ganesh, the elephant-headed deity, purveyor of wisdom, and remover of all obstacles, in which Hindu worshippers all over India honor the god in ritual immersions of his likeness in water. In short, the gag is exceptional, not only for its visual power, its dramatic muscularity, and extravagant whimsy, but for its scarcity in Edwards' *oeuvre*—it will be another twenty years before Blake returns to metaphysical slapstick. (The film will be *Skin Deep*, and by then the director's ontological preoccupations will have soured him considerably.)

Michele's love has given Hrundi the courage to shed his pretensions, the Hollywood edifice has collapsed, and *The Party* draws to a close in a joyous cacophony of suds. It looks like one hell of a good time, but for Blake Edwards and Peter Sellers it was anything but. During *The Party*, Sellers' biographer Ed Sikov reports that the relationship was so tense they would only communicate through the assistant director.[64] And yet, somehow their collaboration produced Hrundi V. Bakshi, a character that stands alongside Sellers' Chance (*Being There*) in superhuman gentility and grace. Bakshi's every move is born of Chaplinesque compassion, but without, as Roger Lewis said, the Tramp's "winsome and dewy eye on the audience."[65] Sellers manages to evoke a man of intense privacy, an incredible feat from any actor, but even more so from a slapstitician. For in physical comedy, buffoonery easily gets the better of inner glow, and even Monsieur Hulot—the tree to Bakshi's apple—is deficient in this department. Tati may be charming, nostalgic even, but he is without gravitas. Sellers is most certainly not.

Unfortunately, the critics thought otherwise. *The Party* has "all the charm of a two-reel comedy," wrote *Variety*, "as well as all the tedium when the concept is extended to ten reels." It gets worse: "The direction is lazy—static medium shots abound—and [it] resembles photographed vaudeville acts . . . the latter-day new freedom of the screen permits exploitation of the gag that has been, and will remain, a laugh getter only from the pimply teenager and the cloddish adult: What to do when all available bathrooms are in use?"[66] As was their custom, the critics lambasted Edwards for his alleged childishness, though perhaps now, with the benefit of forty years' hindsight, they might see *The Party* the way it deserves to be remembered: as the film that brought slapstick out of the past by way of the greatest gag opera Hollywood had ever seen. The box office, however, didn't bat an eye: *The Party* was Blake's fourth consecutive commercial disappointment. Despite these years of tremendous artistic development, Edwards hadn't seen a hit since *A Shot in the Dark*, but you wouldn't know it to look at him. In 1968, he was a happy man. There was a new woman in his life.

4

BLAKE BURNS
1968–1974

DARLING LILI (1970)

Lili: If I continue with Major Larabee, it will just be a matter of time before they discover I'm the one they want. On the other hand, if I stop seeing the Major and the flow of information stops at the same time then they'll know immediately. Interesting situation.

When Blake Edwards met Julie Andrews on his way to therapy, his fourteen-year marriage to his second wife, actress Patricia Walker, was breaking—if not already broken—up, and his drop in Hollywood stock wasn't making anything easier. Slapstick, meanwhile, seemed to have run itself out. If audiences weren't taking it old-fashioned in *The Great Race*, politically in *War, Daddy?* or à la mode in *The Party*, it was reasonable to assume they didn't want it at all. So what did they want? And if Blake figured it out, could he give it to them? Should *he* give it to them? Edwards was in crisis: if there were movie gods out there, now was the time to pray. Or see his analyst five days a week, which meant driving his Rolls-Royce convertible into Beverly Hills, where he kept passing Julie Andrews in her own car, at the corner of Sunset and Roxbury Drive, on her way to her own therapist. One day they pulled over. And that was it. It's *10* meets *The Man Who Loved Women*.

Blake and Julie had met several years earlier at a party Peter Sellers gave at the Beverly Hills Hotel to celebrate the completion of *A Shot in the Dark*—"It was a cursory meeting with just the usual bullshit," Edwards recalled—and then again at Goldwyn Studios, where they were both shooting, she on *Hawaii*, he on *War, Daddy*, and each in the midst of crumbling marriages. They began to see more of each other (now intentionally) throughout *The Party*, taking weekends (now with their children) at Malibu and Gstaad, and speaking (now seriously) about the possibility of working together. In the story Blake had in mind—a World War I story—Julie would play Lili Smith (alias Schmidt), an English singer turned German spy ordered to pry secret military information from the American officer Major Larrabee (Rock Hudson), but falls for him instead. This poses a considerable problem for her nation and her heart, but when she discovers that Larrabee is involved with a stripper called Crepe Suzette, she resolves to go for Germany. She reveals American military secrets, and Larrabee is busted for it (they think he's the double agent), when Lili, who has fallen deeper in love with him, begins to have second thoughts. But how will she save him without exposing herself?

The timing couldn't have been better. In 1968, both Blake and the studios were facing a recession, and Julie Andrews, the second highest grossing film star in the world (after John Wayne), could save them both from calamity. All over town the plan was to capitalize upon the recent success of *The Sound of Music*, the picture that brought in $135 million for Twentieth Century Fox. Hollywood was self-medicating with an overdose of roadshow, and suddenly the hills were alive with *Doctor Dolittle*, *Hello, Dolly!*, *Paint Your Wagon*, *Chitty Chitty Bang Bang*, and at Paramount, the ambitiously titled *Darling Lili, or Where Were You the Night You Said You Shot Down Baron von Richtofen?* Robert Evans, Paramount's new vice president (accent on vice) and head of production—now quite comfortable playing Irving Thalberg*—signed Julie Andrews in what was deemed "the prize casting coup of the year."[1] He said, "We consider *Darling Lili* as one of the most important productions Paramount has scheduled for roadshow in recent years."[2] Everything was at stake, but the odds were spectacularly good: the next *Sound of Music* was in the bag.

When production began, the film's budget was set at $11 million. A great deal of it was spent on *Darling Lili*'s venerable vehicles, which included a 1917 Cadillac limousine, a 1912 Renault Landaulet, two Delages (1910 and 1912), two Darracqs (1911 and 1913), a 1908 Austro-Daimler, a two-seater Corre La Licorne of 1913, two Panhard-Levassors (1914 and 1915), three Renaults (1908 and two from 1912), a 1911 Overland, a 1906 Ford Model N two-seater, a 1917 Model T Ford, a 1913 Studebaker, and early vintage Peugots. And then there were the planes—exact replicas of those which flew over Normandy and the Argonne during World War I— three Fokker D7s, two Fokker Triplanes, two Pflaz D3s, two SE5As of British origin, two French-built, a Luciole and a Stampe biplane, and a German-modeled Morane.[3] All this, shot on locations throughout Europe (which included the Bois de Bologne estate of the Duke and Duchess of Windsor), for what executive producer Owen Crump called "a chic comedy with an Ernst Lubitsch touch."[4] Production was scheduled to last just over a hundred days.

That was March 1968.

---

* The legend goes that it was Norma Shearer, Thalberg's widow, who cast Evans as Thalberg in *Man of a Thousand Faces*.

19. *Darling Lili* (1970) It was late in the decade and America was changing its image. But what did that mean for Julie Andrews? With the help of Blake Edwards—a man obsessed with image—she would initiate a career-long striptease, beginning here in *Darling Lili*, and ending in *Victor/Victoria* ten years later, making it the longest seduction in screen history. (Courtesy of the Academy of Motion Picture Arts and Sciences)

Five months and an additional $3 million later, nothing seemed to be going right. Bad weather made aerial photography an impossibility, the crew was often delayed for weeks at a time (in Dublin, even an entire month),[5] and a student rebellion in Paris forced production to relocate to Brussels. "Nothing like this has ever happened in my life," Edwards said, "You wouldn't believe it, but you name it and we had it . . . I never want to go through anything like this again."[6] To help subsidize the film's soaring expenses, Paramount enlisted the support of the Commonwealth United Corporation, who agreed to issue Paramount $31.2 million in debentures and a $10 million promissory note in exchange for a cash sum and partial rights to *Darling Lili*. A whole year later, about the time the film was to be released, the CUC had suffered its own financial difficulties, permanently impairing the loan formerly credited to Gulf + Western (Paramount's parent company). In the meantime, G+W had entered into three transactions in which the credit was exchanged for a combination of cash and property, the value of which G+W failed to record accurately. The loss they suffered on the debentures they kept a secret.*

The CUC fiasco was just one of the many symptoms of the epidemic. Throughout Hollywood, studios in financial straits were being turned over to conglomerates. Now the suits answered to bigger suits, and according to Robert Evans, the pictures got smaller.

> The big honchos, Harry Cohn, Louis B. Mayer, Jack Warner, were all gone now. They had been owners, not employees. . . . Power was not ours to dictate, but rather be dictated to us. Film was no longer an art to be nurtured, but a commodity to be sold. The Zanucks were gone—the boards of directors were in. Making announcements to save jobs came before the passion to create.
>
> I was a throwback. . . .[8]

With the change in power came a change in pictures, and *Darling Lili*, a film that straddled two eras, was lost in the shuffle. In the post-*Bonnie and Clyde* world of low, low budgets (and high returns), grandiose barn burners like *Lili* were not only fiscally unwise, but with Vietnam still burning in the east, seemed socially and politically irrelevant, irresponsible even. The

---

* In 1979, The Securities & Exchange Commission charged Charles Bluhdorn, Gulf + Western's CEO, with "numerous violations of anti-fraud, anti-manipulation, reporting and proxy provisions of Federal Securities Laws."[7]

time was right for independent financiers to break in with three-million-dollar movies, and in came the likes of Altman, Ashby, and Coppola, brandishing their iconoclasm like a call to arms. In a flash, studioism was passé, and the American movie dream had been revised.

Into this came Edwards' *Darling Lili*. Perhaps appropriate to the circumstances of its production, the film takes as it subject the deceits innate in war, art, and love, and how they present challenges to the legibility of things. While the most duplicitous of Edwards' films (and that's saying something), *Darling Lili* is about more than artifice, it is about the art of artifice, and is stylized accordingly. Throughout the picture, our perceptions, literal and figurative, are continually revised, reversed, and contradicted. Truth in this world is fleeting, and reality, that thing we thought we knew for sure, is as unreliable as a double agent. Apply this thinking to story, character, genre, camera movement, and even to individual images themselves, and *Darling Lili*'s aesthetic organization becomes clear (and by "clear," of course I mean "unclear"). For instance, the film begins in darkness.

From out of the darkness comes a singing voice. The camera cranes into the black and as it does, a bodiless face fills the frame. It's Julie Andrews (Lili Smith), and she's singing. But where is she? Is this a dream sequence? Is it a live performance? If so, is Julie Andrews' character playing a character or is she playing herself? Or perhaps none of this is "real" and it's just being imagined. But who's imagining it? By keeping us in the dark Edwards induces his audience to entertain a limitless array of narrative possibilities. As the scene unfolds, those possibilities will narrow until the facts of the scene are made known to us. Until then we are, as Lili will later sing, in no-man's-land. But for now, her song is "Whistling Away the Dark." *Often I think this sad old world | Is whistling in the dark | Just like a child who late from school | Walks bravely home through the park. . . .* Just then, Lili walks passed a vertical line of colored lights. But they're too abstract to place her for us. She walks on, and as flare spreads through the lens, she glides by a stage light and then a curtain. So this is a theater. She is a performer, but is this a public performance? Or is she imaging herself onstage? The camera pulls back from the close-up into the wide shot, revealing a row of footlights and a dotted rim of starlike glows that line an invisible balcony. *So walk me back home, my darling | Tell me dreams really come true | Whistling . . . whistling . . . | Here in the dark with you.* Now the flare has exploded into decorative, almost psychedelic patterns so strong Julie is nearly obliterated from the frame. The lighting effect is undoubtedly dreamlike, and lends credence to the theory that this "performance" is in fact onstage for no one at all.

The instrumental begins. As Lili spins, the camera, quite surprisingly, starts to spin with her. If Lili were actually onstage, we would expect the audience's point-of-view shot, but Edwards takes it in another direction. Rather than cut to the audience's point-of view shot—the static proscenium shot is, after all, one of his favorite compositional techniques—which would finally show us where we are, Edwards delivers a cinematic maneuver so connected to Lili's subjectivity, so independent of stage restrictions, it's hard to believe this scene is set in an objective, external reality. As Lili repeats the chorus, the camera pulls back to where it was when the number began, and she fades into the darkness once again. The song ends.

Darkness again. And applause. Applause? The house lights come up and we're in a packed theater. Ah, so Lili was performing in objective reality after all. This cut from darkness to the theater, the first cut in the film ("Whistling Away the Dark" was all one take, the longest in Blake's career)[9] describes its central thematic tension: the collusion of private and public personae. To convey this theme, Edwards will manipulate, violate, and integrate musical spaces, which, as Lili's national and personal allegiances shift, will become increasingly malleable until the lies of her private and public lives can be contained no longer. When her mask starts to drop, the barrier between audience and performance (her performance) will go with it. When she assumes a guise, when her identity is obscured by love and country, the artifice of her musicality will be most evident. That's when the number will reveal her lies.

Beginning with "Whistling Away the Dark," the most subjective number in the film, is Edwards' way of introducing us to Lili at her most authentic. Although the sequence presents the idea of artificiality, this is truly the "offstage" Lili, a depiction of a woman free from the duplicitous crises of her professional life. Because Lili turns the entire auditorium into a performance space—the audience sings, too, and some even join her on stage—the artificiality of the theatrical backdrop is rendered insignificant. Everyone sings in unison; there is no separation between audience and performer. At this moment, Lili is not a chanteuse, but simply one of the British citizens. The songs they sing, "Pack Up Your Troubles in Your Old Kit Bag," "Keep the Home Fires Burning," and "It's a Long, Long Way to

Tipperary," are songs of English national heritage, and unlike the Mancini and Mercer compositions that dominate the film, are *real-life* tunes of glory. Accordingly, they work in service of this display of Lili's genuineness. But then the credits roll and we are reminded of cinema. Yes, this is *Darling Lili*! A film! A constructed reality! (The threat of artifice is waiting in the wings.) These first two numbers ("Whistling" and the Brit medley) show two congruous sides of the authentic Lili. One is Lili's Lili; the other is England's stage Lili. And the moment the light comes up, they are united in musical harmony. To drive home the point, flowers are rushed up to Lili from the audience. Where there is no fourth wall there is no differentiation.

Of course, this is a lie. There *is* differentiation. Lili Smith is actually Lili Schmidt, a German spy only *playing* an English patriot. (Actually, she's of mixed parentage, a real girl in no man's land. So what is her performance? What is her reality?) The next number, "The Girl in No Man's Land," illustrates precisely this predicament. The song begins with Lili's close-up as she's singing, and on the field behind her stands a guitar player and an accordionist. Unlike the opening of "Whistling Away the Dark," which intended for narrative ambiguity, the presence of on-screen musical accompaniment instantly designates this pasture as a performance space. But is there an audience? Once again, Edwards has concealed key information in order to manipulate (and very cleverly) Lili's relationship to duplicity. Right now, the performative potential of the number is limited—the singer is (mostly) alone—but this image of partial artificiality is soon interrupted. Lili walks forward and the camera follows her, revealing an audience of wounded soldiers and their nurses. This *is* a performance. *When night is falling / She comes calling / the girl in no man's land / She comes to cheer them / and be near them / a dream they understand.* Now Lili comes "when night is falling"; no longer is she singing it away. This "dream," like her political disloyalty, straddles two worlds, life and death, although her description of *The angel who at close of day / comes round to kiss their cares away* seems closer to the latter. The melody is sweet, a lullaby even, but, like everything else, it lies. Lili is not the kind of angel you want hanging around. And yet, she sure looks like an angel. Her purple costume and matching flower pin describe a character of Maria von Trapp/Mary Poppins goodness and virtue. But that's a lie too. Even the Julie Andrews screen persona has deceived us.

In this number, Lili is spatially and ideologically farther from the audience than she was in the Brit medley. Although there is no literal stage here, the spatial separation is prominent enough to represent the division between her assumed allegiance (England) and her actual allegiance (Germany).* In the next number, "Smile Away Each Rainy Day," the divide widens again (the song advises its listeners to *Be like old Mr. Noah | When it starts to pour | Make fun at trouble | Though you're seeing double*). Before, during "The Girl in No Man's Land," she was photographed from behind the audience in a shot that visually, though not spatially, intermingled them (thanks to the telephoto lens, space only *appears* compressed). But that was only the illusion of sameness. The camera angle lied, depicting a spatial continuity that didn't really exist. Here, in wide shot, with the audience on the left side of the frame and Lili on the right, the territorial segregation is even clearer. But not only is she divided from the audience she is also divided within herself, a conflict expressed in the consecutive pairing of "The Girl in No Man's Land" and "Smile Away Each Rainy Day." In the first song, *night is falling*, and in the second, *love light[s] up the sky*. One is riddled with autobiographical truths (private reality) and the other is a hollow cliché (public deceit). Her smile is the mask she wears for France.

The cancan number that follows does not belong to Lili. She is an observer here, and compared to the dancers, utterly sexless; she is all politics and no desire. Meanwhile, Lili's lies are becoming increasingly more problematic. Now French intelligence *and* William Larrabee are won over: they believe Lili and her part, that of English ally, are one and the same. That's double the duplicity, and in "I'll Give You Three Guesses," Blake dramatizes it musically. For the first time, we see the audience *before* we see Lili, a fact that lays great emphasis on the artificiality of the number. The spectator's point-of-view shot is perfect proscenium, a theatrical frame that underlines the staginess. And that's not all—artifice is just as evident in the number itself. The backdrop, for instance, is absurdly two dimensional, and Lili's costume—a dead ringer for Andrews' "Jolly Holiday" dress in *Mary Poppins*—is a puffed up parody of purity. Edwards cuts to the back of the auditorium and seems to lose Lili on the stage (so small is she in the frame it is as though the on-camera proscenium arch has annihilated her). Placing her in the same shot as the audience draws a

---

* This is not true of the extended cut of the film. The 107-minute director's cut (which is actually *shorter* than its forerunner) has eliminated the shots of Lili merging with her audience.

lying parallel between them, one that says they're on the same side, but tossing daisies into the audience is the closest she comes to crossing the divide which, only days ago, she could very easily negotiate. And so we see that Edwards' presentation of the number is riddled with brilliant contradictions, and from the looks of it, the "guessing game" Lili sings of will be impossible to win. She is fraught.

All this is reversed in the reprise. Later in the film, after Lili learns of Larrabee's affair with Crepe Suzette, she performs "I'll Give You Three Guesses" yet again, making explicit all the irony that was only latent in the original. The new rendition takes the form of a striptease, though considering the look of anguish on her face, it seems Lili's breaking from more than just her costume. Indeed, she's breaking from Larrabee, and from the lies: she will not pretend not to be a double agent any longer. Accordingly, Edwards has no need to show us the stage (this is not a "fake" performance). Instead, he cuts into the audience for reaction shots and cuts back to Lili's close-up for the number. They are not in the same shot (as they have been before), but the smash cutting works to the same effect: the lines between English audience and performer are clarified and her purity of intention is restored. No longer are Lili's allegiances confused in the manner of the spatial ambivalence we saw in "The Girl in No Man's Land." Now it's a matter of her versus them. As the cutting indicates, the slash in Smith/Schmidt has never been stronger. She's a spy again.

The final number of the film occurs after Lily has denounced her duplicitous national allegiances. Now that it is known that she was spy, there is nothing left to conceal and Lili can appear before the audience as her true self: a half-English half-German heartbroken chanteuse. In this spirit, the number returns to "Whistling Away the Dark," and so does the subjectivity technique inherent in Edwards' original presentation. The shot, which includes a spinning haze of red flare, is almost an identical copy of its predecessor, and implies the re-emergence of Lili's authenticity, though this time the Allied soldiers are seen waiting in the wings, indicating that the formerly permeable lines of national identity have been reinstated. Lili has solidified the boundaries between war and love. End of film.

As we have seen, Edwards' use of the musical number has chronicled Lili's evolving relationship to her own duplicity. "Whistling Away the Dark" and the Brit medley evoke truths about Lili which "The Girl in No Man's Land" and "Smile Away Each Rainy Day" will contaminate, but by the time Lili sings "I'll Give You Three Guesses," Edwards' cinema reeks of artificiality. The two reprises that end the film, encores of "I'll Give You Three Guesses" and "Whistling Away the Dark," depict Lili as totally genuine—shattered, but with her emotional integrity restored. With all these stage-bound contradictions, what can we surmise of Blake Edwards' attitude towards performance? Is it, to paraphrase Picasso, the lie that tells the truth? Or is it, as Lili would have the French and British citizens believe, a happy, lying, entertaining divertissement? And which is *Darling Lili*? Does it smile away each rainy day or does it whistle in the dark? (*The Pink Panther* smiles—doesn't it?) From this point forward in Edwards' career it will be tough to say. *The Party*, so to speak, is over, and tonal shifts are more acrobatic than ever.

To best express this dichotomy, Edwards has structured his musical presentation upon the notion of doubles. Songs in *Darling Lili* arrive in pairs, some consecutively, some in reprise, but all in response to our heroine's emotional and political fraudulence. But it is song, more specifically, the theater, that allows her to pull it off. Is Edwards making remarks about the artist's ethical imperative? To find out, let's consider the film's first musical pairing: "Whistling Away the Dark," conveyed in a moment of unmitigated darkness, is overturned by a round of British anthems designed by Lili to banish the war from the minds of her audience. One embraces the darkness, and the other whistles it away. Edwards' coupling of "The Girl in No Man's Land" and "Smile Away Each Rainy Day" has a similar function. The former tells of private sorrow, and the latter, well, smiles it away. Here we have two sides of Lili: the plaintive exile and the cheery entertainer, or in other words, the latent German spy and the Englishwoman trying to cover it up. Likewise, Lili's second rendition of "I'll Give You Three Guesses" reverses the phoniness of her first, and viewed together, they are, like the film's other musical pairings, two sides of the same wooden nickel. Even the two versions of "Whistling Away the Dark" express warring aspects of Lili's identity crisis. At first, Edwards' cinematic treatment of the number appears to repeat itself—a face in the darkness, a crane in—but soon we discover that this is not the "private" performance it once was, but a semipublic performance designed for the benefit of a handful observers waiting in the wings. It represents the peaceful fusion of public and private persona.

The film is so riddled with illusion and contradiction it is difficult to be decisive about any of it. One thing is certain, though; in the world of Blake Edwards, where the only thing that's true is the fact that nothing is true, we can be secure in our insecurity. Edwards' application of the rack focus (which assumes in Darling Lili an aesthetic privilege atypical of his films before or since) translates this idea by bleeding foreground into background (or vice versa) as Lili's perception of one reality gives way to another. What we believe to be the subject of the shot is in fact only a façade, and with the flick of the focus the real subject emerges. The most dramatic example of this technique occurs when Lili awakes after a romantic night with Larrabee. An extreme close-up of a rose precedes a very slow, sensual rack focus (we are meant to feel the focus pull) that reveals a rose bouquet in the midground of the frame. Slowly, the camera tilts up, rack focuses again, and takes us deeper into the shot to discover another plane of roses and Lili behind, admiring them all. Three visual "layers," disclosed in succession, are uncovered like a box within a box within a box. Truth is being embellished and contradicted—it is evolving—before our unbelieving eyes. Lili walks into the room, and, to follow her, Edwards zooms out, tracks right, and pans left. An entire garden of roses fills the shot, Lili walks camera right, as we pan with her and find more roses. It's a gesture of Ophulsian majesty, winsome and lyrical, unusual for Blake, but right at home in Darling Lili. It is one of the most staggering cinematic gestures in the film, and perhaps even of Edwards' entire career.

Optical reorganization runs all throughout Darling Lili, and, in addition to rack focuses, takes the form of zooms, cranes up and down, and expertly crafted lateral movements. Quite frequently, Edwards will begin a scene with a close-up on some seemingly innocuous item of the mise-en-scène, only to zoom back (most often abruptly) to the wide shot in an optical switcheroo that seems to negate itself (think of the film's first shot, the ornate single take in the dark). This is not what it seems, the shot says. The zoom, as opposed to a dolly or track, represents not a change in spatial relations (the camera doesn't modify its distance from the subject) but a purely technical abstraction of physical relationships. Consequently, it gives the impression of movement, not movement itself, and as such, reflects illusion, not true-to-life continuities. Beyond utilitarian, the zoom in Darling Lili is an expressive device in and of itself, and like Edwards' dissolves (not cuts) between scenes dovetails with the notion of changeability. The dissolve, which takes us from one time/place to the next, suggests that temporal boundaries are as inconstant as spatial ones, and complements the constant to-and-froing of Lili Schmidt/Smith.

Dialogue in Darling Lili can have the same effect.

Lili: Would it be indiscreet to say that I missed you?
Larrabee: No.
Lili: To say that I missed you terribly?
Larrabee: Not quite.
Lili: Desperately?
Larrabee: Possibly.
Lili: Passionately?
Larrabee: Definitely.
Lili: Would you settle for desperately?
Larrabee: I'll settle for passionately.
    They kiss.

With their fierce rhythm and dizzing semantics, these eroticomic debates are crafted on the same ideas of contradiction and embellishment. In other words, they do to conversation what the rack focus does to perception. And if we hear in them the music of the screwball, it's because Edwards's nostalgia for movies past has emerged once again. Equally anachronistic is the character of William Larrabee, whose valiant adieu, "I fly at dawn," seems, as Lili says, "a bit unnatural." But there is method in the mannerism: call it bygone gallantry. Indeed *Darling Lili* is is not just nostalgic for an era when going to war was considered glorious, but as these little flourishes indicate, for a cinema gone by. Stuart Byron writes,

> If Edwards is the "last conservative" in a political sense, he may be the "last classicist" in an aesthetic one. His films exist on that thin edge between slapstick and lyricism where once stood Ford and McCarey and Renoir. As lyricism is an expression of grace and slapstick an expression of the lack of it, so Edwards is always so much in control that he can switch from one mood to the other with effortless ease.[10]

Genres switch, moods switch, visuals switch, allegiances and affections switch. And now eras switch; with all its démodé romanticism, *Darling Lili* looks more like *Mata Hari* than M*A*S*H.

Old fashioned, yes, but was it out of touch? The executives thought so, and Blake frantically struggled to recut the picture—the longer he took, the more injurious the investors' interest rates—and soon production costs reached $24 million. The studio was in a bind: cut their losses or just keep cutting? With Edwards' attachment to Julie Andrews now public, Paramount had him right where they wanted him. If the film flopped, their fall guy was ready made. The rumors about the misappropriation of funds were already in circulation: many thought *Darling Lili* nothing more than the most extravagant film of a honeymoon ever mounted.

Finally, in June of 1970, the film was released—to complete critical bafflement. So maligned was *Lili* by public humiliation, the *Hollywood Reporter* deemed it "impossible to approach objectively."[11] *Variety* opined, "Somehow the situations and premise don't quite jell despite the fact that this is supposed to be a comedy, or is it?"[12] According to the *Saturday Review*, "Blake Edwards can be accused of inconsistency of style, social irresponsibility and a disconcerting disregard for how difficult it is for people to get from one place to another in time of war."[13] But for Charles Champlin, the film's contradictory angles were fundamental to its charm. He saw *Darling Lili* as "a skyscraper erected on Rice Krispies . . . like getting Horowitz to play chopsticks."[14] And yet, there is a dark side to Champlin's analogies; they describe a capricious overindulgence—classical studio filmmaking overstaying its welcome. Alas. Those that saw a fleck of gold in the rubble might agree that Edwards' "use of the formal means at his disposal—the zoom lens, the crane, color—displays a knowledge of their emotional effect that surpasses most working directors."[15] But they were few.

In the end, *Darling Lili* earned over just three million dollars. With the flopping of Robert Wise's *Star!* in very recent memory, the value of Julie Andrews was now in serious question. But Blake saw it differently. To him, the problem had more to do with timing than his wife. Audiences obviously were not ready to see her spending time in the shower, going to bed with leading men, or baring her breasts on screen. Nor were they even ready to think of her remarried. Both on screen and off, her changing image was at odds with the chaste maternal icon the world desperately wanted intact. "I guess everybody felt Mary Poppins was getting soiled or something," Blake remembers. "I'm positive that all those extraneous elements hurt *Darling Lili*. . . . It's still hard to talk about now [in 1977], it was that painful."[16] Well aware that Andrews' wholesome-nanny persona was incompatible with the new America, the studios promptly erased her from production. She was dropped from the film of *She Loves Me* (Julie was actually paid $1 million *not* to appear in it), and her starring role in Blake's forthcoming adaptation of Irving Berlin's *Say It with Music* was reneged by MGM soon thereafter. The Hollywood blitz to recreate *The Sound of Music* had officially closed, and the career of Julie Andrews had come full circle. Blake's film had crushed her. The honeymoon was over.

20. *Darling Lili* (1970) On location with Mr. and Mrs. Blake Edwards. (Courtesy of the Academy of Motion Picture Arts and Sciences)

WILD ROVERS (1971)

Joe Billings: *Even if you did get the money sooner or later*
they'd be bound to catch up with you.

THE CAREY TREATMENT (1972)

Angela Holder: *Cops and doctors!*

Blake Edwards' estrangement from his real-life father may or
may not shed light upon the (growing) significance of male/male relationships in his work, but its unquestionable that whether homo- or heterosexual, these couplings are conveyed with a depth of tenderness that rivals
even his most compelling portraits of male/female love. These unique
relationships are modeled on mentor/apprentice roles and often beget a
dominant male and passive "female" in correlation with the outmoded
heterosexual template. Evident as early as *Mister Cory*, the male/female
disparity in same-sex friendships will earn a position of prominence here
in Edwards' later films. As we move towards *10*, *Victor/Victoria*, and *Switch*,
these partnerships will be complicated by healthy challenges to conventional gender responsibilities, as presented by Edwards with shrewd and
loving nuance. *Wild Rovers*, a picture Blake once called his best,[17] returns
the mentor-apprentice model to the fore, and remains, perhaps in consequence of that distant father, one of the director's most personal, startling, and strangely elegiac works.

The film follows Ross Bodine (William Holden) and Frank Post (Ryan
O'Neal), two tired cowboys who yearn for adventure, decide to rob a bank,
and retire to Mexico with the money. When their employer's sons discover
they've gone missing, they set out after them on what proves to be a long,
slow chase to the border. Like many Westerns, *Wild Rovers* is about open
spaces, both geographical and emotional. "I think it's very important to
show the vastness, the loneliness, the boredom and natural beauty of the
West of that period," Edwards said, "because that loneliness and boredom
are the main motivating factors that affect my principal characters."[18] The
aesthetic is set in place immediately: the first shot of the film, an unmov-
ing image, long and wide, holds back as we watch two horseback sil-
houettes traversing a mountain path. There is no music, only the sound of
hooves on dirt and the intermittent *cha-chink* of the saddle. Right away we

know that this is not going to be a triumphant John Wayne story, or spittoon-spitting, pulse-pounding Man with No Name epic, but a plaintive movie about stillness, the inevitability of death, and the dreams in between. A barren landscape delivers all that.

With this shot, the West is reduced to its emaciated essence. There is no glory in it, only the tedium of work, and certainly none of the high-adrenaline genre cornerstones we'd expect of a cowboy picture. (When it finally comes, even the requisite bar fight is drained of fanfare. The standard musical cue is thrown out for cracking wood and glass, sounds which, rather than fill the soundtrack, seem only to enhance its emptiness.) In time, we realize that Edwards is going to great lengths to make *Wild Rovers* into an anti-Western threaded with antigenre set pieces. The bank robbery sequence, one of the genre's staples, has no shoot-out or taut editing, but only chuckles, shrugs, and sighs to break the silence. The scenes themselves are long and conveyed with a monotony that belies whatever tension we think we should be feeling. Granted, it's a strange narrative strategy, maybe even self-destructive, but it serves the director's vision well.

Even Philip Lathrop's camera squanders the potential for high drama. Throughout the film, domestic interiors are haunted by darkness, thick shadows keep faces from legibility, and camera movement is about as likely as good luck. We hear only the ticking of the clock; it's the Western Bergman never made. "I'm going to be careful not to overlight it," Lathrop warned. "One thing I want to do is avoid the slick mechanical gadgetry that we use so much in making pictures today—things like helicopters and obvious dolly shots and zoom lenses. I think that these would be very false in relation to a period Western."[19] It's a prosaic aesthetic, and it's exactly what our duo is trying to escape.

Indeed, on first glance, it appears we are a long way away from the likes of *The Pink Panther* and *A Shot in the Dark*, but upon further consideration, when examined within the context of Edwards' interest in calamity, *Wild Rovers* echoes in darkness what the Clouseau movies show in light. Gags crop up in both worlds, but where in *The Pink Panther* they spare us from having to worry about anyone's safety (Clouseau of course, can't be injured), in *Wild Rovers* they are burdened by the very real fact of mortality. "There's one thing for certain," says Bodine to Post. "What's that?" he responds. "Can't get any worse." A moment later some ogress leans over a balcony and empties a chamber pot onto their heads. It's a bitterly funny

21. *Wild Rovers* (1971) While filming in Arizona, William Holden and Ryan O'Neal forged a close relationship both on-camera and off. Seen here in a shot MGM pulled from the film's original publicity campaign (and replaced it with one of the stars at a manly distance, holding guns), they represent a culmination of Edwards' lifelong investment in male intimacy. (Courtesy of the Academy of Motion Picture Arts and Sciences)

splurch, reminding us that we are never out of the woods for good. (In Blake Edwards, that's a good rule of thumb.) Things can always get worse, and in fact, they almost definitely will. It's no less than man's fate, and in *Wild Rovers* it's inescapable. "What I've written," Blake says, "certainly isn't Shakespeare, but it is tragedy."[20] The existentialist has openly usurped the comedian and the splurches follow suit. In time they will merge, but for now, the laughs are limited to an unprecedented minimum. Furthermore, *Rovers'* splurches, unlike the accidents that befall Clouseau or Hrundi, are not justified or instructive. Simply put, they are dramatically frivolous (contrary to the kind of narrative logic we saw in *The Party*), and appear harsher in their superfluity, but they are significant because they describe the film's bleak outlook: shit happens.

As we have seen, paradoxical strands of cynicism and romance mark Edwards' work of this transitional, slapstick-deprived period. Beginning with *Darling Lili* and continuing on through *The Tamarind Seed*, the Edwardian tension between old-world chivalry and the threat of modernity surfaces with unprecedented bitterness. To contemporary audiences, it exposed the antagonistic counterrevolutionary in Edwards; *Wild Rovers*, as a film that simultaneously resists tradition and progress, is a case in point. The film is so blatantly nostalgic in sensibility viewers of 1971 must have regarded it not only as a movie about the past, but *from* the past; unlike *The Wild Bunch* and *Little Big Man*, *Wild Rovers* has no revisionist ambitions, and though it reinterprets the genre in many ways, it does so without the ironic attitudes inherent in the era's most successful Westerns. *Rovers* is neither hip nor square, but like Lili Smith, stuck in a no man's land between two Hollywoods. We see it in the casting: William Holden, a classical studio star, sharing the screen with Ryan O'Neal, a symbol of classicism's decline. That's its Edwardian duplicity.

Edwards' nostalgia had many opponents, but none more terrible than MGM's new president, James Aubrey. In 1969, the studio was $85 million in the red, and the man who gave America the television sitcoms *Mr. Ed* and *The Munsters*, inspired the title character in Jacqueline Susann's *The Love Machine*, and whom John Houseman nicknamed "the Smiling Cobra," was brought on to rescue it from financial ruin. His plan was simple: "Cut back and then move cautiously forward." According to Aubrey, whipping MGM into shape necessitated the sale of Dorothy's ruby slippers, the suit Spencer Tracy wore in *Inherit the Wind*, and a boatload of other treasured originals. "When we got here," he said to an interviewer, "we drove around the lot. We said, 'Get rid of that—Andy Hardy's Ford—and get rid of those *Ben Hur* steps.' We had no layers of sentimentality, no nostalgia hang-ups. The people in the back seat of the car cried."[21] But the big tears were saved for the sale of 187 acres of back lot and the staggering 58 percent of MGM personnel that were laid off. "Jungle" Jim called a dead halt on prestige productions like Fred Zinnemann's adaptation *Man's Fate*, turning his attention to B movies and luring horny teenagers. Under MGM' motto, *Ars Gratia Artis*, Aubrey nixed the Julie Andrews musicals *She Loves Me* and *Say It with Music*, green-lit *Shaft*, and decreed, "The Days of Indulgence are over and we'll walk the line between domination and discipline."[22]

According to Edwards, that line was crossed in the cutting room. After previewing *Wild Rovers*, the Cobra cut twenty minutes from the finished film and tried to give it an upbeat ending (a difficult task considering it's a tragedy). "There was no discussion," Blake recalled, "an integral part was simply removed."[23] Journalist Herb Lightman had followed the film since production began and printed his reactions to Aubrey's cut in the July 1971 *American Cinematographer*.

> Gone is the opening montage, with Frank Stanley's lyrical images that so aptly set the mood of the film. Gone is the gutsy man-to-man breakfast sequence that so firmly established the protagonists in their milieu. The dramatic in-depth confrontation between Karl Malden and his sheepherder arch enemy, which culminates in slaughter of the sheep, as well as both men, has been telescoped into a quick montage with voice-over narration. One complete sequence which, to me, provided motivation for the entire last half of the picture, has been totally deleted. The downbeat, but honest, ending has been trimmed and tied off with a reprise of the horse-breaking montage that numbs the tragedy and gives the audience a little final lift. Perhaps the audience, never having known all this was part of the original cut, will not miss it—but I will.[24]

"It was my best film," Edwards said, "and he butchered it. I beseeched them; they still butchered it."[25] The film's technical achievements garnered critical approval, especially Lathrop's photography, but once again it was Edwards' genre play that put them off. Speaking for the whole, one critic wrote, "The mood is broken regularly with pratfall humor, also some dehumanizing slow-motion ballets of death."[26] Holden's performance faired well, O'Neal's less so, and the film died at the box office. One can only wonder if Edwards' original cut would have faired any differently. But at 136 minutes, it doesn't seem likely.

It was then that Blake began to think seriously about leaving Hollywood. He'd been scapegoated twice now, and after the ruin of this, his favorite and most personal picture, he wasn't about to let it happen again. The public embarrassment was too much, and with a six-film box-office slump, perhaps there was wisdom in early retirement. He and Julie could pack up the kids and take them to London or Gstaad, or live safely in Malibu reclusion far from town. "But then I did a foolish thing," he remembers, "I allowed myself to be coerced or seduced or whatever. Aubrey got me in and he even apologized and he said, 'But here's a project—*The Carey Treatment*—that I know you're right for and we'll stay out of it.' He was lying through his teeth—he was actually out to crucify me."[27] Blake agreed to the picture, but his instincts were right. *The Carey Treatment* was dead on arrival. Midway into production, the Cobra had reneged on promised script changes, cut two weeks off shooting, set a release date that made it impossible to finish editing, and utterly mutilated the ending.[28] But by that point it was far too late. All Blake could do was run for cover. The film's three screenwriters took refuge behind the pseudonym James P. Bonner, and Edwards sued to have his name taken off the picture, but he lost.[29] The film's autopsy should be carried out accordingly.

The Carey Treatment begins as Dr. Peter Carey (James Coburn) joins the staff of a prominent Boston hospital. There he befriends Dr. Tao (James Hong), a brilliant surgeon, who is arrested when Evelyn Randall, daughter of the hospital's chief doctor, dies after her emergency abortion. Things look bad for Tao, but Carey is determined to prove him innocent. *Carey* then goes from hospital procedural to detective movie. Considering his facility with hard-boiled vernacular ("look out for the goods"), his leather and denim combo, and his dangling cigarette, we might think of Peter Carey as more of a P.I. than an M.D. As a pathologist, Dr. Carey is essentially a medical detective, and stylistically the film jumps from one genre to the other. At first, the two narrative strains seem diametrically opposed; the white, bright, tight compositions of the hospital hallway convey an atmosphere of rational orderliness, but when Carey and Tao head out for a drink, they end up at a bar smothered in the moody shades of noir. The snappy exchange that follows suggests that these guys might fill out trench coats a little better than their scrubs.

When a cut-up rich girl is brought to the hospital, Tao is blamed for a botched abortion and thrown in jail. Just as Marlowe in The Long Goodbye stands by his friend Terry Lennox, Carey never loses faith in Tao. Thus begins a series of detective fiction's greatest tropes: the rich daughter mixed up with the wrong people is right out of The Big Sleep, and so is the man sent out to blackmail Carey; the sex photographs he snags are pure Chandler, too, and so is the dirty blonde with the too-good name of Angela. Trust Blake Edwards to turn a story about who knocked up the little sister into a murder with a female at its core. That's the kind of genre turnaround he loves, and it's what makes his sensibility so well suited to film noir. Where there is duplicity there is mystery, and in Edwards they are perfectly syncopated.

The director's use of veils, obstructions, and other highly angular surfaces assume an expressionistic character that complements noir. Façades in Edwards often demonstrate comic ironies of appearance and reality, but here in The Carey Treatment they are exclusively ominous. As in Experiment in Terror, one of Carey's spiritual predecessors, Edwards is heavily reliant on techniques of voyeurism to convey anxiety. High and low angle shots abound, often hand-held, and windows are everywhere, often dominating shots from both inside and out of Carey's home. A particularly large one looms over his bed, allowing the peeping tom easy photographic access to the lovemaking beneath. Shots of and through microscopes, along with a shot of Carey and Tao looking through a pane of glass into the operating room, emphasize the value the film places on surveillance, which, in every Edwards film since He Laughed Last, has never once been reliable.

Even glass itself becomes an important visual component. We see it in windows, microscopes, and quite pointedly in Lydia Barrett's (Jennifer Edwards's) bedroom in the form of mirrors. The blocking of the scene is designed around these reflective surfaces, which never seem to let poor Lydia out of their sight. Wherever she turns she is met with mirror. The surfaces are oppressive in this case—imposing affronts to her lies—and with their ready-made symbology, induce the cherised noir theme of doubles. But the film's most impressive glass display, in which a massive beaker consumes the right half of the frame, brings to mind the expressionistic exaggerations of laboratory horror. Indeed the glass is so prominently featured the human figures within the shot are almost forgotten in Wellesian deep space, and when Carey steps behind the glass, we see his likeness distorted as in a fun-house mirror. It's a bit of ominous whimsy that turns Carey, the pathologist, into an object of pathological inquiry. He is "under glass" in much the same way that the dead body of Karen Randall (Melissa Torme-March) was laid out under the coroner's plastic sheet. Glass containment, therefore, bespeaks of mortality, the now palpable threat of going under the microscope. No wonder there is a window overlooking Carey's bed; it makes him vulnerable to the danger of the gaze, which in Edwards portends power and death.

There are other instances of glass, but sadly, formal patterns do not a movie make. If they did, masterpieces could be ordered by catalogue and colored by number, and The Carey Treatment, for all of its genre crossing and fractured imagery, might amount to more than a minor hospital whodunit. But it doesn't. "Written, directed, timed, paced, and cast like a feature-for-tv,"[30] the film was regarded as piddling entertainment, and Blake, for having "an eye for spanking fresh visuals and no ear, whatsoever, for what his prettily-photographed people are saying."[31] But was it Blake or his films that was too sleek? Julian Fox considers both angles:

> Presenting the strange case of Blake Edwards. A few years ago one would have said that Edwards was the one American director to have discovered the precise formula for glossy, commercial success—amusing script, good production values and high grade cast. But somewhere around his fourth or fifth film ago he seems to have lost his touch, and his films— although still viable and entertaining—have been near misses with press and public alike. Is it that the values have become too glossy, the effects to calculated and the content too thin?[32]

It's tough to say what The Carey Treatment might have been if Aubrey had behaved, though unlike Rovers, it is safe to assume that it was never headed for greatness. Another director might have brought out the story's latent complexity, but for Blake Edwards, it was the wrong material at the wrong time. And it was the last straw. He took stock of the Hollywood around him and to his disgust saw that his situation was not unique. James Aubrey was merely a symptom of the epidemic.

> Like a lot of other directors as angry as I am, I believed Aubrey wanted to turn MGM back into a movie studio. I eventually realized nobody at MGM was interested in being in the movie business at all. Certainly no one there was interested in making good movies. Nobody knew how. In

fact, MGM executives were antagonistic to artists. They wanted, demanded mediocrity.[33]

In 1972, Blake picked up his family and moved to Gstaad.

Back in Hollywood, the feeling of antagonism towards Aubrey mounted steadily, and he resigned in 1973. By then of course he had torn down MGM's famed Lot 3, the former home of the river dock from *Show Boat*, as well as *Mrs. Miniver's* English village, and the small-town street Judy Garland lived on in *Meet Me in St. Louis*. (The film *Wild Rovers* was the last Lot 3 ever saw. It was razed to make room for high-rise housing.) After all this (and more), Aubrey managed to stop the bleeding—but the scars remained. All over town, the phrase "they don't make 'em like they used to" was put into circulation, and has been there ever since. *Time* reported, "Under Aubrey, MGM churned out profitable, medium-budget schlock like *Skyjacked* and *Black Belly of the Tarantula*; directors often charged him with philistine meddling, and he alienated many of them," but "as a financial auteur, Aubrey may have deserved an Oscar."[34] Thankfully, they do not award statuettes in that category.

Meanwhile, far, far away in his chateau in Gstaad, Blake began to work on a screenplay. It was a black comedy about Hollywood.

THE TAMARIND SEED (1974)

Jack Loder: No one is to be trusted, nothing is to be believed, and anyone is capable of anything.

After his public renunciation of Hollywood, Blake Edwards had no intention of ever directing again. Instead, he planned to just spend his time writing. And just for himself. He began to fill out an idea he had about a respectable middle-aged man in hot pursuit of the most beautiful woman he had ever seen . . . , something about a suicidal director . . . , one about a woman pretending to be a man pretending to be a woman—and for a whole year, refused, one after the next, every directing opportunity that came his way. He was interested only in the creative autonomy he had at the typewriter, and moreover, deeply, deeply depressed. Julie, meanwhile, had been offered a contract to tape a number of television specials in London for Sir Lew Grade, and as Edwards remembers, it was "an offer that was very difficult to refuse. If it had just been a TV series, Julie wouldn't have done it, but there were films involved, too."[35] It had been a long time since Julie worked in films (*Darling Lili* was four years ago) and the offers weren't exactly pouring in. And so, the family packed up, moved to a house in Chester Square, and in time Blake began to relax. "It took a while," he said, "but I started feeling better as soon as we got there. I directed a couple of Julie's TV shows, wrote some and had a great time doing it. It was a good change of pace for me."[36]

The Tamarind Seed was one of the projects Grade had in mind for Andrews, and when it came time to talk seriously about directors, Edwards' name quite naturally came up. Delighted at the prospect of filming Evelyn Anthony's novel—and for the relatively low cost of $2 million—Blake agreed. The material struck familiar chords, and recalled ideas he honed on *Darling Lili*. Their thematic continuity does makes a strong case for auteurists, invoking the famous fallacy that a really good filmmaker really makes only one film, and he makes it over and over again. But if that's so, and repetition is an indication of a strong point of view, then *The Tamarind Seed* does not compromise Edwards' standing as, well, a director with Blake Edwards' point of view. The film describes a trust game between a former Soviet spy, Feodor Sverdlov (Omar Sharif) and a heartbroken Britisher, Judith Farrow (Julie Andrews), contains its share of remarks like

"How are you going to survive if you can't tell the difference between one lie and another?" demonstrates an interest in voyeurism, and espouses a view of sexual and political duplicity that might appeal to traveling businessmen in want of something to read between flights. In other words, this is Edwards material, but without the Edwardian treatment.

There are a few directorial indentations, however, including some of the optical fanciness he impressed upon Lili, but they are without the same strength of purpose. Part of the problem is that, more so than any other Blake Edwards movie, The Tamarind Seed is deeply unfunny. In fact, it is Blake's absolutely unfunniest film. For the first time, the director has dived headfirst into the shallow end of sincerity without any humor raft to keep him afloat. That's not to say that Blake Edwards is unequipped to handle a "serious" situation, but that even at his bleakest, he has always found a way to deliver the antidote. And yet, since The Party, it's a tendency that's been growing ever scarcer. Examining this point in his career, one might wonder at the gradual vanishing of the splurch, and even call into question the relevance of these films to the progression of Edwards's cinema, when in fact, the sequence described in "Blake Burns" provides a necessary foundation for the darker turn in Edwards' comic sensibility that is still to come. With these films as a reference point, we can better contextualize the existential crises of pictures like 10, S.O.B., and Skin Deep, and understand Edwards' return to slapstick not as recourse, but as the germination of ideas that sprouted here. After The Party, which took narrative and deepened it with gags, the next logical step was to take gags and deepen them with greater feeling. For Edwards, that means greater pain; it's what his experiences in the 1970s, both professionally and ideologically, were all about.

The Tamarind Seed, meanwhile, is a picture burdened by an uncharacteristic excess of sincerity both in front of and behind the camera. Unlike Darling Lili, Seed is largely shot in straightforward, unencumbered close-up and medium shots, which tend to do the work the dialogue has already accomplished. Pictorial beauty enriches many of these compositions, but Freddie Young's knack for a shoreline sunset seems only to refer to Barbados, and leaves the telling of the tale to the script. However, the film does take a clever approach to the voice-over, which in Edwards' hands becomes an unexpected agent of political and emotional disconnect. After the soon-to-be-lovers conclude their museum discussion about an actual tamarind seed, we cut to a night sky and then pan down to the dance floor.

In each other's arms now, Judith and Feodor dance soundlessly while the remainder of their unfinished conversation plays out on the audio track. The close-up of Judith's face lets us know that these voices originate in her thoughts, and indicates the split that has erupted within her (her body is present; her mind is past). Thus, if Miss Farrow's story describes her conversion from I'm Through with Love (I'll Never Fall Again) to Falling in Love Again (Never Wanted To), it follows that voice-over, a signifier of emotional disconnect, will gain in frequency and length as the film progresses. Examine the film and the logic holds: The Tamarind Seed begins with an extended interior sequence, and when Judith finally abandons herself in love, the voice-over fades away.

Also, Edwards' handling of voice-over spotlights the great fate debate that persists between Judith and Feodor. "The truth is there are no standards, only experience," the Marxist says, but Judith is not so sure. Placed within the context of the film's structure—the alternation of courtship scenes with political scenes back home—these dialogues foretell what we may already suspect, that the political and romantic dramas will inevitably converge. These parallel narratives lend credence to the film's theory of fate, but with the addition of voice-over they also enforce a feeling of voyeurism that makes the familiar problem of appearance/reality relevant once again. The Judith/Feodor affair looks fishy from the political point of view, but then again, so does the political point of view look fishy to Judith and Feodor—and the discrepancies come through the voice-over. Furthermore, Edwards has stuffed his film with shots of looking and watching, through windows or from a distance, and for the same reason that the film's superb title sequence opens with a close-up of Julie Andrews' eye and that Margaret's lighter is actually a camera in disguise. In Blake Edwards, everyone's undercover. The Tamarind Seed just lends the idea a political metaphor.

But no one is more undercover than Julie Andrews, the actress. As in Darling Lili, the casting of Mrs. Edwards in a non-nanny role (she wears a bikini!) respects the film's concern for crises of identity, in relation to both the character and the real-life woman playing her. But The Tamarind Seed is much subtler in its revision of the Andrews persona. Simply, it relegates Judith Farrow's sexuality to the past. As a character trying to repress a burdensome sexual history, Farrow is somewhere in between Maria von Trapp and Lili Schmidt, imbued with sexual potential, but not sexual energy. Whether we don't want to her break the mold or she's unable to do it, the thought of Julie getting to first base has always felt just a little not quite right, like Vincent Price telling a bedtime story to infants. But now, after having been criticized for casting his wife as Lili, a part the public deemed inappropriately hot, Edwards has responded by turning it down just a notch. The Tamarind Seed therefore represented a public healing of the Andrews image; a husband's attempt to reintegrate a complex interpretation of his wife, but without pushing it beyond the comfort zone he apparently violated with Darling Lili.

"The Tamarind Seed is a movie-movie," wrote Judith Crist, "plain and pure, the kind of romantic adventure we used to get when Irene Dunne and Bette Davis clashed accents and melted hearts respectively and respectably with Charles Boyer and Paul Henreid, when lovers could be 30-plus and gorgeous and talk in the moonlight instead of in the sack and dance cheek-to-cheek and even say, so help me, 'They're playing our song.' "[37] But of course twinkle does not a picture make. "While the nostalgia for that almost vanished form is justifiable, the slackness of this picture is not."[38] That from Richard Schickel, this from Frank Rich: "The movie seems to be the work of a craftsman who has lost touch with himself—and that's a sad development for those of us who have identified Blake Edwards' work with the best of commercial American movie making during the past ten years."[39] At a time when movies were making money for breaking new ground, a film that explicitly cites itself as a disciple of Hitchcock's was vulnerable to both the cognoscenti's veto and the popular shrug. Whatever money The Tamarind Seed brought in it brought in from Europe.

The Tamarind Seed may not have been much, but it allowed Edwards time to repair. Whatever they said, he was a director again. But if he had any intention of restoring his reputation as one of the world's leading filmmakers, he needed to go back to making movies that made money— scratch that, a shit load of money. To do it—if he could do it—Blake would have to change course entirely, and veer from personal projects back to his blockbuster days. That much was irrefutable, and as far as his next project was concerned, it meant only one thing: the Pink Panther had to return.

5

PANTHER PICTURES
(BLAKE BANKS)

SELLERS LIVES:

THE RETURN OF THE PINK PANTHER (1975),

THE PINK PANTHER STRIKES AGAIN (1976),

REVENGE OF THE PINK PANTHER (1978)

> Inspector Clouseau: I see you are familiar with the
> falling-down-on-the-floor ploy.

With the exception of the little-seen *Inspector Clouseau*, Bud Yorkin's pallid 1968 attempt to capitalize on the Panther craze, the franchise had gone untouched for a decade. After 1964, the year of *A Shot in the Dark*, Edwards turned his attentions away from the Panther to focus on a more personal cinema. The next ten years, the most formative of his career, saw Edwards enrich his auteursmanship, diversify his narrative concerns, and develop his comic trademarks throughout. Blake was growing even when it hurt (*Darling Lili*) and when no one seemed to care (*Wild Rovers*), but when he lost his patience (*The Carey Treatment*) and went into exile (*The Tamarind Seed*) the audacity all but left the screen. By 1975, it was nearly extinct. In Edwards' defense, *The Return of the Pink Panther* was a necessary financial foothold, but as is often the case with box-office bait, the meat was duller than the hook. The same goes for *The Pink Panther Strikes Again* and *Revenge of the Pink Panther*. Despite their intermittent sparkle, they do little to advance Edwards' artistic personality, offering instead a (kind of) developmental trajectory independent of his primary creative arc that culminates in 10, *S.O.B.*, and *Victor/Victoria*. About the distinction, Edwards said,

> I found I could get things done—other projects like 10—that I wanted to do by agreeing to another *Panther*. So I was—"coercing" isn't the right word—I guess to some extent I would try to coerce Sellers into doing it because I wanted to do other things. And I think he probably was agreeable because he wanted to do other things too.[1]

Studio dependence can surely yield studio independence, and *Return of*, *Strikes Again*, and *Revenge of* should be considered accordingly, with one eye on the lens and the other on the diamond.

The fabulous Pink Panther diamond has been stolen again and in *Return of the Pink Panther*, Clouseau is sent to Lugash to recover it. Naturally the inspector suspects Charles Litton (Christopher Plummer), the notorious phantom, but it turns out Sir Charles has been framed by Lady Litton (Catherine Schell), his very own wife. In the end, Clouseau is promoted to chief inspector and Dreyfus, mad with spite, is checked into a sanitarium.

Edwards' proven aesthetic of apathy, the distant, slightly obstinate camerawork we saw in *The Pink Panther* and refined in *A Shot in the Dark*, is almost entirely missing from *The Return of the Pink Panther*. The first two Clouseau films presented a world of perfectly ordered compositions, manicured frame lines, and an overall sense of compulsive precision,* as if the stringent demands of camera and mise-en-scène were conceived in hilarious contrast to Clouseau's idiocy. Here instead we have an aesthetic of *empathy*, one that favors Clouseau in close-ups, bold camera movements, and a rapid, highly controlled cutting pattern, all of which, when added together, are profoundly anti-splurch.

In both *The Pink Panther* and *A Shot in the Dark*, splurch scenes are shot in long takes that enhance the feeling of Clouseau's ineptitude, and therefore the laugh. Conversely, the cut-up sequences that characterize *Return* have the effect of streamlining the action in a way that makes Clouseau appear more adept, and where Edwards once kept the camera still to denigrate the idiot inspector, he now uses camera movement to ennoble him. The first Clouseau–Cato battle, for example, opens as the inspector steps into his apartment. In no time, he suspects Cato is up to something, and carefully searches the bedroom, the kitchen, the dining room, and the living room —and the camera pans with him from one space into the next. *Clouseau is important enough to follow*, the shot says, and follow him it does. Edwards is so committed to Clouseau in *The Return of the Pink Panther* that his technique approaches a kind of subjective alignment. But it's too close. Because we are placed *with* Clouseau it's harder to laugh *at* Clouseau.

The battle is fought throughout the entire apartment—considerably larger since we last saw it—and upgrades into a full-blown kung fu scene.

---

* "I'm kind of an obsessive-compulsive type."[2]—Blake Edwards

22. *The Return of the Pink Panther* (1975) Peter Sellers at fifty, still hilarious, but with a weariness less fun to splurch. (Author's collection)

Everything is amplified: the size of the apartment, the physical variation, the camera movement, cutting, and the sound track, but in drawing our attention away from the ironic behavior (a servant commanded to attack his master) to the action of the fight, Edwards inadvertently downgrades the humor and upgrades Clouseau from klutz to Schwartzenegger. What's more, *Return's* depiction of Clouseau is, contrary to the notion of the splurch, surprisingly kind. To a certain extent, though, it was unavoidable: it had been ten years since 1964 and Sellers had aged a great deal. His new slouch, budding jowls, and thinning hairline render *schadenfreude* almost impossible, and without his compelling authoritative outbursts (this Clouseau is more inept than pompous), the comic contrast of the splurch is weakened.

Whereas *A Shot in the Dark* behaved like *The Pink Panther* never happened, *The Return of the Pink Panther* conducts itself with self-aggrandizing esteem. Now that Clouseau was a commodity, it was incumbent on Peter Sellers to "do" him, and apparently it was incumbent on Edwards to give him the star treatment he felt the character deserved. Since the first two pictures, the awarding of the 1965 Oscar for animated short to DePatie-Freleng for *The Pink Phink*, the accompanying broadcast of *The Pink Panther Show*, and Mancini's hit recording of his famous theme, the *Panther*'s reputation had become giant, and *Return*'s opening credits—a celebration of the *Panther*'s notoriety and cinematic eminence—reflect as much.

The film's promotional blitz was equally extravagant. Now that pink was gold, over four hundred and fifty pieces of merchandise, from pink dolls to pink talcum powder, were marketed in over forty countries around the world[3]. Between treatments at the La Costa resort and spa, the press had ample opportunity to enjoy an advance screening of the film, a live performance of Mancini and his orchestra (with special appearance by Johnny Mathis), and all the pink tennis balls, pink T-shirts, pink hats, and pink bags they could stuff into a pink bag. Perhaps won over by the pink crazy foam, the *New Yorker* called *The Return of the Pink Panther* "one of the most delicately cataclysmic studies in accident proneness since the silents,"[4] and everyone else seemed to agree. The picture, which cost just over $2 million, returned it fifty times over at the box office, and a repeat performance was announced. "We were encouraged in many ways to do another," said Blake, "not the least of which was money and ownership."[5]

In 1976 came *The Pink Panther Strikes Again*. The story picks up after Dreyfus (Herbert Lom) escapes from his sanitarium, kidnaps Professor Fassbinder, and bullies him into building a doomsday weapon. With the machine Dreyfus will be able to intimidate the world's leaders into killing Clouseau (though why Dreyfus doesn't use the machine to kill Clouseau himself, I don't know). Of course, Dreyfus fails, and Clouseau liberates Fassbinder (and daughter) just in time. This film—the fourth *Panther*—is the most Hollywood literate, crammed as it is with references to specific films, genres, and even its hallowed past. It all begins in the title sequence, a chase between Clouseau and the Pink Panther set in an old movie palace. This time, though, the iconic feline doesn't refer to the notorious diamond (the film has made no reference to the jewel thus far) but to its own legacy. It's the *film* that strikes again.

Still in the credits sequence: cartoon Clouseau sits down in the front of the theater, the lights dim, and the Panther starts the projector. Hitchcock's famous silhouette wobbles across the onscreen screen and Mancini parodies his theme music. Just then, the silhouette is lifted off—it was a disguise—and we see the Panther holding Hitch's shadow on a stick. The Panther's next disguise is Batman, and then King Kong, Julie Andrews (!), Dracula, Gene Kelly, Buster Keaton, and Bob Fosse, all with Mancini riffs to match. The idea here is that *The Pink Panther Strikes Again* "plays" the genres to match the Pink Panther's changes in character. When the Panther is Hitch, the *Panther* is suspense. When he is Gene Kelly, the film is musical. Etcetera. As *Strikes Again* unfolds, the notion will be recapitulated in Edwards' tandem use of disguise and parody. For instance, when the real-life Clouseau is disguised as Quasimodo, a (quite inspired) gag sends him into the towers of Notre Dame. Later into the film, when Dreyfus is playing at *The Phantom of the Opera* (organ, castle, cackle),* we get a Transylvanian-type setting evocative of Count Dracula, the genre's greatest villain. There are countless other references: James Bond, *Jaws*, Bruce Lee movies, and even *Dr. Strangelove* are referenced with the accompanying visual and/or aural tropes of each.

The film, like Inspector Clouseau, is a master of disguise, and by the same token a master of self-parody. The Cato attacks, Dreyfus' madness, and even the hilarious brutality of the gag have been amplified so far beyond their original incarnations that much of their success turns upon the audience's memories of *Panthers* past. But upping the ante is more than simply parody; it's Edwards' protection against redundancy. Now that we are *Panther* veterans, he can use our knowledge of the film's ritualistic past to (paradoxically) increase the sense of spontaneity. When Clouseau steps into his house at the outset of *The Pink Panther Strikes Again*, we can expect—and even look forward to—an attack from Cato. To keep the surprises surprising, Edwards hits us with the one-two punch of distraction and genre variation. Crosscutting between Clouseau looking for Cato to Dreyfus spying on Clouseau, he can divert us from the now very familiar setup, and splitting the narrative point of view, also create suspense, which tonally

---

* This is an in-joke. Herbert Lom played the Phantom in Terence Fisher's version of 1962. The film is thereby referencing both itself and cinema's past.

"tricks" us out of our expectations. Similarly, in the fridge splurch, Clouseau opens a refrigerator expecting to find Cato (a reference to *Return of*), but he's not in it. Clouseau keeps looking and looking and finally the extraordinary length of the sequence succeeds in erasing Cato from our minds. By the time Clouseau gets into bed for the night, Cato's attack is totally unexpected. Thus has Blake refreshed the form.

The final Cato attack in *The Pink Panther Strikes Again* works in exactly the same way. The scene begins with the threat of danger (Clouseau: "Cato?"), but we are distracted by a change in genre (a James Bond parody), a change in tone (this is a seduction scene), another change in genre (musical: Tom Jones, actually), a change in visuals (deep reds dominate, bubbles float around), and then AAAAAAAAAZZZZAAAA! Cato attacks, the Murphy bed bounces back, bursts through the wall, and Clouseau, Cato, and Olga Bariosova (Leslie-Anne Down) go flying into the moat. Once again, the servant has thwarted his master's sexual escapades, but he owes his success to the picture's facility with self-parody. In fact, *The Pink Panther Strikes Again*'s sense of parody is so pervasive it even doubles its own characters. Superintendent Quinlan (Leonard Rossiter) and Section Director Alex Drummond (Colin Blakely) are Scotland Yard's echoes of Dreyfus and François, and as the film progresses, they will develop the characteristics of their predecessors. Just the same, Clouseau has his doppelgangers in the form of assassins, each dressed in the inspector's trademark tweed hat and trench coat. The list goes on; jokes are repeated ("rheum" for "room"), scenes are repeated (interrogation of manor inhabitants à la *A Shot in the Dark*), and actors are repeated, though in different roles (most notably Graham Stark). In the words of Inspector Jacques Clouseau *de la Sûreté*, "It is obvious to my trained eye that there is much more going on here than meets the ear."

"This one is harder for me than *Return of the Pink Panther* was," said Blake. "That was kind of a lark. This one is a real chore. When I'm being commercial—not to put down being commercial—it's harder to generate the same kind of madness and spontaneity."[6] Apparently Sellers felt the same way. Edwards remarks,

> He would sulk, he would get into black moods, he would withdraw, and he would punish himself by not being able to do something. If he couldn't get a handle on it . . . it would frustrate the shit out of him, and he would become worse and worse and worse in order to justify the fact

that he couldn't do it. He would blame it on somebody else, blame it on conditions, blame it on God—blame it one anybody except Peter Sellers. And he was very cruel to people during those periods. He would threaten, even pretend physical violence, like he would beat somebody up. If it wasn't so sad, it was laughable.[7]

Herbert Lom recalls that relations between Blake and Peter got so ugly they reverted once again to communicating through written notes. "Blake showed me [Lom] telegrams he had received: 'You are a rotten human being.' 'You are shit and I can afford to work without you.' 'I don't need you to get work, Love Peter.' "[8] The picture grossed $100 million.

By that time Blake had convinced himself it was over. "I thought, 'Oh boy, we're getting into a sick area here, it's dangerous, it's too much grief.'"[9] Nevertheless, with Sellers' health on the decline, he made a deal for *Panther* five, "feeling like a man condemned to an illness for a year with the promise of a cure at the end."[10] That illness turned deadly in *Revenge of the Pink Panther*, their next and final film together. The picture begins as mafia man Philippe Douvier (Robert Webber) orders a hit on Chief Inspector Clouseau, now the most prominent gendarme in all of France. To lure his prey, Douvier poses as an informant and tells Clouseau where he can find a famous criminal called the French Connection. Clouseau bites, heads to the location, and switches clothes with a transvestite, but when the cops find a dead drag queen, they think it's Clouseau. The real Clouseau, meanwhile, uses the opportunity to navigate the mafia world undetected, and with the help of Douvier's mistress, Simone, plans his revenge on Douvier, which takes him to Hong Kong (Cato comes too), where masquerading as a mafia godfather allows him to infiltrate Douvier's criminal network and take it down.

The Pink Panther introduced Clouseau. *A Shot in the Dark* perfected him. *The Return of the Pink Panther* acknowledged the film's legacy and *The Pink Panther Strikes Again* parodied it. *Revenge of the Pink Panther*, the darkest in the series, poignantly reverses everything, offering up a new, vulnerable Clouseau as we have never seen him before. The arrogant cover-ups ("Sir, you should have your architect investigated") and the pretentious authoritarianism ("Facts, Hercule, facts!") have been stripped away, and in their place Blake has instated a world that completely overwhelms the inspector. Without his masks of infallibility, Clouseau is meek and defenseless, utterly lacking resilience, and as a result, for the first time in the series, miraculously prone to change. It's a new idea in Edwards, and it gives him the opportunity to develop a signature slapstick tinged with melancholy, one that 10, S.O.B., and *Skin Deep* will see polished.

An unusual thing happens early on in *Revenge of the Pink Panther*. Returning to his apartment, Clouseau, visibly worn by the night's events, unveils to François (André Maranne) a startling weakness.

> François: Why don't you get out of those wet clothes? You could catch pneumonia.
> Clouseau: Yes, I know that, I know that. I will do as soon as I get home provided that that idiot Cato does not attack me first.
> François: Why don't you just tell him not to?
> Clouseau: Believe me, it's not that easy. I have given him instructions to attack me whenever possible and it has now become a matter of pride for him to try to outsmart me.

Clouseau is actually afraid. What's more, Clouseau's Toulouse Lautrec getup—beard, ruffles, and all—enhances the effects of his age and undermines whatever virility he has left. The old man peeks around his front door, carefully steps into his apartment, and calls out to his invisible assailant. He picks up a bugle horn and sounds a pathetic blast. "Cato!" An upstairs neighbor yells at him and he shouts back, "I am trying to save my life, Madame." By the end of the sequence, Clouseau has not defeated Cato. Servant and master are now equals (we see both are covered in paint, the gag has visualized the new relationship), and this reversal of power—unprecedented since the time of the franchise's inception—will be accompanied by a substantial change in narrative structure, one that underlines the theme of Clouseau's helplessness. As we will see, Cato's newfound power over Clouseau is matched by Edwards' decision to allot him greater dramatic emphasis; that is, Cato will take diegetic and extra-diegetic control over *Revenge of the Pink Panther*, and all, of course, at Clouseau's expense. But first, Clouseau "dies."

Up until now, Clouseau has been impervious to death. He has always (unknowingly) dodged the bullet at the right moment, and has always been (wrongly) credited for the kill. He has escaped damage and pain, and because of it, has never had to confront mortality. But all that changes now. To realize his protagonist's about-face, Edwards has injected *Revenge of the Pink Panther* with touching death-related gags. After Cato's white

Peugeot explodes, supposedly killing Clouseau, the inspector is seen walking through the woods, alone in the dark, wearing the clothes of the transvestite who tried to assassinate him. The double-pronged splurch, which takes swipes at Clouseau's mortality and masculine virility, deftly unites sexual and physical decay. Humiliation turns to fear when the police come, and, finding the inspector in drag, take him off to an insane asylum. Despite Clouseau's pleadings, they do not recognize him. Clouseau is dead—this man in drag is an impostor. To escape from the asylum, Clouseau disguises himself as Dreyfus: once again, the disguise actually discloses. Equating Clouseau and his enemy adds a fearful irony to the splurch, which again diminishes his veneer of immortality. And it gets worse: returning home, Clouseau finds that in his absence Cato has turned his apartment into a brothel and opium den. Spying the platform shoes under Clouseau's trench coat, Madame Woo guesses at Clouseau's sexual tastes. She commands Tanya the Lotus Eater to come in, and in walks a leather-clad dominatrix. She snaps her whip around Clouseau's neck, throws him to the ground and he protests, "I warn you, Tanya the Easter Lotus, I am opposed to the women's libs! Man is the master and the woman's place is in the home!" The splurch, Clouseau's physical impairment, belies his chauvinist sensibilities, but the irony of the situation is so heavy it makes humor impossible. Madame Woo smiles at Clouseau's offscreen cries of pain, and says, "another round-eye bites the dust."

After the scene ends (Cato has saved Clouseau from Tanya's whip), the master confides in his servant. "The whole world believes that I am dead. No one will know that it is me as I glide through the underworld like a shadow." Embracing the facts of his own fallibility, Clouseau has taken the first step toward change. Edwards accompanies this revelation with a highly mannered bit of lighting, entirely out of line with the *Panther's* stylistic customs. In it, Clouseau steps toward the camera, light fades from the screen, and a green glow shines on his face. Darkness has washed away the outer world, leaving us with an otherworldly, almost intimate image.* That this revelation occurs in an Oriental setting—an atmosphere associated with spiritual recognition—is no accident: Clouseau has been enlightened. Henceforth, the acceptance of weakness will characterize his

---

* Darkness was part of Edwards' stylistic strategy. Cinematographer Ernest Day noted, "A good 75% of what we've shot has been night—and quite moody night."[11]

actions, not the customary cover-ups and authoritarian outbursts. In this context, the splurch is obsolete. What will physical abuse accomplish that it hasn't all ready? Nothing—Clouseau, for the first time, has changed.

That Clouseau requires the assistance of Cato to break into Le Club Foot speaks to his newly acknowledged weakness. Partnering with "the little yellow man" belies any semblance of authority he would try to maintain. Though he may verbally abuse Cato (and receives the appropriate physical torment), we know by this scene that he needs him. He also needs Simone (Dyan Cannon) to rescue him. Would the old Clouseau allow himself to be rescued? And by a woman, no less? She takes him back to her apartment and what follows is an uncharacteristic display of vulnerability. Compared to his seduction of Maria Gambrelli back in A Shot in the Dark, a scene rife with innuendo, the scene at Simone's is conspicuously lacking in "masculine" demonstrations of power. She's the one who gives him a robe and she's the one who mixes him a drink. (Who's the damsel in distress now?) There are no gags here and no masks, only intimacy. "When you have been killed as many times as I have," Clouseau says, "you get used to it, believe me."

Simone and Clouseau, disguised as a Chinese couple, head off to Hong Kong to get the bad guys. In line with the incumbent transformation, Cato has replaced Clouseau as the new gag force of the film. Physical ineptitude, no longer the province of the enlightened Clouseau, has reversed, and he can regain his authority—but this time, it is earned, not feigned. Once again, the transformation is in the costume: Clouseau appears before the villains as The Godfather, cotton balls and all. And then it happens. Immediately following Clouseau's coup de grâce, the transaction he needs to nail his enemies, one of the villains slaps him with a congratulatory pat on the back. A cotton ball goes flying out of his mouth. Looks are exchanged. Just then, a befuddled Clouseau loses his footing and tumbles off the scaffolding. "He must be a cop! Get him!" (Cue the car chase.) The pratfall that busts Clouseau is momentous, insofar as it stems not from his incompetence but from his success. He does not trip until they have celebrated him, and it is not his blundering that causes it. Someone does it to him. Therefore the splurch is not indicative of his inability, but to the contrary, it is indicative of theirs. That's a Panther first.

The film's penultimate scene shows Clouseau receiving a medal of honor. The award ceremony has a few bits of slapstick (the sword, the misstep, the tie), but they are overwhelmed by the earnest visual authority of Edwards' composition. Les gendarmes are forcefully arranged on all sides, a picture of strength, music swells—and splat. Clouseau will always be accident-prone, Edwards seems to say, but never has he been so valiant. This is clearly a different Clouseau; still klutzy, but changed nevertheless. And if there are still any doubts in the audience's mind about Clouseau's conversion, the next scene, the film's last, will surely put them to rest.

Clouseau's car, the Silver Hornet, stops in front of Simone's apartment, the inspector steps out, and bounds up to her door. They wave when they see each other. The music is tender. "I'm so sorry I'm late," he says. Clouseau helps her into the Hornet, he shuts the door, and the car collapses. In the old days, he would cover the splurch with a declamation of officialdom, but now he apologizes. The splurch, it appears, no longer threatens him. In fact, without the capacity for humiliation, Clouseau has disarmed the splurch into a plain old harmless gag. The final shot sees them walk hand-in-hand away from the camera, down the wet Parisian street, and into the night. It's a true "romantic" coda, the standard couple-affirming image we see in love stories. Clouseau has been formally honored, the gag has lost its power over him, he got the girl, and Cato is nowhere in sight. The *Panther*'s inner and outer worlds have changed, Clouseau has changed, and it is to the acceptance of weakness and mortality that we owe his betterment.

SELLERS LIVES ON:

TRAIL OF THE PINK PANTHER (1982),
CURSE OF THE PINK PANTHER (1983),
SON OF THE PINK PANTHER (1993)

*Cato: Sometimes when you do something long enough you
miss it even though it was painful.*

"The last time I saw Sellers," Blake Edwards recalled, "was on a Christmas in Gstaad, Switzerland. My family and I were in a local disco, and I saw Sellers and his wife come in. And they wouldn't acknowledge us. By then, he was not speaking to me. And I watched from a distance, and I watched him have a fight with his lady and leave.

About half an hour later my son came in—he was meeting us there—he sat down and said, "Dad, I just saw Peter Sellers." And I said, "Yeah," and he said, "He's standing across the street. I thought it was a statue." And I said, "You're kidding. It's snowing out there!" He said, "Yes, he looks like a snowman, it's the weirdest thing I've ever seen!"

I thought, "Well, it's Christmas, and it's crazy, at least for me, to play the game of not speaking or talking. In spite of the problems, there were good times too." So I excused myself to Julie and said, "I'm going to go over and say something to him."

I walked out, and it was spooky—he had a coat on, but he was just standing there. I mean it was snowing heavily, and he was covered with snow, he hadn't moved, it was like he was catatonic. So I walked across the street to him, and I walked up to him, and he acted at least like he hadn't seen me coming or heard me. And I said, "Peter," and he was just standing there, and he kind of snapped out of it, and he looked, and he saw it was me, and he didn't know quite what to do with it. I said, "Peter, go home or get inside. You're going to catch cold." And I kissed him on the cheeks and said, "Merry Christmas" and walked back into the place. And as I walked through the door, I looked back, and he was still standing there. That's the last time I ever saw him.[12]

Between *Revenge of the Pink Panther* and *Trail of the Pink Panther*—a film about dying and a film about grief—Peter Sellers went from *Being There* to not being. He died in 1980, his body cremated at Golders Green to the tune of "In the Mood."

But the franchise lived on. This is a fact that invites cynicism, and rightly so, but before we dismiss the next decade of *Panther* sequels as purely remunerative undertakings, let's remember that Blake Edwards has had a longstanding investment in remakes. As far back as the original *Pink Panther*, in 1964, a picture that can trace a direct lineage to the silents, Edwards has proudly worn influences on sleeves. *The Great Race* names names explicitly and *A Fine Mess*, try as we might to forget it, conjures the same gods. *Gunn* is a remake of Edwards' hit show, his made-for-TV movie *Peter Gunn* follows suit, and the 1970s give birth to *Panther* triplets, but it is the 1980s that produced Edwards' most consistent string of remakes. *S.O.B.*, though original, demands a consideration of Edwards' past, and toys playfully with the translation from its real-life source material to its Hollywood incarnation. The idea of remaking, of revising, is essential even to the film's storyline.

Victor/Victoria and *The Man Who Loved Women* are remakes, and *Sunset* is plainly concerned with the process of adaptation, not simply from the point of view of Hollywood, but from the revisions of memory. And so too is *Switch*, a riff on George Axelrod's *Goodbye, Charlie*, which is about a man who is remade into a woman. Realities (always plural) have always been a source of great fun and anxiety for Edwards, who so often struggles with the contentions of simulacra. And what else is *Son of the Pink Panther* but a copy of a copy of a copy of a copy of a copy of a copy of a copy? There are variations of course, but as live-action cartoons, these films must not change too much for fear of defying their central premise, that Clouseau will always bounce back. In that assertion there is enough pathos and irony to last through more than a couple of remakes before the inevitable intentions of mortality present themselves. This is the contradiction that gives the sequels their punch. *The Return of the Pink Panther* shows a considerably older Clouseau and *Revenge* threatens him with the possibility of his own extinction. It is no surprise that a film like *10* follows right behind. After all, Blake had dying on the mind. *Trail of the Pink Panther* does too.

Like the sequels to follow, *Trail* faces death head on. Sellers is gone, and if the series is to continue, his absence must be dealt with. The films of

1982, 1983, and 1993 approach the issue in different ways, but all are alike in their suffering. Sellers is irreplaceable; the very thought of continuing without him seems shameless beyond belief, and if the disaster of Bud Yorkin's *Inspector Clouseau* was any warning, the only person who could stand in for Sellers was Joe Dunne, his body double. For whomever assumed the role, whether it's Ted Wass, Roberto Benigni, or Steve Martin (in 2006 or 2009), filling the shoes would be a losing battle. But Edwards was no stranger to the difficulty. He had for sometime tried to resist working with Sellers, hoping instead to find replacements in his own career (on occasion he did), but he could never shake Peter entirely. Sellers was inimitable—even to the man who swore never to work with him again. So why continue? Why try to raise the dead? To some, it was cruel disrespect—Sellers' widow won a lawsuit filed under a claim of this sort—but to Blake it was more than an artistic challenge, it was an answer to one of his greatest crises: loss. But honestly, the money didn't hurt.

Indeed the very thought of making a Peter Sellers movie without Peter Sellers sounds more like the subject of a Blake Edwards movie than an actual film. And in fact, insofar as "actual" suggests a cinematic narrative of, as Lehman and Luhr observe, a series of recorded events, *Trail of the Pink Panther* was purely notional:

> Hollywood filmmaking is largely premised upon a notion that the camera records aspects of a profilmic event that includes the actors. The actors, in other words, *were present* when the film was made. . . .If a film of a film is not primarily a record, then it must be primarily a construct. Hollywood films emphasize their recording aspect and not their construct aspect. *Trail of the Pink Panther*, however, emphasizes its construct aspect, not its recording aspect.[13]

Edwards' sixth *Panther* is composed of old Sellers footage, some of it familiar, some of it *very* familiar, some of it unseen outtakes from previous *Panthers*, and some of it entirely new, written and shot expressly for *Trail* and *Trail* alone.

There is more premise here than story: Clouseau's latest efforts to locate the missing diamond end in his disappearance, and the journalist Marie Jouvet (Joanna Lumley) sets out to pick up the missing pieces. Some familiar faces maintain that Clouseau has to be alive (Sir Charles, for one, believes he can't die), we see a few flashbacks, meet a few new characters

(Père Clouseau, *par exemple*), and by the end, Jouvet concludes that Clouseau must be out there somewhere.

Like S.O.B., *The Man Who Loved Women, That's Life!*, and *Switch, Trail of the Pink Panther* is consumed with death, dovetailing perfectly with *Revenge of the Pink Panther*. Taken together, the two films depict Clouseau's existential crisis and his memorial, but have, significantly, skipped his death (or is it disappearance?) along the way. In *Trail*, Edwards turns this uncertainty into a metaphysical exploration of immortality, about the absence of life *and* the absence of death. Fittingly, no one in *Trail of the Pink Panther* believes Clouseau has actually died. And why should they? After nearly ten hours of watching him survive the most dangerous situations without even the slightest scratch, we have little reason to accept that something as minor as a plane crash could actually take Clouseau down with it. When Charles Litton (David Niven) tells Jouvet that he refuses to believe Clouseau has died, he isn't merely expressing denial in the Kübler-Ross sense, he's stating a hard fact about *Panther* reality, that deathlessness is likelier than death.

David Niven and Capucine, whom *we* remember from *The Pink Panther*, set up a series of memory "flashbacks," which are actually just snippets yanked from their film of twenty years before. "To my dying day," Litton begins, "I will never forget that old man trying to cross the street." We cut to the corresponding scene in *The Pink Panther*: a wide establishing shot takes us to a deserted piazza at nighttime. Edwards cuts again to the man, and then his point of view of a car racing down the street. This segment is presented from the old man's perspective, but it's *his* point of view, not Litton's, and therefore violates the flashback's subjectivity. Litton himself is nowhere to be seen, which means there's no way that this is his memory. No wonder the "memory" is presented exactly as it was in *The Pink Panther*. That's how Sir Charles remembers it; he is speaking not as a character, but as moviegoer who has seen the *The Pink Panther*.

Although this is diegetically impossible (no film of *The Pink Panther* exists within the world of *The Pink Panther*), it spotlights the meta-structural fabric of Edwards's film. Litton is not speaking as himself, but as David Niven, a man who saw the film and was involved in its production. The actor, in other words, in an "interview" with Marie Jouvet, is remembering the actor Peter Sellers. All at once, the pretense of a fictional narrative about a missing detective gives way to a confessional about a missing friend. But were Sellers and Niven really friends? According to the eulogy Niven delivered at his memorial service, it's impossible to say. "It was a joy and a privilege to have known him for so long. Yet how many of us really did know Peter? After twenty-five years of friendship, I had to ask myself."[14]

The incredible ambivalence of character, the pastiche of Litton and Niven—itself matching *Trail*'s own collage-like structure—speaks to Edwards' own ambivalence towards Sellers. "I've become more generous in my forgiving and forgetting," Blake said. "I wish he were still here with all his craziness, and I wish he were well. I'm not sure that I wish to make another film with him, but I wish for those times."[15] This about a man who he once compared to Hitler?[16] It's a contradiction embodied in *Trail of the Pink Panther*, a movie that suggests that the process of forgiving and forgetting demands a schizophrenic blend of memory and fiction. "Litton's memories," after all, are nothing but old film clips. From Blake's point of view, this is a fictional forgiving memory of the very funny side of Sellers, the comic genius who brought great joy into the world. But isn't Blake forgetting something? What about the *real* Sellers, the offscreen maniac?

"The way you make peace is to forgive and forget," Blake continues "and the way you forgive and forget is to try to understand why people are like that."[17] Comedy helps us to understand Sellers' madness, and the process of forgiving, of selecting memories, becomes analogous to watching the hilarious scenes from the film. Through Litton, we have seen Edwards select pieces of his own past, glorious bits of Clouseau to help him remember Peter when he was good, but they do little to help Blake/ Jouvet understand Sellers when he wasn't. Enter Clouseau's father (Richard Mulligan), a feeble French winemaker. He relates to Jouvet, not his personal recollections of his son, but young Jacques' own memories. We flash back once again, though this time it isn't to old *Panther* clips, it's to new footage—scenes from Clouseau's youth. Unlike Litton's memories, these aren't stained with the problems of point of view and selective recall. There is no discrepancy between *Père* Clouseau's recounting of the events and the events themselves. Why? Because *Père* Clouseau isn't flashing back, Blake Edwards is. The nature of the scenes reveals they are reconstructions of easily recognizable film conventions, even direct citations to movies past, and not, as *Trail*'s narrative suggests, actual events.

Blake is using cinematic lore to stand in for Clouseau's past. What he doesn't know about his main character (alias Peter Sellers) he has filled in with imagination, which, in these scenes, he equates to filmmaking. A close-up of pictures in a photo album prompts the transition into the "past," a device that suggests at the importance of representation, of making pictures, as it relates to designing memories. The first "memory" demonstrates baby Clouseau's unusual talent for projectile urination. It may seem an inconsequential aside or even another meaningless gag, but in actuality it refers back to a matching scene in Trail's title sequence, in which the credit "Story by Blake Edwards," is sprayed out in Clouseau's pee. The comparison suggests that this is not a piece of fact from Père Clouseau, but imagination from the mind of the storywriter. Edwards is the rememberer here, and he's using references to pictures past—specifically, Sergio Leone and The Bridge on the River Kwai—to blur the lines between actual history and movie history.

Memories, movies, the echoes felt by Jouvet and Père Clouseau, and the dogged conviction that he just can't die, all point to the possibility of Clouseau's metaphysical endurance. Even if Clouseau were dead, Trail of the Pink Panther has indicated that he couldn't stay that way. At the end of the picture, Marie Jouvet turns directly into the camera and poses a question that goes unanswered. "Did Inspector Clouseau really perish in the sea as reported," she asks, "or, for reasons as yet unknown, is he out there someplace plotting his next move, waiting to reveal himself when the time is right?" As she speaks, the camera glides over island cliffs to reveal an expanse of ocean. Panning left onto a patch of green, we see Clouseau overlooking the sea (Edwards' favorite metaphysical setting). We might actually believe it, were it not for the voice-over that brought us here. After all, as a part of Jouvet's closing statement, these pictures are purely speculative. We cut to a double of the same shot, but this time, Clouseau is not represented by a body double, he's drawn in animation over an ocean at nightfall. Drawing a parallel between Clouseau as a flesh-and-bones actor and Clouseau as a cartoon figure, Edwards has recapitulated his point about the preservative qualities of cinema. So long as there are doubles and a camera to record them, Clouseau's death will indeed be impossible. When the animated figure turns around, we see that it's actually the Pink Panther in the inspector's trench coat. Just then, the Panther unfastens his coat, spins around and flashes the camera. But he has no body. Inside his coat is blackness. From the dark unspools a highlight reel of Clouseau's greatest moments, beginning with his first slip on the globe, twenty years earlier, in The Pink Panther. The panther's body, in other words, is cinema, which is why Clouseau lives: movies won't let him die.

Immortality, after all, has a big commercial upside, proving once again that a dead horse, when beaten, becomes a cash cow. But the critics held their noses (and rightfully so). The *Los Angeles Times* called *Trail* "a melancholy affair that makes us feel the loss of Sellers all over again,"[18] and Vincent Canby wrote, "Not all the material is terrific, but all the memories are fond."[19] Not so for Sellers' widow, Lynne Frederick. She sued MGM/UA and Edwards' production company, claiming they had used Sellers' likeness illegally, violated his contract, and tarnished his work. Frederick said that Peter's agreement with Edwards never granted him the right to make a feature of unused footage, to which her lawyer added, "Sellers was something of a perfectionist" and believed the outtakes were not "particularly funny or worthy of his talent."[20] Testimony revealed that Sellers had on several accounts refused to make to a film from the cutting-room floor, but did his right to posthumously control use of his performance extend to his beneficiaries? The court ruled that it did, and awarded the widow nearly $2 million in damages. United Artists appealed, maintaining that they had full copyright on the *Panthers* and were never prohibited from using footage that did not make the release prints. But they lost. And if the lawsuit didn't drive home the point that this was their last doomed film with Sellers, the box office certainly did: *Trail of the Pink Panther* did very poor business.

There was little consolation in *Curse of the Pink Panther*, Edwards' second-to-last *Panther*. Because of glitch in the Interpol computer (Dreyfus at it again), inept Clifton Sleigh of the NYPD (Ted Wass), mistaken for the world's greatest detective, is selected to recover Clouseau. What follows (and indeed what precedes) is unfunny. For many reasons, those who remember Clouseau rather enjoy life without him, and in a concatenation of familiar events, fail to assassinate Sergeant Sleigh. The film, unfortunately, goes on, and eventually Sleigh trails Clouseau (still alive!) to a cavernous health spa overlooking the Mediterranean run by Countess Chandra (Joanna Lumley), where he discovers that Clouseau has actually had a face transplant and now looks exactly—I mean, *exactly*—like Roger Moore. No one is not confused when, at the end of the film, Sir Charles, Lady Litton, and Sir Charles' nephew, George, yacht off with the diamond.

Edwards' casting of television comedian Ted Wass, in whom Edwards saw "a certain vulnerability,"[21] is the film's single addition to its tired heritage. Plucked from the suds of the TV show *Soap*, Wass was purely a TV personality before he got the *Curse*. Only two starring roles in small-screen features preceded his transition to films, and after Dudley Moore turned down the part, Wass signed up. We get our first glimpse of him undercover on a Manhattan street corner, dressed in drag and—you guessed it—utterly incompetent. But there's a catch. Where Clouseau would try to cover up his ineptitude, Sleigh makes no attempt.

> Sleigh: You gotta a light, big boy?
> Charlie: Cliff, uh, broads don't call guys "big boy" anymore.
> Sleigh: Oh. Right, Charle.
> *Charlie, another agent, leans in to light Sleigh's cigarette.*
> Charlie: I thought you didn't smoke.
> Sleigh: I figured it kinda goes with the look.

Cliff inhales and erupts into a pathetic coughing fit. We see he has no capacity for arrogance, so what's the point of splurching him? As Wass said in the film's press release, Sleigh is "earnest, but never pompous. He doesn't have Clouseau's vanity, or superb self-confidence."[22] Clouseau needed a good pie in the face, but Sleigh, it seems, just needs to throw one.

Janet Maslin wrote that *Curse* was "Not unfunny, and not really an offense to the memory of Inspector Clouseau, it's merely a movie with very little reason to exist."[23] The *Los Angeles Times* was generous: "Gimmicky, yes, but Edwards can take age-old gimmicks and recycle them into novelties";[24] but the *Hollywood Reporter* saw something bigger, a problem that ran deeper than the film itself. "Any studio that opens a film on a Friday afternoon in mid-August without press previews or preliminary fanfare obviously suspects the film is in deep trouble. And in the case of Blake Edwards' *Curse of the Pink Panther*, his seventh in the series, I suspect that MGM/UA is quite right."[25] The film grossed $1.6 million on 812 theaters opening weekend, a pathetic sum for any big picture, let alone the seventh film in the most successful comedy franchise of all time.

Blake blamed MGM for the flop, alleging that MGM/UA and Frank Rothman, its chairman and chief executive officer, "conspired together" to "frustrate and prevent the economic success of *Curse*."[26] They buried the film, Blake said, violating their verbal agreement to spend $3.5 million promoting it in the weeks prior to and following its release. "It is ludicrous," Rothman returned, "to assume that MGM/UA would do anything other than to maximize the results of a film that MGM/UA financed." To Edwards, it was a $180 million difference in opinion. Meanwhile, MGM filed a $340 million cross-complaint that cited Edwards for gross mis-

23. *Curse of the Pink Panther* (1983) Tedd Wass filling Sellers' impossibly large shoes as Sergeant Clifton Sleigh of the NYPD. The "Instant Companion" beside him—the third inflatable joke in the movie—redundantly splurches an already splurched man. (Author's collection)

management of funds and fraudulent spending back on *Victor/Victoria*. The studio contended that if there was any loss it was theirs, and Edwards was to blame for spending "large sums on unnecessary expensive items, extravagant or non-existent living expenses, and chauffeur expenses."[27] (Of the $18.6 million it cost to make *Victor/Victoria*, for instance, $445,000 was spent on cars.) Incensed to find his name vilified in the press, Edwards counter-countersued on the grounds that MGM/UA libeled him and his wife by disseminating copies of the fraud suit to reporters, an accusation that added $400 million to the damages. By the time the dust had settled, the combined grand total came to $1.414 billion.[28] Now *that's* a good opening weekend.

The dispute was settled out of court, and Blake took a ten-year hiatus from *Pantheriana*. The period of 1983 to 1988 was wildly inconsistent artistically speaking, but in financial terms, largely second-rate. His return came with *Skin Deep* in 1989 and continued on through *Switch*, but in the meantime, the *Panther* trademark had been caught up in legal limbo: MGM/UA had become MGM-Pathé. Under Giancarlo Parretti, the company's new chairman, the studio's financing agreement with Edwards had fallen through, and the unborn *Son of the Pink Panther* turned into another rights dispute. The new MGM, after failing to honor the contract, prohibited Blake from looking elsewhere for funding. Naturally, the deadlock put Edwards in a difficult position; not only did MGM refuse to make the film, they refused to let Blake take it anywhere else. Edwards charged the company for breach of contract and fiduciary infractions.

When Alan "Laddie" Ladd Jr. replaced Parretti, he green-lit *Son* again, though Gerard Depardieu, who had been interested the first time around, was no longer available. Then came the decision to cast Roberto Benigni, spurred on by a viewing of Jim Jarmusch's *Down by Law*. In Benigni they found was a wise investment; his film *Johnny Stecchino*, the highest grossing Italian film ever, launched him into superstardom, and garnered the financial attention of Aurelio De Laurentiis who, in the most expensive acquisition ever paid by an Italian distributor, exchanged $14 million for the film's Italian-language distribution rights—nearly half the film's budget.

The studio jumped headfirst into marketing. There was no question that the series' fan base, though loyal, had aged considerably. The teenagers present for *The Pink Panther* now had children who may or may not have any concept of the franchise, and considering that the successes of the previous films were built upon return customers, it occurred to MGM that a few focus groups might come in handy. What, they asked, did the new generation know about *The Pink Panther*, *A Shot in the Dark*, *The Return of the Pink Panther*, *The Pink Panther Strikes Again*, *Revenge of the Pink Panther*, *Trail of the Pink Panther*, and *Curse of the Pink Panther*? As it turned out, not much. To the new generation, *The Pink Panther* was a feline Hugh Hefner with monocle and cigarette; they knew the cartoon, not the inspector. (It had been fifteen years since the last *Panther* made a box-office impression, with *Revenge*, in 1978). And so, to marry the film's live-action legacy with the youth's cartoon awareness, MGM hired Geoffrey Edwards to direct a $1 million title sequence in which Bobby McFerrin would scat with the cat. Thus begins *Son of the Pink Panther*, a film made forty whole years after the original, Blake Edwards' thirty-seventh (and to date final) directorial feature.

The film follows Gendarme Jacques Gambrelli (Roberto Benigni) and his Clouseau-like efforts to find the kidnapped Princess Yasmin (Debrah Farentino). The story sees Dreyfus (Herbert Lom) fall for Jacques' mother (Claudia Cardinale), who reveals that Clouseau is actually her son's father; and after a Middle East shoot-out to save the princess, it concludes in what may be the franchise's most nauseating revelation: Clouseau's son has a sister.

Right away, we see that Jacques Gambrelli, Clouseau's illegitimate son, has inherited many of the qualities that made his father a box-office favorite. He is, in the words of his mother, "Foolhardy, accident-prone, pig-headed, courageous . . . accident-prone." Indeed Gambrelli is pure spin-off, a seasoned catastrophist capable of sending Dreyfus into convulsions, and from Gambrelli's very first onscreen tumble (his bike hits a car and sends him over), Dreyfus senses the presence of a family brand. The film's title, *Son of the Pink Panther*, should give us some indication that the chief inspector's worst fears will be realized: Clouseau lives on. And *Son of the Pink Panther* confirms what we already suspected, that spiritual regeneration—the posthumous transference of personae—is not only possible, but with Blake Edwards, quite likely.

In *Son of the Pink Panther*, that transference is biological. The character of Jacques is not merely an honorary Clouseau in the manner of Sleigh, but an actual Clouseau, an authentic copy with a destiny to fulfill. In fact, the presence of the father is so strong in young Jacques (though he has no idea who his real father is) that he is said to have considered Clouseau his hero. Of course, it goes without saying that Clouseau should be the hero of every rookie gendarme, but as the mise-en-scène indicates, junior admires more than just his father's international celebrity. Perched over the fireplace in Jacques' bedroom are two miniature dolls, replicas of Stan Laurel and Oliver Hardy. Jacques Gambrelli, we see, is a *fan*: his father's son *and* his audience. The scene in Dreyfus' hospital room, for instance, sees the chief inspector in bed with a broken leg suspended in a cast, and splurch-ready. As the hospital television makes plain, the slapstick ahead is a direct and literal quotation of a Marx Brothers routine. The film is *A Day at the Races*, and in it, Groucho, Chico, and Harpo wreak havoc in an operating room as Margaret Dumont looks on to the tune of "Well, I never!" Jacques smiles at the sight of it, picks up what he believes to be the remote control, and presses a button that claps Dreyfus' bed into paroxysms of the highest order. Edwards cuts back and forth from the television to Dreyfus, from Dreyfus to the television, hammering home the point that life is imitating art, when in fact it was Gambrelli himself—the Marx Brothers fan—that incurred it.

When Jacques disguises himself as a doctor, we might think he has inherited his father's fluency with masks, but it is actually from Groucho that Gambrelli borrows this disguise (the quotation is quite literal: in *A Day at the Races*, Groucho's Dr. Hackenbush is a veterinarian posing as a human doctor). The extended "doctor" routine between Gambrelli and the villainous Hans (Robert Davi) may indeed resemble Clouseauvian slapstick in sheer ineptitude, but it is closer to Marxism in sensibility. Benigni's style is actually the opposite of Sellers'; if Clouseau were a doctor, the comic irony would reside in the schism between his confidence and his ability—splurch—but Gambrelli has no confidence. Like the Marx Brothers, he is all goofiness, and though biologically founded, it comes from a natural admiration for clowning. Why else would he declare, "That felt good!" after a hearty pratfall?

And his idea of showmanship doesn't end there. A committed performer, Jacques is also a singer and a declaimer of Shakespeare and Byron, and, as we see, associates the concept of perfomance with his father's memory.

> Jacques: Why did you pretend that my father was an Italian French horn player?
> Maria: Well, for one thing it explained your interest in music. Actually, Clouseau played the violin. Not well, but passionately.

Being a musician or a performer is a continuation of Jacques' inheritance. In the picture's opening credit sequence, the symbol of passing the baton is applied literally. In it, Henry Mancini (musical father) offers his baton to the Pink Panther (his son, his creation) who proceeds to conduct a studio orchestra in a performance of his theme song.

So here we are again, back to the Edwardian concept of performance. Consider, for instance, the *Panther* series' overwhelming, almost ridiculous repetition and recycling of actors. Not just Sellers, Lom, Kwouk and the one or two others who recur throughout, but the inescapable group of faces that pop up again and again, from *A Shot in the Dark* to *Son of*, and in different roles every time. Graham Stark is a perfect example: He has gone from Hercule (*Shot*) to Pepi (*Return*) to Hotel Clerk (*Strikes Again*) to Balls (*Revenge*), back to Hercule (*Trail*), then to a waiter (*Curse*) and then, finally, to Balls again (*Son of*). Even if we do not know his name, we recognize his face. "Hey, isn't that . . . ? Wasn't he . . . ?" Yes it is, and yes he was. Casting Joanna Lumley as two different women (Jouvet and Chandra) in two consecutive films may appear to be a mere directorial convenience, but the juxtaposition of roles yields a clever variation on Edwards' internal doubling. Jouvet and Chandra are from one vantage point pure opposites—one is good, the other is evil—and from another perspective, continuations of the same narrative through-line; Jouvet spends *Trail* looking for Clouseau, and Chandra spends *Curse* living with him. We might consider Cardinale's "role" in the same light. In 1964 she played Princess Dala in *The Pink Panther* and now, thirty years later, Blake has cast her as Maria Gambrelli, a part that we associate with Elke Sommer. Not only has she changed identities, but she has stolen someone else's! This constant shuffle of actors and characters is so blatant in its misappropriation of identity that one can see in it the notion of transference reinterpreted as a kind of repertory theater. As long as the company survives, Clouseau's legacy will live on.

But it didn't. "Blake Edwards has nothing fresh or funny to add to the old ideas," went *Variety*, "Too bad that [his] specialty, the elaborate orchestration of sight gags with hilarious payoffs, is almost absent here, replaced by vulgar slapstick humor and a few effective gags."[29] The *Los Angeles Times* was worse: "Edwards actually sets the stage at the end for a sequel. Is there anybody out there who would want to see it? More to the point, would Edwards want to make it? His work here is so spiritless that the idea of his doing a sequel is positively harrowing. Either that or it's the best joke in the movie."[30] Here's hoping for the latter.

6

BLAKE BOOMS

1979–1982

10 (1979)

George: If you were nineteen, and twenty years from now you were
dancing with your wife . . . or girlfriend you knew in high school
and you said to her, "Darling, they're playing our song," do you know
what they'd be playing? "Why Don't We Do It in the Road."
What the fucking hell kind of era is that?

To fully appreciate the importance of 10 in the trajectory of Edwards' work, it will serve us to consider his creative life in terms of one overarching ambition composed of many smaller supporting ambitions. The big one, of course, is the development of slapstick storytelling. The others, which include (in chronological order) the manipulation of appearances, the problems of gender, the mutability of genre, the invention of personal style, the reinterpretation of the Andrews persona, the struggle to work in the new Hollywood, and a whole host of others, Edwards has used to give purpose and meaning to his slapstick. To do so, he spent his career fusing the gag with his supporting ambitions, understanding that the strengthening of one by the other (which I've called the splurch) would restore silent-era comedy to the present world. And it didn't stop there. As we've seen, since *The Pink Panther*, Edwards was not content merely to make a films dotted with slapstick like *A Shot in the Dark*, *The Great Race*, and *What Did You Do in the War, Daddy?*, but wanted instead to produce whole dramas out of physical comedy as he did in *The Party*, where the splurch doesn't just comment on the action, it moves it from one moment to the next. But there were problems along the way, problems like *Darling Lili* and *Wild Rovers* and *The Carey Treatment*, which seemed, in their solemnity, to distract him from the main line of his career. From the vantage point of today, though, we can see that in fact the opposite was true. And it begins here, with 10: as a thoroughgoing slapstick narrative consumed with emotional crisis, a film that owes its success not just to the structural integrity of its splurching, but to the depth of the despair that preceded it.

Back in Gstaad after *The Carey Treatment*, buckling under the deepest of depressions, Edwards found solace in writing, and discovered that rather than kill the comedy, his emotional pain—like the physical pain of Clouseau—only enhanced it. He realized that trauma after trauma after trauma wasn't just miserably tragic, but could actually be funny, and that breaking the pain barrier of the heart revealed a theory of slapstick that didn't just pertain to the idiot klutzes up there on the screen, but to every human being in his lowest, darkest moment. From now on, Blake saw, nothing would be unfunny. Depression, divorce, suicide, artistic heartbreak, they would become his whoopee cushion, and 10, S.O.B., and Victor/Victoria would be his proof. In these films (and Skin Deep to follow), Edwards would take the gag into the contemporary world by growing it up with torment. But would anyone care? They didn't the last time he got personal in the early seventies (Wild Rovers), and even berated him for it. To recover, he retreated to the Panther trilogy of 1975–78 and resuscitated his commercial viability, but as an artistic director independent of the mega-franchise, Edwards' place in Hollywood was still precarious. One misstep and it would be back to Clouseau.

And then one day, as he was being chauffeured to work in Brussels, Blake had an idea. "We pulled up to a stop sign and there was a bride, and I could not see her face. With that veil and all that stuff, I couldn't see what she looked like. In those few moments . . . I thought what would happen if I were unattached in a wonderful romantic European city, and I looked over and I saw, and it only happens in books, the girl of my dreams in the next car and she was on her way to get married."[1] Changing that European city to Las Hadas, Mexico, and that "I" to George Webber, Edwards composed the screenplay of what is arguably the greatest serious comedy of adult slapstick ever written for the movies. But, alas, no one in Hollywood felt the same way. Blake found the executives wanted one thing from him, and one thing only: a steady stream of Pink. But that well had run dry. Blake had had it with The Pink Panthers, and now wanted only to reinvent himself. Unfortunately, "reinvention" is not a part of the commerical vocabulary. Edwards was in Hollywood deadlock.

To work himself out of it, he struck a compromise. Blake negotiated a three-picture deal with the newly formed Orion Pictures, a baby production outfit under United Artists, with the proviso that he would deliver them The Ferret, a caper franchise in the style of The Pink Panther, but only after they gave him 10. At the time, it seemed a fair trade; two film forces starting anew, one in search of an old hit, and the other after a new one. From there, he assembled a cast culled from the ranks of Hollywood's old and new. George Segal, resuscitated by the success of Fun with Dick and Jane, agreed to play the part of George; after a four-year hiatus from the screen, Julie Andrews was to return as Samantha (her image was undergoing public reconstruction once again: 10's production files celebrate "busy Julie" and her trip to Nashville where she would "cut an album that will have a 'new Julie' sound.");[2] and Robert Webber, known for playing tough guys, was cast quite intentionally against type as the gay lyricist, Hugh. Finding the actress to play the film's title role was a bit more challenging. Blake tested an awful lot of 9s and 9.5s, and was even considering calling off the search, when he overheard someone at a party talking about actor John Derek's wife. He arranged to meet her, and when she arrived at the office he took one look and gave her the part. The phrase he used was "skidding halt." "But can she act?" Julie asked later that night. "Jesus, I don't know," Blake said. But it didn't matter. He never tested her.[3]

The first day of shooting arrived, and with it came an unforeseen challenge: George Segal quit the movie. The specifics were vague, but Segal's agent, Guy McElwaine, cited "irreconcilable artistic differences" between his client and the director.[4] Segal himself claimed he backed out on account of certain scenes Edwards refused to cut from the screenplay, but that didn't make any sense; they had had meetings right up until he dropped, and as far as Edwards could see, there was nothing wrong. Segal sued, Blake countersued, and the matter was settled out of court.

Two weeks later, Dudley Moore, an actor virtually unknown in America, was given the part. He and Edwards had known each other from group analysis, but at first Blake had other plans for him. Originally, he had approached Moore to play the lead role in The Ferret, the film he had been preparing as his follow up to 10, but when the part of George Webber came his way, Dudley snatched it up. Miraculously, the character was not rewritten. "In 10, I'm really just playing myself," Moore said. "The dilemma that George Webber finds himself in is something that I've struggled with, in one way or another, forever: coming to the reality of things and people."[5] Their collaboration was enormously successful. "Dudley made me feel like I was in remission," Blake said. "I have never been so happy in my whole life. He gave an extraordinary quality to the film—his charm, manner, warmth."[6] It was his breakthrough performance, standing alongside Arthur as the greatest of his too short career. He plays songwriter George Webber, a man desperately unsure about marriage. His girlfriend Sam (Julie Andrews) is a lovely woman, but at forty-two, he'd rather be ogling 10s than sharing quiet nights at home with a soprano. When the most beautiful girl he's ever seen (Bo Derek) passes in a limo, George can't help but follow her—to Mexico.

The film begins before it even begins. And it begins with an end. Over a pitch black screen, we read: "This Film is Dedicated with Love and Respect to DICK CROCKETT." No doubt those who saw 10 upon its original theatrical release must have been a little disoriented by this opening. After the *Pink Panther* movies of 1975, 1976, and 1978, one could imagine audiences expected something a little lighter from a Blake Edwards movie, but this was 1979, and Blake was another year darker.

Over the course of Dick Crockett's thirty-year collaboration with Edwards, he worked as a stuntman, actor, producer, and assistant director, until his death in 1979; 10 was his last film. His memorial, the minor chord that announces the film, will resonate throughout, even during the picture's most hilarious moments. We remember the life of a stunt double as George Webber is thrown down the hill behind his house. And when he crashes his Rolls-Royce into a cop car, we will laugh, but we might also feel an absence. This tension—the unending dialectic between humor and mortality—charges through 10, blindsiding at will. Here's how it works:

> [Blake said] About the time you're convinced you're into a semi-serious film, I hit with the first comedy, the first laugh which is a really good one, not enormous, but now they know something's going on. Then there's quite a little period of time where I kind of tip back into the serious part of drama. . . And just about the time you think they might be getting a little restless, insane, I devastate them.[7]

Apropos, 10's opening title cards are black. One completely fades out before the next fades in, leaving the audience with a moment of complete darkness in between. Fade out—breath—fade in. Using lethargic fades instead of rhythmic cuts, Edwards lends the sequence a wistful melancholy and enhances it with the lonely piano playing on the soundtrack. But wait—lonely? Wistful? What kind of a comedy is this? (Visually speaking, it isn't.) As we will discover, 10 doesn't look like a Hollywood comedy. It doesn't explode with flat, evenly distributed high-key lighting, but is instead obscured by darkness, and often to the point of total impenetrability. Edwards has made his intentions clear: where we expected comedy, we will be given heartache.

Naturally, the first shot in 10 is all shadow. A doorbell rings, and a butler, candle in hand, responds to the call. We follow him down the hall, in a single, hand-held shot taking us to the front door. He opens it, and standing in silhouette is George Webber. "It looks like somebody died,"

24. 10 (1979) Edwards does in 10 what George Webber (Dudley Moore) cannot, marrying the previously divergent forces of emotional sophistication and slapstick, personified here by Samantha Taylor (Julie Andrews) and Jennifer Miles (Bo Derek). (Courtesy of the Academy of Motion Picture Arts and Sciences)

he says. The butler hands George the candle and steps into another room. The shot continues—one long, uninterrupted take—leading George, alone, into the dark house. But how alone is he really? The handheld shot makes this scene feel distinctly voyeuristic, creating the uneasy feeling that George is in fact being watched. The tension is further enhanced by Edwards's clever use of the long take, which prolongs the suspense.

Suddenly, the lights are thrown on and "Surprise!" Dozens of George's friends pop out of the furniture. Edwards has blindsided us with an abrupt shift in tone, one of many, that tells not just of his penchant for genre violation, but of the nature of life. "I have a feeling that maybe an audience is identifying more with a future shock kind of existence," he said, "with things that are rapidly changing—one minute you see this, the next minute you see that. We don't live in such a structured complacent kind of existence."[8] A hard cut takes us to a keyboard, rescuing us, in a sense, from the noise and commotion of the previous shot, and changing tone yet again. Tension is released, Sam Taylor (Julie Andrews) sings beautifully about how "love will chase the shadows away," and the camera drifts gently around the piano to reveal George beside her at the keyboard. Light is everywhere, but a moment later, it's gone: "How do you feel about forty-two?" George asks Sam. (The party has died down. They're sitting alone before the fireplace in a two-shot overwhelmed by darkness.) Sam is lit in a bold orange-yellow light that visually links her to the fireplace, but George on the other hand is nearly obliterated in shadow. Before we know anything about them, Edwards has, with strong, expressive lighting choices, alerted us to a discrepancy in their relationship. "Forty-two what?" she asks him. "You know, years," he mumbles. The entire scene is shot from this angle. Framing doesn't change. Neither actor moves. The effect is one of stifling immobility. George and Sam are stuck, and so George, quite tellingly, flees.

He leaps out of the frame and into the next shot, another static two-shot framed identically to its predecessor. The only difference is this time it is Hugh (Robert Webber) who is framed camera right, where Sam was in the shot before. With this visual analogy, Edwards has established a comparison between George's romantic partner and his professional partner. The shot also introduces what will be a recurring notion in the film (and one that appears throughout Blake Edwards' films), that is, the idea of the bar as a site of male interaction. But exactly what sort of interaction is this? George slides his wineglass over to the bartender. "Could I have some more white wine, Bacchus, my dear?" he asks. Moore's reading on this line is decidedly gay, not to mention the line itself with its hedonistic Greek god and femme "my dear." At first, it seems a strange choice, but as the dialogue progresses we sense that Hugh may be a homosexual himself (a suspicion confirmed in the following scene). Within this context, one might read this playacting literally; George is exploring, if only through a joke, an alternative to his life of heterosexuality (which we saw depicted just moments ago). Thus, the compositional echo between Sam's shot and Hugh's shot signifies a deeper, yet-to-be-realized anxiety in George's character.

A cut takes us to the beach. Larry, a good-looking younger man (Walter George Alton), runs along the shore and stops to chat with an attractive

Malibu-looking couple. Inside at the piano, George, shot from behind a window, steals a glance at them and then turns away. More than simply underlining the theme of voyeurism, the glass divides the young people from the aging man. But because they are reflected in the glass on the same plane as George, the youth-trio appears to be right in front of his face—Edwards' framing is particularly playful here—giving the impression that although George is looking away, he is staring right at them (as if they were on the sheet-music stand he's reading from). Of course, literally speaking, George is inside playing his piano, but in his mind, we know he is out on the beach, and younger than forty-two. Compositionally, we have separateness and the dream of sameness coexisting within the shot. Ideologically, the image presents the reality of age and the wish for youth.

Following a brief professional exchange between George and Hugh (composer and lyricist, respectively)—an exchange that invokes the idea of partnership in its many forms—George gets up from the piano and crosses to the bar (the theme is recapitulated), where he is witness to Hugh's difficulties with Larry (another variation on partnership, this one homosexual)—and then leaves the house. George gets into his Cream Corniche and slips a tape in the tape deck. We then hear Sam singing on the soundtrack; the song is "He Pleases Me," by Mancini and Wells. *He's no more than a man*, she sings. *He's a child to be sure, at times insecure / But he pleases me.* What we see are shots of George ogling younger couples through his windshield and rearview mirror (there's that glass again). Slowing to a stop sign, George casually looks into the car beside him. The significance of the moment is accentuated by an exchange of crosscut point-of-view shots, the first series of its kind in the film. No longer are we simply watching George watch, we are literally seeing what George is seeing: a beautiful young bride (Bo Derek) in the back of her car. Music swells. She turns to look back at George. Her look is vacant. Or is it sad? Doesn't she want to be getting married? Or is she, like George, unprepared for a life of committed monogamy? (Sam sings, as if she were watching, *Why is it I never doubt him / When I've known all along.*) And, as the bride's car pulls off, we cut wide to George's car and zoom in to a close-up on his face. As the first zoom in the film, this maneuver is startling. But it has a purpose: it is in this shot that George decides, for the first time, to turn his benign voyeurism into action. (Cue Sam: *Now and then the very best of men must roam*). George follows the bride's car.

What ensues is a low-speed chase through Beverly Hills. Her car slows in front of the church, George pulls around it, and *bam!*—he smashes head-on into a police car. It's the first splurch in 10, and not only does it blindside tone (the contemplative musical interlude becomes physical comedy), it links George's dilemma—in this case, the problem of mis-directed sexual desire—to the world of slapstick comedy. The splurch owes its effectiveness to excellent camera operating, which limits (and maintains!) the frame to the tip of George's hood ornament from the time the car rounds the corner to the moment of impact (we don't see it coming —the very definition of blindsiding).

From here on in, the greater George's transgression, the harder he will fall. The timing of the splurch, in other words, is syncopated with George's gaze, which is the locus of his desire. In this way, we might regard 10 as a film about a man whose quest for young flesh gradually divests him of his physical control. And as his body goes, his character will alter, and in turn, so will the story. This is a perfect example of dramatic splurching, and in 10, which picks up where The Party left off, it will become the primary drama-turgical component of the film. (Remove a splurch from 10 and the story makes no sense.)

With this in mind, we can understand the car splurch as the motivating force behind George's decision to sneak into the church. After the crash, he curbs the car (he has to: the motor sounds horrible), and from there, tiptoes into the wedding, Clouseau-like, leaving a brightly lit exterior behind for the pallid, underexposed interior of the church, as though it were an institution still stuck in the dark ages, considerably bleaker than the world outside. Cutting to the bride and groom, we see the lighting changes dramatically once again. George lurks in the darkness behind a white bouquet and watches. The priest asks the question. George, rapt, peers over his glasses (again the gaze) to stare at the bride, Jennifer, who herself has commanded the gaze of an entire audience. He waits for the response. Just then, a bee climbs out of the bouquet and up his nose—we cut from an extreme close-up of George's nose to an extreme wide shot of the as-sembly—and George knocks over the flowers and runs screaming out of the church. The instantaneous juxtaposition of spaces (close to wide) doubles the effect of the joke, making a private moment public, and also has the effect of completely losing George in the space. In typical Edwar-dian fashion, the frame has diminished him, making George appear more foolish than ever. Thematically, the splurch reminds us of the dangers of appearance, of the little unseen bee in every pretty white flower. Like George's car accident moments before, it is paired with theme, presented in a style that maximizes the comic effect, results in a character change, and, as we will see, is necessary to motivate the events of the story.

Later that night, Sam and George are eating dinner alfresco. Neither one speaks. "Okay, what's up?" Sam asks. George mumbles some nonsense about biorhythms. "Maybe you are allergic," she says, clearing the dishes, "that bee-sting's awfully close to your frontal lobes," and steps out, leaving George alone. The sound of a neighbor's music draws George to the telescope, and he looks through (the voyeur again) to see a man playing pool with a naked, considerably younger woman. "The son of a bitch across the way has got a bigger telescope than we have," George says from bed, watching television (not Sam).

> Sam: Not *we* have, *you* have. I don't need to peek into somebody else's windows to get my jollies. You're a dirty old man, George, and so is your friend.
> George: He's not my friend.
> Sam: Well he should be. You must know him intimately by now.
> George: I don't watch him, I watch his broads. He's got a hell of a stable over there.
> Sam: Then he must be pretty good in the sack, huh?
> George: What's that got to do with it?
> Sam: Well, unless he's got some new remote-controlled screwing device, how can you keep from watching him too?
> George: I concentrate on the broads.
> Sam: But he's around, isn't he?

This dialogue suggests that Sam might have a better sense of George's homosexual curiosities then even George himself, and Edwards' framing —a fixed, medium two-shot—reinforces it quite plainly. Pairing Moore and Andrews within a single shot and at the same spatial plane, reminds us that we are looking at a heterosexual unit, whether George likes it or not. On the other hand, there are certain visual elements built into the frame that contradict their togetherness. First, and perhaps most striking, is the costuming; George is in black, Sam is in white. Additionally, the composition of the picture—both George's and Sam's heads are "boxed" by props strategically arranged above their bed—suggests a compartmentalizing distance. Like the scene in front of the fireplace, Edwards tells the story of emotional connection and disruption within a single image. A bee lurks within the flower.

Sam leaves in a huff, George gets locked out of his house (in a trademark infantilizing wide shot), and is left with nothing to console him but his not-so-big telescope. Peeping through, he spies a beautiful young redhead (real-life porn star Annette Haven) having sex with his neighbor. And then, from out of nowhere, she turns to the telescope and blows George a kiss. Suddenly we realize she's performing. A hard cut takes us to Sam in song, rehearsing for a large, exclusively male audience. This harsh juxtaposition of performers effectively situates us within George's internal debate. We wonder: whose audience does he want to be? Seeing Sam as an object of the male gaze reminds us of her desirability, and linking her with the preceding pictures of soft-core sex challenges George's perception of her as a sexless prig. What's more, the character she's rehearsing is a parody of the character Julie Andrews is playing. In Blake Edwards' world of things not being as they appear to be, it's significant, if not remarkable, that even in performance, singing "I give my heart to just one man," Sam can't help but be herself.

So what does George want if he doesn't want Sam? His neighbor's lover? The mystery woman who just got married? Or does he want some-one else's life entirely? At therapy, he sheds some light on the confusion: "I don't like middle age. I mean, it's not that complicated, I'd just rather be thirty. Or twenty even. God, you can bet your ass if, to make it, I had to change places with Larry and a life of faggotry, I'd sure as hell give it a lot of consideration." In a *Playboy* interview of 1982, Edwards confessed to having had similar thoughts, and in a similar setting:

> Many years ago, when I began analysis, the first thing I contended with was my own great fear of being a homosexual. That sort of thing is operative in everybody. It's latent and it's there, to one degree or an-other, so why not deal with it? I mean, what's so terrible? You are what you are, and if it frightens you, deal with it.[9]

It's a subject that Edwards has been dealing with (to one degree or an-other) since his earliest films, but in 10, for the first time he deals with it explicitly. That's no small feat for a mainstream Hollywood director, espe-cially considering he's addressing it from the point of view of a man who up until now has demonstrated conventional heterosexual urges. The im-plication—that human desire, like human identity, is never one thing—is an unconventional attitude to say the least, but when it is presented in a mainstream American comedy, it's downright subversive.

When George arrives at the church (the same church where the mystery woman was married), the reverend (framed ironically under a ceiling vent that suggests a makeshift halo) hurries George into his chambers (overexposed windows indicate, once again, that it's darker inside the church than out) so that he may listen to his new song. "You know, George, I'm a songwriter, too," he says, and plays "I Have an Ear for Love,"* a musical reminder that the church is not as it appears and is better suited to showbiz than Godbiz. The reverend sings *When you appear | Though we're in a typhoon | Why do I hear | Snowflakes that fall in tune?* This hat trick of aural inconsistency is right at home with 10's many tricks of appearance, and lays the philosophical groundwork for the great Mrs. Kissel sequence that follows. Beautifully timed and choreographed, this joke saves Edwards from having to make explicit either his main character's frame of mind, or the sham world he's found himself in. Old Mrs. Kissel (Nedra Volz), a gray-haired churchgoer of the hunchback variety, enters a wide shot of George and the reverend from frame right. She does her best to cross frame left, but with her old age and the weight of her tea tray, it doesn't look promising. As is typical, Edwards uses the wide-angle lens, the anamorphic frame, and the imbalanced composition to make Mrs. Kissel's journey appear to be longer and more arduous than it actually is.

The camera pans left, following George and the reverend into the sitting room, and leaving poor Mrs. Kissel in the dust. If she is to reach the coffee table, she's going to have to cross more floor than we (or she) initially thought, and not just laterally, but all the way to the back of the room where George and the reverend are seated, waiting for her to approach. Once again, we see that Edwards' visual comedy relies upon the subtle extension of physical space. As expected, the camera doesn't follow Mrs. Kissel, but maintains an apathetic distance, rendering her, as it does George for his gags, meek and defenseless. Suddenly, the silence is interrupted by Mrs. Kissel's rip-roaring fart. The dog runs out the room and the reverend delivers the immortal line, "When Mrs. Kissel breaks wind we beat the dog." For all its vulgarity, this bit of slapstick is eloquent on the point of George's emotional and ideological impasse. As a represen-

* Mancini: "There's no question about it. It is definitely the worst song I have ever written."[10]

tation of the church and its values, the Mrs. Kissel routine works like the Rolls-Royce and the bee-in-flower splurches; that is, as a warning to George. This one warns against old age and the archaic notions of marriage the church represents.

The next splurch finds George at the telescope again, where he is watching his neighbor in the midst of an all-out orgy. In his frustration, George slaps the telescope, which swings around and knocks him on the head, throwing him off balance and down the hill. We cut to an extreme wide shot of the hill (dramatic spatial change) as the figure tumbles down, lost in brush (diminishment by framing). The image, which emphasizes the great distance George has to fall, reiterates 10's slapstick equation: the greater the extramonogamous temptation, the more harmful the splurch; the more harmful the splurch, the greater its impact on the events to follow. On his way back up the hill, George hears the phone ring (it's Sam) and rushes to the house. But he's missed the call. "Hello?" There's no one there. He slams down the phone and rips it off the table, loses balance, and crashes into the pool. Here is the second of two consecutive great falls, and like the first, which splurches George's misdirected lust, this one ups the ante on his physical upheaval to make the point that to-and-froing between youth and age, bachelorhood and marriage, voyeurism and reality is an offense punishable by slapstick.

From the moment we first see George is in the dentist's office we know he's headed the wrong way. (The reverend had told George that Jennifer Miles, the mystery woman, is the daughter of a prominent Beverly Hills dentist.) Dr. Miles tells George that his daughter is honeymooning in Mexico and Edwards cuts in to George's close-up: four hands choke the frame with dental appliances. They had better remove the cavities today. The drill spins, the nurse infantilizes him (he's no more than a man), and George's face contorts. Afterwards, at the café, he's seen having a difficult time speaking, and an even more difficult time being understood. Again, George's regressive infantilization is visualized through a splurch depriving him of physical self-possession. At the booth opposite George in the café, a young girl sits reading a magazine. He smiles at her; she smiles back. Openly flirting, he sips his coffee and spills it all over his shirt. But this isn't simply a reiteration of an old theme; it's a necessary platform for the elaborate phone charade that follows.

Back home again, George gets to the phone in time, but alas, Sam doesn't recognize his voice. It's the Novocain. He rushes to the bar for a drink. Their mangled conversation is presented in crosscuts between Sam's house and George's, which Edwards differentiates through the contrast of light and dark spaces. Her frame is filled with color; a striking blue sweater, a yellow pillow, and a pair of red roses, but George's space is the exact opposite; black and brown, with the only flash of light in the frame aimed at the phone, Sam's stand-in. Fed up with George, Sam runs out of her house, calling to her son from the stairs, "Josh, do your homework!" "I've already done it," he drones. The proximity of Josh and George suggests Sam has two children to manage, a son and a boyfriend, but a grown man is missing from the equation. It's worth noting, too, that the phone farce, a common device in Edwards, is, like the telescope, conducive to the misrepresentations and misperceptions that perpetuate the splurch. Moreover, it's part of a clearly motivated slapstick chain reaction: though they are separated by time, the dentist sequence, the coffee sequence, and the phone call are bound by the cause and effect of George's desire; they therefore have a direct effect on his behavior, which in turn influences the events of the narrative. It's dramaturgically sophisticated gag work, and it escalates with the telescope (what else?), through which George can see that his neighbor's sex party has reached new heights. He's in wide shot, visually vulnerable, and as the police creep in around his house, legally vulnerable, too. The cops, he realizes, think he's an intruder in his own house. "That's ridiculous, I'm George Webber!" But of course, they can't understand him. And they're right not to. Now that his obsessions have transformed him, George is not George.

Mistaken identities are no mistake in the Blake Edwards movie, and the present madman is no exception. Appearance and reality are at odds once again and must be resolved before truth is reinstated. Then again, perhaps the present incarnation of George is the true George, and the piano-playing sophisticate was just a civilizing ruse. Who's wearing the mask, we might ask, the adolescent or the adult? With the farce of bad timing and misperception in effect—George's and Sam's cars pass on Mulholland—it will be difficult to distinguish one from the other. In the meantime, an inebriated George drives along in a hot, youthful speedster (remember, his Rolls is busted), and pulls up in front of the orgy house (we hear the music coming from within. Mancini's funk parody "Get It On" throbs from inside the house.* The song is so inane that if he were to be restored

---

* "Get it on, get it on, get it on, baby." Repeat. That's the whole song.

to his senses, George Webber, a member of ASCAP, would surely be made sick by it.) Inside, George finds everything he has lusted after: indiscriminate free love with young people of both sexes, and not a drop of monogamy in sight. That is, until he and Sam casually spy each other through facing telescopes.

It is significant that this moment of discovery for Sam and George occurs via telescope, where the act of looking has peaked, and turning upon itself has doubled the perils of misconception. What Sam sees is the boy George has become, not the man he can be; what George sees is the woman he fears, not the woman he loves. Ultimately, neither sees the other for who they are, and when their cars pass each other once again, it seems inevitable that problems of appearance have taken the farce past the point of reconciliation.

George heads for Mexico.

On the plane, he's still drinking. (Alcohol, as we have seen, maintains the relationship between sexual misdirection and physical disability.) From the plane, we cut to Sam in her room. By her bed is a framed picture of her son. But shouldn't it be George? This uncomfortable confusion of man and boy further reinstates her predicament. She picks up a phone and calls George. (The phone, a self-consciously old model, denotes Sam's old-fashioned sensibility, hinting out her outdated feelings toward matrimony.) Meanwhile, in the back of a Mexican taxi, George's body is thrown from side to side. The cab pulls into an extreme wide shot at the hotel entrance. One again, space—and more specifically, distance—is going to be a problem. George falls out of the car, trips over a step, hits a glass door, and stumbles up to registration. The desk clerk hands him a pen he can barely hold and he falls over. It takes the assistant manager to physically carry him into the next shot, another deep-space glimpse into what awaits George. A waiter brings George an extravagant welcome cocktail, which he takes on the golf cart that nearly crashes on its way to his room. (More drinking, more space to traverse.) From these images, Mexico looks less like George's fantasy and more like his personal torture chamber.

This paradise may appear desirable, but in fact it's full of visual treachery. The assistant manager opens the door to the hotel room, and we see that George has fallen asleep standing up. As he is helped inside, we see a room drenched in foreboding; from the bars on the duvet to the grillwork on the windows, the iconography is more suggestive of a prison than a hotel. Vaulted arches and Corinthian columns enhance the feeling of ancient space, as do the primitive idols lodged in little enclaves in the wall. But shouldn't this space be bright? Absolutely not: Taking the church's aesthetic and applying it to Mexico, the site of sexual abandon, Edwards is suggesting that though he may not realize it, George's flight from Sam is not about to lead him into the light, but keep him in the dark.

A hard cut takes us to the beach. A woman frame right, and a fisherman frame left. As the fisherman approaches the shore, we see that it's Hugh. We aren't in Mexico, we're in Malibu, yet another of Blake Edwards' carefully designed illusions. Expecting to see George, we are disappointed—and this is precisely what the scene will be about. A cut places us in a two-shot of Hugh and Sam, the telephoto lens compressing the space between them, which in graphic (and emotional) terms brings them closer together (George and Sam have never been shot this way). "He's more trouble than any man I've ever known," she confides, calling George "exhaustingly childish." To illustrate the point, Edwards cuts to George struggling to negotiate a hanging bridge on his way to the bar. To our surprise, he arrives intact, and, sliding up to Don, the barman (Brian Dennehy), places his order. A piano tinkles in the background.

After George's unsuccessful attempt at apologizing to Sam (on the phone, of course), the pianist plays "Laura" while he and Don listen in reverent silence. The song evokes another tale of sexual obsession. In it, the sophisticated older man falls for the younger girl he can't have. Laura, like Jennifer, is "only a dream," full of deceit, and for the men who watch her, the ultimate illusion. "They don't write music like that anymore," George says. "Each of us is a product of an era. That music is my era." The song ignites the composer in George. He is becoming himself again, but this time, with an appreciation for the glory of the old (see the epigraph to this chapter). "You know something," Don says, "I like your songs." A musical relationship has emerged, and unlike his partnership with Hugh, George's association with Don is free of sexual inadequacy. Without the corrupting force of youth (in Hugh's case, Larry), George can cultivate a successful male friendship, and resolve the "problem" of his latent homosexuality.

His manhood, though, is still in question. From the bar, George goes home with Mary Lewis (Dee Wallace) who has recognized George from one of Truman Capote's parties (what kind of evening was that?). Back at George's room, their kiss turns into a pratfall off the balustrade (the splurch is infidelity to Sam), and rather than show us what follows, Edwards defies our voyeuristic curiosities with a cut to a thatched window. The image is restrictive and fatalistic, and sets the mood for the upcoming exchange. A pan right delivers us through a few moments of dark, empty space, ending on a postcoital close-up of Mary Lewis, framed left of center, in a composition that underscores her emotional isolation. "George?" she asks. "Is it me?" From offscreen, we hear "No." (Now we understand that what looked like postcoital wasn't really; another visual trick.) It appears that George's manhood is so deeply threatened he isn't even worthy of being in the shot. Spatially, Edwards has, one again, reduced George to the margins. But this time it isn't as a gag. "Some of us don't bring out the man in men," Mary says.

The following sequence invokes the same theme, and is set, quite naturally, where the distinction between males and men is acutely evident: at the beach. George is introduced into the scene long after it begins, effectively compromising his dramatic value. Likewise, his entrance is presented in one of Edwards' multipurpose wide shots, which does the double-duty of graphically trivializing George while making his trek across the hot sand seem even longer. Despite the heat, he's dressed in sweatpants and a sweatshirt, a costume that, in revealing none of his skin, reveals all his insecurities. Those insecurities are confirmed both by the towel gag (sliding across the hot sand on yellow towels) and by the fact that he needs to piggyback on a waiter to get into the water. Both are assaults to his body, which since last night with Mary has continued to splurch him. Moments later George is wading in the sea, sandwiched by two extremes of ridiculous manhood. To his left, a man wearing a T-shirt with a cat on it; to his right, a former marine who "refuses to be carried." All three are exposed when Edwards cuts to the wide shot to show a young surfer riding out into the ocean (this "real" man, as we will discover later, is Jennifer's husband).

In the following sequence, George's crisis of masculinity takes the form of a crisis of voyeurism. His hungry gaze upon Jennifer's body is interrupted the moment she opens her eyes at him. George looks away, ashamed. For the first time, the act of watching is unavailable to him, and robbed of his "telescope," he alters his fantasy. He can't look out, so now he looks in to watch a fantasy play out before his mind's eye. We watch what he's imagining: he and Jennifer kissing in the waves à la *From Here to Eternity*. The explicit film reference enhances the notion of scopophilia (we *watch* movies), and more specifically, the conventional notions of manhood at play in the picture itself. The fantasy, although tender, is subject to Edwards' gentle condescension; the slow motion effectively parodies the sentiment. The same can be said for the film's most iconic moment. In it, we see Jennifer running down the beach in slow motion. She is moving towards the camera, the ocean water glittering at her back. The reverse shot of George is almost an exact match—*almost*. He's running down the beach, but the sand looks drier, the surf is intermittent, and the light is flatter than it is in her shot (also, he's wearing a sweat suit, not a bathing suit). What's more, the telephoto lens, having compressed space, creates the illusion of stationary movement, as if these characters were running along a treadmill. George runs, and runs, and runs, but for what? The shot indicates that he's not going anywhere. Into their close-ups, the cutting tempo increases, the music crescendos (still the parody of a love scene), and yet, neither figure is ever in the same shot. Crosscutting gives the illusion of unity, but it fact, George and Jennifer could be on different beaches entirely. There's a fly in the ointment (but what an ointment!).

It appears that the fantasy sequence ends when the score drops out and we cut back to George sitting on the shore. But it only *appears* that way. The shot that follows—Jennifer running towards the camera, ocean shimmering behind her—is so similar to her shot in the fantasy, we might wonder if George's subjectivity has washed into reality. The following cues indicate as much: Jennifer runs into a low angle, and with little bits of flare dancing around her head, is framed against the sky like one of Riefenstahl's Olympians. She's bigger than life, maybe even more than a 10. (Back in his therapist's office, George called her an 11. "You said there was no such thing as a 10," his analyst reminds him. Edwards' camera is with the shrink.) Either way, the difference between what's "real" and what isn't has ceased to matter. The point is they have been confused by George's false fantasy of manhood, and in the following sequence the fantasy is perpetuated. After the "Riefenstahl" shot, the camera continues with Jennifer, following her back down to her beach towel. As we pan down, we see that George is missing from his spot behind her. Nondiegetic "rescue music" swells, and from out of nowhere, George is sailing a rescue boat out in the ocean. Huh? Where did he find the boat? How did he get so far out to sea? The temporal and dramatic improbability of the scene that follows—watching George save Jennifer's husband—not to mention the shark fin(!) chasing after them (there's even a bit of *Jaws* in the score), makes the whole thing look ridiculous. But it is explicitly ridiculous, and made so by an abrupt shift in genre (of course, typical of Edwards) that speaks not only to the problems of perception (ours as an audience; George's as a man) but, for the first time in the film, proffers George a physical dominion that runs contrary to the splurch.

The absurdity of it registers on Hugh and Larry's faces as they watch George the hero on TV. Now, for the first time, George has become the object of the gaze. His newfound "masculinity" has placed him on the other side of the telescope. "I've gotta call Sam," Larry says, reaching for the phone. Of course, as a token of voyeurism (and therefore false perception), the television undermines the authenticity of George's conversion to manhood. As we have observed, the gaze betrays, and in this case it betrays Hugh and Larry. We cut to their point-of-view shot—a close-up of the television—and pan left to a shot of Sam watching from her bed. We're surprised to find ourselves in a new location. It's a little Edwardian sleight of hand, pairing visual illusion with philosophical misperception.

Back at the bar, Don toasts George. "To your very good health." Clink. But the bar is dark, empty, and silent. Where is the conqueror's celebration? Where are the spoils of masculinity? George crosses to the piano and speaks into a tape recorder, "This is a new one, Hugh." What follows is a musical interlude as sad, as personal, and as moving as any moment in the whole of Hollywood comedy. Fantasy has failed, and for the first time in the picture, George Webber is stripped of self-denial. Had he continued to operate under false pretenses, it would be the perfect time to splurch him, but he is utterly authentic here, and gives Edwards nothing to take down with slapstick. Childish pretensions of masculinity have finally been cast aside, and in their place blossoms the true manhood that can only come with the sadness and wisdom of forty-two years of life. George's musical soliloquy indicates as much: as a proclamation of self it's pure, but poignantly, his playing is formless. Like him, it has no shape or direction (when he is seen playing with Sam later in the film he will find melody again), and fittingly Blake cuts back to the old fantasy of Jennifer running down that beach. Perhaps George isn't as strong as we thought; perhaps he's headed for infidelity, and Blake nailed it when he said that great comedy is based on human frailty.[11]

In no time, George is at Jennifer's doorstep, and from the moment he steps into the room, Edwards makes clear the insurmountable distance between them. For one, his glimpse of Jennifer's reflection in her puny bathroom mirror reinstates his voyeuristic impulse; and for another, the great, imposing formal composition that frames their discussion in the sitting room lends the scene its staid, unnatural quality, with a rigorous symmetry that underscores George's uneasiness. That Edwards has resisted the opportunity to splurch George here, at a juncture rife with slapstick potential, is all the proof we need of his conversion. This is a picture of a man with a firm grip on his reality.

But not for long. George and Jennifer move on to an intimate dinner, dance, and then return to her room for some music. Her choice surprises the middle-aged man. "I don't know why," he says, "but I wasn't expecting Prokofiev." She hands him a joint. "Did you ever do it to Ravel's Boléro?" Boléro? This free-lovin' hippie is into orchestral music? If so, George has misjudged his fantasy; from the way things are going, it looks like this 10 for looks might rank a 42 for age. Once again, George's desire ignites, but this time—for the first time—it isn't because of how she looks, it's about who she is. There is nothing to splurch, George's lust for surfaces is gone, and suddenly they're in bed. But the record stops.

"Start it again," she says.

"What?"

"The music. It's better if you start right at the beginning. Please?"

George leaps out of bed—"Hurry," she says—and he runs to the record player. As the lovemaking proceeds, we might begin to notice that the splurch is being gradually reintroduced; Jennifer pulls his hair (ow), gets on top of him (oh), and drags her cornrows across his mouth (ew). But if George has resolved the illusion problem, why is Edwards doing this to him? The answer is on its way.

The phone rings: it's Jennifer's husband. The shot is wide, enveloped in darkness. While a lighting scheme of this kind could be used to establish intimacy, in this case it all but obliterates its subjects. In fact, the real subject of the image is blackness itself, which in Edwardian terms connotes the blackness of blindness. As if on cue, the splurch returns: Jennifer goes over to the record player and restarts Boléro (for the third time) and George knocks himself on the headboard. He's clearly bothered about the phone call. "What the hell did you get married for?" he asks. As George is discovering, free love and romance can't mix, and sex, though it might appear otherwise, goes deeper than voyeurism. "I thought maybe you thought that I was something more than just a casual lay," George says. "Why did you think that?" Jennifer replies. The tables have turned—another trompe l'oeil—and George Webber, the great objectifier, has at last been objectified. He is within her gaze, and he doesn't like it. Their in-bed debate recalls the argument George and Sam had in their own bed just days before, and the silent contrast between them motivates the action our soon-to-be hero is preparing to take.

"I don't think I really have a problem, George."

"That's your problem," he says, and gets out of bed.

A dramatic upsurge of violins takes us from Jennifer to Sam. She's singing before a packed audience, fitted from wig to corset in eighteenth-century costume. The lyric, "I Give My Heart Just to One Man" reminds us that even when she's on stage, Sam is most decisively speaking for herself. Though she is performing, there is no transformation, no discrepancy between appearance and reality. In fact, the stage enhances her true self, proudly declaring her age (this time as a character over three centuries old) and her unabashed, albeit traditional (there's age again) commitment to one lover. But the number is incomplete; Edwards gives us just the end. In fact, since the very first time they sat down together at the piano, George and Sam's musical interludes have been fractured. Either they have been cut short or prematurely abandoned. The only musical sequence Edwards has presented in its entirety is George's piano solo, but even that, from the songwriter's point of view, was deficient. What they need, Edwards is seeming to indicate, is completion not just in each other, but in song, and considering George is the composer and Sam is the singer, it is only logical that they should find that resolution together—which is where the film began and indeed will end.

George heads to Sam's and asks her to dinner. "Your phone's been busy all day," he says. At last, George has cast off the faulty interlocutor, made misperception impossible, and replaced it with person-to-person contact. Now farce is no longer a contender. However, Sam declines George's invitation. Instead, George calls Hugh. They talk *on the phone*, a significant detail suggesting that this relationship is not only repaired, but relieved of homosexual dilemma. Now all is right: whereas the film began with George and Hugh together and George and Sam on the phone, it has ended with George and Hugh on the phone and George and Sam . . . together?

George is at the piano now, alone. Without Sam's vocal accompaniment, the composer is forced to do the singing. *It's easy to say it's over*, he begins. *It's easy to say we're the best of friends.* Clearly, he's singing about the end of a romance, and then, Sam walks in the door, our expectations are reversed, and Blake wins the hand again. She sits down next to him and the camera glides from the far end of the piano to a tightly framed two-shot of the reconciled lovers. This movement is the *exact opposite* of the camera movement that introduced us to Sam and George nearly two hours of screen time ago. But instead of starting at the keyboard and drifting away, the shot starts away, drifts around the piano, and ends at the keyboard (George and Sam have returned to music, not pulled away from it). Edwards has encased his story in two sibling shots which, like bookends, hold between them an entire shelf's worth of material on the hilarity and sadness of getting older. They sing together: *You could search the years away / That old cliché is the first of May / To old or new love / It's easy to say, as easy as ABC / I love you, love you, love you.* George jokes that he was going to call the song "I Love You, Samantha," but "some hack" got there first. The hack he is referring to is none other than Cole Porter, and the song, written for *High Society* (another story of matrimonial jitters), suits the moment perfectly. It tells of pure, monogamous devotion: *I love you, Samantha / And my love with never die / Remember, Samantha / I'm a one-gal guy.*

But neither is ready for marriage. At George's proposal, Sam lovingly declines. She goes the kitchen and we cut to the point of view of George's neighbor's telescope. Through the peephole—the image literally reduced to a circle in the center of the frame—we watch George get up from the piano and step out of the shot. He has put on *Boléro.* All seems well, save for the music, which reminds us of George's secret (Sam knows nothing of Jennifer), a past that may be read as a hint of infidelities to come. Or does the inclusion of Jennifer's "presence" in this new monogamy indicate that George has successfully incorporated youth into age? A facile filmmaker might have resolved George's ideological crisis with a sweeping dismissal of youthful inhibition, or even heralded his acceptance of middle-agedom and monogamy with unequivocal clarity. But Blake Edwards does neither. Instead, he turns up the ambiguity by playing out the scene through the telescopic iris. The voyeur's point of view certainly sexualizes Sam and George, which seems to resolve an important question in their narrative, but like everything else on the other side of the lens, it's prone to misrepresentation. So what is it misrepresenting? At the close of an entire feature spent watching watchers, the answer to that question is finally up to us; after all, now we're the ones looking through. And like that, 10 ends where it began: in the dark.

The film garnered almost unanimous praise. Andrew Sarris called it "a brilliant and ultimately poignant sex farce with more out-and-out belly laughs than any movie in years. Edwards has justified the faith invested in him for twenty years by diehard Edwardians like myself,"* adding, "a vintage Hollywood director has brilliantly demonstrated that the American cinema can be as 'personal' as any."[12] The film was a hit, one the biggest of the year, and secured Orion's place as one of the strongest new production houses around. Riding high on his new success, Edwards requested that Orion temporarily postpone *The Ferret* and allow him to begin production on S.O.B., his seditious fable of Hollywood hell. Amazingly, Blake was given studio approval and preproduction began on his most personal film to date.

But they are not long, the days of wine and roses. Once Orion got wind of the picture's soaring budget, they pulled the plug, and abruptly canceled their deal with Edwards. Blake was crushed, but he would not let himself forget what the comic Mort Sahl once said to him: survival is the best revenge. And from that point on, he adopted it as his motto. Blake's producer Tony Adams once observed, "Blake has said that Clouseau subscribed to the 11th commandment: Thou shalt not give up. That's pure Blake. He never gives up."[13] "S.O.B., I'm going to do," he said to Lehman and Luhr. "I just *am* going to do it because when you see 10, you will see that it is my statement more than anything I've done before and S.O.B. is just the next step. And I am going to do it one way or the other."[14]

* Sarris recalibrates after *Blind Date* in 1987. (See his article "The Bitter Essence of Blake Edwards," *Village Voice*, May 5, 1987.)

S.O.B. (1981)

Ben: It's all bullshit.

There was a time when Blake Edwards was Hollywood's favorite director. It once seemed that there was no genre beyond his mastery and no investment he left unreturned. Studios loved him, Godard loved him, and Julie Andrews loved him.

To Paramount executives in search of the next *Sound of Music*, pouring money into his *Darling Lili* seemed like the perfect way to keep old Hollywood bankable, and so they set Blake up with just about everything the director of a World War I spy-musical-comedy-melodrama could want, from period Studebakers to authentic aircraft on loan from the Royal Air Force, and of course, Hermes Pan. It was expensive, but it was movies.

Cut to months later. When chronic bad weather put a halt on production, Paramount found itself pouring more and more money into *Lili* just to keep her afloat. Thankfully, Commonwealth United Corporation came to the rescue in 1969, and loaned Paramount's parent Gulf + Western a certain humungous sum it was later revealed they were unable to make good on. That's when the ulcer began to hemorrhage. Debt piled up, and it seemed even if the movie was a hit the studio would have a difficult time rebuilding itself. But the movie wasn't a hit. In fact, the movie flat-out bombed, Paramount was nearly destroyed, and Blake was blamed for the whole thing. The scapegoating was merciless; he received one of the most hideous professional, artistic, and personal denigrations in the studio's history. Bob Evans said Blake was responsible for "the most flagrant misappropriation of funds I've seen in my career," the critics were abrupt, and the fans were downright angry. How could he allow Julie Andrews to do a burlesque? A burlesque. *Julie Andrews*. How could he do it? It was like watching your mother lap dancing.

But it gets worse.

Hoping to start fresh, Edwards struck a new deal at MGM, and began work on *Wild Rovers*, a dark and mournful Western he believed was his best film to date. His best, that is, until it was mutilated by studio chief James Aubrey, a.k.a. "Jungle Jim," a.k.a. "the Smiling Cobra." The reptile ripped nearly forty minutes from the picture (more showtimes that way), but it didn't matter (the picture flopped), and for a moment it seemed Blake would leave Hollywood for good. But the Cobra turned on the charm, and with a flash of its scales lured Blake back to work on The Carey Treatment, consenting to a completely laissez-faire (fingers crossed) production. By the time Blake realized he had been tricked, it was too late. From the very beginning, Aubrey was haunting the production through two-faced producers he used as informants, and rogue editors hell-bent on cutting happiness into a movie that was supposed to be about rape, drugs, and murder. Blake tried to get his name taken off the picture, but he failed. He claims never to have ever seen a full cut.

It gets worse. (Have we broken the pain barrier yet, Leo McCarey?)

He sank into a depression so deep, it seemed he'd never recover. His Hollywood, the town that raised him a third generation filmmaker, was now out to eradicate him. "The need for a scapegoat in reverse," he said, "is more important to them then either the commercial or artistic wisdom of a particular course."[15] S.O.B.s always ran Hollywood, but now they were destroying it.

Broken, Blake moved to Switzerland. He planned never to direct again.

The years to follow consisted mostly of cinematic wound licking; he wrote and wrote, and at Julie's insistence, returned to directing, though sadly, The Tamarind Seed was a Wiffle ball in the wind, and Panthers three, four, and five were at best inconsistent. But Clouseau padded the Swiss account quite nicely, and in time Blake was ready to take another stab at Hollywood. To Orion Pictures, a newly formed production outfit, the box office streak he recovered with the Panthers was reason enough to take a risk on 10. They were young, he was getting old, but to everyone's shock and delight, the $30 million comedy went on to gross over $300 million. Blake was back.

He happily agreed to reteam with Orion on The Ferret with the understanding that they would finance his dream movie, the project nearly every studio deemed too dirty to touch: Hollywood S.O.B. By that time, the script was something of a secret legend around town, and rumors about its real-life counterparts flew from commissary to overpriced commissary. But no one wanted it—and why should they? Who wants to see a movie about why Blake Edwards hates Hollywood? (Furthermore, who wants to finance it?) Orion jumped in headfirst—the impossible, it seemed, was about to happen—but disputes over budgetary costs on The Ferret precipitated an about face, and Edwards found himself spurned again. Pre-production stopped dead in its tracks, and both pictures were given the boot.

Fortunately, when Orion dropped the ball, a move Edwards called "unconscionable, immoral and unethical,"[16] Lorimar was right there to pick it up again, and signed Edwards to a three-picture deal that included, after S.O.B., a sci-fi comedy/drama called *Far Out*, and the upcoming *Victor/Victoria*. Eager to make the transition to features, the television production company approved the film's $12 million budget, and granted Blake total artistic supremacy, meanwhile ending their distribution deal with United Artists in favor of a new agreement at—of all ridiculous ironies—Paramount, one of the studios S.O.B. was indicting.

At 7:45 A.M. on March 20, 1980, after eleven years of delays, Blake completed the first shot of S.O.B. A bottle of Dom Perignon was popped, and on the beaches of Paradise Cove, cast and crew raised their glasses to a director on the verge of vengeance. The toast occurred at the foot of the $500,000 beach house the production had been granted special permission to build, and for a rare moment, everyone forgot that it would be torn down after filming. Present were some of Blake's most loyal collaborators, from Bill Holden to Craig Stevens of *Peter Gunn* and *Gunn* to cinematographer Harry Stradling, and a reunion of other company players who had each been a part of Edwards' longstanding battle with Hollywood, some since the very beginning. And they all had a part in the movie.

Here's what it's about: Hollywood producer Felix Farmer (Richard Mulligan) is having the worst day of his life. His movie *Night Wind* bombed, his wife left him, and he can't even manage to kill himself. In a flash of insane inspiration, he gets the idea to recut his picture into a porno starring his wife, Sally Miles (Julie Andrews), American's G-rated sweetheart. To do so, Felix buys back the film from the studio, and convinces Sally it's in her best interest to show her boobies on film ("Felix, darling, some of her fans still think she doesn't go to the bathroom"). It looks like Farmer's about to get away with the whole thing when the executives nail him on a loophole and steal the film away from him. That's when Felix really goes really crazy and tries to kidnap his negative, but is stopped dead by a bullet. Hollywood memorializes him with a phony funeral, but his best friends—the people who really love him—do him the honor of burning his corpse off the shores of Marina del Rey.

The pain begins after the film's opening scene—a musical parody in the early Andrews style—when we cut to a Malibu shoreline to watch an expository paragraph scroll up the screen. It reads:

Once upon a time in a wonderful land called Hollywood there lived a very successful motion picture producer named Felix Farmer. He owned three beautiful houses, he had two lovely children, and was married to a gorgeous movie star. The people who ran the studio where he worked loved and admired him because he had never made a movie that had lost money. Then one day he produced the biggest most expensive motion picture of his career and it flopped. The people who ran the studio were very angry at Felix because they lost millions of dollars. And Felix lost his mind.

If it wasn't clear from the film's opening number, its autobiographical agenda is now officially stated, but not just to those who know something about Edwards' personal life or the events leading up to S.O.B.'s production, but to everyone watching. Anyone who can appreciate the implications of a filmmaker making a film about a filmmaker will begin asking themselves the question Blake's characters have been considering since his earliest films: How much of this is true? Or, in Edwardspeak: is this real or bullshit?

Indeed Blake Edwards is no stranger to the filmed memoir. Throughout his career, he has produced autobiographical movies of all genres, and with varying degrees of explicit self-reference. These can be traced back as far as *Days of Wine and Roses*, and include works as ostensibly preposterous as *The Great Race* and *The Party*, neither of which is without traces of Blake's autobiographical inclinations. Of course, it goes without saying that no work is exempt from the intimate influences of its creator, but when it comes to films like *10* and S.O.B., those influences assume unequivocal significance. In the case of the former, one need only be familiar with the most basic fact of Edwards' home life—specifically, his marriage to Julie Andrews—to wonder if her characterization of Sam has any relation to offscreen reality. The same can be said of nearly every Edwards/Andrews collaboration (culminating, as we will see, in *That's Life!*), but what makes S.O.B. distinctive amongst the Edwards/Andrews partnerships is that its commitment to the dramatization of the filmmaker/actress relationship— and by extension, the perils of depiction—plays directly into the director's lifelong examination of objects and their reflections.

On the one hand, we have Mr.and Mrs. Edwards, on the other, their film likenesses. But S.O.B. ups the ante by adding a third level of (mis)reading; Julie Andrews is remade as Sally Miles, America's Sweetheart, whom

Felix Farmer (remade from Blake Edwards) remakes into Sally Miles, star of soft-core porn. "I've always been interested in the roles we play," said Edwards to an interviewer. "The different people we are essentially. As we sit and talk here now, we're both different people from when we get up and go talk to so-and-so over there."[17] Naturally, between Sally's personae, there is a great cleavage (innuendo intended) that tells of Hollywood's funniest and most tragic problem: bullshit.

S.O.B., or Standard Operational Bullshit, is the primary thematic and stylistic determinant of the film. Thematically, bullshit is self-evident throughout the picture. With the exception of Felix, every character and every scene is perpetually involved in matters of misrepresentation, but for the studio players, figures like David Blackman (Robert Vaughn) and Eva Brown (Shelley Winters), misrepresentation takes the form of willful deceit. Simply put, they are all liars, with the primary difference being that suits use lies to destroy while Felix and his cronies use lies to survive. Tim Culley (William Holden), despite his maturity, seems to be living the life of a teenager; Dr. Irving Feingarten (Robert Preston) is happier as his own patient; and Ben Coogan (Robert Webber) is a nervous P.R. man, trying his best to keep anxiety from blowing his cover. As in *The Party*, authenticity is at the mercy of phoniness, and show business is only the business of *show*.

Remarkably, S.O.B. finds an aesthetic for bullshit. Beginning with the first scene, a number that makes *Mary Poppins* look like *Caligula*, S.O.B. *visually* represses physical urges. The nursery room setting undermines the inherent eroticism of the bursting canon and out-popping jack-in-the-box and Julie's song, "Polly Wolly Doodle," regresses her to presexual infancy. This is the bullshit of asexuality, and it contradicts the truth of the offscreen identities of both Julie Andrews and her fictional alter ego, Sally Miles. Genre-wise, this opening number plays a similar role, using the time-tested film-within-a-film device to trick us into believing that S.O.B. is going to be something that it isn't.

If sexuality is visually repressed in S.O.B., then so is the body's second favorite impulse—death. So miserable is Felix Farmer over *Night Wind*'s B.O. disaster that he decides to kill himself, sampling the whole buffet of do-it-yourself dying from hanging to asphyxiation, but all with the same unfortunate result: survival. Farmer's aborted suicides are conveyed through Edwards' aesthetic of bullshit by which spatial repression—the actual subordination of Felix's body within the frame—reflects the diegetic urge to deny Farmer his emotional authenticity. In his first suicide attempt,

Felix shuffles into the garage, gets in the Cadillac, closes the garage door, turns on the engine, and waits. Here, his body is contained within two dark spaces—the garage and the car—removed from the public eye, and almost entirely at rest. Felix tries to kill himself again—a few more times, actually—once, by putting his head in the oven (containment), and again, by putting a gun to his head, which is, expectedly, hidden under a sheet. Each failed suicide indicates the same thing: Felix's pain, his interior impulse, is visually denied in the world of the film, evincing that in S.O.B., graphic and emotional containment are of a piece. Thus the aesthetic of bullshit.

When Culley, Irving, and Ben arrive, they hide Felix in the upstairs bedroom. Significantly, none of them seem to take any interest in their friend's emotional troubles, only in his physical whereabouts. Protecting him requires that they protect his body, through not from physical harm, but from public perception (in Edwards, perception is the most bullshit thing of all). Whether it's keeping Felix upstairs, or injecting sedatives into his body, their goal is to keep up the bullshit image of his sanity and the way they do it is by keeping him hidden. Even in terms of narrative and dialogue, Felix is contained. For the first act of S.O.B.—the section we might call "The Reign of Bullshit"—Felix Farmer is as silent as Buster Keaton. He is grief stricken beyond speech and barely able to walk. Furthermore, though the first act of the film is set almost entirely in his own house, Felix's drama is subordinated to the farcical goings-on that take place downstairs (remember, he is upstairs), and for long stretches of film, the story seems to forget him almost entirely. If we find ourselves asking, "What happened to Felix?" it's because S.O.B., at this stage in the film, cannot tolerate his hurt. It must cover him up. So it changes the subject.

Meanwhile, there's a dead body on the beach. And unsurprisingly, no one seems to care. No one, that is, except for the dead man's dog standing by, howling into the night. (In fact, the only sound pre-verbal Felix makes is an imitation dog howl. The comparison suggests a brotherhood of neglected pain.) Since physical containment and denial are cornerstones of the aesthetic of bullshit, it follows that their opposite, expression and exteriority, are part of the aesthetic of authenticity. When this formula is applied to Felix's botched suicides, S.O.B.'s gag structure becomes apparent. Consider the containments: a garage, an oven, a bedroom, spaces sequestered in death. After an authentic gesture of self-destruction (hanging, suffocation, toxic inhalation), these spaces begin to break down. At the point of breakage, slapstick occurs. The car breaks through the garage and into the sea; the noose snaps and Felix falls through the floor; Dick Benson (Larry Hagman) pulls him out of the oven and Felix spills onto the ground. Edwards is using physical comedy to represent the conflict between containment and expression, which he posits through the use of open/public and closed/private spaces.

But wait. What kind of perverted gag would splurch a genuine man? If Blake's slapstick is intended to dramatize the transformation from pretension to humility (in S.O.B.'s terms, from bullshit to truth), then what business does it have knocking Felix to the floor? The simple answer is: it doesn't. Because Felix begins the movie as a gagged man—Night Wind has already splurched him beyond recall—the physical whacks he encounters aren't intended to humiliate him, but to splurch the S.O.B.s around him. Felix Farmer is their agent, not their opposition. Accordingly, when he falls through the first story ceiling (a segue from private to public, repression to expression), he doesn't injure himself like George Webber would; he injures others, those villains of bullshit like Polly and Wilbur Reed (Loretta Swit, Craig Stevens). Later, David Blackman and Dick Benson get the same treatment and for the same reason. (David is splurched by a perpetually broken middle finger; Dick by perpetually bad timing with a golf cart).

We are beginning to see that Edwards' aesthetic of bullshit is expressed visually through public/private spatial relationships and his slapstick gags are arranged at their various points of contact. But there's more. The first act of the film, a bravura sequence that describes Hollywood's reaction to Felix's infirmity, utilizes a thrilling structural device, something akin to narrative simultaneity, to enhance the bullshit aesthetic. Indeed it is simultaneity of all kinds—be they visual, dramatic, kinetic, or aural—that maintains the farce. And it is farce that maintains the satire. "You try, but ultimately you can't make sense of nonsense,"Edwards says. "That's why the only way for me to approach dramatizing the insanity of Hollywood was to make a satire."[18] That insanity—the Standard Operational Bullshit from which his film gets its name—erupts in frenzies of simultaneous misrepresentation. The genre of farce, in other words, is indigenous to Hollywood ideology.

The farce of narrative simultaneity represses Felix Farmer. For instance, the rapid, incessant crosscutting between characters as they respond to the news of Felix's suicide draws our attention away from the one person whose dramatic conflict forms the center of the story—Felix! Likewise,

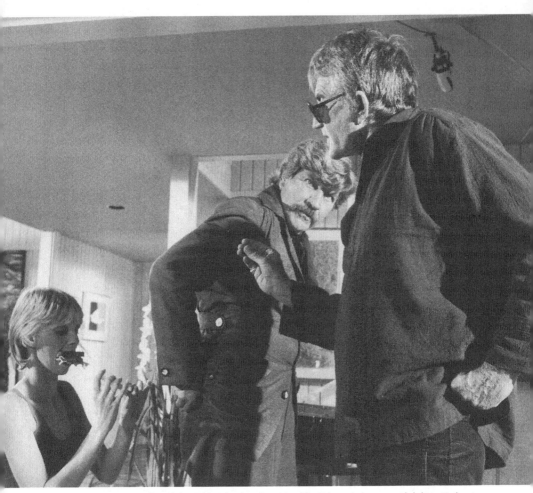

25. S.O.B. (1981) Blake Edwards showing Jennifer Edwards how to stick it to Robert Preston. Penetration—breaking in or breaking out—is a common theme to the splurches in S.O.B. (Courtesy of Jennifer Edwards)

Blake uses visual simultaneity to draw attention away from Felix. Compositionally, he will literally bury Felix within the wide shot, either in the background or periphery of the frame, behind objects, people, or reduced by spatial depth, and all in service of the aesthetic of bullshit. (When Felix falls through the ceiling, or waddles downstairs or through doors, he is never the subject of the shot.) Here, the B.S. is everything else that goes on around Felix—no one notices the man trying to end his own life. And in bold contrast to Felix's silence, Edwards' bullshitters overdose on dialogue. People talk, yell, argue (but no one communicates) creating an atmosphere of aural simultaneity that completely upstages our protagonist. What all this tells us is that there is no place in S.O.B., either dramatically or stylistically, for a man of Farmer's pain.

The anarchy increases after every one of Felix's failed suicide attempts because the physical damage Felix leaves in his wake opens up new spaces of simultaneity. The hole in the ceiling, for instance, creates an additional plane of depth through which continuous action can coexist. Thus, kinetic simultaneity—the perpetual motion integral to farce—is also compatible with Edwards' visual subordination of Felix. And is there a better aspect ratio than the anamorphic frame for enhancing kinetic anarchy? When it's Edwards' frame, certainly not. In his hands, the very wide screen is ruled by the precise choreography of perfect farcical rhythm. One actor's entrance is another's exit, and the offset balance rights itself. At their peak, these balletic reshufflings are syncopated to the whimsical pitch of Feydeau, and like all other facets of audio/visual/dramatic simultaneity in S.O.B., integral to Edwards' farce of repression and misrepresentation.

One of the challenges to creating and maintaining farce is that it requires both spatially and temporally contained environments. For this reason, it is most frequently seen on the stage, where a fixed proscenium keeps bodies within close and constant proximity to one another. In film, the "stage" is always being redefined, which poses a problem to directors trying to create finite spaces. Edwards addresses this problem quite ingeniously through his use of the telephone, which not only dramatizes the notion of bullshit (voices, after all, are only representations of their speakers—we've seen this in 10), but keeps characters within close contact at all times. This is a cinematic correlate to a theatrical device, and keeps up the fast-paced rhythm necessary to maintain simultaneity. The telephone also serves a very practical purpose here: it takes farce from out of the boudoir and into the twentieth century; the peepholes and disguises of Darling Lili and Victor/Victoria have been cast aside. Even The Pink Panther, for all its farcical invention, could still use its cartoon aesthetic to justify the artificial "stage" that the genre demands, but S.O.B. is unquestionably here and now. When considered within this context, the achievement is even more remarkable.

All this comes to a screeching halt when Felix, emerging from under a blanket in a symbolic rebirth, realizes that unbridled sexual expression will save his career. "We sold 'em schmaltz," he yells, "they want sadomasochism!" At this moment, the repressive aesthetic of bullshit becomes an aesthetic of exteriority. The new Felix Farmer communicates in exaggerated gestures, is shot in close-up after close-up, talks nonstop, and shouts and runs everywhere. Simultaneity of all kinds virtually disappears, the farce begins to dissipate, and Farmer can be the star of his movie. He leaves his home for the first time and S.O.B.'s physical setting expands. Its panoramic ensemble separates into a few narrative strands, and our main character's physical and emotional vitality finally come into relief. The deal he makes with Blackman and his henchman, for instance, is set on *Night Wind*'s soundstage after he emerges (opposite of containment) from behind a jack-in-the-box, microphone in hand. In an absolute one-eighty from his former self, he wants to be seen and heard. He wants to express himself.

Going from private to public spaces, Felix finds he must contend with the problem of representation. Throughout S.O.B., representation (or "image" as it is sometimes referred to) is prone to all kinds of bullshit interpretations and manipulations, most of which bear no relation to their original's actuality. At home, Farmer's wife, Sally Miles, behaves one way, but on the screen, as we have seen, she is a completely different person. Her house itself is a monument to representation (mirrors are everywhere), decorated with portraits of women (including Sally as Peter Pan) in many styles. These paintings, like *Night Wind*, portray a respectable, "high"-art taste, but considering what we know about Sally Miles (who swears and threatens to kill Felix), they are related to her own personality in image only. If this sounds anything like the "real" Julie Andrews, then Edwards has made his point. But doesn't his film begin "Once upon a time . . . " as though it were a fairy tale? What's autobiographical about that? Perhaps S.O.B., like everyone in it, is subject to the same kind of bullshit approach to reality.

Indeed the film is peppered with so many references to Edwards' own life it is difficult to know what's real and what's invented. The jogger that dies on the beach, for instance, is Herb Tanney (credited as Stiffe Tanney), Blake's own personal physician. His daughter, Jennifer Edwards, plays Lila, one of the hitchhiking women of easy virtue Culley picks up on his way to see Felix. (Ironically, the doctor dies of a heart attack, and the daughter is turned into a sex kitten. It's a very in joke, but Edwards is using casting to make the same points about the treacherous lure of singularity.) Julie, of course, plays Sally; Shelley Winters, in girth and personality, bears a striking resemblance to former Hollywood super-agent Sue Mengers; and Felix's editor, Ralph Himmler, shares the same first name as Ralph Winters, A.C.E. If *Night Wind* doubles for *Lili*, then Blackman doubles for Bob Evans, which means his wife/girlfriend is probably Ali MacGraw, and Sam Marshall, the actor she's having an affair with, is undoubtedly Steve McQueen (note their initials). But as Edwards' films teach, there is never a one-to-one relationship between reality and fiction. In fact, *S.O.B.*'s fiction-to-reality ratio is complicated by allusions to other legendary fictions. In theme and narrative structure, for instance, *S.O.B.* looks a lot like *Singin' in the Rain* (a film about Hollywood's image/authenticity problem), and the casting of William Holden within the context of Tinseltown indictment evokes *Sunset Boulevard*, the greatest indictment of them all. (There is also reference made to the death of Barrymore, but we'll get to that in due time.)

And yet, in the final analysis, exactly who is what and how much isn't of primary importance. What matters is that Edwards is using Hollywood's fictional and factual past to make *S.O.B.* into a factual and fictional recounting of his life. In the second portion of the film, a section devoted to Felix's fight to overcome bullshit with authenticity, he decides the most effective way to save his career is to turn *Night Wind* into a money-making porno. For the film's great moment, Sally Miles will show her breasts in defiance of the phony "Smiles" propaganda (as explicit a reference to *Darling Lili* as there ever was). This hypersexual and death-drenched version of "Polly Wolly Doodle" has revised its iconography to suit Felix's new vision; Jack (in-the-box) has become "Jock," the toy cannon, well, shoots smoke, and the ballerinas have turned into Salomés. In narrative and imagery, the actual sequence is candid beyond analysis, but Edwards makes a handful of choices that warrant deeper exploration. The most prominent of these occurs when Sally enters the devil's mouth and encounters a darkened inner sanctum walled with endless reflective surfaces. In each case, the multiplicity of figures speaks to her problem of identity, responding (quite literally) to the image crisis. Edwards presents the tension between the real Sally Miles and "Smiles," her Peter Pan persona, in split screen when she rips off her top, at once on the left and right sides of the frame. This moment completely undoes the former aesthetic of bullshit by liberating a truth formerly repressed, and in the face of it, it follows that any S.O.B. present would suffer a splurch. Thus Polly Reed, propped up in a full-body cast, screams and falls forward on her face. At the moment of impact, her mummy-like mold breaks (containment becomes exposure). Authenticity, it seems, is finally having some effect. The proof? Cast and crew of *Night Wind* observe a moment of silence in memory of Burgess Webster (Stiffe Tanney), the jogger who collapsed on the beach earlier in the film. In this fashion—through the juxtaposition of comic and somber moods—Edwards will gradually begin to strip away the bull to reveal the ultimate truth: death.

"Throughout his work," wrote Jack Ellis, Edwards "uses familiar genre materials in fresh and ingenious ways, juxtaposing scenes of apparent verisimilitude with those of wildly improbable farce and parodying the pretensions of his heroes."[19] Mapping out the breast-baring sequence in these terms, we can observe the juxtaposition in miniature. The commemorative moment of silence (verisimilitude) is followed by Polly's escape from hospital (parody), which is followed by Sally's first encounter with "Jock" (verisimilitude *and* parody), followed by dressing-room shenanigans (parody), and then take two (verisimilitude), and the response to take two (parody). Is S.O.B. having a schizophrenic break of its own? When Felix is brutally shot to death after a Keystone Kops-ish chase, it certainly appears so. One might experience this tonal conflict as a matter of directorial indiscretion, but in fact it isn't: Farmer's assassination represents a return to bodily repression, and heralds S.O.B.'s definitive departure from containment. Until this point, we've accepted farce as the norm, but now that it has been stripped away, we see that S.O.B. is a tragedy all along, struggling to get out. Edwards has expanded the idea of bullshit to include genre itself.

Felix's death, though it may seem to represent the triumph of Hollywood bull, is, from a structural perspective, the exact opposite: it is an expression of Edwards' own authenticity. Having so boldly killed off his protagonist at the end of act two, he has subverted traditional story structure, and turned S.O.B. into the kind of authentic personal expression Felix was after. This, ironically, avenges Felix's death. The studios may have the weaponry, the picture is saying, but the vision is what counts. We might remember the following exchange:

Felix: Sane and miserable or insane and bursting with creative joy and happiness—*that's* the point, Culley. And in the final analysis who says, 'He's sane, therefore he should,' or 'He's insane therefore he shouldn't'? Culley, come on. Even if I'm wrong—and I'm not—I'm full of fire, Culley. I'm a blazing comet.

26. S.O.B. (1981) Both Julie Andrews and her character Sally Miles face decisive moments in their careers, as producer Felix Farmer (Robert Mulligan) begs to see some skin ("It's just one shot!"). With them are Ben Coogan (Robert Webber, center) and Tim Culley (William Holden, right, in his final film). (Author's collection)

Culley: Comets burn out, pal.

Felix: But ah, my foes and oh my friends, it gives a lovely light.

Expression of authenticity, regardless of its merit, is all that matters. That's a lucky break for Felix, considering the quality of his own work. With titles like *Love on a Pogo Stick*, *Invasion of the Pickle People*, *Pagan Plunder*, and of course, *Night Wind*, it's safe to say we're not in the province of high art. And judging from the little we've seen of Night Wind, in either version, it seems we're correct to think little of Felix the auteur. But how does that translate to the real life of Blake Edwards? "I wanted to communicate not only a sense of the industry's craziness," he said, "but also some of my own, since I'm a part of it."[20] This admission brings up an important discrepancy; Farmer is a producer, Blake is a director. Why? Because S.O.B., unlike 8½, is not about an artist, it's about the bottom line. Felix never indicates he thinks anything of Night Wind as a work of art, and in fact, when we're first introduced to him, he's shuddering over its bad box-office report, not a bad review. Focusing on the plight of the producer, Edwards isn't playing the whiny old Hollywood-destroys-artists card, but is after something much greater: the end of an era. He said,

> Harry Cohn operated on the principle that if he gave you your way, he'd either have the benefit of your being right or have a scapegoat if you were wrong. So if you fought hard enough for something, you could get his authorization, if not his approval. To this day, for all that the style of the studio executive has changed, the need for a scapegoat in reverse is more important to them then either the commercial or artistic wisdom of a particular course.[21]

Bastards always ran Hollywood, but now the S.O.B.s were destroying it.

If it were to end with Felix's death, the movie would not only forfeit its anti-Hollywood structure, it would deprive the bullshitters of their chances at redemption. With that in mind, Edwards cuts to juke box and pans left to reveal Culley, Coogan, and Feingarten drinking at a bar.* The image—one long, static three-shot—is unprecedented in S.O.B. Until now, when they have been photographed together, the three muscatels were seen at different spatial depths, in constant motion, and generally prone to the chaos of simultaneity. This shot replaces all that with a straightforward, visually uncluttered picture, and represents the beginning of an aesthetic of authenticity. That the change occurs in a bar is no accident. From What Did You Do in the War, Daddy? to Skin Deep, when Blake Edwards puts guys in a bar, it's to watch them open their hearts.

---

* Culley plays Sinatra. The first time we hear him listen to the Chairman of the Board, he's coasting down the PCH playing "Young at Heart." The song seems innocent enough, but the lyrics speak to Culley's problem of misrepresentation: old on the outside, young on the inside. The Sinatra he plays at the bar, "All the Way," reverses all that. It's a song about loving, not "fairy tales can come true."

Coogan: It's the damnest shame. There are so many things I've done and so many things I didn't do, and I should have, and I didn't, and I—

Feingarten: Darling . . .

Coogan: Come on, I want Culley to beat the shit out of me so I can feel better.

Feingarten: But, brother sinner, even though I completely understand your need for purgation—

Coogan: Do you? Do you really?

Feingarten: Ben, there isn't a man among us with half a conscience who doesn't keep a hair shirt as a permanent part of his wardrobe.

Coogan: What does that mean?

Feingarten: Can you explain it to him, Culley?

Culley: It's not easy. There are so few people in this town with a conscience.

Coogan: I'll tell you one thing, I am not going to that bullshit funeral. It's . . .

Feingarten: Hypocritical.

Coogan: It's bullshit!

The process of shit purgation begins right away. At O'Ryan's funeral home (note the homonym of "Orion"), Coogan can't keep himself from farting and pissing all over the place. It seems like sophomoric bathroom humor, but it is actually a profound (okay, sophomoric *and* profound) approbation of Ernest Becker's theory of anality (outlined in the Introduction to this book). Later that night, the muscatels quite literally purge Felix's own body from O'Ryan's, which, as Coogan has stated, represents "that bullshit funeral." Like the final scenes in *The Party*, this sequence embraces slapstick as antidote to false values (that is, false image values), and exorcises them by the splurching of Felix's dead body.

That night, during a private wake they hold for Felix, Coogan gets up and kisses Felix's cheek.

Coogan: God, that was . . . *blech!*

Feingarten: But your gesture was magnificent. It was *blech* because that's not Felix.

Coogan: What do you mean? Who is it?

Feingarten: No, no, no. Not even "who." Just something Felix walked around in. But it's important because it serves as a reminder to those that loved who he was.

The doctor's distinction is both thematically and stylistically resonant. In a surprisingly spiritual turn, he has proclaimed human flesh S.O.B.'s final perpetrator of misrepresentation. Sally Miles, naked or clothed, is still in possession of a body that wrongly filters the expression of her inner self, whatever that may be. After all, if we're talking about authenticity, a true spirit that cannot be contaminated, and the materialization of any physical thing subjects it to distortion, then the expression of self is compromised, and therefore bullshit.

The muscatels have gone from repressing the body (S.O.B.'s first act of farce) to liberating it, a transformation that reenacts Felix's own transformation from containment to expression. In visual terms, this change in values is met with the kind of frank pictorialism we saw in the bar scene. Felix's wake, which functions as another bar scene, complete with male bonding and alcohol, is photographed without duplicitous simultaneity, in extended, shallow-space three-shots that enhance the sense of growing sincerity. The first shot of the wake begins with a gentle forward glide, a gesture that creates an intimate space, and is lit with partial shadowing that contrasts with the flat, extremely artificial colorizations of the film's former aesthetic of bull. In fact, the mise-en-scène has been desaturated to the most basic tans and browns; the color of feces, earth, and Jack Daniels. Material values have been renounced, and this is what remains: an honest to goodness asceticism. And the body is material too. That is why Felix's friends burn his corpse at the end of the film. It's an act of pure authenticity, and also a homage to Hollywood lost. Legend has it that after John Barrymore's death, his cronies Errol Flynn and Raoul Walsh repaired to a local bar, drank, toasted their friend, and then said goodnight for the evening. From there, Walsh headed to the funeral home, arranged a deal with the caretaker, and took Barrymore's body to Flynn's house. When he got home, Errol Flynn saw the body sitting up in his living room. Even Feingarten's adieu, "Good night, sweet prince," matches Barrymore's epitaph. The analogy reminds us that Felix's death isn't only sad to those who loved him, but to those like Blake Edwards who remember Hollywood when it was good.

As he was finishing up *Victor/Victoria* in England, Edwards got word that the marketing people at Paramount were reneging on the big S.O.B. publicity junket they had promised him. Instead they had planned a press screening at the studio and an informal meal at the commissary. It made sense to Paramount to publicize a movie about a movie with a party on the lot, but to Blake, it was only an excuse. They were cutting corners, he thought, skimping on a movie they wanted to bury out of contempt for him and the film that ridiculed them. What's more, they had arranged to release S.O.B. the same weekend as *Raiders of the Lost Ark*, and do it with an ad campaign that was all about Julie's breasts. Blake despised it, but his hands were tied; this was a studio matter. Paramount's Barry Diller explained, "We'll advertise and support the film in a way that reaches the consumer."[22] Surely they wouldn't deliberately destroy one of their own movies? If S.O.B. did well, Paramount did well, and if they deemed Edwards' promotional strategy impractical, that was their prerogative. But Blake was still unsatisfied. Paranoid, coherent, or somewhere in between, he did what Felix Farmer might have done: he took it away from them. Think of it as life imitating art imitating life.

Edwards put up $200,000 of his own money to arrange the junket he believed his film deserved, and that meant full airfares for visiting press, weekend accommodations at the Beverly Hills Hotel, a postscreening dinner party at La Scala, breakfast the next morning back at the hotel with one-on-one cast interviews in poolside cabanas, and then, later that night, a gala dinner dance in the Crystal Ballroom. But it didn't come off: on the final evening, there was countersabotage. Uninvited limo drivers broke into the hotel to distribute copies of the *Los Angeles Times* in which were printed the ads Edwards vetoed. Naturally, it was expected that the contemptuous folks at Paramount were behind it. Edwards was so irate he actually tried to buy back S.O.B. from Lorimar so he could distribute it himself (*viva* Felix!).[23] They turned him down.

When it was released, the film was met with incredulity. Critics knew S.O.B. was something, though what exactly they couldn't say. Blake's customary tonal fluctuations were the source of some confusion, for others the satire was too misanthropic, and some thought it just downright unfunny. Vincent Canby, though, saw something else. His defense of the picture, "Why 'S.O.B.' deserves to be S.R.O.," first appeared in his native *New York Times*, and then, eleven days later, *Variety* reprinted it in its entirety. Here's the gist:

Very rare is the American director who has the power and mania to explore his own psyche with the grace and occasional mercilessness of

a Truffaut in his Antoine Doinel films and the far bleaker *La Peau Douce*,
or with the poetic and economic abandon of a Fellini in 8½, *Juliet of the
Spirits, Amarcord*, and the current *City of Women*.

It isn't only the Hollywood system that inhibits such filmmaking. We
tend to regard such self-absorption by film directors (though not by
novelists and playwrights) as unseemly, show-offy, un-American. Mod-
esty is the third Yankee virtue. It comes directly after godliness and
cleanliness, even though a gigantic ego is almost as important in successful commercial cinema as talent.

Thus the audacity, nerve, originality, and courage of Blake Edwards'
S.O.B. . . .Sometimes there's nothing quite as exhilarating as being able
to bite the hand that feeds you, but then S.O.B. isn't a bite. It's a six-
course meal of palms, knuckles, and fingers. There's never been an
American film exactly like it.[24]

That Julie Andrews' breasts fill out the better part of S.O.B. may be reason
enough to declare it Blake Edwards' masterpiece, but the fact is, Canby's
right; it happens to be an extraordinary film in its own right.

VICTOR/VICTORIA (1982)

Toddy: To quote the immortal bard, "Love looks not with the eyes, but with the mind. Therefore is winged cupid painted black."

Lorimar had agreed to make *Victor/Victoria*, and in October of 1980 preproduction on the film began. Two months later, there was bad news: Lorimar's film division had suffered serious losses and budget over-runs, and was forced to the pull the plug. However, the day before Christmas, Blake got a call from David Begelman, MGM's new production chief, who had been hired to undertake the monumental task of gearing up MGM's production from five to fifteen pictures a year, and *Victor/Victoria*, he told Edwards, would be one of them. Under Begelman, MGM (which became MGM/UA in 1981) practiced a vulture policy, swooping down on troubled productions like *Victor/Victoria* and snapping them up. They in-creased the film's size and budget, deciding not to shoot on location in Paris, but just outside London at Pinewood Studios. At its height, the production spread into fifteen sound stages, two of which opened up into four hundred continuous feet of Paris in the thirties. This double stage was *Victor/Victoria*'s pièce de résistance, housing the film's snowy boule-vard of live buildings, some of which reached as high as three stories.

Edwards' script, adapted from the 1933 German film *Viktor und Viktoria*, tells the story of Victoria Grant (Julie Andrews), an unemployed chan-teuse, who meets Carroll "Toddy" Todd (Robert Preston) in a restaurant swindle that turns them into fast friends. Soon after they move in together, Toddy convinces her that she could be a successful gay drag queen ("a woman pretending to be a man pretending to be a woman?"), and takes her to audition for Andre Cassell, one of Paris' leading theatrical agents. Victoria gets the job, and before long she is the toast of Paris. The macho gangster King Marchand (James Garner) instantly falls for her (him?), but when he finds out that Victor is actually Victoria, she tells him that they must masquerade as homosexuals to uphold her assumed identity and maintain her career. He agrees, reluctantly. As the film ends, Toddy sur-prises everyone by becoming the new Victor, and Victoria and Marchand come out of the heterosexual closet for good.

Perhaps it's best to start with the first shot. With this simple stroke, Blake introduces the major conceptual and stylistic devices that he will develop throughout the film. It begins with a conventional establishing shot of a Paris street scene: high above the ground, snow falls, a horn blasts, and figures cross from one sidewalk to another. In the foreground stands a red storefront and very green telephone booth, in the background a royal blue building. The title "Paris 1934" fades in, and, gently, the camera pans left to reveal a window—we've been looking at a view from an apartment—and continues into a bedroom, past a wall photograph of Marlene Dietrich (in a tie), and over to a close-up of a sleeping man (this is Toddy). The camera holds. A moment of expectant silence follows. We anticipate some kind of verbal or physical action from the actor, but instead, a young man (previously concealed) hoists himself up from behind Toddy, gives him a once-over, and gets out of bed. End of shot.

Here we have bold colorization, long ago and far away, windows and perception, tricks of illusion, gender-bending performers, and reversals of expectations—the primary components of *Victor/Victoria*. Let us then take these elements as they have been presented. First, there is color, and a lot of it. From Norma's yellow dress to the red-red roses in the restaurant, every frame of *Victor/Victoria* is saturated in the cartoonist's palette. Colors are taken to an extreme beyond reality and enhanced by art director Rodger Maus' eye for coordination. Whole spaces are often composed in entirely one shade, like King Marchand's hotel room, a space muted in "masculine" bluish-gray from the walls to the pillows, and Victoria and Toddy's yellow-filled suite. This amounts to an impossibly mannered world in contradiction to Edward's specificity of time and place. On one hand, we are given a realistic idea of where and when we are (Paris, 1934), and on the other, a fantasized interpretation of it. So which is it? Like everything else in *Victoria/Victoria* (or Blake Edwards, for that matter), it is neither one exclusively—it is both.

Windows are used to represent the *bothness*. Like the stage, they turn voyeurs into audiences, offering them a way to watch and make (false) assumptions about the appearance of things. In this first shot, for instance, Edwards' pan left from the street into the bedroom challenges our assumptions by disclosing a previously concealed bit of exposition. It *appeared* that we were outside, above a Paris street, but it was *revealed* that were actually inside, looking through a reality-reversing window. Additionally, the transition from public space (exterior street) to private space (interior bedroom) reflects Edwards' continuing interest in the semipermeable divide between how we present ourselves and how we really are. To dramatize the arc from the phoniness of a single identity to an enlightened acceptance of inner duplicity (in other words, the story of the film) Blake will violate the seemingly obstinate boundary between musical performance spaces and audience spaces. Once gender identity is deconstructed, the fourth wall can fall. This means that in *Victor/Victoria*, duplicity is not seen as deceitful, but as the remedy to gender stereotypes, which in their polarity—one is either "manly" or "feminine"—are actually phonier than a woman pretending to be a man pretending to be a woman.

It's an idea introduced in the first shot. Just take a look at Toddy's picture of Dietrich: Master of the cabaret, a musical form that reached a pinnacle between the wars (hence 1934), Marlene is the fairy godmother of *Victor/Victoria*. But first, a bit about cabaret: significantly, the word itself has origins in "camberet," a Middle Dutch term meaning "little room." The small size is essential to the creation of intimacy between performer and audience, and conducive to blurring the line between proscenium and spectator. If this is where we like our torch songs to be sung it is because our proximity to the singer casts his/her interpretation in an immediately autobiographical light: there appears to be no performance because there is no stage. Think of *Morocco* and how easily Dietrich crossed into the audience. She is, like Victoria, riddled with contradictions of identity and gender on screen and off, and like Edwards' *Lili*, caught in the wartime conflict of national allegiance. Add to this the Svengali and Trilby implications of her films with von Sternberg (mirrored in the Toddy and Victoria relationship),* and she becomes a perfect match for the world of the film.

Leaving Dietrich (we're still in the first shot), the pan left continues to Toddy's bed. The music stops, there's a pregnant moment, and then a half-naked *man* gets up from behind him. In this typically Edwardian reveal, the treason of appearance invalidates our expectations, but what is unique about this particular epiphany is that it is doubled. First, a body is revealed. Second, the body is revealed to be male. (The shot and the gender deceived us.) The prominence of the mirror in the shot underscores the problem of appearance and cues a world of infinite variation where visual "reality" is never secure. The same can be said of spoken reality.

---

* There is also the meta-cinematic reading of Blake and Julie, not to mention George du Maurier's novel *Trilby*, which Blake had at once time wanted to adapt. (In fact, Victoria even wears what is known as a "Trilby" hat in the film: it looks like a fedora, but with a narrower brim.)

27. *Victor/Victoria* (1982) How many homosexuals here? King Marchand (James Garner, left), Victoria Grant (Julie Andrews, center), and Carroll "Toddy" Todd (Robert Preston), are all gender benders extraordinaire, but does that make all of them gay? Or is that not the point? (Author's collection)

Toddy: Cab fare, Richard?

Richard (*stuffing a wad of Toddy's cash into his pocket*): No, I've got to pay some bills.

Toddy: You could at least leave me enough for breakfast.

Richard: Toddy, one would suspect you think I'm mercenary.

Toddy: Try "unscrupulous."

Richard: You get your money's worth.

Toddy: I think we both get my money's worth.

Negations are reversals of reality actualized through speech. A says "x," B responds with "x-1," A retorts with "x-1-1," and then B comes back with "x-1-1-1." In short, a series of cumulative amendments results in a fresh disclosure. Like his gag structure, Edwards' banter takes a given assumption ("Cab fare, Richard?"), and turns it into dignity-wounding splurch ("I think we both get my money's worth"), such that each line renders the previous false. The analogy to topping the topper readily applies.

Problems of identity persist in Victoria Grant, the prim and proper coloratura we meet near the start of the film. Her audition is a cute little ditty called "Cherry Ripe," and it de-eroticizes Victoria almost to the point of childishness (in fact, Andrews used to sing the song as a young soprano). Unsurprisingly, Labisse, the club owner, is not interested. He wants va-va-voom. She pleads, insisting that with a little practice she could give it to him, but he's not having it. "Lady," Labisse says, "that is like a nun saying with a little practice she can become a street walker." The word "nun" suggests an autobiographical bond between Victoria and Julie Andrews. Both character and actress have been rejected for their apparent sexlessness, but by the end of *Victoria/Victoria*, Edwards will restore it to both of them. Andrews said, "There are always those who say, 'Oh, I wish she'd do something else' or 'Oh, God, why did she try it; she should be sticking to all those lovely films.' So I'm damned if I do and I'm damned if I don't."[25] It's true. *Darling Lili* took it too far, and *Star!* didn't take it far enough. So what's the right balance? Moreover, how do you sex up a woman whose sexuality can be taken only with spoons-full of sugar? *The Tamarind Seed* tried to bury it in backstory, 10 forfeited it to Bo Derek, *S.O.B.* parodied it, but in *Victor/Victoria* Edwards grows it up.

Like everything else in *Victor/Victoria*, his answer requires a careful reorganization of performance and audience spaces, and it begins with "Cherry Ripe," the first number in the film, where, appropriately, the distinctions between role player and observer are ideologically and visually at their clearest. Without the tricks of transvestism and homosexuality to complicate her relationship to the audience, the line between what is real and what is not is stated plainly in crosscuts between Victoria and Labisse. We have performer in one image and audience in the next and everyone knows who everyone is. Of course, that's the problem as Edwards sees it. These are show people and homosexuals after all, and playing with private parts can get tricky when the parts keep changing.

For example, in Toddy's "Gay Paree," a number he sings at the gay club Chez Lui, the audience actually seems to upstage him. Most of the time, in fact, they are together in the same shot. There is no raised stage to distinguish him from them (unlike "Cherry Ripe"), indicating that in this space, performance exists on both sides of the footlights. But what does that mean? Toddy's musical lead-in offers some insight: *When people speak of Gay Paree / They think that when they say Paree is gay / They mean that gay Paree is gay / It is! Not in a way Paree / Was gay and yesterday Paree / It means today that gay Paree is gay!** Blake cuts to a two-shot close-up of two men (or women) in drag sitting in the audience, suggesting that, though they are offstage, they are, by the very subject of the song, a part of the number. For the same reason, the shots of Toddy performing are composed with the backs of spectators' heads in the foreground of the frame, and by the end of the number Toddy is actually singing from within the audience.† What is Edwards getting at here? Why has he gone to such lengths to draw parallels between performance and audience? Because in Chez Lui, gender is an Edwardian utopia where role playing is universally accepted and the metaphor of performance can be liberated from the stage.

One of Edwards' cleverest statements about performer/audience relations occurs not on stage, but in a restaurant. Because they are performers, and therefore comfortable with the idea of role playing, Toddy and Victoria can turn just about every setting into an informal show venue. This particular one sees Victoria's attempt to stage some cockroach blackmail she hopes to turn into a free meal. Unfortunately, the bug gets away from her and turns what was intended to be a performance into an authen-

---

* The wording is intentionally convoluted. Even the word "gay" has two identities.
† Edwards' presentation of "You and Me," Toddy and Victoria's delightful side-by-sider, is designed with the same visual strategy and for the same reason. Stage/audience lines are irrelevant to those who have already accepted the arbitrariness of gender.

tic situation. But because Blake has given us privileged information about the insect's whereabouts, we know that this "scene" is really real and that Victoria is not acting at all. The waiters, though, suspect otherwise. They've seen customers pull the same kind of stunt and accuse Victoria of rigging the whole thing. In short: it was a fake scene that became real but that was *perceived* as fake. This illusory triplet looks ahead to the blurred lines that Victoria will establish between the genders, and, from within the context of the film's milieu, assumes theatrical connotations.

In this scene (or is it "scene"?), the various dramatic roles—performer (Victoria), fooled audience (waiters), and knowing audience (Toddy)—are strongly enunciated by mise-en-scène and camera. The lace curtains behind the table foretell the actual curtains that will run the length of Victoria's stage, while the windows behind those curtains remind us of Edwards' dangerous game of voyeurism. Furthermore, intercutting Toddy's close-up with a wide shot of Victoria fighting with the waiters allows Edwards to establish a theatrical relationship between Toddy (knowing audience) and Victoria (performer) / waiters (fooled audience) by bestowing upon him the act of watching; when Edwards goes wider to shoot all the participants in one image, Toddy is placed far enough to the left of the frame to physically distinguish him from "the scene." All of this theatricality comes to a visual climax when the bug lands on a fat lady and full-blown restaurant pandemonium breaks out. Just then, Blake cuts to the building's exterior. Through the row of windows, passersby stop to watch the chaos within. From their spot on the other side of the glass, the flying plates and tumbling bodies surely look like an act. But, like so many others, they only see the outside. Without question one of the most glorious images in all of Edwards work, this lunatic tapestry hammers home the point that in *Victor/Victoria*, changes of identity can happen even to those spectators who don't believe they are part of the role playing.

If changes on stage prompt changes in the audience, then there is often no need to distinguish between them. What makes Toddy and Victoria so well suited for one another is that they appreciate this, the value of their malleable identity(ies).

Victoria: How long have you been a homosexual?
Toddy: How long have you been a soprano?
Victoria: Since I was twelve.
Toddy: I was a late bloomer.

For homosexuals and performers, the lines between onstage and offstage are as blurry as those separating "male" and "female." But not so for King Marchard and his moll Norma. For them, there is no overlap between the masculine/feminine polarity. If they are going to be changed for the better, then King and Norma must accept both literal and figurative performance, both the kind that they watch, and the kind that they try to avoid in gender differentiation. To illustrate this transition, Edwards will gradually reconfigure stage/audience spaces such that, by the end of the film, the boundary will go from firm (as demonstrated in "Cherry Ripe") to flexible and forgiving (as they were, happily, in "Gay Paree").

It begins with Victoria's first number as Victor, "Le Jazz Hot." Like "Cherry Ripe," the stage/spectator boundaries are carefully maintained. Throughout the performance, when Blake cuts to a reaction shot (and there are many), he does so without including any part of the stage in the frame, indicating that role playing hasn't yet crossed over into the audience to play havoc with gender. That is, King's gaze, his fascination with Victoria, is still heterosexual, and the visual and sexual boundaries are still intact. But all that changes as soon as the song ends. During Victoria's curtain call, Blake cuts to a wide shot of stage left, placing, for the first time in the number, audience and performer in the same image, confirming that the identity-related transition is imminent. The tuxedoed man who hands Victoria a bouquet is confirmation. His audience-to-stage crossover paves the way for yet another breakage in the façade. And here it comes: a drum roll from the orchestra . . . Victoria removes her wig . . . and . . . *she's a man.*

Quite naturally, this reveal comes as something of a blow to King Marchand's sense of gender stability. If he had the hots for a guy playing a girl, does that make him gay? If so, does that make him less of a man? What is "man" anyway, but a set of cultural conditions we enact everyday? The moment the wig comes off and King's sexuality is questioned, he has, like a stage performer, to play the role of "male." Indeed, backstage after the number, we see that masculinity is mask-unlinity for both Marchand and Victoria, a part they both are playing for the benefit of their audiences. So who's the real performer now, King? And who's the audience? What good is the fourth wall when life is a cabaret, old chum?

According to "The Shady Dame from Seville," none at all. At three points in the number, Victoria breaks the illusion by looking directly into the camera, and for a split second (sometimes even longer), the two distinct worlds of stage and audience are united. The lyrics, *One day came a world famous matador* and *It's best to say nobody knows* prompt the fissures, and quite appropriately so; both lines refer directly to the offstage drama (the first to Marchand, and the second to his sexual ambiguity). On the subject of lyrics, the dramatics described in "The Shady Dame from Seville" closely resembles the narrative of *Victor/Victoria*, and much more so then "Le Jazz Hot," a number that seems not to comment on the film's offstage action. As the movie unfolds, however, the onstage "performances" will gain in dramaturgical consequence, yet another indication that stage is pouring into audience. Victoria's wink into the camera is demonstrative of precisely this fluctuation, as are the breaking glass and popping champagne bottles, which are set off at the end of the number by Victoria's trademark high note. These gags service the same principle: onstage events have had some effect on the offstage, and with steadily mounting impact.

In keeping with this pattern, Blake cuts to a two-shot of Andre and Toddy applauding wildly as they glance over the audience. The fact of their spectatorship—not on the spectacle, but on the other spectators—underscores Marchand's new role as a man with a gender conflict. Even Squash is watching King. Edwards' point seems to be that his "performance," the identity that has masqueraded as masculinity, is under full scrutiny just as he is scrutinizing Victoria's identity. ("There is no better reactor than Jim [Garner]," Blake said.[26])

The proverbial tables take another proverbial turn in "Crazy World," which is essentially a pictorial duet between Victor and King, one that lyrically and cinematically fails to discriminate between stage and audience. She sings autobiographically, *Crazy world / Crazy world / Full of crazy contradictions / like a child / First you drive me wild / And then you win my heart / With your wicked art*. Applying "art" to King represents his official induction into the world of gender-bending performers. And so does the shot: in one clear continuous take, Blake visualizes a direct, one-to-one relationship between performance and audience. At this point in the story, both King and Victoria are perceived as homosexuals, but as tends to be the case in Blake Edwards, perception is misconception. Beginning with a close-up of a red carnation against total blackness, Edwards pulls back to reveal (there's that word again) Victoria's hand on a piano and follows it up her arm to her face, half in shadow. Without a single cut, the camera begins a lateral clockwise drift and maintains it through a full 180° rotation. Now that it is behind Victoria, the camera has placed her and the audience in the same shot. Not only does this move represent the climax of the off/on-stage convergence, it reenacts the public transmission of private longings.* Apropos, the cinematic presentation does not distinguish between them. And so, when Victoria tosses that red carnation to Marchand, it represents Edwards' coup de grâce to the artificial borderlines known as gender. Now the whole audience notices King. Though he is sitting amongst the spectators, Victoria has effectively taken him out of the closet to join her on the "stage."

But there is a problem. King and Victoria aren't gay. She's pretending to be a homosexual to keep her career and he has sacrificed the role of "masculinity" in respectful deference. Naturally, both illusions must be righted. In the visual vocabulary of *Victor/Victoria*, this means that stage/audience lines must be restored. In this fashion, the third reprise of "The Shady Dame from Seville" corrects the confusion by entirely eradicating illusion. Though Toddy is in drag and literally onstage, his pointedly pitiful attempt at appearing female renders the entire act too absurd to be real. Unlike Victor's successful transformation, this transvestism is a parody of femininity, one that aims not for deceit, but for a kind of exaggerated buffoonery that sets Toddy's naturalized masculinity into relief. Though he may be a homosexual in a dress, Toddy's maleness has never been more palpable. And neither has Victoria's femininity. She watches the show from the audience. End credits roll.

At last, it seems Blake Edwards has solved the Julie Andrews problem. Having cast Andrews in a part that requires her to conceal and then reveal her sexuality, Blake has made it possible to complete, before our unwilling eyes, his wife's erotic development. To pull it off, Edwards wedded our want for dramatic resolution—that is, to see Victor transform back into Victoria—to his personal want to see the sexless Mary Poppins image transform back into Julie Andrews. "What is healthy about comedy," Edwards says, "Is that it can attack your prejudices, undermine your defenses. And to do all this, it works almost subliminally. Unlike tragedy, where you 'steel yourself' for the pain, the grief, the suffering, comedy is so entertaining that your guard is down. So the things the author or the director wants to say he can smuggle in, under cover of laughter, much more easily."[27] With our guard dropped, Edwards can bootleg some of

* *Darling Lili's* "Whistling Away the Dark" contains similar stylistic and dramatic information.

Julie's sex appeal just as easily as he can traffic some pretty consistent theories on his perception polemic. And as always, the splurch is his courier of choice.

Though *Victor/Victoria* is not a committed gag-narrative in the manner of *10*, there are several significant instances of visual comedy. First and foremost, there is the matter of the exploding wine glasses and champagne bottles. Beginning with "Cherry Ripe" and topping itself throughout the picture, this gag, generated by Victoria's high note, speaks of the real woman hidden under the man under the woman, telling us (and Monsieur Labisse), that this sound is too feminine to be believed. The same principle applies to Norma's battle-ax gag. When it suddenly punctures a closed door at King and Squash's crotch level, the analogy to male weaponry becomes blatant. (Norma, a phallus carrier? In Blake's world, certainly. She may not be a man, but that doesn't mean she can't act like one.) Later, after she's escorted to the train track (a scene that courts *Some Like It Hot*), she rips off her coat to expose the lingerie beneath, and a bystander looks up and spills onto the tracks. But his nosedive isn't in vain. Edwards uses the pratfall to espouse the film's central point, that looking can be dangerous. Consequently, anyone Blake's camera catches peeping through windows is going to get it: Squash is snowed on, the ubiquitous waiter (played by the ubiquitous Graham Stark) tumbles over railings, and Private Investigator Charles Bovin (Sherloque Tanney) misses a barstool, gets electrocuted, has his finger crunched in a closet door, and then gets a mallet whack to that selfsame place.* Edwards' musical presentation espouses the same ideology: that is, that Victoria's routines do to King what slapstick does to almost everyone else. But because *Victor/Victoria* is a musical, it will rely on musical performance, not physical recrimination, to reform its hypocrites. The result is Blake's most pleasant comedy, one that exchanges bone breaking for some good old-fashioned gaiety. No doubt, this was partly responsible for the picture's popular reception and what earned it so many comparisons to Lubitsch. Arthur Nolletti, Jr.:

---

* "Sherloque" is a ruse. The actor here is the Edwards' family physician Herb Tanney, who since *Darling Lili* has been making cameos in Blake's movies, and all under assumed names. In *Lili* it was "Sascha Tanney" and in *Wild Rovers* it was "Studs." After that came Serge, Sado, Senilo, Stiffe, Sidi Bin, Schweitzer, Shep, Stanley. . . .It goes on. From one film to the next, Blake delights in making Herb suffer. In *S.O.B.* he's the jogger whose dead body goes unnoticed on the beach.

One is reminded of the oft-repeated maxim that bedroom doors in Lubitsch's films always played leads without ever getting billing. In *Victor/Victoria*, which is clearly a sophisticated comedy in the Lubitsch vein, the same holds true for closets and windows. What, in fact, would Edwards' characters do without these two indispensable signifiers of spying? Obviously, very little.[28]

Anything that allows for seeing without being seen is going to be instrumental to farce. What makes *Victor/Victoria* so well suited to this format is its commitment to the gender debate, which offers Edwards numerous opportunities to deconstruct the sexual personalities of those on either side of the window, or perhaps more appropriately, the closet. Adjoining rooms provide safe settings for those urges/identities which, when exposed by flung-open doors, erupt into chaotic revelations. King and Squash, for example, hide not to protect themselves from physical harm, but to repress their inner emotional duplicity. Since closed doors keep them from these difficulties of self-disclosure, it follows that Squash would have to break one down before he can come out to his boss (which he does).

Victor/Victoria brought Edwards some of the best reviews of his career. "Get ready, get set and go—*immediately*—to the Ziegfeld Theater," wrote Vincent Canby in the *New York Times*, "where Blake Edwards today opens his chef d'oeuvre, his cockeyed, crowing achievement, his *Duck Soup*, his *Charley's Aunt*, his *Hotel Paradiso*, his *Some Like It Hot*, his urban *As You Like It*, and maybe even his *Citizen Kane*, which his film resembles in no way whatsoever."[29] Stanley Kauffmann, a newcomer to team Edwards, called the film the best American film farce since *Some Like It Hot*,[30] and *Variety* invoked Lubitsch by name.[31] It was the kind of press that foretells of a director's ascension into the comedy firmament, but of course, it wasn't unanimous. Andrew Sarris named the film "the most engaging entertainment of 1982," but his feet never left the ground. "*Victor/Victoria* is hardly the occasion for hyped-up apocalyptic criticism," he continued. "It does not mark the end of one world or the beginning of another. It is instead a bridge between the past and the present, and it assumes an amiable reasonableness in the audience."[32]

The apocalypse Sarris refers to erupted from the film's treatment of homosexuality, which in 1982, a landmark year for Gay Hollywood, was a hot and sensitive topic. Within the span of a few months, the studios released such ostensibly gay-centric works as *Personal Best*, *Making Love*,

Partners, and *Victor/Victoria*, stirring up a great many viewers, and raising the question of queer cinema: namely, what is it? To some, *Victor/Victoria* only used homosexuality as a story device to explicate the conflicts of its straight characters, treating gay issues as hurdles to be overcome, not maintained. Is this true? If so, does it make *Victor/Victoria* a lesser film? Vito Russo, author of *The Celluloid Closet*, thought so. He wrote,

> Unfortunately, Edwards' cowardly handling of the sexual politics in *Victor/Victoria* stopped short of any radical statement the film might have made. A love affair between Toddy and James Garner's bodyguard, played by Alex Karras, could have been revolutionary. Instead, the one shot of the two in bed together shows them fully clothed, propped up primly like two maiden aunties. Thus, a chance to eroticize the asexual sissies of the Thirties was lost.

He concludes that *Victoria/Victoria*, "For all its high-flown dialogue about heterosexual insecurity with homosexuality . . . is as straight as the values it pretends to challenge."[33] Ed Sikov disagrees:

> Alex Karras' affable Mr. Bernstein presents precisely that gay image which Hollywood has been chronically unable to tolerate in the past, namely one in which gayness is not a metaphor for something else, not the single most recognizable feature of a personality, and not an expression of heterosexual anxiety in the guise of a gay boogie man.[34]

Could both be right? Perhaps *Victor/Victoria* endeavors not represent queer cinema, but simply be a gay-conscious straight story with a view of human sexuality that tolerates both opposites within a single individual. By the end of the picture, Marchand may end up with a woman, but considering the chain of events that got him to Victoria it seems unreasonable to categorize him as definitively straight. Far from diminishing its assertions about gender, the film's tolerance of Marchand's complete arc expresses not just straight or gay—either would be an oversimplification—but the full panorama of in-between. Deciding upon either polarity is to negate what makes Edwards Edwards: a subjective multiplicity demonstrative of no sexual sensibility but his very own.

That year, *Victor/Victoria* received seven Oscar nominations, a rare distinction for an American comedy. Those honored were Patricia Norris (costumes), Rodger Maus, Tim Hutchinson, William Craig Smith, and Harry Cordwell (art direction), Julie Andrews (best actress), Robert Preston (best supporting actor), Lesley Ann Warren (supporting actress), Henry Mancini and Leslie Bricusse (best music) and Edwards himself (best adapted screenplay), but *Victor's* single Oscar win went to Mancini and Bricusse. The film garnered a host of Golden Globe nominations and other awards—notably the César for *meilleur film étranger*, the David di Donatello for best screenplay of a foreign film, and the WGA Award for best adapted comedy—and hurried Edwards to the peak of critical and popular acclaim. With no shortage of offers, Blake once again faced the familiar, though still precarious, question of how to use his recovered power. In the past, he had used hits to lengthen his studio leash and push the artistic envelope to its breaking point, but he had since learned his lesson. Either he could stray from the Blake Edwards the world wanted to see while the real Blake Edwards suffered the consequences (see *Darling Lili*, etc.), or he could give them the *bimps* and *meuths* they wanted (read: once wanted) and pretty much secure his place atop Hollywood, dig in his heels, and get comfortable again.

Better safe than sorry (right?)*

* Please see "*Panther* Pictures: Sellers Lives On" for a discussion of *Trail of the Pink Panther*, *Curse of the Pink Panther*, and *Son of the Pink Panther*.

7

BLAKE BREAKS
1983–1988

THE MAN WHO LOVED WOMEN (1983)

David: I love watching women.

MICKI + MAUDE (1984)

Rob: I'm happy and suicidal!

A FINE MESS (1986)

Ellen: Do I smell like onions?

There is no getting around it: the next five years of Edwards' career were not good. Vacillating between diluted studio jobs and filmed therapies, Blake saw his work of this period alternately compromised by an excess of laurel-resting and navel-gazing. His abusive relationship with Hollywood had finally gotten co-dependent, and try as he might to break away from it, he always found himself back for another beating. But this time the S.O.B.s weren't the only ones to blame. With *The Pink Panther* twenty years in the past, the splurch was finally showing its age—and so was Blake. *The Man Who Loved Women* and *That's Life!* are needlessly heavy, *Micki + Maude* and *A Fine Mess* are heedlessly light, and although *Blind Date* and *Sunset* represent returns to form, it's only form they return to. Where was the innovation of Blake's youth? Where was the dazzle? Gone, it seemed, in the haze of whine and dozes.

The first time Blake sought psychoanalytic counsel was in the early fifties. As a hypochondriac and one-time morphine addict, he would meet vicious circles of actual and invented pain as what began as somatic injuries—a broken back, a broken neck—and ended up psychic. From morphine Blake turned to drugs and alcohol. "Madness was creeping up on me," he remembers. "I was frightened, in terror. I was just in the most profound depression and had the most terrible anxieties." Bound up in his relationship problems was the remembered trauma of his mother's suicide threats, and the deep jealousies and manipulations she had conditioned into him. "You find yourself immediately talking about all the forbidden things that childhood made forbidden—and, obviously, the most profound part of that was sexuality."[1] Edwards endeavored to put it all into *The Man Who Loved Women*, an "Americanization" of Truffaut's 1977 film (Blake was careful not to call it a remake), which he co-wrote with his therapist Milton Wexler. The picture describes a psychosexual picaresque through the mind of artist-in-midlife-crisis David Fowler (Burt Reynolds) as he beds Louise and Agnes and Courtney and Nancy and Janet and eventually his therapist Marianna (Julie Andrews), who narrates in flashback, trying to maintain scientific detachment, while carrying on the "do you really think we should be doing this?" bit until she finally decides she shouldn't.

David Fowler shares with fellow creatives George Webber, Felix Farmer, and Zach Hutton (Skin Deep) a sex problem that plays out voyeuristically. Obsessed with their own masculine decay, these men find perverse relief in body watching. Blake Edwards knows a great deal about the tricks the eyes play on the heart, and has developed an elaborate system of visual illusions to represent them. Throughout the filmography, characters torn by their difficulties with doubles are often met with the camera's eye for slick surfaces, bold colorizations, and other seductive (ultimately hollow) representations of the pretty veneer of things. The truth about skin-deep splurches many of them, but they tend to come out the better for it. David Fowler, though, is the exception; his eyes lead him to his death. The first time we see Fowler, he's looking at a pair of legs through the window of his gallery (the gallery itself is a place where people come to look—David is, after all, a sculptor; surfaces are more than a pastime, they're how he makes his living). He follows her, and a solitary splurch—about the only one in The Man Who Loved Women—comes after. Hot on the trail, David nearly gets hit by a car, trips backward, and flies into the back of a truck. The slapstick turns grizzly when, at the end of the film, he sees Legs crossing Rodeo Drive, runs after her, and is mowed down by a Rolls. The hospital doctor says he'll survive, which he does, though not for much longer. A leggy nurse steps in, David reaches after her, and falls to his death.

David's house is a voyeur's paradise. It's walled in glass, filled with objets d'art, vantage points, and uninterrupted sight lines. One night David picks up a sweet-looking hooker (Jennifer Edwards), takes her back to his studio and watches her. He simply watches her. The implication is that, to David, women are art: targets of masculine scrutiny, things of beauty, but hardly real people. Enter Marianna, David's analyst. Because the locus of David's problematized desire is in his eyes, their sessions take place in a honey-colored cubicle free of visual distractions. There are no windows, sculptures, or vistas in Marianna's office. Edwards further demystifies the act of looking by reducing his formal treatment of these scenes to an abstentious minimum in which long takes go uninterrupted by camera movement. As is the Freudian custom, David spends the fifty-minute hours looking *away* from his doctor. Only after an opportune earthquake disrupts the session's calm does David glance over at Marianna to see her legs reflected in a mirror. Scopophilia is reintroduced, Pandora's box opens, and a love affair begins. The courtship includes a trip to the ballet—Hollywood's favorite way to indicate a changed man—reminding us that when the stage is present, the problem of perception can't be far off. That they're seen watching *Swan Lake* is further indication that David, like Siegfried, is tragically susceptible to the way things appear.

Blake Edwards' unconventional use of voice-over addresses this conflict between David's exteriority and Marianna's interiority, and adopts a free-associative structure that allows him to shift from scenes that take place inside of David (flashback), to scenes that take place outside of him (present). But there's a hitch: the entire film is Marianna's flashback. That means that David's subjectivity is placed within hers. What we see, then, is only Marianna's impression of David's interiority—the doctor's diagnosis of her patient—not his own. This is essential to the character's tragedy: he never becomes introspective, meaning he is all exterior. In these terms, *The Man Who Loved Women* is actually a film about a woman remembering a man remembering women, and uses narrators like Victoria wears genders: to divest us of our supposed hold on the veracity of what we see.

The movie was generally disliked. Neither Burt Reynolds' box-office cachet nor the film's distinguished pedigree, which included Ralph Winters, Haskell Wexler, and Milton Wexler, was enough to save it, disproving the short-lived theory that Burt was a sure thing and two Wexlers were better than one. We can only wonder if Blake wonders at what went wrong. Should he have cast Dustin or Warren? (He tried.) Should he have shot the picture in his regular wide-screen format? Should he have used the chipper new ending Columbia asked him to?

Burt and Blake weren't fazed, and soon after the film's completion, approached Clint Eastwood to star (with Reynolds) in Blake's tough little Prohibition comedy, *Kansas City Jazz*. Retitled *City Heat*, the bantery buddy movie was ready to begin shooting when Eastwood and his writer/director reached an impasse. According to Eastwood biographer Patrick McGilligan, Blake had "mysteriously dropped"[2] Clint's inamorata Sondra Locke from the picture in favor of casting—and this via Richard Schickel's biography of Eastwood—Jennifer Edwards, Blake's daughter.[3] In came script disputes and personality disputes (Burt Reynolds likened the Edwards-

28. *The Man Who Loved Women* (1983) Looking, watching, spying, and/or objectifying are a constant lure (and ultimately torment) to the Edwardian lothario. David Fowler (Burt Reynolds), seen here in an art gallery, has directed his glance from one representation to another. (Columbia Pictures/Photofest)

Eastwood collaboration to Stanley Donen tap dancing with Gary Cooper⁴), and finally, out of deference to the star, Warner Brothers fired Edwards in favor of director Richard Benjamin. Blake had his name taken off the picture.*

"It broke my heart,"⁵ Edwards said. Perhaps it was in this frame of mind that he consented to direct *Micki + Maude*, a film that seemingly required less of him than it does of us. It tells the story of Rob Salinger (Dudley Moore), who loves Micki (Ann Reinking), but never gets to see her

---

* The screenwriter credited on *City Heat*, under the pseudonym "Sam O. Brown" (note the initials, inspectors), is none other than Mr. Edwards in disguise.

because she's always working. Maude (Amy Irving), on the other hand, is adorable and available, and very suddenly, also pregnant. And incidentally, so is Micki. For three trimesters, Rob somehow manages to keep them both in the dark by running around like a man in a farce, which he is. After Micki and Maude deliver their babies at the same hospital at the same time in adjoining rooms (sloppy bigamy, but really fun), Rob's deceit is at last discovered, and Micki and Maude bar him from seeing their children. But he is Dudley Moore, which means before long both women are back in love with him. Customary Edwardian tendencies are at play: the problem of monogamy, the strength of the male duo, scenes of voyeurism and performance, and, of course, the great masculine crisis.

Rob gets off lightly for an Edwards protagonist. Unlike George Webber (who gets skewered), he isn't interested in the typically masculine pursuit of flesh, but the so-called feminine world of child rearing. Conversely, the androgynously named Micki plays the "masculine" role of career-oriented parent, unable to devote time to children. (Even Maude's father, a professional wrestler, is a device of gender inversion; he cries, discusses interior decoration, and hugs.) If he is a bigamist, why doesn't Rob get splurched? Because his bigamy is sincere: he is *genuinely* in love. As opposed to most of Edwards' men, Rob's infidelity comes from an excess of affection and not the lack of it. He's a feminized lothario, not a chauvinist, and thereby renders Edwards' process of moral rectitude redundant. Accordingly, Blake will deny slapstick opportunities throughout *Micki + Maude.* The scene in the doctor's office, for example, a generous contrivance that offers Blake two wives and one waiting room, lends itself to the kind of dumb show we saw in *The Pink Panther*, and a proscenium-minded single take clears the air for thorough splurching, but physical comedy is declined at every turn. Save for a slight gag montage at the end of the film (running into a tree, soapsuds), Rob pays for his minor misdeeds in a little sweat and embarrassment.*

Despite these deviations from his directorial insignia, *Micki + Maude* is typical Edwards when it comes to the master shot. Entire scenes play out in one take; the camera is often fixed, and coverage is scarce. The exchanges between husband and wives (namely Rob's with Micki) are not subjected to directorial comment of any kind—Blake opts for a more objective van-

---

* Pauline Kael: "It's puzzling that a director with Edwards' mastery of sight gags . . . would come up with a picture as visually undistinguished as this one."[6]

tage point—a tactic that frees him from having to weigh in on the problem of bigamy. It's a cunningly conceived bit of neutrality, and crucial to getting us on board with Rob, but in its moral indifference undermines Blake's facility with comic humilation. The director redeems himself in the film's bravura third act, but in large part it is inaccurate to classify *Micki + Maude* as a Blake Edwards movie. Gender explorations are present, and the notion of duplicity is contained throughout, but they are merely utilitarian story points. Screenwriter Jonathan Reynolds elaborates:

> Columbia said to me, "We've got this great idea about a man who gets his wife and his girlfriend pregnant at the same time," which I thought would be pretty smarmy if the guy were played by Warren Bcatty. So in order to make the character sympathetic, I concluded he had to be the loving, maternal figure desperate for babies and the other two had careers on their minds (or at least Micki did, which allowed Rob to fall for someone whom he felt loved him).[7]

The material was appropriate for Edwards, but was too mild to play to his strengths. "Once again," *Variety* wrote, "the director has proved that he is a master farceur, probably the foremost practitioner on the scene today of the sort of romantic comedy at which Hollywood used to excel."[8] Yes, but let's not mince words here: the picture belongs to Dudley Moore. "He is the only actor I can compare to Sellers in terms of physical comedy and his understanding of humor," said Blake. "That's particularly important for those sequences in which the camera becomes a proscenium, giving Dudley's finely tuned comedic instincts to play within the framework of a scene as it unfolds because, rather than guide my audience into looking here or there, I allow them to see a lot of things going on at once."[9] The comic freedom the master shot allows an audience was, in a manner of speaking, prevalent on the set. There was Blake's omnipotent fart machine, which if deployed at the right moment could splurch anything, and someone in a gorilla costume who broke out of a closet during a take and tried to seduce Dudley.

Blake Edwards intended *A Fine Mess* to be a remake of the classic Laurel and Hardy short *The Music Box*, and planned on improvising his way through the picture the way he did in *The Party*, but studio interference and bad test screenings forced him to reconceptualize. Sadly, the picture became a meaningless, awesomely mind-numbing exercise in emptiness. The story follows Spence (Ted Danson) and Dennis (Howie Mandel) as they get themselves into a situation involving a couple of gangsters, a racetrack, and breathtakingly enormous suppositories. The bad guys who know they know too much run them all over Los Angeles, but when the cops catch up with them after Howie Mandel's cringeworthy/memorable escapade in drag, they capture the heavies and free the heroes. The whole thing is so aggressively indifferent to the tenets of cinema narrative it achieves a kind of monastic transcendence. Does this suggest that Edwards was after an anarchy so pure he had to drain his film of content to get there? If so, and there is majesty in steadfast senselessness, then A Fine Mess is Blake's coronation. But all this seems unlikely; A Fine Mess is not a good bad movie, it's just a bimbo.

The headline in Variety read, "Laurel & Hardy, RIP."[10] "I can't think of a single reason for anyone to see it," Andrew Sarris wrote, "but I remain interested in Edwards' ideas about comedy, even when they seem completely misguided at first, second, and third glance. After all, it took me a decade to come to terms with The Great Race. Unfortunately, A Fine Mess may take a century."[11] Columbia predicted this kind of response and changed the movie's release date from Christmas 1985 to May 16 of the following year, and then bumped it up again to August. Test screenings indicated that unlike Edwards' recent continuum of male-menopausal movies, A Fine Mess was well matched to younger tastes, and late summer would be an ideal moment to lay the bait, but the kids didn't bite. Whether Blake's original cut was more palatable we'll probably never know, but either way, the miserable studio experience left him, once again, outraged at Hollywood, and he vanished from the scene. But this time he didn't go to Europe, he went to Malibu, and he took his whole family with him.

THAT'S LIFE! (1986)

Gillian: Let it out.

Blake knew that if he wanted to make *That's Life!* his way, he would have to finance the picture himself, and so he put up $1.5 million of his own money, used the family home in Malibu as his main location, and asked the actors to defer payment. He also invited co-writer Milton Wexler to be a regular presence on set, and not just to give notes, but to lead the company in analysis. Blake said,

> It was almost like group therapy. We would sit and talk about this character and what they would say and what they wouldn't say and where they were coming from, and he would conduct a seminar in a way that we would eventually get up and shoot.[12]

That's Life! wasn't just an experimental picture, in Edwards' hands it was experimental treatment. For the first few weeks of production, he had created an artistic and therapeutic utopia absolutely unique in the history of movies. But there was trouble in Paradise Cove.

When the Local 695 discovered that *That's Life!* was a nonunion shoot, they wrote an open letter in the *Hollywood Reporter* alerting the heads of both the Screen Actors' Guild and the Directors' Guild of America that Tony Adams and Jonathan Krane, the film's producers, had not been granted waivers from IATSE (the International Alliance of Theatrical Stage Employees), and urged the guilds to pull their members out of the production. The DGA and SAG responded that they had in fact signed contracts with Edwards' Malibu Productions, and would therefore be in violation of their own agreement if they were to strike. But there was a backlash to the backlash. Morgan Paull, a chief representative of Actors Working for an Actor's Guild (a subdivision of SAG), expressed support of the Local 695 on behalf of his organization, while Charlton Heston, himself a prominent figure in AWAG (Actors Working for an Actors Guild), spoke out in defense of SAG. Almost overnight, the guild split in two, and just as fast, a picket line erupted outside Edwards' home. Meanwhile, Adams and Krane issued a counterstatement that said, "Waivers were requested from IATSE prior to commencement of principal photography, which we understood were granted, and which we relied upon."[13] The production itself was basically uncompromised by the fiasco, although Edwards' favorite cinematographer, Harry Stradling Jr. (who had shot S.O.B., Micki + Maude, and A Fine Mess), was forced out by the American Society of Cinematographers, and replaced by Tony Richmond.

In time, though, the union crisis was resolved and *That's Life!* resumed. The film is set the weekend of Harvey Fairchild's (Jack Lemmon) sixtieth birthday. The poor guy's a nervous wreck and scared out of his mind, though for the wrong reasons; while he's kvetching, his wife Gillian (Julie Andrews) is waiting for her biopsy results. The Fairchild children come in next, bringing with them neuroses of their own and not a single one aware of their mother's potential illness. Julie clutches at her throat periodically to remind us of what nobody is talking about, but that changes when the doctor comes to Harvey's party to bring her the news—good news. Everything is going to be okay.

Blake Edwards juggles realities. Going all the way back to *High Time*, he has demonstrated a keen interest in combining genres and narrative attitudes that on first glance appear to be irreconcilable, on second glance look mad, and on third glance, maybe, hybridize opposites into new and unprecedented forms. Perpetually poised in in-betweens, these works are conflicted not just within themselves, but amongst themselves. How do we locate the heart of an artist when it straddles films as stylistically and emotionally diverse as *The Party* and *The Tamarind Seed*? How do we—rather, how does he—reconcile those cartoon visions with his psychoanalytic concerns?

That's Life! doesn't try to modernize the slapstick idiom, but submits instead to a full-blown realism tied to biographical ground and tempts us to read it with a one-to-one eye for representation and real life. S.O.B. also shares certain prominent commonalities with its creator—not the least of which is a burning desire to sexualize Julie Andrews—but unlike *That's Life!*, it's firmly grounded in the splurch. Slapstick advances the predicament of Felix Farmer a few paces past reality and helps us untangle what is authentic from what is phony. Not so with *That's Life!* For starters, Blake Edwards shot the film at his house, with his money, and his family. In it, Julie Andrews plays a celebrated singer and family matriarch; Emma Walton, her daughter, and Jennifer Edwards play her daughters; Chris Lemmon, son of Jack (who plays Mr. Fairchild), assumes the role of the son;

and Felicia Farr, Jack Lemmon's real-life wife, plays a kooky medium who gropes her way into curing his impotence.

"Everybody was dealing with themselves," Blake said, "everybody but me. I just sat back and let Jack be me, to some extent."[14] But to what extent? The director has demanded a biographical reading and then has complicated it. His conflation of private life with the public life of cinematic representation is, like Lili Smith/Schmidt's conflict, riddled with the problems of duplicity, but this time it isn't the lies of the characters we're dealing with, it's the truths of the actors playing them. Watching the picture we might ask, Is this a home movie? Or is it a fiction made to look like a home movie? Did Julie Andrews *really* have a cancer scare, or is that something they made up? (Did Emma Walton *really* name her dog Chutney?)

Problems of reality/imagination get fuzzier when we consider that *That's Life!* was largely improvised. Lemmon described it like this:

> Blake developed the characters, the story, how the characters would behave . . . but we helped put in the words. Of course, Blake was still the director. He said, "do this," "do that," "develop this more," or "forget that." But we, the characters, spoke very much as we felt we should.[15]

So what was scripted and what was improvised? If certain of these scenes are improvised and potentially reflect the experiences of the actors who play them as they play them, then these aren't just characters we're watching, but spontaneous evocations of the actor's real selves. In that case, there is no performance, "acting" must have quotations around it, and *That's Life!* is actually a kind of documentary in disguise. Many of these questions are impossible to resolve, but like Buñuel's surrealist documentary *Las Hurdes*, it's only the asking that matters.

To gain insight into the mystery, it is necessary to examine the picture's formal elements. Perhaps the most curious visual feature of *That's Life!* is that it abstains from the stylistic traits we expect of improvised (or partially improvised) filmmaking. Going all the way back to *Breathless*, arguably the apex of movie extemporaneousness, we find a highly pragmatic cinema, one that must forego the tradition of control in deference to the needs of spontaneity. Since then, Godard's handheld camera, extended scenes of dialogue, and grainy black-and-white film stock have become mainstays of the impromptu aesthetic, and helped to pave the way for American independents like Cassavetes whose movies, like *That's Life!*, are populated

29. *That's Life!* (1986) The Fairchild family, speckled with autobiographical ties. Pictured here are father Harvey (Jack Lemmon, center), mother Gillian (Julie Andrews), with daughter Megan (Jennifer Edwards, left), son Josh (Chris Lemmon), and daughter Kate (Emma Walton, daughter of Julie Andrews). (Author's collection)

with the director's friends and family. By contrast, the formal composition of *That's Life!* walks a line between naturalism and mannerism, and is as conflicted and enigmatic as its central conceit.

The early portion of the film—in which the relationship between Harvey and Gillian is at its rockiest—is photographed with a passive camera that holds back in wide-shot and permits the actors improvisatory leash to negotiate the space without amending it with cuts and/or movement. When the Fairchilds meet at the end of the first day, Blake shoots the meeting at the bottom of the stairs, in a frame cluttered with distractions. This is not a "carefully selected" image in either composition or beauty, but seems as though it were captured on the fly. And yet, despite its apparent randomness, the shot is expressive in its immobility; it describes Harvey's chaotic emotional state and the disconnect in his marriage. In other words, it's carefully directed. But reality isn't. And thus the contradiction of real and artificial persists: Edwards' use of the picture is both objective in its encouragement of actor-agency *and* interpretive in its visualization of their emotional states.

Equally conflicted is the film's transition from the feeling of extemporaneity to intimacy. As *That's Life!* continues and the Fairchilds are drawn together, Edwards abandons the wide shots for single close-ups. In the family dinner scene, for instance, the illusion of a directorless film has evaporated. We see here a more conventional, controlled cinema, as relegated by a higher frequency of cuts between speakers. Once initiated, the transition from wide to close continues to expand, going from the dinner table to Gillian and Harvey's bedroom scene, to its culmination: a shared close-up of Harvey and Gillian dancing cheek-to-cheek after her secret has been revealed. Intimacy, the camera says, is now possible. It ranks with the closest of human close-ups Edwards has ever shot.

Seen under a magnifying glass, there are certain moments that break entirely from the film's dream of naturalism in favor of the dominant Hollywood aesthetic. Certain close-ups of Andrews are Streisanded with diva-glow, and the film's finale—the down-to-the-last-minute reveal that Gillian will be okay—comes at a moment only Hollywooden logic would allow. Weary of her voice, Gillian is about to sing, and almost divulges her secret when her doctor appears from the shadows and gives her a happy sign. Wouldntyaknowit. Additionally, the film's deliberate composition is affirmed by several gags—the "holy water" (filled with liquor), the crabs scene, and Father Baragone's (Robert Loggia's) slip on his way to the podium—which splurch, as they did in 10, the religious figure and the adulterer.

Although *That's Life!* was not a box-office success, its negligible overhead turned a nice profit for its principals. The critical reception was generally favorable; some praised Edwards' experimentalism, others accused him of self-indulgence. And yet, amongst the lukewarm, a few observations stood out. Janet Maslin, a frequent champion of Edwards' work, came to his defense once again. Where others nailed him on charges of self-plagiarism and downright irrelevance (things like "who cares about the whiny rich?"), Maslin, in a lengthy appreciation of the film, compared *That's Life!* to emeritus masterpieces like *All That Jazz* and *Fanny and Alexander*.[16]

It was a personal triumph for the director—and much needed. Blake's life, throughout the production of *That's Life!*, was filled to the brim with the kind of personal, professional, and creative tensions we see manifested in the film itself; it is built of inner stylistic contradictions, it has a conflicting relationship to Blake Edwards' other pictures, it was shot amidst fervent union opposition, and finally, as an experiment in autobiographical filmmaking, it stands in counterpoint to a career marked by lavish entertainments. Even the humor in the film is contrapuntal, but that's life.

BLIND DATE (1987)

Walter: What does "lose control" mean?

In 1986, Cybill Shepherd's pregnancy put *Moonlighting* on a fourteen-week hiatus, which allowed Bruce Willis enough time to break into movies. With *Blind Date*, made at TriStar for $16 million, Willis had his first starring role, but at that time, before his superhero image had been solidified, he was known for playing smoothies like David Addison from *Moonlighting*, and his work in features was expected to follow suit. Instead, Edwards signed him to the most antithetical role imaginable: Walter Davis, the corporate-minded discombobulate in *Blind Date*. It was certainly a risky move, especially on the heels of Sean Penn and Madonna, who had just dropped the picture, but Edwards assured the studio there was no need to worry. He was after all quite practiced in casting against type. There was the transformation of Hepburn into Holly to remember, and of course the ongoing sexification of Julie Andrews (not to mention what *Peter Gunn* did to Craig Stevens and what *Days of Wine and Roses* did to Jack Lemmon), but Willis was different. Though he was known, he was not yet a movie star.

Meanwhile, screenwriter Dale Launer's original draft of *Blind Date*, rewritten by Leslie Dixon and Tom Ropelewski, and revised again by Edwards, emerged without his credit, and Launer decided to fight it. The script went into arbitration. According to Launer,

> I know there were scenes added where someone crashed into a bakery and becomes covered with flour and later someone with all of their clothes on jumps or falls into a swimming pool or someone tosses something into a woman's cleavage. . . .[17]

Launer argued that despite the new material, the new writers hadn't altered the script's structure, which remained overwhelmingly his own. The Writers' Guild decided in favor of Launer—and Edwards protested. "I actually tried to get my name taken off the script," Launer says, continuing,

> My experience with Mr. Blake is without question the worst experience I've had in the motion picture business. He refused to talk to me, refused to even have someone tell me he wasn't going to talk to me. He

was shooting my script but was unwilling to have any communication with me whatsoever. No apologies. Nothing. Kind of a big . . . uh . . . fuck you. So, as a result, I think the guy's kind of a prick.[18]

Stories of this kind are all over Hollywood. On more than one occasion, Edwards has threatened physical combat against his enemies (Felix Farmer, in S.O.B.: "I warn you, my hands are lethal weapons!"), and is notorious for causing problems when things don't go his way. "There are two sides to Blake Edwards," Anthony Cook reports. "Depending upon who you talk to, the man is either a pixie or a hellion."[19] It seems the reality of it is if you're an actor, he's a pixie, and if you're anyone else, learn jujitsu.

Screen credit aside, Blind Date, a screwball comedy about a yuppie who falls in love with the gag, is unquestionably a Blake Edwards movie. Walter Davis (Bruce Willis), a businessman on the rise, has anarchy written all over him, but he must sublimate slapstick to impress his superiors. Nadia Gates (Kim Basinger), the high priestess of drunken calamity, accompanies Walter to a Very Important Dinner, splurches authority left and right, and gets him fired in the process. At first he hates her for it, but in typical eighties fashion he learns that the gag is mightier than the briefcase, and spends the rest of the movie discovering his inner havoc. (It's Days of Wine and Roses, but funny.) In the classical Hollywood style, he follows his slapstick angel all the way to her fiancé's house, and intervenes just as she's about to marry him.

The opposition between composure and recklessness is an ideal setting for Edwards' gag reflex, and it's in play almost instantly. Blind Date opens with a measured pan from Walter's bedroom to his living room, beginning with a guitar by the bed and ending with Walter asleep on a table in the living room. Walter has done to his musicality what the shot has done to the guitar; that is, he has left it behind, he has sublimated it. The sequence that follows conveys this tension between inner authenticity and money-hungry yuppie, and does so through a series of minor gags, all presented with Edwards' impeccable sense of momentum. The radio alarm sounds, jolting Walter from his sleep—he's late for work. Now fumbling before the mirror, he ties a tie around his forehead, straightens the knot, and then realizes his error: ties belong around the collar. He makes the necessary readjustments and then bolts. The gag has answered the question asked by the guitar. Walter is not corporate at heart.

30. *Blind Date* (1987) Where there is pretension in Edwards, there is a loose cork jonesing to break free. The 1980s were made to be splurched, and *Blind Date* lights the fuse. From left to right: Walter Davis (Bruce Willis), Nadia Gates (Kim Basinger), and George Coe (Harry Gruen), as the yuppie businessman incarnate. (Author's collection)

The wide shot of the office interior does the double duty of enhancing the physicality of the impending gag and accentuating the austerity of the professional world. Edwards' penchant for hard, sleek lines is given prominence in the wide shot, and contrasted with the tempestuous effects of slapstick makes the polarity appear more extreme. Walter runs from camera right to camera left, crashes into an office employee (paper goes flying) and continues onward. Perpetual motion places him at odds with the rigidity of office life—the gag recapitulates—and Edwards' indefatigable use of camera movement keeps the tempo lively. From there, an extended Steadicam shot leads Walter from the cubicles into the elevator and then over to his meeting. In a single take, the actor walks "into" the camera, to the right of the camera, to the left, and even when he's standing still in the elevator (going down) the exterior changes as the glass box flies from one floor to the next. Combining multiple screen directions in such a cramped space of time compresses activity and makes the motion appear doubly frenetic. It is, by the same reasoning, the perfect setting for the gag, but Edwards deliberately sublimates it. We know Walter is gag-prone when he's alone (we've seen it twice already), and so we expect it to recur, especially now, only seconds before the big meeting, but like the guitar it is repressed by the businessman in Walter. As for the other side of him, the side that craves music and anarchy, the side that would throw up if it ever found out about office-Walter, that side Nadia will take care of.

Their blind date gets underway at an art gallery. Another long take, handheld this time, establishing improvisational intimacy between Walter and Nadia as they walk around the room, and in its continuity, picks up all the little moments between the lines. However, the moment Nadia's ex-boyfriend David (John Larroquette) is introduced, Edwards breaks the shot with a cut, suggesting that montage is an impediment to romantic rapport, and that the screwball rudiments of banter and motion have been broken. When David takes a swing at Walter (who evades) and lands in a sculpture, we know that the worlds of business and art can never commingle. That gag says that inner authenticity, when externalized through art, is staunchly opposed corporate pretension. That being the case, it is fitting that Walter and Nadia's first kiss is set in a recording studio. The scene is covered in wide shots.

Off they go to the restaurant where the Very Important Dinner is set to take place. Of course, we know it's important because the waiters are French—is there a better indication of snobbery in the movies? Like Walter's fellow businessmen, these hierarchy-obsessed elitists are poised for a splurching, and thanks to Nadia's low alcohol tolerance, all it takes is a little booze and she's off. (A waiter gets champagne in the face.) Walter loves her for it—we see his latent fondness for anarchy surface—but when her mayhem turns to the company table, he must sublimate. Nadia, meanwhile, can't be stopped, and after she tears the wig off Mr. Yakamoto's concubine, all hell breaks loose. False hair, one of Blake Edwards' favorite displays of duplicity, is put to good use here, exposing the Japanese chauvinism behind the geisha. "You're entitled to fifty percent of your husband's assets," Nadia whispers to the concubine. "Fifty percent?" she asks. Nadia's splurch has become a fiscal castrator, chopping down men where it really hurts—in their pockets (she actually rips pockets off jackets, a little sight gag that plays on the metaphor)—making her a proponent of yuppie domination. Walter's fired.

Now Nadia has David *and* Walter on her case. Their attempts at repressing her—David with unrequited love, Walter with anger—are quite naturally offset by a gag sequence that does its best to splurch it out of them, but fails. It begins as David crashes his car first into a pet store and then a paint store, continues as Walter drops off Nadia at a house that is literally pulled away, and tops off the topper when David crashes into a flour depository. Finally, at a posh Los Angeles dinner party (the peak of yuppie pretension), David and Walter fall off the balcony in acrobatic unison and onto the cake below. Both are humiliated by the gag because they are opposed to it—if they loved Nadia for who she was, not what she did, they'd learn to love the gag—but in the meantime, the more Walter fights the splurch the harder it beats him, until the topper can be topped no more and he is thrown in jail.

By the time he is released, his orientation to the gag has changed. The next morning, Walter's brother Ted (Phil Hartman, perfectly cast) picks him up in his shiny new Lincoln, a car that represents Ted's business (he is a car salesman), and therefore a target for the splurch. But this time, for the first time, Walter is doing the splurching. On the drive home, he asks, "New car?" "Yes," Ted replies from behind his shades, and Walter leans forward to puke on the carpeting. The vomit expresses his disgust for everything his brother's car represents; business, affluence, and yuppie chic—everything Walter once aspired to. The new Walter is different, though. He's disheveled, cranky, and in terms of the splurch, won't contain his impulses. In other words, he's becoming like Nadia, and when he finds her hungover in bed, the comparison is made clear; she herself is disheveled, cranky, and won't contain her impulses. He approaches her, breaking the bed frame; she slides off and pulls herself up again. They fight through the whole scene, but Edwards knows—and the presence of physical comedy confirms—that their reckless authenticity is not pulling them apart, but bringing them together. To make his point, he shoots the exchange in a master shot. As in their first conversation, the spatial and temporal continuity of the shot allows for intimacy, and considering there's a mattress in the middle of it all, this scene is less conducive to hostility than to love—slapstick love. From now on, physical comedy will assume a positive connotation.

Later in the film, when Walter tries to save Nadia from David, he is seen falling out of the Bedfords' tree, into their pool, and even hiding under their bed. (He now wears Hawaiian shirts.) And yet, Walter isn't splurched by the gags. In fact, the pratfalls and other minor setbacks that befall Walter actually protect him. The tree, the pool, the bed; these things conceal him from his opponents, and introduce a protective slapstick into Blind Date, culminating in Walter's liquor-into-chocolates initiative. This deliberate, premeditated gag summons is intended to free the inner havoc from Nadia who is, as this very moment, on her way to the altar with David. Symbolically, it represents the completion of Walter's arc from gag denier to gag exploder. And as we hear "speak now or forever hold your peace," the physical outburst takes effect. With Walter revealed, Nadia drunk, and a pool between them, the lovers leap into the air, splash into the water, and into each other's arms. They kiss.

The film's problematic last moment sees the reunited couple embrace beside a two-liter bottle of Coke. Are we supposed to believe that Nadia has given up drinking? If so, is the implication that the gag has been "rightfully" banished? Considering Walter's transformation, all this seems utterly unconvincing (even dumb),* but it is not without precedent. Indeed the endings of 10, Skin Deep, and Breakfast at Tiffany's express an Edwardian doubt about romantic longevity, and Experiment in Terror, Days of Wine and Roses, Gunn, and S.O.B. make it look downright impossible (in Micki + Maude, it quite literally was), but if we take the whole panoply of Edwardian relations into account we might recover a little hope. All we have to do is look at the men. For every fractured heterosexual romance in Blake Edwards' films there is an equally stable friendship, whether at the bar, on the trail, or in the wings. Where there is no sex there is no strife, and even when the friendships end (as in Wild Rovers and S.O.B.) they end because of external pressures (death in both cases), not because of duplicity or any other kind of Edwardian no-no.

Blind Date went on to take in $87 million, but you wouldn't know it to look at the reviews. The New Yorker was kinder than most: "The movie plods along with a jokey but dispirited air, like a sketch in a Bob Hope special. When things get slow, somebody falls into the pool."[20] Janet Maslin saw more, countering, "The perfect gag, as orchestrated with supreme professionalism by Blake Edwards, is something that proceeds in

* TriStar was at the time a subsidiary of Coca-Cola.

stages. It has a beginning, a middle, an end, and maybe even a postscript or two."[21] (Without knowing it, she described topping the topper.) It's true that the picture can't withstand the pressures of prolonged consideration, but there's no denying it's exemplary regulation of slapstick, especially those scenes involving Kim Basinger, who turns it out with the beauty and precision of Carole Lombard. In physical comedy, Edwards rarely affords women the same opportunities he does men (largely because his female characters are too reasonable to be splurched), but Basinger, since *The Man Who Loved Women*, has provided him a notable, wonderful exception. In that picture, Edwards made sure her character paid the price for adultery, and gifted Basinger with gags that showed off her propensity for slapstick, as well as his eye for advancing untapped talent, a skill that was paying off for him (and for them) as far back as 1964. Although Sellers' genius had been unleashed to the English, it was *The Pink Panther* that brought him the international megastardom he retained to his dying day. Similarly, Edwards turned good into gold with the likes of Dick Shawn, Richard Mulligan, John Ritter, and Ellen Barkin (not to mention Dudley Moore and Robert Preston, who in *10* and *Victor/Victoria* gave the richest performances of their lives), while the less fortunate cases (Howie Mandel? Ted Wass?) are perhaps better off forgotten, though worth mentioning for the same reason: Blake delights in revising popular personalities as much as he does the identities of his characters. TriStar recognized it in his work with Bruce Willis, and on the occasion of *Blind Date*'s massive success, signed them up for another picture.

SUNSET (1988)

Alfie Alpern: Thank you for remembering.

If Edwards' commitment to Sunset can be quantified in his commitment to period authenticity, then it is to the film's designers that he owes his victory. The film's Dusenbergs, Packards, and Rolls-Royces came in at around a million dollars a piece, and when the time came for it, were demolished with the same love and respect with which they were made. Real locations were used whenever possible, even if it meant shlepping the crew out to the farthest reaches of California just to shoot a railway sequence that survives in less than a minute of Sunset's 102. Admittedly, there were some misguided attempts at rear-projection technique (the IntroVision process proved too restrictive), but on the whole, Edwards opted for mostly live recreations of Hollywood circa 1928. He snatched up Art Deco locales like they were going out of style (which they had), and in the case of the Academy Awards finale, used the back of Bullocks Wilshire for exteriors and Wiltern Theater down the street for the grand staircase shoot-out.

Coming off his big Date with Bruce Willis, Blake Edwards found the ebb and flow of his box-office potential had drifted in his favor once again, and the boss men of Culver City were prepared to pay. And in the case of Sunset, their money is on the screen. It survives in the decor of design team Rodger Maus, Richard Haman, and Marvin March, and in the costumes of Edwards-regular Patricia Norris (who was nominated that year for an Oscar). The production's concern for authenticity extended to the pages of Variety, which announced an open-casting call for "FAMOUS MOVIE STAR LOOK ALIKES OF 1928," listing names and their ages in the designated year. The list of twenty-four stars included some of Blake's idols; Stan Laurel (age thirty-nine), Oliver Hardy (thirty-seven), Harold Lloyd (thirty-six), and Buster Keaton (thirty-four) were among them, but unfortunately, not all of them made it to the finished film.

Despite its body count, Sunset is Blake Edwards' most optimistic Hollywood tale. It tells the story of the real Wyatt Earp (James Garner) after he's called into Hollywood to act as technical advisor on a Tom Mix (Bruce Willis) movie. But when a dead body is discovered at a local bordello, Wyatt and Mix's talents are really put to the test. The duo snoops its way right up to studio head Alfie Alperin whom, just after the 1927 Academy Awards, they bust for more than one murder.

Although the word Sunset is never mentioned in the film, the feeling of nostalgia, of an era's twilight, is felt throughout. The picture is awash in a golden glow and favors close-ups of a softer, forgiving approach to portraiture, as though the film itself were trying its best to remember happily. Thankfully, it's generous in its recollection: autumn is everywhere in *Sunset*, warm light pours in from all sides, and earthen tones of the American West fall through it like tumbleweed. This is not the 1928 of history books; it is a memory of 1928 dressed up with yearning for Hollywood's past. But memory is prone to revision, and as the king of movie duplicity, Edwards knows it better than most; indeed Wyatt's motto, "It's all true, give or take a lie or two," applies to his film as much as it does to the concept of nostalgia.

Movies play tricks on us. *Sunset* opens as a Western—a stagecoach flies over the hills with Tiomkinesque musical accompaniment—until we hear "Cut!" Oh, it was just a scene, and that man isn't a cowboy, he's Tom Mix, movie star. But of course, it isn't *really* Tom Mix, it's just Bruce Willis playing Tom Mix, and not even the real Mix, but a fantasized recreation of him (the story of *Sunset* is untrue, after all), and although Tom Mix and Wyatt Earp actually existed, what we're watching never occurred. If lying is a crime, *Sunset* is saying, then movies should be locked away. And not just the Tom Mix movies within *Sunset*, but the movie *Sunset* itself. We have our proof in Mancini's non-diegetic emulation of Dimitri Tiomkin. This bit of score is not source music coming from an element within the film, but a stroke of trickery trying to pass itself off as *Sunset* music. In fact, it has less to do with the film we're watching than with the film we're watching being filmed.

But it doesn't end there. The movies within the movie aren't simply not real, they're actual lies. Take the filmed shoot-out, for instance. From behind the cameras, Wyatt Earp observes the brawl with a squint. "This is inauthentic," he's thinking, and to prove it we cut to a flashback (a rare maneuver in Blake Edwards) that shows us what a real Western standoff looks like. And it looks more like *McCabe and Mrs. Miller* than *Sunset*; its flat light and dull colors are all shot with an unflattering telephoto lens that drains the epic sprawl from the scene. "Was that okay for you?" the director asks Earp after the take. "Okay for me," he says. "I mean, was that really just like it?" Wyatt waves him off. "Just like it." It's a blatant lie, but

31. *Sunset* (1988) Bruce Willis and Blake Edwards study the monitor between takes. Blake's shirt was to his eighties' wardrobe (see Illustration 25) what the turtleneck (see Illustrations 1, 10, and 18) was to his sixties', that is to say, an omnipresence. (TriStar Pictures/Photofest)

nobody knows the difference. Nobody, that is, but Tom Mix, who has the good sense to ask for clarification, and Wyatt's responds with pantomime.

> Marshallin' and actin' ain't too far apart. I remember one time, I wasn't packin' my six gun and Doc Holliday, he got drunk and he was just roarin' . . . he was gonna shoot my earlobes off. So I went for a hideout gun [Wyatt reaches into his jacket]. Fortunately, he thought I had one [Wyatt removes a cigar].

It's a performance about a performance, implying that Earp is just like any other actor, and lays the groundwork for Edwards' next shot. A magnificent crane pulls back from atop a cargo cart to reveal the busy back lot.

Grips, Indians, and chorus girls cross between soundstages, and there's Wyatt Earp in the middle of it. In this crowd, his authentic attire looks like just another costume, and for a moment turns the real-life sheriff into just another contract player. When the legend becomes fact, print the legend: that's the Western according to Earp. Give or take a truth or two.

Michael Alperin (Dermot Mulroney) is sure Wyatt isn't who he says he is. To prove himself, Earp tells a charming little anecdote about Mary Jane Canary, alias Calamity Jane. (Jane herself was a real-life frontierswoman, also prone to exaggerations about her own past. Her experience in Buffalo Bill's Wild West show—a traveling vaudeville of Western "heritage"—was as "reliable" as Wyatt's own.) Though brief, their exchange is thematically significant. Ironically, Michael is wrong in believing Wyatt is lying about his identity—he is in fact Wyatt Earp—but he's right in thinking him a liar. After all, who is Wyatt Earp but a self-constructed phony? Like Tom Mix, he's an actor with an image to maintain, but the role he's playing is himself. When he sits down to be interrogated by Chief Dibner (M. Emmet Walsh), Wyatt's manner is so clichéd in its evocation of "the Sheriff," it seems as though he's performing a part. He takes no pauses before he speaks, reveals no signs of weakness, and carries on with the kind of smart-ass poise we call Hollywood tough-guy. We've seen it many times before—the cowboy sizing up the marshal—but in this case, the tables are turned. Who's the real authority here, the appointed man behind the desk, or the man "playing" "Wyatt Earp"? By the end of the scene it's certain that the fake is the real thing: Edwards gives Wyatt close-ups, but Dibner gets mostly mediums. The victor is clear.

What is less clear, though, is the kind of movie *Sunset* is turning out to be. After his interview with Dibner, Wyatt is summoned to the palatial home of Christina Alperin, wife of studio head Alfie Alperin (Malcolm McDowell). When they meet, Mrs. Alperin is shot in half-shadow, and the film's score, Western until now, sounds a lonely horn. She takes Wyatt outside so they can be alone. There she confides in him. Her husband's a bad man, she says, and her son's in trouble. Can he help her? Wait: A rich and desperate blonde (with an accent) and a rough-and-tumble lawman? The marshal's getting more hard-boiled by the second. "I'll pay whatever it costs," she says. Wyatt stops her, "I'm not for hire." Of course he isn't. After Philip Marlowe, what respectable P. I. would be? Is *Sunset* cultivating a strain of noir? It has the femme fatale; now all it needs is the murder.

Enter the Candy Store, a high-end brothel with movie-star look-alikes for hookers. Like Wyatt, "Mae West" and "Greta Garbo" are walking amalgams of fact, posing the question, what is a legend but a reconstruction of the truth? The first shot inside the Candy Store confronts the dilemma the only way it can—with an illusion. Shot through what appears to be a glass partition, Tom and Wyatt make their way into the brothel, and before we have long enough to figure out that the partition is really a mirror, the surface slides back (oh, it's a door!), and out steps a man in tuxedo. Actually it's a woman (Mariel Hemingway), and she goes by the hermaphroditic name of Cheryl King. In a world of doubles—a very noir concern—King is her own gender double, and represents the Edwardian fascination with sexual duplicity. Generally in Edwards, the discrepancy between appearance and reality is used for comic effect, and when misrepresented is met with a retaliating gag, but there are no splurches in noir, no just comic force intended to restore order to the doubling. And where there is no humor, there is only confusion (think of Clouseau without the splurch). It follows that film noir is the evil twin of the Blake Edwards comedy.

What is unique about Sunset is that it represents a collaboration of both twins, and, like Wyatt, is juggling personae. We see it visualized at the scene of the crime, a bungalow behind the Candy Store. The shadow play is gentle here, though unmistakable; ambience has assumed a new visual precedence, richer in contrast, and with an emphasis on practicals that gives the room a jagged volatility. The Alperin home, in much the same way, is fractured with mild expressionistic gestures. These are evident in wrought-iron grillwork on the front door, the crooked shadows on the staircase, and of course, the venetian blinds, a veritable touchstone of noir stylistics. Paul Schrader elaborates:

> As in German expressionism, oblique and vertical lines are preferred to horizontal. Obliquity adheres to the choreography of the city, and it is in direct opposition to the horizontal tradition of Griffith and Ford. Oblique lines tend to splinter a screen, making it restless and unstable.[22]

Schrader notes an antipathy to the classical Western aesthetics of D. W. Griffith and John Ford, an observation that speaks to Sunset's schizophrenic split of genre and style. Edwards' eye for sturdy, balanced composition, perhaps the most striking visual characteristic of the film, is utterly opposed to the psychological aberrancy we encounter in noir. But to cinematographer Tony Richmond, the opposition was his artistic focal point:

I tried to shoot the exteriors with strong shadows and backlight, in the traditional John Ford Western image, and for the interiors I shot closer to the reality of what Hollywood looked like in the twenties. . . .A lot of the buildings in those days in this part of the world, regardless of how large they were, tended to have very small windows presumably to keep the sun out since there was no air conditioning. This enabled me to light a lot of our day interiors with strong shards of sunlight streaming in from outside.[23]

These contradictions run rampant through Sunset. The combinations of Western/noir, lying/truths, history/fiction , and the problems of performance, amount to a highly fraught cinematic environment.

This (con)fusion dovetails with Sunset's investment in the Edwardian problem of identity. That's why the combination of noir and Hollywood, both contingent on doubling, provides Edwards with the perfect Sunset setting. And that's why Tom Mix is the perfect hero. According to Jeanine Basinger,

Tom Mix' life story, though interesting, isn't a patch on the one invented for him by Fox publicists. He is a classic example of the Hollywood tendency to take what was more or less true and embroider it, as if it were one of his own cowboy shirts. . . .The publicists at Fox convinced Mix that it was in his best interests just to go along with the nonsense, because it was all business, and the business was that of selling images and stories to the public. He was told he could tell anyone the truth in private if he wished to, but publicly he was to endorse the legend. Mix more than endorsed it, he embraced it, and to this day it is difficult to tell fact from fiction.[24]

The spirit of invention continued on-screen as well. Compared to actor William S. Hart, whom Basinger calls "stark and realistic," Mix's cowboy persona was "flamboyant and flashy." She continues,

Hart performed his action sequences as realistically as possible, but Mix liked to wow an audience. Instead of just getting on his horse and riding well, he would show off—standing up in the saddle or jumping on his mount while the horse was at full gallop.[25]

Just as the audience knows Count Victor Grezhinski is only playing Victoria, so Tom Mix's audiences expected him to affect the cowboy showman. As real fakes, they are exemplary of Blake's favorite paradox, that what is imagined can often be mistaken for the truth. In that contradiction is the definition of legend, memory, and historical fiction made fact. That's Sunset. And that's movies. Give or take a lie or two.

One can only wonder if a different combination of genres could have saved the film from critical reproof, though in the case of Vincent Canby, it seems doubtful. He wrote, "Mr. Edwards' finished film remains little more than a fanciful idea photographed. It's not quite a murder mystery, not quite a satiric send-up of old Hollywood, not quite a comedy. It's a plot that unravels on its own, without characters, without anything, not even a point of view. It's a zombie."[26] Rather than enhance one another, the communion of narrative styles does just the opposite, and instead suffers in excess of Edwardian ambition. For others, the film failed on account of its lack of Edwardianism. "There are few of his own specialties here: none of those gems of physical humor, those beautifully protracted and choreographed set pieces. Instead, the film relies on décor, plot and dialog—and dialog is Edwards' great weakness as a scenarist."[27] Ironic: too much Edwards, and then not nearly enough. Which was it?

We might find a scapegoat in the Directors' Guild strike of June 30, 1988 which forced Blake to shoot at a hurried pace. If he had intended to wrap before production was put on a guild-wide halt, he would have had to break his comfortable working-day schedule and push on into late nights and evenings. He was never one for many takes, but in the case of Sunset, maybe a few more would have done him good. For whatever reason —lack of comedy, over-ambition, poor reviews—Sunset was a box-office loser and Blake was met with picking up the pieces once again. There was some talk of co-writing another film with Wexler, this one based on the true story of Koko the gorilla, the animal who was said to have grieved over the death of her cat.[28] Lehman and Luhr mention that in Blake's version of the story, entitled Helen and the Lord, the gorilla actually uses sign language to communicate that the cat went to God.[29] The film was mercifully never made, but the ecclesiastical component hints at the coming of a strange, though not unprecedented turn in Edwards' career.

8

BLAKE BOWS

1989–1991

SKIN DEEP (1989)

Zach: Not being able to screw is as bad as not being able to write.

Independent financing from Joe Roth and James G. Robinson's Morgan Creek took the pressure off Blake. "It's bad enough dealing with one studio executive," he said, "let alone a committee. This way, as long as I'm on budget nobody much cares how long I shoot."[1] Deferring his salary and casting his film with relatively affordable talent, Blake earned a little more leash, and for the first time since *Victor/Victoria*, now seven years in the past, found himself making personal slapstick comedy without studio interference.

To be sure, *Skin Deep* and *Switch*, Edwards' last two non-*Panther* movies, owe their emotional and metaphysical resonance to the director's new-found creative autonomy as much as they do to the fresh autobiographical perspective he has returned to his comedy. The renewed artistic vigor would be a welcome relief from the work between *The Man Who Loved Women* and *Sunset*, films which suffered from an excess of rancor and a fatigued, if not worn-out sensibility. For Andrew Sarris, the problems went back to unsettled business.

> My own penultimate judgment is that Edwards has never completely succeeded in exorcising all the demons of anger, bitterness, and resentment that surfaced in S.O.B. Hence, his undeniable facility as a filmmaker is coupled with an emotional detachment that causes an increasing skeletonizing of his farce mechanisms. As an Edwardian of longstanding, I do no regret my critical commitment, but like so many other phenomena of the '60s, what I once took to be a new wave of the future has turned out to be a receding wave in the past.[2]

Had Edwards' career ended here, Sarris would have been absolutely correct. Though *The Man Who Loved Women*, *Micki + Maude*, *A Fine Mess*, and *Blind Date* all found contemporary settings for gags, the gags themselves were anachronistic and largely skimped on modern ideas. With its overtones of yuppie anxiety, *Blind Date* came the closest, but considered in the company of *10* and *S.O.B.*, it does little by way of deepening the splurch with fresh feelings, fusing instead a screwball ideology into a 1980s setting. The update Blake needed he got in *Skin Deep*. All it took was a little soul searching.

"I long for a meaningful, monogamous, healthy relationship," Zach Hutton (John Ritter) says, "And I was sure I had it with Alex, but the truth is, in the deep dark silence of my considered conscience, where there's just me and me, the unmitigated truth is, I want it all." That's *Skin Deep*. "I want a loving, faithful, caring, caretaking wife," he continues, "and I want to make love to everything else in long skirts, with bare feet and ripe, juicy mouths. Little boy-girls with small firm breasts and tight asses. Rubenesque round women with big Mother Earth breasts and green eyes. God! I could go on and on." In fact he does, and for it faces the banana-peel's punishing morality. The film that results is a love story about narcissism, a comedy about tragedy, and a sex farce without any sex. Like many of Blake's other late-greats, it is also a catalogue of artistic paralysis and sexual surplus.

Take, for instance, the first scene of the film: Through the bars of the second-story balustrade, we watch a woman slip cautiously past the front door and into a large house. Inside, she casts a long shadow. The composition is unbalanced. The colors are mute. As in the opening images of *10*, *Skin Deep* begins with visual obscurity: the bars initiate a deeply unstable graphic metaphor (we wonder, "is this home a prison?") into a supposedly comic narrative, effectively toying with audience expectations and genre conventions. On one level, Edwards is creating an atmosphere of illusion (as we will soon discover), and on another level he is challenging our ideas about comedy. From the looks of it, we say to ourselves, this isn't a funny environment. The tone is all wrong, the music is too forceful, and of course, the images ring with suspense. But this as we know is Blake Edwards. And those who know that his films often begin like films by anyone but Blake Edwards will not think of this opening scene as atypical. We can recognize the face even behind the mask. Blake said,

> I was told, "Listen, comedy is not dramatic. You know, you can't mix the two." But what I wanted to do was mix them. . . . A producer said, "No, ridiculous. You can't. This is a comedy. If you open that picture this way they won't know it's a comedy."[3]

Naturally, nothing, not even genre, goes deeper than skin in *Skin Deep*. Perhaps this accounts for the film's abundance of sleek, angular forms and tendency to favor shallow depth of field. Rarely, if ever, do we have any sense of great space or distance. Figures crowd the extreme foreground of the frame, and interiors dominate the film, placing clear physical restrictions on what we can and cannot see. Close-up and medium shots rule, and if we ever go long, we're never far from a wall. The metaphor is clear enough: our field of view is limited. There are notable exceptions to the rule, the earliest of which occurs here, during the film's opening sequence: the woman we have been watching (she will later identify herself as Angie) catches sight of Zach at the end of a long hall. Her vision here is, literally speaking, *deep*. In fact, throughout the entire sequence, her point-of-view shots are punctuated by deep focus and through-doorway shots, images that connect to the idea of heightened perceptibility, of going past the surface of things.

She cocks a gun and points directly into the camera. We are now in Zach's point-of-view shot (the gun is aimed "at us") a change of subjectivity that brings with it a change in physical space. The woman is backgrounded now by closed blinds, a flat surface that initiates us into the visual motif of Zach Hutton (John Ritter). In Zach's reaction shot, his startled face is framed against the flat headboard of his bed, and as more complications are added to the scene (such as the introduction of the *real* wife) the shots get wider, longer, deeper, the effect of which is not only depict the mounting intensity of Zach's situation, but also—continuing with Edwards' clever manipulation of space—to visually represent the dissolution of one façade (or flat space) after the next. And Edwards has picked the perfect situation for this technique: in this first scene, a nimble shuffling of comic reversals, the woman who *appears* to be Zach's wife catches him fooling around with what *appears* to be Zach's girlfriend. These assumptions are overturned by the appearance of Zach's *real* wife, whose introduction forces, yet again, another reading of the situation.

Apply the same ideology to Zach's visits with his therapist (wonderfully played by legendary choreographer Michael Kidd), and what emerges is a gradual transition from shallow space (their first meeting is shot all from one angle—and flat) to deep, three-dimensional space (their final meeting is delivered in a tracking shot that starts behind them and drifts around, stopping in front of them). Once again, this visual progression describes the deepening of Zach's emotional awareness. Surfaces, in other words, have been replaced by dimension. But we're getting ahead. At this point, Zach still has a long way to go. He's lost his wife, his mistresses, his gun can't fire, and his typewriter is sitting at the bottom of the pool.

"I threw out that typewriter," Alex explains, "because it represents everything that could have been loving and lasting and wonderful, and everything that wasn't." Thus, without his typewriter, without his ability to create, Zach has lost the ability to be a loving, wonderful man. The will to restore that manhood, in all its myth and meaning, is what drives Zach, just as it drove George Webber and countless Edwards protagonists before them, to recover their typewriter, or piano, or film, or sculpture, or whatever talent they lost with the women they have forgotten how to love. Unfortunately for them, they're driven to find the answer in sex (we know it won't work; the splurch tells us so).

According to Edwards' precise system of ethics, the proximity of gag to the eruptions of Zach's libido means that sex can't be the solution to his problems. Trailing a beautiful woman, Zach crashes his car; ogling a twenty-something in a hotel lobby, he's chased out by her rock-star boyfriend and trips down the stairs; trailing another beautiful woman into a spa, he finds himself buckled to a bed where he receives high-voltage electric shock therapy, and the list goes on. Each instance deprives Zach of his physical control, exposing the true fragility lurking beneath his suave exterior. He may begin his seductions like "a man," but in the end, we see Zach is nothing more than a broken-down boy. And, as always, the splurch is what goes beneath skin-deep to show us *real* character. Without it, Blake's worlds are unjust, anarchic, and screaming with lies. But Zach Hutton doesn't see that. As a man in the midst of the chaos, he sees only the pratfalls, and not the force behind them. He doesn't go deeper. He doesn't question why, all of a sudden, he's being splurched left and right. Or why, in the midst of hilarity, he's consumed with depression. And why should he? What character in the history of slapstick comedy has stopped, thought about his place in the comic universe, and wondered at why the filmmaker is slapping him with humor? Zach Hutton may be the first: late in the *Skin Deep*—after days of solitude and meditation—he realizes what Blake Edwards has known for the past thirty years of moviemaking.

Zach throws open the door to his best friend (Joel Brooks)'s beach house and cries, "There is a god and he's a gag writer!" Just then, a huge tsunami wave comes crashing into the house and throws Zach across the room. It is as though God has answered, "Yes Zach, and here I am." As the only splurch in the film *not* motivated by Zach's lust, his eureka is further proof that the slapstick preceding it must have been administered by a just and ethical intelligence. So there is a god! (Though, unfortunately, one with a masochistic sense of humor.) But why Zach Hutton? Why, of all Blake's protagonists, is Zach the only one to gain awareness of the metaphysical laws of Edwardian comedy? Many have come before him, many have tripped, slipped, been smashed or crashed, but none have been enlightened by the divine scheme.

The difference is Zach is a writer. This places him, like a priest of comedy, one step closer to the Ultimate Writer, the G-g Writer, making his search for spiritual fulfillment, which began the moment Alex launched his typewriter into the pool, no different from his search for the muse. After all, if God really is a gag writer, then the road to nirvana is paved with shtick. Along the way, the devout observer will realize that the splurches he suffered were not only punishments from on high, but, for the failing writer, blessings in disguise, the stuff of great screenplays and literature. Now that he has suffered (as we laughed), Zach can turn around and laugh at his suffering, and having recovered his sense of humor, he can write again. And he does. And so did Blake:

> I was in the middle of a divorce. I decided I'd have a party at the beach and invite all my friends, who would make it easier on me . . . but I freaked out, I couldn't bear all the fun, all the noise. I went down to the beach, put myself in the yoga position and looked out at the sea. There was a big full moon, like a movie set. It was bright yellow, and the sky was purple. No clouds. And as I was sitting there contemplating, I noticed that the moon had disappeared suddenly. I thought, "What the fuck is that?" And at that second I was hit by a tsunami wave—which had been predicted—and it rolled me under the house. When I finally came up out of all this seaweed and sand, I could hear the party going on up above. Nobody had any idea that I was under there with a mouth full of sand. And of course it struck me as funny.
>
> I crawled out from under the house and staggered into the house next door, where a writer, Johnny Bradford, lived. . . . So I opened the gate and walked through, laughing my ass off, went up to the porch and opened the door. And there Johnny Bradford was with his wife, sitting at this little candlelit dinner. And that's when the big second tsunami hit. It came through that courtyard of his house like something coming out of the barrel of a gun, and hit me and blew me into their house and

right into their table. We all ended up covered with water and scream-ing with laughter. I said, "One day I'm going to do this in a film." A true, true moment.

I went to bed and slept in all this sand. The next morning I got up, and went into the bathroom, opened the door—and there was my soon-to-be-ex-wife with a .38 cocked and pointed right between my eyes.

I took the gun away from her. I'd been trained to do that for over thirty years. But I looked at her and thought, "Boy, you never know. You laugh at what God has to say about tragedy and then think it's all been resolved, and the next thing you know you're facing a loaded .38." There's a lot of drama waiting right around the corner, and a lot of humor, too: even the gun.

He goes on,

If I didn't have comedy, I wouldn't have survived this far. Comedy is always the saving grace. If I can find the humor in a situation. . . Sometimes it looks like it isn't going to happen. Sometimes I think, "Where are you? I need you to give me the insight that will save me." And only one time has it gone far enough that I felt, "I don't want any more of this. I can't put up with this anymore." One time I really contemplated suicide.* And getting rid of that impulse turned out to be one of the funniest moments in my life.[4]

Physical and emotional pain inhibit humor, which inhibits transcendence. Reverse the logic and you have enlightenment. Therefore, physical and emotional pain, by transitive property, bring upon the comic awakening.

Skin Deep's visual logic supports this transformation. First, and perhaps most obviously, Edwards has set Zach's epiphany out of doors in direct opposition to the limited spaces that define the early parts of the film. On the beach, the vistas are wide. We have depth: physical, emotional, and now spiritual. At this point, Zach's voice-over makes a welcome appear-ance: "I've never felt like this before," he says to himself, "I'm seriously unhappy. This is not the bush league blues. We're talking major league depression here." The voice-over takes the introspection up a notch. If we're hearing Zach's thoughts, this must be serious. Just to make sure he isn't kidding, Blake has an attractive blonde walk down the beach. Zach

---

* See this book's Introduction for the full story.

32. *Skin Deep* (1989) "I'm a desperate man, doctor," says Zach Hutton (John Ritter, right) to Dr. Westford (Michael Kidd, left). Hutton's search for meaning, which ends in the revelation that God is a gag writer, retroactively imbues ontological significance into Edwards' *oeuvre*, but it begins here, where so many baffled Edwardians begin, on the couch. (Author's collection)

doesn't follow her—there's no gag here. Instead, he walks down to the beach and actually *prays*. Voice-over again.

That this scene is set at the beach is no accident. Time and again, Blake's characters reach the seaside at moments of great spiritual need. Think of 10: George's fantasy, Sam's heart-to-heart with Hugh. Think of S.O.B.: Felix tries to drown himself, and later he's buried at sea. Throughout Blake Edwards' films, bodies of water are imbued with an almost religious significance. They provide the setting for intense personal meditation, bursts of love, and most often bouts with death, showing up in times of great desperation when nothing seems to be going right. In *That's*

Life!, Gillian Fairchild's breakthrough happens on the beach, and following her husband's failed attempt at adultery, we see him standing in his underwear, defeated, on the balcony of one of his unfinished houses, staring out to sea. It is one of the most spectacular pictures in all of Edwards' films; a man stripped of his clothing, diminished by the architectural skeleton that surrounds him, sexually impotent, and afraid of death—it could be Zach Hutton twenty years later. The vantage point has changed, but the ocean remains the same.

"I'm so miserable I want to fucking shoot myself," Zach says to his therapist, "but I can't because I'm afraid to die. How's that for fucked up?" Blake has done this before—promised comedy and delivered pain—but never to this extent. In *Skin Deep*, his thorough examination of the subject turns on his evocation of Zach's interiority, which comprises the structural foundation of the narrative. It's easy to forget, but much of the film takes place in Zach's memory, from within his head. Indeed he (and the picture) leaps ahead and back in time with the free-associative ease of a patient speaking with his analyst. Perhaps unsurprisingly, Blake's interest in psychotherapy is more prominent here than it ever has been. In the past, Edwards' therapists have served as expositional devices (as in 10, we get George's story laid out quite clearly), for laughs (as in the *Panther* films, when Inspector Dreyfus is driven crazy by Clouseau), and have even been misused (the aimless emotional noise of *The Man Who Loved Women*), but never has the director applied psychotherapy—in both ideology *and* dramatic organization—to such a successful end.

The story, in other words, is told in a manner as scattered as the man who tells it, and as it/he reaches resolution, it/he will right it/himself by restoring chronological order to the fragmented narrative/psyche. Simply put, Zach needs to learn how to tell his story. Only then can he write. But before that happens, he's a mess—the film is a mess—revealed in short, even staccato snippets. Consider Zach at the bar, telling Barney (Vincent Gardenia) about how he got thrown out of his house. We cut to a typewriter flying through the air, the scene plays out, the typewriter sinks, and Zach's voice over fades in, "It's over, but I still love that woman," and another cut takes us to Zach and Jake, who apparently have been discussing the events we just witnessed. But the flashback never ended. Typically, we would return to Barney, to the present, to signify the end of the memory. But Blake is trickier that that. Leaving the flashback unresolved—like a minor chord hanging in the air—the director has threatened the audience's sense of time, twisting our minds out of chronology in much the same way as Zach's mind searches back and forward through his life. Later, Zach walks into a party his pal Sparky (Peter Donat) is giving, with a woman we've never seen before and will never seen again. Where did she come from? Where does she go? We can't say. All we get is a piece of her story, just as we get only a piece of the realtor Zach sleeps with. In three shots—he sees her, she sees him, they have sex—we are given the entire account of their relationship. The same goes for Molly (Julianne Phillips). The decline of her affair with Zach is told in a single cut: first Zach is serenading her to "The Most Beautiful Girl in the World" (cut) and then, during his version of "My Romance," she's setting his piano on fire. How much time elapses between the cuts? Does she hate him, or does she just hate Rodgers and Hart? The details are unclear; all we have are fragments.

The opposite is true of Zach's scenes with Alex, his ex-wife. These are long, sometimes very long sequences, and entirely without ellipses. The implication is that, in her company, Zach's mind can find the order it seeks, and experience at long last a consistent relationship with time (no wonder he's still in love with her). Whether it's their break-up scene, their dinner scene at home, or Zach's pathetic efforts at thwarting her wedding, the Zach/Alex phrases unfold with uncharacteristic chronological determination. In Skin Deep's story terms, it implies Alex brings out the writer in him (the photograph of her Zach keeps by his typewriter indicates as much), and as we will see, she also corrects Zach's very Edwardian pursuit of skin deep. When Zach realizes that he's gone to bed with a female bodybuilder (Raye Hollitt) we laugh not just because exterior no longer matches interior, but because we're witness to a reversal of so-called manhood. At last, Zach's macho arrogance is undone by a woman he calls "Mrs. Arnold Schwarzenegger,"* who pins him to the bed in a splurch of false machismo. The next morning, Zach awakes to find himself in the midst of an aerobics class. Nearly naked, and surrounded by bouncing women, he is forced into the workout, and rather than lust after them, he's seen full of fear.

Through the glow-in-the-dark condom episode—perhaps Skin Deep's greatest splurch (and indeed one of the more balletic gags in Edwards' career)—the director raises similar questions about the illusion of mas-

---

* In an early draft of the script, Zach murmurs, "I feel like Maria Shriver." The line makes the gender shift even more explicit.

culinity, though with a stronger implication of homoeroticism. The two penises in question (alias Zach and Rick) seem more concerned with wrestling each other than with getting into bed with Amy. And by reducing his characters to the colored glow of their condoms (the lights are off, remember), Edwards posits a graphic metaphor for the obliteration of identity through libido. Remove those condoms and what's left behind? Darkness. That's what Zach Hutton doesn't want to face. But can he change? Dr. Westford, Zach's analyst, doesn't think so. "Don't you know by now that changing one's basic character is next to impossible?" he asks his patient.

> Zach: No. I don't know that. Jesus, Doctor, if I thought I couldn't change, I wouldn't come see you in the first place.
> Dr. Westford: I didn't say that you couldn't.
> Zach: You just said it was impossible.
> Dr. Westford: I said it was next to impossible.
> Zach: Well, shit, Doctor. "Next to" isn't that far removed.
> Dr. Westford: If it were, there'd be no analysts.
> Zach: Not an entirely unhappy prospect, Doctor.
> Dr. Westford: Did I ever tell you the story about the scorpion and the frog?

In order to get across the river, the scorpion has to ride across on a frog, who agrees to take him on the condition that the scorpion won't sting him. In the middle of the river, the scorpion stings the frog anyway. As he's drowning, the frog asks, "Why did you do that?" The scorpion responds, "I'm a scorpion. It's in my character." (An early draft of Skin Deep was called The Scorpion.) So is Zach a scorpion?

Blake doesn't think so. "Skin Deep ends on a happy, hopeful note," he says. "Zach realizes he has to change, and he does to some extent, but his basic character is still intact. At least he has changed enough so that he has gotten back on track as far as being productive, creative. Stopping drinking—that's a big change, an enormous change, when a man wants to stop drinking and get back to writing. Of course, he'll slide back occasionally into old patterns, but one hopes at this point that he will at least recognize what he's doing, and be able to manage it better."[5] But is this truly as happy and hopeful as the writer/director says? Judging by the film's ending, probably not. Although we see Zach in bed with Alex, their resolution is not quite convincing. Like the final shots of Breakfast at Tiffany's, Days of

Wine and Roses, *Blind Date*, and 10 (and others), the suggested and actual meanings are in conflict, giving one the sense that though this may be a fade-out, the cycle might repeat itself. Perhaps we are more like Clouseau than we would like to believe.

And Blake Edwards the filmmaker is no exception. At the time of *Skin Deep*'s release, many critics chastised him for self-plagiarism. "As his comedies accumulate," wrote Vincent Canby, "some a lot less funny than others—Blake Edwards appears to be bent on becoming the definitive chronicler of life as lived by a small group of privileged, mostly superfluous Southern Californians."[6] But Edwards spins it differently:

> I've been accused of following a certain theme from 10 and *The Man Who Loved Women* and that kind of thing. [*Skin Deep* is] sort of the next step in the evolution of a man in search of his mortality or immortality and a phenomenon that has always interested me, and that is part of my life and of a lot of middle-aged guys. How difficult it is for any of us to change our basic character.[7]

"This is a theme in a number of Blake's films," Tony Adams agreed, "the idea that it is difficult, if not impossible, to change the essence of one's character. As a matter of fact, the working title [of *Skin Deep*] when we were shooting was *Change*."[8] There was even a period when the film was conceived as a sequel to 10, entitled (as one might have hoped) 11. That draft opens opens with George Webber at the piano, serenading Molly with "My Romance." A moment later, she's setting his piano on fire. (Right away, we see that George, despite what we might have hoped, hasn't changed.) This very same scene appears in *Skin Deep*, but of course, the pianist is Zach. In fact, the entire script for 11 is practically a scene-by-scene rehearsal for *Skin Deep*; "George" has been changed to "Zach," "Sam" to "Alex," and "Hugh" to "Sparky." Suddenly, Zach's ubiquitous musicality assumes new relevance. His clash with the rock star, his competitive exchange with Alex's Juilliard-trained son (once "Josh," now "Greg"), and his spontaneous performances of "Have You Met Miss Jones?" and "You Better Change Your Ways" are really vestiges of George Webber. But does that mean Edwards hasn't changed? Is he stuck in material he should have laid to rest years ago? Were it to respond, his next picture would answer in the negative.

SWITCH (1991)

Amanda: If I'm gay, then Clint Eastwood's a transvestite.

The second half of Blake's career, those two dozen films that began with *Darling Lili* and his fall from Hollywood grace, is marked by a considerably darker turn in his work, namely with respect to his treatment of death. In these films, the Reaper makes no bones about tone or genre, but crops up everywhere, with a disregard for context that has earned him a bad reputation, and as we see, slapstick comedy is no exception. "Black comedy" seems an applicable designation for such pictures, but the term falls short of films like *Skin Deep* and *Switch*; their humor does not come from making light of dark situations like the slapstick suicides of *S.O.B.*, but rather from the cracks of light between the dark, alternating from high highs to low lows, but rarely if ever maintaining both at once. Indeed *Skin Deep* and *Switch* are simply manic-depressive, and, because they perpetually break even with their own tonal standards, remain beyond classification. Furthermore, these consecutive works are unique in the *oeuvre* for their direct confrontation with man's ontological predicament, latent until now.

Existential conflict has never been far from Edwards' comic world (even Holly Golightly had her "mean red" nights), but before 1989 it was different: there wasn't a god. Mercifully, he makes cameos in both *Skin Deep* and *Switch*; in the first we feel him, and in the second, we see him. (Actually, the god of Blake Edwards must be referred to as "s/he," for when the deity finally appears in *Switch* [shafts of light, by the way] it has a woman's voice and a man's voice.)* If indeed God is the gag writer Zach believes him/her to be, then prayer is the want of a joke, and the splurch—even though it comes at the expense of Edwards and his characters—is in truth a vessel of divine wisdom. Only after responding to the reasons for a pratfall can they be righted. This is how grace is imparted upon Edwards' characters, and nowhere is this truer than it is in *Switch*, Blake Edwards' last good movie.

"The genesis for *Switch* was probably *Victor/Victoria*." Blake said to an interviewer. "I got fascinated by that sort of complicated situation of a woman playing a man playing a woman playing a man—whatever it was,"

---

* Conversely, *Switch*'s Devil is male without female counterpart. That's why he's in hell.

adding, "I didn't think of it as a comedy. I really didn't—anymore than I approached *Victor/Victoria* as a comedy."[9] The unusual blend—typical for Edwards, but problematic for studios—had a greater chance of making it into theaters if the project could find independent financing, and so Blake enlisted the support of Arnon Milchan's Regency International and casting talks began. Ellen Barkin was Blake's first choice. "She understands, I think, her masculine side," he said, "most of us walk around denying those separate sides exist . . . and I don't think she denies it."[10] The backers, though, were reluctant, and after a period of stalling, the money fell through. The project was put aside for a year, and in 1990, after *Sea of Love* delivered Barkin into the big time, Blake returned to the idea of *Switch*, and approached the HBO–Cinema Plus partnership. They agreed to a budget of $14 million and Warner Bros. signed on to distribute. They also agreed to Barkin, now an A-list star, as well as Jimmy Smits, Lorraine Bracco, and JoBeth Williams, whose account of Edwards' improvisational/collaborative process remains one of the best descriptions of his technique.

> Blake is one of the calmest directors I've ever worked with. He's relaxed and the whole set is relaxed. Most directors feel time pressure and they're constantly rushing around and whipping the crew into shape, but Blake will sit and look around the set. And we're all kind of sitting there, waiting, ready to shoot. For about ten minutes you can see the wheels turning in his head about what we can do in this room. What kind of physical comedy can we create here? And he'll just sit there, quietly, looking around without anybody bothering him. And then he'll say, "Well, let's try—" and then it starts. And then you try it that way, and then someone says, "Well, what if I do so-and-so?" And then someone adds, "Well, what if there's sexy lingerie wrapped around the gun?" And then the whole thing just mushrooms.
>
> It's a really fun way to work and it's perfect for comedy because as much as you can prepare ahead of time about doing a comic scene, you have to feel it in the moment. You have to be in the space. You have to see what the props are. You have to see what the potential is in order to make the fun stuff happen.[11]

Williams' emphasis on time and space ("in the moment," "be in the space") speaks to the importance of Edwards' long takes in wide-shot which, by extending visual and temporal parameters, allow actors to experiment and encourage strong comic chemistry. "It's great for actors interacting with other actors, and I'm sure it works for the comedy. It's hard to be funny by yourself. We do very long takes, and he [Blake] doesn't do things in bits and pieces, he doesn't do too many takes."[12]

In one such instance, a journalist from the *Village Voice* was present. Though what he saw was cut from the film, it stands as an example of Edwards' unceasing sexual curiosity:

> On a Culver City soundstage that once served as the setting for Rhett and Scarlett's squabbles and romantic lashings, two sexy women are making out on a bed. Lorraine Bracco's mouth slides down the length of Ellen Barkin's twitching body—from breasts to her midriff, her head finally disappearing between the star's writhing thighs before Barkin, giggling hysterically, her eyes popping, struggles to pry herself loose, jumping up and climbing over Bracco's perplexed head to declare, "If I was going to do this with any anybody, I would do it with you. But it's not going to be anybody."[13]

Under pressure to satisfy a wider market, Blake was forced to cut the heat from the scene, but it just goes to show that at seventy years of age the director was still pushing the sexual envelope. Not even Billy Wilder in his advancing years could muster the same sense of purpose; neither did Lubitsch, Sturges, or Cukor, as they rounded the last lap, find a way to up the ante one more time.

When womanizer Steve Brooks (Perry King) is murdered by vengeful girlfriends, God and the Devil agree to give his soul one more chance on earth, but this time, they decree, if he wants to get into heaven, he has to make a woman love him. So he's sent back, but this time *as a woman*. Now Steve is Amanda (Ellen Barkin), his best friend Walter (Jimmy Smits) can't keep his hands off him, and every woman he's interested in thinks he's a lesbian. Who picks up the check now? One night, Steve—I mean, Amanda—wakes up in bed with Walter, discovers he's pregnant, and quite miraculously, has the baby girl, dies in childbirth, and ascends to heaven.

The splurch in *Switch* resides at the intersection between the drive of mental will (Steve within) and the restrictions placed upon it (Amanda without) by the androgynous Almighty. We can conclude therefore that every time Amanda stumbles in his/her high heels or trips into a dress we see evidence of what Ernest Becker calls the human condition. "Nature's values are bodily values," he writes, "human values are mental values, and though they take the loftiest flights they are built upon excrement, impossible without it, always brought back to it."[14] Which is stronger, the man within or the woman without? And which one is real? What we see or what we feel? This is predicament of the existentialist and, as we see in *Switch*, the transgendered. Both share the human dream of overcoming biological restriction. Taken to its logical extreme, that is the dream of overcoming death.

If we were to prevail over the restriction, we can transcend genetic limitation and become godly in our ability to control body with mind. Becker again: "When Freud talked about 'the feminine side of his nature' he could just as well have been speaking from the strength of his ego rather than its weakness, from his own single-minded determination to engineer his own immortality."[15] Anyone who can will themselves to alter the very mortal fact of their sex can, in symbolic terms, reverse decay and live on. *Switch* reinforces the idea, both explicitly (Amanda goes to heaven) and conceptually, in its recapitulation of the theme of rebirth. The first and last shots of the film, for instance, feature the blue sky quite prominently, which in structural terms, speaks to narrative circularity. Thus Edwards marks *Switch* with a plentitude of circles, and often pairs them with the life-giving image of water. Steve's exes, Felicia, Liz, and Margo, gather like a coven of witches in a bubbling cauldron of a jacuzzi which, shot from overhead, is contained in a perfect circle. They try to drown Steve, and, thinking they've killed him, retreat to safety in the bedroom only to find he has re-emerged, zombielike, to chase them about the room. Margo reaches for the gun and pops him one. She kills him, but his life isn't over. When he returns to earth as a woman, Steve/Amanda is seen hovering over the toilet (water, circles) when he realizes what's happened. This sheds light on the very first post-title image: an extreme close-up of a golf ball. Steve, in his office, putts it into a plastic hole, sinks the ball, and waits for it to shoot back to him. Return, rebirth.

But there is something greater at work here: *Switch* marks the first time Edwards has built a film around a comedienne. There was Kim Basinger in *Blind Date*, who represented a significant step forward for the Edwardian slapsticienne, but her character was only splurch-maker and was not susceptible to change. All that changes in *Switch*. It takes Ellen Barkin into the male-dominated forum of slapstick comedy. And that was no easy task: from the first days of cinema, clowning has always been a man's show. Indeed the roll call of silent greats—Chaplin, Keaton, Lloyd, Laurel,

Hardy—rarely includes a single dame. Mabel Normand, quite understandably the love of Mack Sennett's life, might pop up occasionally, but when she does it's generally in a kind of apologetic drag. Jeanine Basinger writes,

> Because she was so small, she could disguise herself as a boy in baggy pants, a flannel shirt and a loose cap, and because of her athletic ability, get away with it. . . . In America, we ask our women to sacrifice glamour if the situation calls for it, because we prize the "good Joe" quality in women. A heroine needs to be able to roll with the punches, take it on the chin, and dish it out as necessary. Mabel Normand could and did do all this in spades, and she more or less defined the tradition.[16]

There is a precedent for women in slapstick, but as the story of Mabel teaches, masculinity was always in attendance. Molly Haskell adds,

> The comic spirit, particularly in the rambunctious, anarchic forms of silent comedy, or the debunking shafts of verbal wit, is basically masculine in gender and often anti-feminine in intention. A woman can display humor in the diluted forms of sarcasm or "personality," but if she indulges in either the athletics of the clown or the epigrams of the wit, she risks losing the all-important status of a lady.

And therefore,

> While a male comedian can have sex appeal—in fact, his humor may contribute to it—a female comedian (and how few there have been and, of these, how few have been "sexually attractive!") automatically disqualifies herself as an object of desire.[17]

But what of that *other* woman's slapstick, the one where a woman can take a pie, and not forego her sexual charisma?

Basinger cites Lucille Ball and Betty Hutton, but their interpretations of slapstick, though distinct, have that Normandesque girl-in-pants quality. As Trudy Kockenlocker in *The Miracle of Morgan's Creek*, Hutton is always whacking Eddie Bracken, and pulling at him, and breaking down. She's a truck, a torrent, a wrecking ball, and handles her dress like a pair of overalls. Lucy is a step closer, though, but one never calls Mrs. Ricardo alluring. The most famous sequences in *I Love Lucy* (grapes, chocolates, Vitameatavegamin) are, sexually speaking, neutral. True, Lucy does not

33. *Switch* (1991) If only they gave Pulitzers for comedy, Ellen Barkin would have won at least two—one for slapstick, and the other for acting—making her, in *Switch*, that all-too-rare thing in contemporary movies: a true physical comedienne. (Author's collection)

conceal her feminity like Mabel Normand, but she does not celebrate it either.

Before Ellen Barkin in *Switch*, there was really only one actress who did: Carole Lombard. She was knockout *and* knockabout, the only true glamour klutz, and as slapstick's screwball queen, lead author of the splurch. Out of this tradition, Blake pulls *Switch*'s best switch, creating a fully realized slapstick role for a woman. It's a singular accomplishment in his work, and since Lombard, distinct in the history of cinema. In consequence, Barkin's performance is doubly resonant; first, as a demonstration of the actress' formidable comedic skill, and second, in the director's (thematically appropriate) reversal of comic convention. Even by Edwards' standards, the part of Amanda Brooks is uniquely layered. Whereas Julie Andrews in *Victor/Victoria* never had to play a man playing a woman (when Victoria was "in drag" she was only playing herself), Ellen Barkin, as a woman playing a man *trying* to play a woman, must triple-filter her performance. (For Victoria, it's only the illusion of an illusion; for Amanda, it's several realities compounded.) That's quite a task for an actress. What's more, the question of Amanda's sexual identity, unlike Victoria's, is never addressed conclusively. She is both a sex all her own and complicated beyond recognition, making *Switch* not a gender-bender, but gender-blender.

At first, though, the gender lines are clear. Even when Steve becomes Amanda we can see that deep down she's actually Steve—the splurch tells us so. She wears his suit, throws her arm around buddies, and sits with her legs open. If we laugh, it is because we know this is not "feminine" behavior (in this way, her slapstick resembles Normand's in its proximity to drag). Amanda's slow entrance into the bar, her high-heel struggle, is presented in a long dolly shot, the kind of setup Edwards designs to emphasize the physical comedy. Because the gender lines are clear, the laughs (and gags) come harder. This is a bender, not blender. As Edwards moves into blender, the comic discrepancy lessens, we lose track of the contrast, and *Switch* switches into a new tonal realm. The slapstick dissipates. The ironic long takes give way to sincere close-ups. "Is this a comedy?" we ask. "Is Amanda a woman?" Who knows? When Amanda turns her head to check out an appealing woman, we see not a man in drag, but a lesbian. And so does Walter. He asks, "Hey, you're not gay, are you?" Amanda responds, "Hey, if I'm gay, then Clint Eastwood's a transvestite." But wait—a woman who ogles other women? That's gay, right? Isn't it? Yes, but only from the outside. Inside that woman's body, after all, Steve is one hundred percent straight. The lines are clear. In time, though, Steve (Amanda's masculine core) begins to fade. She learns to wear high heels. She stops struggling with her hair. Her physical facility improves (that's Edwards-speak for "mind is aligning with body"), and as we've seen before, when a character overcomes the gag, it means that justice has been restored and the splurch can be retired. We lose Amanda's inner Steve, which means we lose slapstick, which means we're not in comedy anymore. With problems in gender have come problems in genre.

When splurches start popping up in the middle of the love scene between Amanda and Sheila Faxton (Lorraine Bracco), we might wonder, what is homosexuality? "I felt my pantyhose were strangling me," she says in narration (the use of voice-over enhances her inner split). The scene ends as she faints off-camera. Though what we see indicates one truth (lesbians), Blake's clever placement of the gag reveals another (there's a man in that body). Amanda is still Steve and not, as it would appear, a lesbian. She's only *pretending* to be a lesbian to get the Faxton account.* In other words, Steve has declined the opportunity to have what is, from his position, heterosexual sex. (Confused yet?) The old Steve would have been all over Lorraine. The old Steve, who before his "death," was so excited by the prospect of Sapphic erotica (see the jacuzzi scene), has rejected his fantasy—a quintessentially male fantasy—in favor of . . . what? Margo, Steve's former girlfriend, suggests that because Amanda/Steve is still a male chauvinist, s/he is repulsed by the very thought of homosexuality. If that is so, and Amanda cringes at the thought of gay, then how can s/he have heterosexual sex? Must Amanda sleep with Walter? Amanda/Steve is caught in limbo: s/he cannot be gay and s/he cannot be straight. But that's impossible! She must be one or the other . . . mustn't she? (He?)

Amanda may not be a lesbian, but that doesn't rule out the possibility that Steve is gay. When Amanda takes Walter back to her apartment (he's drunk), the two go to bed—and in the same bed. Blake then cuts to the East River as a man's body pulled out the ocean. It's Steve's body. Literally, we are being told that Steve is dead. Metaphorically, he has been excised from Amanda's body, engendering her pure woman. Thus, any sexual transaction between her and Walter is now, symbolically speaking, heterosexual, and the question of identity and gender has been put to rest. Steve began as a heterosexual and Amanda will end as one. A cycle has been completed. But look again: though it conveniently appears at the moment of intercourse, the discovery of Steve's death actually changes nothing about Amanda. (Steve hasn't disappeared, only his body has.) And so, when morning comes and we find out Walter and Amanda have had intercourse, we may consider it a homosexual act. Then again, this is *Switch* and the potential for both narrative/sexual possibilities doesn't rule out the coexistence of both. It is unclear.

Very few critics responded well to *Switch*. "Edwards's idea of what men and women are is crass and thirty years out of date," wrote David Denby. "What he's done is impose role-reversal jokes, some good, some bad,

---

* Steve works in advertising. It's the ideal metaphor for his situation.

onto these retro stereotypes."[18] He has a good point. Blake's jokes *are* based on tired stereotypes, but his attitude towards human sexuality is not. So where does that place the film on the spectrum of old-fashioned to progressive? For *Variety*, somewhere in the middle: "*Switch* is a faint-hearted sex comedy that doesn't have the courage of its initially provocative convictions. Undemanding audiences will get a few laughs from the slapstick emanating from the notion of a man parading around in a woman's body, but older, more sophisticated viewers will no doubt reject the tired farcical conceits and resent the copouts of the second half."[19] And yet, despite all this, Michael Wilmington of the *Los Angeles Times* "saw something very interesting: a sense of modern confusion about sexual roles [and] social masks. There's honest emotion and questioning in its stylized, movie-movie surfaces. It's a post-Sexual Revolution comedy about trying to find a sense of responsibility—or empathy or humanism— in the midst of sexual chaos."[20] Exactly.

Unlike *Switch*, *Some Like It Hot* and *Tootsie* acquiesce to normalcy. Men learn their lessons from drag and by the end of the films they can cast off their wigs. "Nobody's perfect" speaks to the switch in all of us, but Wilder's and Pollack's films end there. Edwards takes it farther, and once he arrives, doesn't go back. When Steve/Amanda has his baby, he is not magically restored to his first act self. There is no celestial contrivance to unravel the gender complications, only, as Patrick McGilligan calls it, "sexuality as a continuum."[21] This is not the closing message of the conventional Hollywood film, but a subversive narrative tactic that embraces complication and obscurity. It suggests that when the construct of gender clashes with the fact of biology every erotic act is simultaneously heterosexual and homosexual. *Switch*'s dramatization of precisely that ranks it with cinema's most subversive inquiries into human sexuality, the pulls of nature and freedom, and the near-impossible business of selfhood.

If Blake was depressed by the critical response to Son of the Pink Panther, the cloud lifted two months later as he headed down Sunset Boulevard to the Directors' Guild of America to accept his Preston Sturges Award, which, judging from the caliber of its two other recipients—Richard Brooks in 1990 and Billy Wilder in 1991—ranks with the most precious and specialized prizes in all of Hollywood. A joint tribute by the Writers' and Directors' guilds, the Sturges Award is given in recognition of those who have distinguished themselves in both writing and directing, and unlike the Oscar, it is not handed out yearly, but only when a body of work demands it. After fifty years in radio, television, and film; twenty years after trying to leave town for good; after Darling Lili and The Carey Treatment and Wild Rovers, and after S.O.B., Blake was about to join the ranks of the cinema's greatest hyphenates, who in the spirit of Sturges, their patron saint, had achieved a mastery of word and image. Just check Blake's movies against Sturges' Golden Rules of Successful Comedy and the reason becomes clear:

> A pretty girl is better than a plain one
> A leg is better than an arm
> A bedroom is better than a living room
> An arrival is better than a departure
> A birth is better than a death
> A chase is better than a chat
> A dog is better than a landscape
> A kitten is better than a dog
> A baby is better than a kitten
> A kiss is better than a baby
> A pratfall is better than anything.

With the exception of the fifth, Blake was as orthodox a follower as there ever was, perhaps more so than even Wilder.

Billy himself was in the building the night of October 24, 1993. The impish cherub waddled up to the stage, and with not so much as a glance at the standing ovation that might have kept a prouder man from speaking, addressed the room in the Austrian accent he once described as a mixture of Arnold Schwarzenegger and Archbishop Tutu. "Blake Edwards," he began. "I knew him, I liked him."

> But there was nothing special about him. [Audience laughter] But then one day I ran a picture—something called 10—and I said, Wait a minute . . . this is good. This maybe is a little bit too good. [laughter] So I went out and I got myself something like twenty Blake Edwards pictures. And I suddenly found myself seeing the pictures of a truly great picture maker. Sure, he makes a flop! But if he makes a flop, it's a tremendous flop! In my opinion, the so-so director, he never is a failure, but he never is a success. He just kind of wiggles along somehow and he gets another picture, and two other pictures . . . but, my god, Blake Edwards, you know when he comes with something you know it is with a fist! It can hit you in the stomach or it can make you laugh and not forget what you have seen. [Looks up] Blake, I would like you to know that I have a tiny little treasure safe with the pictures that I love and among them are two of yours. There should be more but [laughter] I'm no longer young, you know, my eyesight . . . Let's see, they are 10 and . . . the other picture which I love very much . . . [Searches his notes] I must find exact title or it is no good . . . It was that wonderful picture of yours . . . [laughter] . . . uh . . . um . . . [Searches his notes] that don't . . . *Breakfast*, uh . . . *Breakfast at Tiffany's.*[1]

With that, Billy Wilder sidestepped down into the audience, reached a hand out to Jack Lemmon, and shuffled slowly to his seat. He wore a gray suit that night. His bow tie was blue.

Soon thereafter, Blake followed with his acceptance speech. He thanked Julie and Tony Adams and then he stopped. He looked out over the audience. "Last but not least," he said, "I want to thank Billy."

> Whether you know it or not Billy, you have always been my mentor. I think the first director that I really took note of was Mr. Lubitsch, but I didn't have the opportunity to get to know him or to really be involved with his work other than sitting in an audience and thinking, "Oh my god, isn't that wonderful?" He just put the camera on the door and people came in and out and you wondered what went on in that other room. I was just enraptured by it. And then along came Billy. And as

34. Fifth Avenue, October 2, 1960. Blake Edwards on the first day of filming *Breakfast at Tiffany's*. (Courtesy of the Academy of Motion Picture Arts and Sciences)

proof of how important Billy has been in my career in my life, sometime ago when I first began, one of my early films was run at a producer's home one night, and someone who shall remain nameless for the moment came to me and said, "Billy Wilder was there and he saw it and you know what he said? He said, 'You know it's shit, but it's funny shit.'" [Audience laughter] Now, had anybody else said that—this is proof of how I feel about Billy—I would have taken exception to it. But I didn't. I said, "My god! Billy Wilder thinks I make funny shit!" I mean, that's all I needed. So, whether it's shit or it isn't—whatever it is that I try to do well—I try to do well. And I hope it's funny.[2]

Bring Your Smile Along (Columbia, 1955)

Producer: Jonie Taps; Screenplay: Blake Edwards and Richard Quine; Cinematographer: Charles Lawton, Jr.; Editor: Al Clark; Music: Morris Stoloff; Songs: "Bring Your Smile Along" (Benny Davis and Carl Fischer), "If Spring Never Comes" (Bill Carey and Carl Fischer), "The Gandy Dancer's Ball" (Paul Mason Howard and Paul Weston), "Don't Blame Me" (Dorothy Fields and Jimmy McHugh), "Side by Side" (Harry Woods), "When a Girl Is Beautiful" (Allan Roberts and Lester Lee), "Mama Mia" (Ned Washington and Lester Lee)

Starring: Frankie Laine (Jerry Dennis); Keefe Brasselle (Martin Adams); Constance Towers (Nancy Willows); Lucy Marlow (Marge Stevenson); William Leslie (David Parker)

Running time: 83 minutes

He Laughed Last (Columbia, 1956)

Producer: Jonie Taps; Screenplay: Blake Edwards, from a story by Edwards and Richard Quine; Cinematographer: Henry Freulich; Editor: Jack W. Ogilvie; Music: Arthur Morton, supervised by Fred Karger; Songs: "Save Your Sorrow for Tomorrow" (B. G. De Sylva and Al Sherman), "Strike Me Pink" (B. G. De Sylva, Lew Brown, and Ray Henderson)

Starring: Frankie Laine (Gino Lupo); Lucy Marlow (Rosemary Lebeau); Anthony Dexter (Dominic); Dick Long (Jimmy Murphy); Alan Reed (Big Dan); Jesse White (Max Lassiter)

Running time: 76 minutes

Mister Cory (Universal-International, 1957)

Producer: Robert Arthur; Screenplay: Blake Edwards, from a story by Leo Rosten; Cinematographer: Russell Metty; Editor: Edward Curtiss; Music: Joseph Gershenson

Starring: Tony Curtis (Cory); Martha Hyer (Abby Vollard); Charles Bickford (Biloxi); Kathryn Grant (Jen Vollard); William Reynolds (Alex Wyncott); Henry Daniel (Earnshaw)

Running time: 92 minutes

This Happy Feeling (Universal-International, 1958)

Producer: Ross Hunter; Screenplay: Blake Edwards, based on the play For Love or Money by F. Hugh Herbert; Cinematographer: Arthur E. Arling; Editor: Milton Carruth; Music: Frank Skinner; Song: "This Happy Feeling" (Jay Livingston and Ray Evans)

Starring: Debbie Reynolds (Janet Blake); Curt Jurgens (Preston Mitchell); John Saxon (Bill Tremaine); Alexis Smith (Nita Hollaway); Mary Astor (Mrs. Tremaine); Estelle Winwood (Mrs. Early); Troy Donahue (Tony Manza)
Running time: 92 minutes

This Perfect Furlough (Universal-International, 1959)
Producer: Robert Arthur; Screenplay: Stanley Shapiro; Cinematographer: Philip Lathrop; Editor: Milton Carruth; Music: Frank Skinner; Song: "The Perfect Furlough" (Skinner, Diane Lampert and Richard Loring)
Starring: Tony Curtis (Lt. Paul Hodges); Janet Leigh (Lt. Vicki Loren); Keenan Wynn (Harvey Franklin); Linda Cristal (Sandra Roca); Elaine Stritch (Liz Baker)
Running time: 93 minutes

Operation Petticoat (A Granart Production for Universal-International, 1959)
Producer: Robert Arthur; Screenplay: Stanley Shapiro and Maurice Richlin, suggested by a story by Paul King and Joseph Stone; Cinematographer: Russell Harlan; Editor: Ted J. Kent and Frank Gross; Music: David Rose
Starring: Cary Grant (Lt. Comdr. Matt Sherman); Tony Curtis (Lt. Nick Holden); Joan O'Brien (Dolores Crandall); Dina Merrill (Barbara Duran); Arthur O'Connell (Tostin); Gene Evans (Molumphrey); Richard Sargent (Stovall); Gavin MacLeod (Hunkle); Dick Crockett (Harmon)
Running time: 124 minutes

High Time (A Bing Crosby Production for Twentieth Century Fox, 1960)
Producer: Charles Brackett; Screenplay: Tom Waldman and Frank Waldman, based on a story by Garson Kanin; Cinematographer: Ellsworth Fredricks; Editor: Robert Simpson; Music: Henry Mancini; Songs: "The Second Time Around" and "Nobody's Perfect" (Sammy Cahn and James Van Heusen)
Starring: Bing Crosby (Harvey Howard); Fabian (Gil Cuneo); Tuesday Weld (Joy Elder); Nicole Maurey (Helene Gauthier); Richard Beymer (Bennerman); Patrick Adiarte (T. J. Padmanabhan); Yvonne Craig (Randy Pruitt); Gavin MacLeod (Thayer); Dick Crockett (Bones McKinney)
Running time: 102 minutes

Breakfast at Tiffany's (A Jurow-Shepherd Production for Paramount Pictures, 1961)
Producer: Martin Jurow and Richard Shepherd; Screenplay: George Axelrod, based on the book by Truman Capote; Cinematographer: Franz F. Planer; Editor: Howard Smith; Music: Henry Mancini; Song: "Moon River" (Mancini and Johnny Mercer)
Starring: Audrey Hepburn (Holly Golightly); George Peppard (Paul Varjack); Patricia Neal ("2E"); Mickey Rooney (Mr. Yunioshi); Buddy Ebsen (Doc Golightly);

Martin Balsam (O. J. Berman); José Luis de Vilallonga (José); John McGiver
(Tiffany's salesman)
Running time: 114 minutes

Experiment in Terror (A Geoffrey-Kate-Blake Edwards Production for Columbia
Pictures, 1962)
Producer: Blake Edwards; Screenplay: Mildred and Gordon Gordon, from their novel
   Operation Terror; Cinematographer: Philip Lathrop; Editor: Patrick McCormack; Music:
   Henry Mancini
Starring: Glenn Ford (John Ripley); Lee Remick (Kelly Sherwood); Stephanie Powers
   (Toby Sherwood); Ross Martin (Red Lynch); Roy Poole (Brad); Ned Glass (Popcorn)
Running time: 123 minutes

Days of Wine and Roses (Jalem Productions through Warner Brothers, 1962)
Producer: Martin Manulis; Screenplay: J. P. Miller, based on his television play;
   Cinematographer: Philip Lathrop; Editor: Patrick McCormack; Music: Henry
   Mancini; Song: "Days of Wine and Roses" (Mancini and Johnny Mercer)
Starring: Jack Lemmon (Joe Clay); Lee Remick (Kirsten Arnesen); Charles Bickford
   (Ellis Arnesen); Jack Klugman (Jim Hungerford)
Running time: 117 minutes

The Pink Panther (The Mirisch Corporation through United Artists, 1964)
Producer: Martin Jurow; Screenplay: Maurice Richlin and Blake Edwards;
   Cinematographer: Philip Lathrop; Editor: Ralph E. Winters; Music: Henry Mancini
Starring: David Niven (Sir Charles Lytton); Peter Sellers (Inspector Jacques
   Clouseau); Robert Wagner (George Lytton); Capucine (Simone Clouseau);
   Claudia Cardinale (Princess Dala); Brenda de Banzie (Angela Dunning); Fran
   Jeffries (Greek "cousin"); James Lanphier (Saloud)
Running time: 113 minutes

A Shot in the Dark (A Mirisch and Geoffrey Production through United Artists, 1964)
Producer: Blake Edwards; Screenplay: Blake Edwards and William Peter Blatty, based
   on plays by Harry Kurnitz and Marcel Achard; Cinematographer: Chris Challis;
   Editor: Ralph E. Winters; Music: Henry Mancini; Song: "Shadows of Paris"
   (Mancini and Robert Wells)
Starring: Peter Sellers (Inspector Jacques Clouseau); Elke Sommer (Maria
   Gambrelli); George Sanders (Benjamin Ballon); Herbert Lom (Chief Inspector
   Charles Dreyfus); Tracy Reed (Dominique Ballon); Graham Stark (Hercule
   Lajoy); André Maranne (François); Burt Kwouk (Kato)
Running time: 101 minutes

The Great Race (Jalem Productions through Warner Brothers, 1965)
Producer: Martin Jurow; Screenplay: Arthur Ross, from a story by Arthur Ross and
Blake Edwards; Cinematographer: Russell Harlan; Editor: Ralph E. Winters; Music:
Henry Mancini; Songs: "He Shouldn't A Hadn't A Oughtn't A Swang on Me,"
"The Sweetheart Tree" (Mancini and Johnny Mercer)
Starring: Jack Lemmon (Professor Fate/Prince Hapnik); Tony Curtis (The Great
Leslie); Natalie Wood (Maggie DuBois); Peter Falk (Max); Keenan Wynn
(Hezekiah); Arthur O'Connell (Henry Goodbody); Vivian Vance (Hester
Goodbody); Dorothy Provine (Lily Olay); Larry Storch (Texas Jack); Ross Martin
(Baron Von Stuppe)
Running time: 150 minutes

What Did You Do in the War, Daddy? (The Mirisch Corporation and Geoffrey
Productions, released through United Artists, 1966)
Producer: Blake Edwards; Executive Producer: Owen Crump; Screenplay: William Peter
Blatty, story by Blake Edwards and Maurice Richlin; Cinematographer: Philip
Lathrop; Editor: Ralph E. Winters; Music: Henry Mancini
Starring: James Coburn (Lt. Christian); Dick Shawn (Capt. Cash); Sergio Fantoni
(Capt. Oppo); Giovanna Ralli (Gina Romano); Aldo Ray (Sgt. Rizzo); Harry
Morgan (Maj. Pott); Carroll O'Connor (Gen. Bolt)
Running time: 119 minutes

Gunn (Geoffrey Productions, released through Paramount Pictures, 1967)
Producer: Owen Crump; Screenplay: Blake Edwards and William Peter Blatty, based on
a story and characters created by Blake Edwards; Cinematographer: Philip Lathrop;
Editor: Peter Zinner; Music: Henry Mancini; Songs: "I Like the Look" (Mancini and
Leslie Bricusse), "Dreamsville" (Ray Evans and Jay Livingston)
Starring: Craig Stevens (Peter Gunn); Laura Devon (Edie); Ed Asner (Jacoby); Sherry
Jackson (Samantha); Helen Traubel (Mother); Albert Paulsen (Fusco); Marion
Marshall (Daisy Jane); J. Pat O'Malley (Tinker); Regis Toomey ("The Bishop");
Dick Crockett (Leo Gracey)
Running time: 95 minutes

The Party (The Mirisch Corporation and Geoffrey Productions through United
Artists, 1968)
Producer: Blake Edwards; Screenplay: Blake Edwards, Tom Waldman, Frank Waldman,
based on a story by Blake Edwards; Cinematographer: Lucien Ballard; Editor:
Ralph E. Winters; Music: Henry Mancini. Song: "Nothing to Lose" (Mancini and
Don Black)
Starring: Peter Sellers (Hrundi V. Bakshi); Claudine Longet (Michele Monet); Marge

Champion (Rosalind Dunphy); Steve Franken (Levinson); Fay MacKenzie (Alice Clutterbuck); J. Edward McKinley (Fred Clutterbuck); Sharron Kimberly (Princess Helena); Denny Miller (Wyoming Bill Kelso); Gavin MacLeod (C. S. Divot)
Running time: 99 minutes

Darling Lili (Geoffrey Productions through Paramount Pictures, 1970)
Producer: Blake Edwards; Screenplay: Blake Edwards and William Peter Blatty; Cinematographer: Russell Harlan; Editor: Peter Zinner; Music: Henry Mancini; Songs: "Whistling Away the Dark," "The Girl in No Man's Land," "Smile Away Each Rainy Day," "I'll Give You Three Guesses," "Your Good-Will Ambassador" (Mancini and Johnny Mercer)
Starring: Julie Andrews (Lili Smith); Rock Hudson (Maj. William Larrabee); Jeremy Kemp (Kurt von Ruger); Lance Percival (Lt. Carstairs Twombley-Crouch); Jacques Marin (Maj. Duvalle); Michael Witney (Lt. George Youngblood); André Maranne (Lt. Liggett); Bernard Kay (Bedfore); Doreen Keogh (Emma); Gloria Paul (Suzette)
Running time: 136 minutes

Wild Rovers (Geoffrey Productions through MGM, 1971)
Producer: Blake Edwards and Ken Wales; Screenplay: Blake Edwards; Cinematographer: Philip Lathrop; Editor: John F. Burnett; Music: Jerry Goldsmith; Song: "Wild Rover" (Goldsmith and Ernie Sheldon)
Starring: William Holden (Ross Bodine); Ryan O'Neal (Frank Post); Karl Malden (Walter Buckman); Lynn Carlin (Sada Billings); Tom Skerritt (John Buckman); Joe Don Baker (Paul Buckman); James Olson (Joe Billings); Leora Dana (Nell Buckman); Moses Gunn (Ben); Victor French (Sheriff); Rachel Roberts (Maybell)
Running time: 113 minutes (theatrical cut); 136 minutes (director's cut)

The Carey Treatment (MGM, 1972)
Producer: William Belasco; Screenplay: James P. Bonner, based on the novel *A Case of Need* by Jeffrey Hudson [Michael Crichton]; Cinematographer: Frank Stanley; Editor: Ralph E. Winters; Music: Roy Budd
Starring: James Coburn (Dr. Peter Carey); Jennifer O'Neill (Georgia Hightower); Pat Hingle (Capt. Pearson); Skye Aubrey (Nurse Angela Holder); Elizabeth Allen (Evelyn Randall); John Fink (Dr. Murphy); Dan O'Herlihy (Dr. J.D. Randall); James Hong (Dr. David Tao); Alex Dreier (Dr. Joshua Randall); Michael Blodgett (Roger Hudson); Regis Toomey (Sanderson); Steve Carlson (Walding); Rose-Mary Edelman (Janet Tao); Jennifer Edwards (Lydia Barrett)
Running time: 100 minutes

The Tamarind Seed (ITC and Jewel Productions through Avco-Embassy Pictures, 1974)
Producer: Ken Wales; *Screenplay:* Blake Edwards, based on the novel by Evelyn
   Anthony; *Cinematographer:* Freddie Young; *Editor:* Ernest Walter; *Music:* John Barry;
   Song: "Play It Again" (Barry and Don Black)
Starring: Julie Andrews (Judith Farrow); Omar Sharif (Feodor Sverdlov); Anthony
   Quayle (Jack Loder); Dan O'Herlihy (Fergus Stephenson); Sylvia Sims (Margaret
   Stephenson); Oscar Homolka (Gen. Golitsyn)
Running time: 123 minutes

The Return of the Pink Panther (ITC, Jewel Productions and Pimlico Productions
through United Artists, 1975)
Producer: Blake Edwards; *Screenplay:* Frank Waldman and Blake Edwards;
   Cinematographer: Geoffrey Unsworth; *Editor:* Tom Priestley; *Music:* Henry Mancini
Starring: Peter Sellers (Inspector Jacques Clouseau); Christopher Plummer (Sir
   Charles Litton); Catherine Schell (Claudine Litton); Herbert Lom (Chief Inspector
   Dreyfus); Peter Arne (Col. Sharki); Burt Kwouk (Cato); André Maranne (François)
Running time: 115 minutes

The Pink Panther Strikes Again (Amjo Productions through United Artists, 1976)
Producer: Blake Edwards; *Screenplay:* Frank Waldman and Blake Edwards;
   Cinematographer: Harry Waxman; *Editor:* Alan Jones; *Music:* Henry Mancini; *Song:*
   "Come to Me" (Mancini and Don Black)
Starring: Peter Sellers (Inspector Jacques Clouseau); Herbert Lom (Dreyfus); Colin
   Blakely (Alec Drummond); Leonard Rossiter (Quinlan); Lesley-Anne Down
   (Olga); Burt Kwouk (Cato); André Maranne (François)
Running time: 103 minutes

Revenge of the Pink Panther (Jewel Productions through United Artists, 1978)
Producer: Blake Edwards and Tony Adams; *Screenplay:* Frank Waldman, Tom Clark,
   and Blake Edwards, based on a story by Blake Edwards; *Cinematographer:* Ernest
   Day; *Editor:* Alan Jones; *Music:* Henry Mancini
Starring: Peter Sellers (Inspector Jacques Clouseau); Herbert Lom (former Chief
   Inspector Dreyfus); Dyan Cannon (Simone Legree); Robert Webber (Douvier);
   Burt Kwouk (Cato); Paul Stewart (Scallini); Robert Loggia (Marchione); Graham
   Stark (Auguste Balls)
Running time: 98 minutes

10 (A Geoffrey Production for Orion Pictures, released through Warner Brothers,
1979)
Producer: Blake Edwards and Tony Adams; *Screenplay:* Blake Edwards; *Cinematographer:*
   Frank Stanley; *Editor:* Ralph E. Winters; *Music:* Henry Mancini; *Songs:* "It's Easy to

Say," "No More Than a Man" (Mancini and Robert Wells), "Don't Call It Love" (Mancini and Carole Bayer Sager)

Starring: Dudley Moore (George Webber); Julie Andrews (Samantha Taylor); Bo
Derek (Jennifer Miles); Robert Webber (Hugh); Dee Wallace (Mary Lewis); Sam
Jones (David Hanley); Brian Dennehey (Don); Max Showalter (the Reverend);
Rad Daly (Josh); Nedra Volz (Mrs. Kissel); James Nobel (Dr. Fred Miles); John
Hawker (Covington); Deborah Rush (dental assistant); Don Calfa (neighbor);
Walter George Alton (Larry); Annette Martin (redhead); John Hancock (Dr.
Croce)

Running time: 122 minutes

S.O.B. (Geoffrey Productions and Lorimar through Paramount Pictures, 1981)
Producer: Blake Edwards and Tony Adams; Screenplay: Blake Edwards; Cinematographer:
Harry Stradling; Editor: Ralph E. Winters; Music: Henry Mancini

Starring: Julie Andrews (Sally Miles); William Holden (Tim Culley); Marisa Berenson
(Mavis); Larry Hagman (Dick Benson); Robert Loggia (Herb Moscowitz); Stuart
Margolin (Gary Murdock); Richard Mulligan (Felix Farmer); Robert Preston (Dr.
Irving Feingarten), Craig Stevens (Willard); Loretta Swit (Polly Reed); Robert
Vaughn (David Blackman); Robert Webber (Ben Coogan); Shelley Winters (Eva
Brown); Jennifer Edwards (Lila)

Running time: 121 minutes

Victor/Victoria (Peerford Films, Blake Edwards Entertainment, and Ladbroke
Entertainment for MGM, 1982)
Producer: Blake Edwards and Tony Adams; Screenplay: Blake Edwards, based upon the
film Viktor und Viktoria; Cinematographer: Dick Bush; Editor: Ralph E. Winters; Music:
Henry Mancini; Songs: "Gay Paree," "Le Jazz Hot," "The Shady Dame from Seville,"
"You and Me," "Chicago, Illinois," "Crazy World" (Mancini and Leslie Bricusse)
Starring: Julie Andrews (Victor/Victoria); James Garner (King Marchand); Robert
Preston (Toddy); Lesley Ann Warren (Norma); Alex Karras (Squash Bernstein); Peter
Arne (Labisse), John Rhys-Davies (Andre Cassell)
Running time: 133 minutes

Trail of the Pink Panther (Titan Productions and Blake Edwards Entertainment
through MGM/UA, 1982)
Producer: Blake Edwards and Tony Adams; Screenplay: Tom Waldman, Blake Edwards,
and Geoffrey Edwards; Cinematographer: Dick Bush; Editor: Alan Jones; Music:
Henry Mancini
Starring: Peter Sellers (Inspector Jacques Clouseau); David Niven (Sir Charles Litton);
Herbert Lom (Dreyfus); Richard Mulligan (Clouseau Senior); Joanna Lumley
(Marie Jouvet); Capucine (Lady Litton); Robert Loggia (Bruno); Harvey Korman

(Prof. Balls); Burt Kwouk (Cato); Graham Stark (Hercule); Peter Arne (Col. Bufoni); André Maranne (François)
Running time: 97 minutes

Curse of the Pink Panther (Titan Productions through MGM/UA, 1983)
Producer: Blake Edwards and Tony Adams; Screenplay: Blake Edwards and Geoffrey Edwards; Cinematographer: Dick Bush; Editor: Ralph E. Winters; Music: Henry Mancini
Starring: Ted Wass (Clifton Sleigh); David Niven (Sir Charles Litton); Robert Wagner (George Litton); Herbert Lom (Dreyfus); Joanna Lumley (Countess Chandra); Capucine (Lady Litton); Robert Loggia (Bruno); Harvey Korman (Professor Balls); Burt Kwouk (Cato); Leslie Ash (Juleta Shane); Graham Stark (Bored Waiter); Andre Maranne (François); Peter Arne (Col. Bufoni)
Running time: 110 minutes

The Man Who Loved Women (Delphi Productions and Blake Edwards Entertainment through Columbia, 1983)
Producer: Blake Edwards and Tony Adams; Screenplay: Blake Edwards, Milton Wexler, and Geoffrey Edwards, based upon the 1977 film by François Truffaut; Cinematographer: Haskell Wexler; Editor: Ralph E. Winters; Music: Henry Mancini
Starring: Burt Reynolds (David Fowler); Julie Andrews (Marianne); Kim Basinger (Louise); Marilu Henner (Agnes); Cynthia Sikes (Courtney); Jennifer Edwards (Nancy); Sela Ward (Janet)
Running time: 118 minutes

Micki + Maude (Delphi III Productions and Blake Edwards Entertainment through Columbia, 1984)
Producer: Tony Adams; Screenplay: Jonathan Reynolds; Cinematographer: Harry Stradling; Editor: Ralph E. Winters; Music: Lee Holdridge; Song: "Something New in My Life" (Michael Legrand and Marilyn and Alan Bergman)
Starring: Dudley Moore (Rob Salinger); Amy Irving (Maude); Ann Reinking (Micki); Richard Mulligan (Leo Brody); George Gaynes (Dr. Eugene Glztszki); Wallace Shawn (Dr. Elliot Fibel)
Running time: 115 minutes

A Fine Mess (Delphi V Productions and Blake Edwards Entertainment through Columbia, 1986)
Producer: Tony Adams; Screenplay: Blake Edwards; Cinematographer: Harry Stradling; Editor: John F. Burnett and Robert Pergament; Music: Henry Mancini
Starring: Ted Danson (Spence Holden); Howie Mandel (Dennis Powell); Richard Mulligan (Wayne Farragalla); Stuart Margolin (Maurice Dzundza); Maria

Conchita Alonso (Claudia Pazzo); Jennifer Edwards (Ellen Frankenthaler); Paul Sorvino (Tony Pazzo)

Running time: 100 minutes

That's Life! (Paradise Cove–Ubilam Productions through Columbia, 1986)

Producer: Tony Adams; Screenplay: Milton Wexler and Blake Edwards; Cinematographer: Anthony Richmond; Editor: Lee Rhoades; Music: Henry Mancini

Starring: Jack Lemmon (Harvey Fairchild); Julie Andrews (Gillian Fairchild); Sally Kellerman (Holly Parish); Robert Loggia (Father Baragone); Jennifer Edwards (Megan Fairchild Bartlet); Chris Lemmon (Josh Fairchild); Cynthia Sikes (Janice Kern); Dana Sparks (Fanny Ward); Emma Walton (Kate Fairchild); Felicia Farr (Madame Carrie)

Running time: 102 minutes

Blind Date (ML Delphi Premier Productions and Blake Edwards Entertainment through TriStar, 1987)

Producer: Tony Adams; Screenplay: Dale Launer; Cinematographer: Harry Stradling; Editor: Robert Pergament; Music: Henry Mancini

Starring: Kim Basinger (Nadia Gates); Bruce Willis (Walter Davis); John Larroquette (David Bedford); William Daniels (Judge Harold Bedford); George Coe (Harry Gruen); Mark Blum (Denny Gordon); Phil Hartman (Ted Davis); Stephanie Faracy (Susie Davis); Graham Stark (Jordan)

Running time: 95 minutes

Sunset (ML Delphi Premier Productions and Blake Edwards Entertainment through TriStar, 1988)

Producer: Tony Adams; Screenplay: Blake Edwards, based upon a story by Rod Amateau; Cinematographer: Anthony B. Richmond; Editor: Robert Pergament; Music: Henry Mancini

Starring: Bruce Willis (Tom Mix); James Garner (Wyatt Earp); Mariel Hemingway (Cheryl King); Kathleen Quinlan (Nancy Shoemaker); Jennifer Edwards (Victoria Alperin); Malcolm McDowell (Alfie Alperin); M. Emmet Walsh (Chief Dibner); Richard Bradford (Capt. Blackworth); Andreas Katsulas (Arthur); Joe Dallesandro (Dutch Kiefer)

Running time: 105 minutes

Skin Deep (Blake Edwards Entertainment and Morgan Creek through Twentieth Century Fox, 1989)

Producer: Tony Adams and Joe Roth; Executive Producer: James G. Robinson Screenplay: Blake Edwards; Cinematographer: Isidore Mankofsky; Editor: Robert Pergament; Music: Henry Mancini; Song: "Falling Out of Love" (Ivan Neville)

Starring: John Ritter (Zach Hutton); Vincent Gardenia (Barney); Alyson Reed (Alexandra Hutton); Joel Brooks (Jake Fedderman); Julianne Philips (Molly); Chelsea Field (Amy McKenna); Peter Donat (Leon Sparks); Donn Gordon (Curt Ames); Nina Foch (Marge); Denise Crosby (Angela Smith); Michael Kidd (Dr. Westford)

Running time: 97 minutes

Switch (Blake Edwards Productions and HBO Independent Productions through Warner Brothers, 1991)

Producer: Tony Adams; Screenplay: Blake Edwards; Cinematographer: Dick Bush; Editor: Robert Pergament; Music: Henry Mancini; Song: "It's All There" (Mancini and Marilyn and Alan Bergman)

Starring: Ellen Barkin (Amanda Brooks); Jimmy Smits (Walter Stone); JoBeth Williams (Margo Brofman); Lorraine Bracco (Sheila Faxton); Tony Roberts (Arnold Freidkin); Perry King (Steve Brooks); Bruce Payne (the Devil)

Running Time: 103 minutes

Son of the Pink Panther (Blake Edwards Productions through MGM, 1993)

Producer: Tony Adams; Screenplay: Blake Edwards and Madeline and Steven Sunshine; Cinematographer: Dick Bush; Editor: Robert Pergament; Music: Henry Mancini; Song: "Pink Panther Theme" (Mancini and Bobby McFerrin)

Starring: Roberto Benigni (Jacques Gambrelli); Herbert Lom (Police Commissioner Charles Dreyfus); Claudia Cardinale (Maria Gambrelli); Shabana Azmi (Queen); Deborah Farentino (Princess Yasmin); Jennifer Edwards (Yussa); Robert Davi (Hans Zarba); Mark Schneider (Arnon)

Running time: 93 minutes

APPENDICITIS

HOW TO MAKE A BLAKE EDWARDS MOVIE

Hitchcock's blondes have received some nice publicity over the years, as have his weapons, staircases, and dotty mothers. Buñuel is a foot fetishist, a shoe fetishist, and the cinema's last great lover of a good pair of hands (amputated or still attached), and always enjoyed a crucifix, a priest, a dinner party, a dead body, a dinner party, and a dinner party, but it was clowns and bosoms for Fellini, distant fathers for Spielberg, and what's Ingmar Bergman without a clock? Ranging from informal motifs to full-blown obsessions, these items can assume a conceptual heft as strong as any auteurist tendency. After all, who can deny the importance of servants in Blake Edwards' pictures? Flying custard was practically invented for the pompous ones, and as for their superiors, the Nazis of the buffet, let's rememeber that meringue is best served on a tux. Then again, maybe Edwards' thing for explosions goes no deeper than a hankering to blow stuff up. In any case, without further ado, here they are: mix and match to create your very own Blake Edwards masterpiece.

ANIMALS

"Animals are associated with the unexpected."—Lehman and Luhr

Horses (He Laughed Last), seagull, horses (This Happy Feeling), duck (The Perfect Furlough), sea animals in opening credits (Operation Petticoat), cat (Breakfast at Tiffany's), the Pink Panther (Panther Pictures), polar bear (The Great Race), pigeons, horses, hens, goats, donkeys, cows, and a dove (What Did You Do in the War, Daddy?), Bertie num nums, elephant (The Party), puppies, horses, cat (Wild Rovers), "minkey" (The Return of the Pink Panther), goat, "Does your dug bite?" (The Pink Panther Strikes Again), inflatable parrot, pigeon (Revenge of the Pink Panther), shark (10), dog on beach, rat in the garage (S.O.B.), cockroach (Victor/Victoria), bulldog, pug (Curse of The Pink Panther), Louise's dog, David's dog (The Man Who Loved Women), Maude's cat (Micki + Maude), horses (A Fine Mess), Chutney the dog (That's Life!), monkey, rabbits, Rambo the dog (Blind Date), horses (Sunset), poodle (Skin Deep), psychic's parrot (Switch), Maria's poodle, King Haroak's horse (Son of the Pink Panther)

ANIMATIONS

"If any director has turned live-action characters into cartoon creations, it is Edwards."
—Stuart Byron

Opening titles (He Laughed Last), opening titles (This Happy Feeling), opening titles, transitional effects (High Time), opening titles (Days of Wine and Roses), opening and closing titles (The Pink Panther), opening titles (A Shot in the Dark), opening titles, sing-along (The Great Race), opening titles (Gunn), opening titles (The

Tamarind Seed), opening and closing titles (The Return of the Pink Panther), opening and closing titles (The Pink Panther Strikes Again), opening and closing titles (Revenge of the Pink Panther), singing balloons (S.O.B.), opening titles (Victor/Victoria), opening and closing titles (Trail of the Pink Panther), opening and closing titles (Curse of the Pink Panther), opening titles (Micki + Maude), cockfight (Skin Deep), opening and closing titles (Son of the Pink Panther)

BARS

"Cole Porter, a bartender/personal psychiatrist, an endless flow of Bonsai Sunrises: these are the ingredients that make a bar for Edwards a kind of earthly paradise."
—John Falwell

Happy Club (He Laughed Last), Vollard bar, at the Reno Casino, in the Dolphin Club (Mister Cory), hotel bar (The Perfect Furlough), burlesque bar (Breakfast at Tiffany's), the Roaring Twenties (Experiment in Terror), too many in Days of Wine and Roses, hotel bar (The Pink Panther), the saloon (The Great Race), Valerno café (What Did You Do in the War, Daddy?), Mother's, the Arc, the Monkey Farm (Gunn), moveable bar (The Party), various saloons (Wild Rovers), at the pool hall (The Carey Treatment), "Casablanca" bar, nightclub (The Return of the Pink Panther), Queen of Hearts, Oktoberfest (The Pink Panther Strikes Again), At Simone's, Le Club Foot (Revenge of the Pink Panther), Mexican hotel bar (10), Felix's, Sinatra Bar (S.O.B.) Chez Lui, Matelot, underground dive bar (Victor/Victoria), Bruno's bar (Trail of the Pink Panther), Countess Chandra's bar (Curse of the Pink Panther), Mexican bar (The Man Who Loved Women), red curtain bar (Micki + Maude), Western saloon (A Fine Mess), Freda and Freddy's (Blind Date), the Candy Store, saloon (Sunset), Barney's (Skin Deep), strip club, Pazzo's Bar, Duke's, lesbian bar (Switch), Omar's (Son of the Pink Panther)

CARS

"With few exceptions, a Blake Edwards film plays like an extended Martini and Rossi ad."
—Steve Garbarino

Dan's Rolls, "Just Married" (He Laughed Last), the "ten thousand dollar little buggy" (This Happy Feeling), Kelly Sherwood's yellow convertible (Experiment in Terror), Sir Charles Lytton's Ferrari (The Pink Panther), Inspector Clouseau's Mini (A Shot in the Dark), the Great Leslie's "Leslie Special," Fate's "Hannibal 8" (The Great Race), various army jeeps (What Did You Do in the War, Daddy?), Hrundi Bakshi's Morgan Three Wheeler (The Party), 1917 Cadillac limousine, 1912 Renault Landaulet (Darling Lili), Carey's station wagon (The Carey Treatment), Litton's yellow Mercedes convertible (The Return of the Pink Panther), Douvier's Rolls, the Silver Hornet, Cato's white Peugeot (Revenge of the Pink Panther), George Webber's "ASCAP" Cream Corniche, Sam Taylor's "Sam 1" Mercedes (10), Felix's Cadillac, "Smiles' " Rolls, Culley's Mercedes, Coogan's pink convertible (S.O.B.), George Litton's Ferrari (Curse of the Pink Panther), Agnes' pink Mercedes convertible, Louise's turquoise Roll-Royce, Janet's blue Rolls-Royce (*The Man Who Loved Women*), blue car from the set, Spence's yellow VW, red Cadillac, Phil's truck (*A Fine Mess*), Stoner's VW (*That's Life!*), David's Chevy, Ted's Lincoln, Walter's white car (*Blind Date*), Tom Mix's extravagant white car, the black Cadillac (*Sunset*), Margo's limousine (*Switch*)

CHASES

"What Edwards does excel at, when the Imp of the Comic Perverse whispers advice in his ear, is creating a logically evolving chaos."—Harlan Kennedy

Wedding chase (*He Laughed Last*), Bill chases Janet through the rain (*This Happy Feeling*), "Follow that cab!" (*The Perfect Furlough*), Holden chases Barbara on the raft (*Operation Petticoat*), onscreen in Popcorn's silent movie theater, G-men trail Kelly out of the bar (*Experiment in Terror*), Madame Clouseau followed to the elevator, Sir Charles on sleigh, Sir Charles on skis after Princess Dala, car chase in piazza (*The Pink Panther*), Clouseau and Maria chased out of nudist colony (*A Shot in the Dark*), the Great Race (*The Great Race*), chase around the docks (*Gunn*), dogfights, nighttime car chase to train station (*Darling Lili*), horse-breaking scene, pursuit of Ross (*Wild Rovers*), Carey chases the photographer (*The Carey Treatment*), the Phantom escapes from Lugash museum (*The Return of the Pink Panther*), Clouseau chases Panther in opening titles (*The Pink Panther Strikes Again*), chase to shipyard, chase from shipyard (*Revenge of the Pink Panther*), George trails Jennifer's limousine, Sam and George rush to see each other (*10*), chase out of the studio (*S.O.B.*), chase of Sleigh's taxi from Hotel du Cap (*Curse of the Pink Panther*), Legs (*The Man Who Loved Women*), Rob trails his babies (*Micki + Maude*), chase out of the stables and around the horse track, cop chase under freeways, escalator chase, street chase climax (*A Fine Mess*), low-speed car chase, Walter flees from Rambo (*Blind Date*),stagecoach chase (*Sunset*), chasing Jacques Gambrelli from the hospital (*Son of the Pink Panther*)

CREATIVES

"The emphasis on masks and illusion stresses the fact that many of Edwards' characters are dreamers, enthralled by an intoxicating vision."—Neil Sinyard

Jerry Dennis, Marty Adams, Nancy Willows (songwriters, *Bring Your Smile Along*), Rosemary, Dominic, choreographer (singer/dancers, *He Laughed Last*), Mitch, Nita, Tony (actors, *This Happy Feeling*), Sandra Roca (actress, *The Perfect Furlough*), Paul Varjack (writer, *Breakfast at Tiffany's*), Nancy Ashton (mannequin maker, *Experiment in Terror*), Edie (jazz singer, *Gunn*), Hrundi Bakshi, Michele Monet (actors, *The Party*), Lili Smith (singer/dancer, *Darling Lili*), George Webber (composer, *10*), Felix, Culley, Sally Miles, Sam Marshall (producer, director, actress, actor, *S.O.B.*) Toddy, Victoria, Leclou, the world's greatest equilibrist (performers, *Victor/Victoria*), David Fowler (sculptor, *The Man Who Loved Women*),

Maude Guillory (cellist, *Micki + Maude*), Spence Holden (actor, *A Fine Mess*), Harvey and Gillian Fairchild (architect and singer, *That's Life!*), Walter Davis, Stanley Jordan (guitarists, *Blind Date*), Tom Mix (actor, *Sunset*), Zach Hutton (writer, *Skin Deep*)

CRIMINALS

"No matter how perfect it seems, nothing in a Blake Edwards film is really what it appears to be."—Lehman and Luhr

Big Dan, Max Lassiter, et al. (*He Laughed Last*), Sally Tomato (*Breakfast at Tiffany's*), Red Lynch (*Experiment in Terror*), Sir Charles Lytton, Mme Clouseau, George Lytton (*The Pink Panther*), Dreyfus et al. (*A Shot in the Dark*), Nick Fusco, Daisy Jane (*Gunn*), Ross and Frank (*Wild Rovers*), Angela Holden, Roger Hudson (*The Carey Treatment*), Sir Charles and Lady Litton (*The Return of the Pink Panther*) Inspector Dreyfus and various henchmen/assassins (*The Pink Panther Strikes Again*), Douvier, Guy Algo, Al Marchione, Julio Scallini (*Revenge of the Pink Panther*), King Marchand (*Victor/Victoria*) Bruno Langois (*Trail of the Pink Panther*), Langois, Littons, Chandra (*Curse of the Pink Panther*), Turnip, Binky, Pazzo (*A Fine Mess*), Dutch Kieffer, Capt. Blackworth, Alfie and Victoria Alperin (*Sunset*), Yussa, Arnon, Hanif (*Son of the Pink Panther*)

DETECTIVES

"Edwards films deal with people in the dark, people who must adjust and readjust to the evidence they perceive from the unknown surrounding them. Everyone must be a detective." —Lehman and Luhr

Jimmy Murphy (*He Laughed Last*), house detective (*The Perfect Furlough*), narcotics detective (*Breakfast at Tiffany's*), John Riley and G Men (*Experiment in Terror*), Inspector Clouseau (*The Pink Panther* et al.), Dreyfus (*A Shot in the Dark*, et al.), St. François Chevalier (*A Shot in the Dark*, et al.), Gunn, Lt. Jacoby (*Gunn*), Maj. Duvalle and Lt. Liggett (*Darling Lili*), Peter Carey, Capt. Pearson (*The Carey Treatment*), Quinlan and Drummond (*The Pink Panther Strikes Again*, *Trail of the Pink Panther*), Charles Bovin (*Victor/Victoria*), Clifton Sleigh, Lt. Palmyra (*Curse of the Pink Panther*), Lt. Cranzano and Sgt. Stone (*The Man Who Loved Women*), Hunker and Blist (*A Fine Mess*), Wyatt Earp, Marvin Dibner (*Sunset*), Lt. Laster and Sgt. Phillips (*Switch*), Jacques Gambrelli, Police Chief Charles Lazar (*Son of the Pink Panther*)

DISGUISES/DOUBLES

"There is a tension between appearances and reality in a world which systematically denies direct feeling and camouflages perception."—George Morris

Hodges as doctor, bellhop (*The Perfect Furlough*), scavengers' camouflage, smuggled pig (*Operation Petticoat*), Harvey Howard in drag (*High Time*), Huckleberry Hound masks, Holly's night mask, Holly Golightly persona (*Breakfast at Tiffany's*), Red Lynch as old lady, Red as mannequin (*Experiment in*

Terror), Madame Clouseau changes in the elevator, the Phantom/Sir Charles, George as the "prefect of police," George as the flower delivery man, all attendees of Princess Dala's costume ball (The Pink Panther), Clouseau as balloon man, as Toulouse-Lautrec, as a hunter (A Shot in the Dark), Fate as board member, as man in saloon, also Fate/Hapnik (The Great Race), The Italian-American uniform switch, Gina as nurse, Cash as prostitute, Cash as Nazi, Cash as dead German (What Did You Do in the War, Daddy?), sets of twins in the Arc, Grethers as "Daisy Jane" (Gunn), Divot's toupee, tiara/wig (The Party), Von Ruger as hotel porter, Lili as Smith/Schmidt (Darling Lili), Feodor (The Tamarind Seed), Clouseau as pool cleaner, Clouseau as phone repairman, Clouseau as Guy Gadois, Clouseau as housekeeper, Cato as Japanese waitress (The Return of the Pink Panther), the Pink Panther's disguises in title sequence, Clouseau as Quasimodo, Dreyfus as Claude Duvale, Jarvis in drag, assassin as waitress at Oktoberfest, Tournier's Clouseau disguise, Clouseau as Dr. Schurtz, Clouseau as knight (The Pink Panther Strikes Again), Clouseau as Toulouse-Lautrec, Claude Russo in drag, Clouseau in drag, Clouseau as Dreyfus, Clouseau as priest, Clouseau as sailor, Clouseau as Chinese man, Simone as Chinese woman, Clouseau as the Godfather (Revenge of the Pink Panther), Victor/Victoria, Toddy/Victoria, assorted transvestites (Victor/Victoria), Clouseau as Quasimodo, Henri Botot, and Marie Jouvet (Trail of the Pink Panther), Sleigh in drag, wax versions of Clouseau and Cato, "Instant Companion," Roger Moore as Clouseau (Curse of the Pink Panther), Rob as bearded intruder (Micki + Maude), Dennis as maid (A Fine Mess), Mrs. Yamamoto's wig, Walter as Panda (Blind Date), Tom Mix as Wyatt Earp, "Greta" as Greta Garbo (Sunset), Zach as Genie, "Mrs. Arnold Schwarzenegger" (Skin Deep), Steve/Amanda, Devil in drag, Devil as TV Evangelist (Switch), Jacques Gambrelli as doctor, Cato as rabbi, the "Gambrelli 2" (Son of the Pink Panther)

DRINKERS

"Drink is a common failing of an Edwards character."—Neil Sinyard

Mrs. Early (This Happy Feeling), Holly Golightly (Breakfast at Tiffany's), Joe Clay, Kirstin Arnesen (Days of Wine and Roses), Princess Dala (The Pink Panther), Prince Hapnik (The Great Race), Tinker (Gunn), General Bolt (What Did You Do in the War, Daddy?), Levinson, martini-drinking woman (The Party), George Webber (10), Finegarten (S.O.B.), Père Clouseau (Trail of the Pink Panther), Harvey Hamilcard III (Curse of the Pink Panther), Father Baragone (That's Life!), Nadia Gates (Blind Date), Michael Alperin (Sunset), Zach Hutton (Skin Deep), Amanda (Switch)

DRUGS

"I got into drugs pretty heavily. When you're a real neurotic, to get into heavy drugs is a really bad trip."—Blake Edwards

Holly's involvement with smuggling (Breakfast at Tiffany's), sedative (Days of Wine and Roses), morphine (The Carey Treatment), a fizzy tablet (The Return of the Pink Panther), nitrous oxide (The Pink Panther Strikes Again), the French Connection (Revenge of the Pink Panther), Novocain (10), tranquilizer dart (Curse of the Pink Panther), anesthetic (Micki + Maude), dynamite stimulant suppository (A Fine Mess), The "dope factory on wheels" (That's Life!), "weed" shirt, vitamin shot, B12, adrenal cortex, Sleeping Beauty boilermaker, gentle little pink pills, marijuana, car exhaust (S.O.B.), marijuana (Switch), tranquilizer shot, Novocain (Son of the Pink Panther)

EXPLOSIONS

"The conditions of just being alive are parlous in all Edwards' pictures, even the slapstick comedies."—Myron Miesel

Lassiter's cigars (He Laughed Last), air raids, misfired beach missile (Operation Petticoat), dynamite in Harvey Howard's dream (High Time), Princess Dala's mansion (The Pink Panther), Clouseau's car (A Shot in the Dark), Professor Fate's castle (The Great Race), opening montage (What Did You Do in the War, Daddy?), dynamite at Mother's (Gunn), Hrundi steps on detonator, soap bubbles (The Party), various planes and airfields (Darling Lili), car over the cliff, motorboat (The Tamarind Seed), bomb delivery to Clouseau's apartment, water/soap burst out of the bathroom (The Return of the Pink Panther), Cato impales the TV, Clouseau's apartment (The Pink Panther Strikes Again), Balls' costume shop, Cato's Peugeot, shipyard (Revenge of the Pink Panther), François' car, Young Clouseau's house, The Bridge on the River Kwai explosion (Trail of the Pink Panther), Sleigh's hotel (Curse of the Pink Panther), Zach Hutton's house (Skin Deep), Gambrelli kitchen, grenade blast (Son of the Pink Panther)

HOLLYWOOD

"Despair and darkness lurk beneath the Californian luxuriance."—Neil Sinyard

Sandra Roca, Harvey Franklin (The Perfect Furlough), O. J. Berman (Breakfast at Tiffany's), setting for The Pink Panther, Lt. Christian called C. B. DeMille (What Did You Do in the War, Daddy?), setting for The Party, Pink Panther's imitations of Chaplin, Mickey Mouse, Marx Brothers, references to Casablanca, To Catch a Thief, The Maltese Falcon (The Return of the Pink Panther), Pink Panther's imitations of Hitchcock, Batman, Bob Fosse, King Kong, Gene Kelly, Dracula, Buster Keaton, and Julie Andrews, references to James Bond films, Jaws, Dr. Strangelove, Phantom of the Opera, The Hunchback of Notre Dame and Omar Sharif (The Pink Panther Strikes Again), references to The French Connection, The Godfather, Gigi (Revenge of the Pink Panther), George Webber's Oscars (10), Setting for S.O.B., references to Sergio Leone and The Bridge on the River Kwai (Trail of the Pink Panther), 1930s' movie within movie, Laurel and Hardy remake of The Music Box, Western film within film (A Fine Mess), setting of the film (Sunset), Zach Hutton's screenplays (Skin Deep)

HOMOSEXUALS

"Edwards has a great deal of trouble with endings that strongly affirm the heterosexual couple."
—Lehman and Luhr

Choreographer (He Laughed Last), Harry Ross and Grethers "Daisy Jane" (Gunn), Harry, Gore Pontoon (The Party), Stephenson (The Tamarind Seed), The Queen of Hearts Nightclub (The Pink Panther Strikes Again), Hugh and Larry (10), Toddy and Richard, Count Victor Grezhinski, Squash et al. (Victor/Victoria), Victoria Alperin? Cheryl King? (Sunset), Sparky and Curt (Skin Deep), psychic, Sheila Paxton, lesbians at bar, Steve? Walter? (Switch)

MALE DUOS

"Edwards also attaches significance to a mentor, who takes an interest in the protagonist to help him advance, succeed, and mature."—Myron Meisel

Jerry & Marty (Bring Your Smile Along), Cory & Caldwell (Mister Cory), Sherman & Holden (Operation Petticoat), Charles & George Lytton (The Pink Panther), Clouseau & Hercule (A Shot in the Dark), Dreyfus & Chevalier (A Shot in the Dark et al), Professor Fate & Max, Leslie & Hezekiah (The Great Race), Capt. Cash & Lt. Christian (What Did You Do in the War, Daddy?), Maj. Duvalle & Lt. Ligott (Darling Lili), Ross & Frank (Wild Rovers), Carey & Dr. Tao (The Carey Treatment), Stephenson & Loder (The Tamarind Seed), Quinlan & Drummond (The Pink Panther Strikes Again), Clouseau & Cato, Professor Balls & assistant (Revenge of the Pink Panther), George & Don (10), Victor & Toddy, King & Squash (Victor/Victoria), Rob & Leo (Micki + Maude), Spence & Dennis, Turnip & Binky, Blist & Hunker (A Fine Mess), Tom & Wyatt, Blackworth & Dibner (Sunset), Zach & Barney (Skin Deep), Walter & Amanda Switch)

OCEANS

"I went down to the beach, put myself in the yoga position and looked out at the sea."
—Blake Edwards

Docks (He Laughed Last), miscellaneous beach scenes (Operation Petticoat), San Francisco Bay (Days of Wine and Roses), boat shooting (Gunn), Caribbean, view from Judith's sanitarium (The Tamarind Seed), Hong Kong, shipyard (Revenge of the Pink Panther), Mexico (10), Malibu, Marina Del Rey (S.O.B.), closing credits (Trail of the Pink Panther), the Littons sail into the ocean (Curse of the Pink Panther), David and Marianna sailing (The Man Who Loved Women), the view from Maude's apartment (Micki + Maude), Malibu (That's Life!), final shot (Blind Date), Pacific Ocean (Sunset), Malibu (Skin Deep), East River (Switch), Nice (Son of the Pink Panther)

PARTIES

"Parties fascinate Edwards because at them people play roles."—Neil Sinyard

At Italian restaurant (Bring Your Smile Along), Mr. Dover's (This Happy Feeling), New

Years Eve (*The Perfect Furlough*), various dances (*High Time*), Holly's cocktail party (*Breakfast at Tiffany's*), Roaring Twenties bar (*Experiment in Terror*), boat party (*Days of Wine and Roses*), Princess Dala's dinner party, chalet party, Princess Dala's costume party (*The Pink Panther*), nudist colony (*A Shot in the Dark*), Prince Hapnick's ball (*The Great Race*), Two Valerno street festivals (*What Did You Do in the War, Daddy?*), the party (*The Party*), Carey's house party (*The Carey Treatment*), French Embassy ball (*The Tamarind Seed*), Oktoberfest (*The Pink Panther Strikes Again*), George Webber's surprise party, Webber's neighbor's parties (10), birthday party for nobody (*S.O.B.*), Valencia street festival (*Curse of the Pink Panther*), after-performance party (*Micki + Maude*), Harvey's sixtieth (*That's Life!*), party on Elm and Hill (*Blind Date*), Victoria's house party (*Sunset*), Sparky's party, Zach's book release party (*Skin Deep*), Steve's "surprise" party, Sheila's party (*Switch*)

PERFORMANCES
"Because any notion of the self implies a role that the self will play, Edwards concentrates on changes in role as reflections as changes in personality."—Myron Meisel
"Bring Your Smile Along," "When a Girl is Beautiful," "If Spring Never Comes," "Mama Mia," "Side by Side," "The Gandy Dancer's Ball," "Don't Blame Me," "Every Baby Needs a Da-Da-Dassy," (*Bring Your Smile Along*), "Save Your Sorrow for Tomorrow," "Danny Boy," "Strike Me Pink," tango rehearsal and performance, restaurant guitarists (*He Laughed Last*), horse show, "This Happy Feeling," the play (*This Happy Feeling*), Mambo band (*The Perfect Furlough*), the Prophet on guitar, witch-doctor dance, Auld Lang Syne (*Operation Petticoat*), Harvey Howard sings "The Second Time Around," "Nobody's Perfect," "It Came upon the Midnight Clear"(*High Time*), Holly Golightly sings "Moon River", burlesque dancer (*Breakfast at Tiffany's*), girls on swings at bar, a combo at a jazz bar (*Experiment in Terror*), belly dancer (*Days of Wine and Roses*), Greek "cousin" sings "It Had Better Be Tonight"(*The Pink Panther*), band at nudist colony, flamenco dancers, hula dancer, Russian dancer (*A Shot in the Dark*), Lily Olay sings "He Shouldn't A Hadn't A Oughtn't A Swang on Me", Maggie Dubois and the Great Leslie sing "The Sweetheart Tree" (*The Great Race*), Fake battle (*What Did You Do in the War, Daddy?*), "I Like the Look," "If Only I Could Fly" (*Gunn*), Michele Monet sings "Nothing to Lose", Russian dancers, the Party Poops sing "The Party" (*The Party*), "Whistling Away the Dark" x 2, Brit medley, "The Girl in No Man's Land," "Smile the Rain Away," Hungarian Gypsies, cancan, "I'll Give You Three Guesses" x 2, Crepe Suzette's striptease (*Darling Lili*), Ross sings "Ballad of the Wild Rovers" (*Wild Rovers*), belly dancers (*The Return of the Pink Panther*), Jarvis at the Queen of Hearts, people singing at Oktoberfest (*The Pink Panther Strikes Again*), Clouseau sings "Thank Heaven for Little Girls," Dreyfus eulogizes Clouseau, Clouseau plays dead, Le Club Foot band performs "Move

'em Out" (*Revenge of the Pink Panther*), George Webber sings and plays "It's Easy," the Reverend sings and plays "I Have an Ear for Love" (10), Sally's two versions of *Night Wind*, "Promise Me" (*S.O.B.*), "Cherry Ripe," "Gay Paree," cancan, "Le Jazz Hot," "Shady Dame from Seville," "Chicago, Illinois," Chez Lui drag, "Crazy World," *Madame Butterfly*, "You and Me," Toddy's "Shady Dame from Seville" (*Victor/Victoria*), Clouseau's "Dancing in the Rice" (*Trail of the Pink Panther*), "You Do Something to Me" sung in the streets, 1812 Overture, flamenco dancers in Ole Café (*Curse of the Pink Panther*), jazz combo, *Swan Lake* (*The Man Who Loved Women*), jazz band at governor's rally, string quartet, Rob on camera, Cambodian dancers, Hollywood Bowl, wrestling match, Maude's audition (*Micki + Maude*), stripper, movie within movie (*A Fine Mess*), Kate Fairchild plays sax, band at Harvey's sixtieth(*That's Life!*), Stanley Jordan plays "Treasures," Billy Vera and the Beaters, Mambo Band (*Blind Date*), scenes for the camera, band at train station, Mariachi, Tom's dance number, Alfie's vaudeville (*Sunset*), Zach Hutton sings and plays "My Romance," "The Most Beautiful Girl in the World," "Have You Met Miss Jones?"(*Skin Deep*), Jacques performs *The Barber of Seville*, belly dancer at Omar's (*Son of the Pink Panther*)

PIANOS

"Blake Edwards has always been a kind of hip guy—he liked jazz, he always played it, and loved it."—Henry Mancini

Orchestra pit, Jerry and Marty's apartment, Jenson's office, Italian restaurant (*Bring Your Smile Along*), Happy Club (*He Laughed Last*), Mitch's, Mr. Dover's (*This Happy Feeling*), Helene Gauthier's (*High Time*), at the Arc, Nancy Harris', Fusco's (*Gunn*), Clutterbuck's (*The Party*), Lili's (*Darling Lili*), saloon piano (*Wild Rovers*), piano at Fassbinder Farm, Queen of Hearts (*The Pink Panther Strikes Again*), George's, Hugh's, at Don's bar (10), Sally's, Felix's (*S.O.B.*), Toddy's, in Chez Lui, rehearsal piano in the Hotel Marceau (*Victor/Victoria*), piano in jazz combo (*The Man Who Loved Women*), antique player piano (*A Fine Mess*), Fairchild piano, at André's (*That's Life!*), In Stanley Jordan's studio (*Blind Date*), Zach Hutton's, Alex's, at Barney's (*Skin Deep*), piano in lesbian bar (*Switch*)

POOLS

"As early as This Happy Feeling, Edwards was using water to extreme degrees."
—Lehman and Luhr

Janet falls into a stream (*This Happy Feeling*), wine vat (*The Perfect Furlough*), public pool, rehabilitation pool (*Experiment in Terror*), M. Ballon's fountain, nudist colony (*A Shot in the Dark*), castle moat (*The Great Race*), piazza fountain (*What Did You Do in the War, Daddy?*), behind Gunn's building (*Gunn*), foyer pool, backyard pool, living room pool, subterranean pool (*The Party*), rain puddles outside Lili and Larrabee's hideaway (*Darling Lili*), Litton's, indoor at Gstaad, pond in

Japanese restaurant (*The Return of the Pink Panther*), Seine, castle moat (*The Pink Panther Strikes Again*), George Webber's swimming pool (10), Sally's (*S.O.B.*), Dreyfus' pool, Litton's pool, Langois' pool (*Trail of the Pink Panther*), outside Sûreté, Chandra's mudbath, at the Hotel du Cap (*Curse of the Pink Panther*), at Spence's apartment complex (*A Fine Mess*), Fairchild's pool (*That's Life!*), Bedford pool, pool at Elm and Hill (*Blind Date*), Alfie's pool, Victoria's pool (*Sunset*), Zach Hutton's swimming pool (*Skin Deep*), Margo's jacuzzi, Sheila's jacuzzi, pond in Central Park (*Switch*), at the gym, desert, Omar's (*Son of the Pink Panther*)

SERVANTS

"A pie in the face is an outrage to pumped-up dignity."—Mack Sennett

Mrs. Early (*This Happy Feeling*), Mister Cory, Mr. Earnshaw, William (*Mister Cory*), assistant hotel manager (*The Perfect Furlough*), Ramon, the chef (*Operation Petticoat*), Saloud (*The Pink Panther*), Cato, (*Panther pictures*), Maurice (*A Shot in the Dark*), Hezekiah, Max (*The Great Race*), Levinson, Harry et al; (*The Party*), Bedford and Emma (*Darling Lili*), William (*The Carey Treatment*), Charles Litton's (*The Return of the Pink Panther*), Jarvis, Mrs. Leverlilly and the rest of the Fassbinders' staff (*The Pink Panther Strikes Again*), Guy Algo, Prof. Balls' assistant (*Revenge of the Pink Panther*), Covington (10), Felix's houseman, Sally's chef, Gary Murdock (*S.O.B.*), the ubiquitous Graham Stark and others (*Victor/Victoria*), Arthur (*Trail of the Pink Panther*), Hugo the Houseman (*Curse of the Pink Panther*), director's houseman, Covington (*A Fine Mess*), Cory (*That's Life!*), Various waiters, Jordan (*Blind Date*), Arthur, George, Alperin butler, Victoria's Australian houseman (*Sunset*), Margo's maid Mae (*Switch*)

THERAPISTS AND PHYSICIANS

"The source of his comedy is invariably pain or humiliation."—Neil Sinyard

Big Dan's doctor (*He Laughed Last*), Dr. McCafferty (*This Happy Feeling*), Lt. Vicki Loren (*The Perfect Furlough*), French doctor (*Operation Petticoat*), Inspector Dreyfus' analysts (*A Shot in the Dark, The Return of the Pink Panther, The Pink Panther Strikes Again*), Dr. Peter Carey, Nurse Angela Holder, Dr. David Tao, Dr. Joshua Randall, Sanderson the Pathologist (*The Carey Treatment*), Dr. Claude Duval (*The Pink Panther Strikes Again*), Dr. Paul Laprone (*Revenge of the Pink Panther*), Dr. Croce, Dr. Miles, his nurse (10), Dr. Alfassa, Dr. Feingarten (*S.O.B.*), Dr. Longet (*Trail of the Pink Panther*), ENT doctor, Hotel doctor (*Curse of the Pink Panther*), Marianna, Simon Abrams, hospital doctor (*The Man Who Loved Women*), Dr. Eugene Glztszki, Dr. Elliot Fibel, Nurse Mary Verbeck, Dr. Kondoleon (*Micki + Maude*), Dr. Henry Garfury (*A Fine Mess*), Dr. Keith Romanis, Dr. Gerald Spelner, histotechnologists, anesthesiologists, (*That's Life!*), Dr. Westford (*Skin Deep*), labor and delivery (*Switch*), Italian doctors (*Son of the Pink Panther*)

NOTES

MATTERS OF INTRODUCTION (pp. 2–17)

1. James Agee, "Comedy's Greatest Era," in *Agee on Film*, vol. 1 (New York: Grosset & Dunlap, 1967), 2–3.

2. Ernest Becker, *Denial of Death* (New York: Simon and Schuster, 1997), 31.

3. Jeff Silverman, "Verbal '10's,'" *Los Angeles Herald Examiner*, October 26, 1982.

4. Kevin McKelvey, "Blake Edwards: Making It Whether They Like It or Not," *Hollywood Reporter*, November 24, 1986.

5. Janet Maslin, "Blake Edwards: Laughs amid the Brickbats," *New York Times*, March 5, 1987.

6. Pauline Kael, *5001 Nights at the Movies* (New York: Holt, Rinehart and Winston, 1982), 488.

7. David Thomson,*The New Biographical Dictionary of Film* (New York: Knopf, 2004), 272–73.

8. George Morris, in "Lost in Gloss or Cineaste Maudit: The Strange Case of Blake Edwards," *Monthly Film Bulletin* 51 (1984): 224.

9. Andrew Sarris, *The American Cinema: Directors and Directions 1929–1968* (New York: Dutton, 1968), 91–93.

10. David Zeitlin interview, pp.7–8, Special Collections, AMPAS Margaret Herrick Library, Los Angeles.

11. Mack Sennett,*The King of Comedy* (San Francisco: Mercury House, 1990), 137.

12. Ibid., 90.

13. Jean-François Hauduroy, "Sophisticated Naturalism: Interview with Blake Edwards," *Cahiers du Cinéma in English* 3 (1966): 24.

14. Kirk Honeycut, "His Pain, His Gain," *Los Angeles Times*, May 5, 1991.

15. Steve Garabino, "The Silver Panther Strikes Again," *New York Times* Magazine, August 8, 2001.

PROLOGUE (pp. 21–24)

1. Stuart Byron, "Confessions of a Cult Figure," *Village Voice*, May 8, 1971, 56.

2. Henry Mancini with Gene Lees, *Did They Mention the Music?* (New York: Cooper Square Press, 2001), 85.

3. Patrick McGilligan, "Blake Edwards: Jumping Around," in *Backstory 4* (Berkeley: University of California Press, 2006), 89.

4. Jean-François Hauduroy, "Sophisticated Naturalism," 22.

5. Anthony Cook, "Survival Is the Best Revenge," *Gentlemen's Quarterly*, April 1989, 323.

1. BLAKE BEGINS (pp. 29–41)

1. The Preston Sturges Award Writers Symposium, Writers Guild Theater, October 23, 1993, audiotape at WGA Shavelson-Webb Library, Los Angeles.

2. Anthony Cook, "Survival Is the Best Revenge," *GQ*, April 1989, 323.

3. *He Laughed Last* film review, *Variety*, July 20, 1956.

4. *He Laughed Last* film review, *Hollywood Reporter*, July 20, 1956.

5. Dave Kehr, "Blake Edwards" in *The International Dictionary of Films and Filmmakers* (St. James Press, 2001), 292–94.

6. Myron Meisel, "Blake Edwards (1922)," in *American Directors*, vol. 2, ed. Jean-Pierre Coursdon and Pierre Sauvage (New York: McGraw-Hill, 1983), 117.

7. *Mister Cory* review, *Weekly Variety*, January 16, 1957.

8. "Curtis' 'Mister Cory' Crashes High Society," Philip K. Scheuer, *Los Angeles Times*, March 14, 1957.

9. David Zeitlin Interview, Special Collections, AMPAS Library, 16.

10. Andrew Sarris, *The American Cinema: Directors and Directions 1929–1968*, 92.

11. Peter Lehman and William Luhr, "Too Much to Do, Not Enough Time to Do It," *Wide Angle* 3, no. 3 (1979): 55.

12. Stuart Byron, "Blake Edwards" in *The National Society of Film Critics on Movie Comedy*, ed. Stuart Byron and Elisabeth Weis (New York: Viking Press, 1977), 94.

13. Philip K. Scheuer, "Debbie in Pleasant Comedy," *Los Angeles Times*, June 19, 1958.

14. Jack Moffitt, "Hunter-Edwards Pic Sheer Farcical Joy," *Hollywood Reporter*, March 18, 1958.

15. *The Happy Feeling* film review, *Variety*, March 18, 1958.

16. Myron Meisel, "Blake Edwards (1922)," 118.

17. Jean-François Hauduroy, "Sophisticated Naturalism," 23.

18. *The Perfect Furlough* film review, *Variety*, October 8, 1958.

19. "New Pictures," *Time*, February 9, 1959.

20. Jean-Luc Godard, *Godard on Godard: Critical Writings by Jean-Luc Godard*, ed. Tom Milne (Cambridge, MA: Da Capo Press: 1986), 149.

2. BLAKE BUILDS

Operation Petticoat (pp. 45–49)

1. Nancy Nelson, *Evenings with Cary Grant* (New York: William Morrow and Co., 1991), 229.

2. Patrick McGilligan, *Backstory 4*, 96.

3. Neil Rau, "Pig Boat Built to Fit Joan," *Los Angeles Herald-Examiner*, April 12, 1959.

4. *Operation Petticoat* Production Code Files, Special Collections, AMPAS Margaret Herrick Library.

High Time (p. 54)

5. Harry Brand, "Vital Statistics on *High Time*," Twentieth Century Fox Publicity, AMPAS Margaret Herrick Library.

6. James Powers, "Brackett, Edwards Turn Out B.O. Bet," *Hollywood Reporter*, September 19, 1960.

7. Philip K. Scheuer, "Bing Collegian—and 'High Time'!" *Los Angeles Times*, September 22, 1960.

Breakfast at Tiffany's (pp. 55–61)

8. Richard Zoerink, "Truman Capote Talks about His Crowd," *Playgirl*, September 1975, 50–51, 54, 80–81,128.

9. Truman Capote, *Breakfast at Tiffany's* (New York: Random House, 1958).

10. Jean-Francois Hauduroy, "Sophisticated Naturalism," 24.

11. Pauline Kael, *5001 Nights at the Movies*, 75.

12. Steve Garabino,"The Silver Panther Strikes Again," 78.

13. Henry Mancini with Gene Lees, *Did They Mention the Music?*, 98.

14. A. H. Weiler, *New York Times*, October 6, 1961.

Experiment in Terror (pp. 62–67)

15. *Variety*, January 4, 1961.

16. Peter Stamelman, "Blake Edwards Interview—In the Lair of the Pink Panther," *Milimeter* 5, no. 1 (January 1977): 20.

17. Jean-Francois Hauduroy, "Sophisticated Naturalism," 24.

18. Erskine Johnson, "Ross Martin as Mr. Blake Is Heaving-Breathing, Sinister," *Los Angeles Mirror*, August 29, 1961.

19. *Show*, May 1962.

Days of Wine and Roses (pp. 69–75)

20. *Days of Wine and Roses*, DVD commentary (Warner Brothers, 2004).

21. Ibid.

22. Richard Lemon, "Go Find Something Wrong with Him!," *Saturday Evening Post*, January 16, 1965, 73.

23. Don Widener, *Lemmon* (New York: Macmillan, 1975), 191.

24. *Days of Wine and Roses*, DVD commentary.

25. Brendan Gill, "Drinking and Cheating," *New Yorker*, January 26, 1963, 122.

26. James Powers, *Hollywood Reporter*, November 29, 1962.

27. Chris Lemmon, *A Twist of Lemmon: A Tribute to My Father* (Chapel Hill, NC: Algonquin Books of Chapel Hill, 2006), 179.

28. Henry Mancini with Gene Lees, *Did They Mention the Music?*, 111.

29. Gene Lees, *Portrait of Johnny: The Life of John Herndon Mercer* (Milwaukee: Hal Leonard Corporation, 2006), 281.

30. Ibid, 280.

3. BLAKE BLOSSOMS

The Pink Panther (pp. 79–87)

1. Jean-François Hauduroy, "Sophisticated Naturalism," 24.

2. Walter Mirisch, *I Thought We Were Making Movies, Not History* (Madison: University of Wisconsin Press, 2008), 144.

3. Interview with author, September 1, 2006.

4. Marty Jurow, *Marty Jurow Seein' Stars: A Show-biz Odyssey* (Dallas: Southern Methodist University Press, 2001), 104.

5. *Los Angeles Herald Examiner*, November 6, 1962.

6. Marty Jurow, *Marty Jurow Seein' Stars*, 104.

7. Director's commentary, *The Pink Panther* DVD, MGM, 2005.

8. David Zeitlin Papers, AMPAS Margaret Herrick Library.

9. Jean-Francois Hauduroy "Sophisticated Naturalism," 24.

10. Michael Starr, *Peter Sellers: A Film History* (Jefferson, NC: McFarland, 1991), 230.

11. Ibid.

A Shot in the Dark (pp. 88–97)

12. Henry Mancini with Gene Lees, *Did They Mention the Music?*, 141.

13. "Tailor Shot in the Dark for Sellers," *Variety*, November 20, 1963.

14. Peter Stamelman, "In the Lair of the Pink Panther," 72.

15. Interview with author, September 1, 2006.

16. Richard Van DerBeets, *George Sanders: An Exhausted Life* (Lanham, Maryland: Madison Books, 1990), 134.

17. *Playboy*, December 1982, 97.

18. Ed Sikov, *Mr. Strangelove: A Biography of Peter Sellers* (New York: Hyperion Books, 2002), 211.

19. Interview with author, September 1, 2006.

20. Director's commentary, *The Pink Panther* DVD (MGM, 2004).

21. Stephen Watts, "No Shot in the Dark," *New York Times*, January 19, 1964.

22. "Strange World," *Rolling Stone*, April 17, 1980, 46.

23. "Unafraid of 007 Mirisch Plotting Clouseau Series," *Variety*, January 20, 1965.

24. Stephen Watts, "No Shot in the Dark."

25. Jean-François Hauduroy, "Sophisticated Naturalism," 26.

The Great Race (pp. 98–107)

26. David Zeitlin Interview, "The $12,000,000 race," AMPAS Margaret Herrick Library.

27. Suzanne Finstad, *Natasha: The Biography of Natalie Wood* (New York: Harmony Books, 2001), 254.

28. Lana Wood, *Natalie: A Memoir by Her Sister Lana Wood* (New York: G. P. Putnam and Sons, 1984), 85.

29. Interview with author, August 28, 2006.

30. Marty Weiser Files, inter-office memo, Special Collections, AMPAS Margaret Herrick Library.

31. Warner Brothers press release for *The Great Race*, March 4, 1965.

32. Mack Sennett, *The King of Comedy*, 139.

33. David Zeitlin interview, "The $12,000,000 Race."

34. Mack Sennett, *The King of Comedy*, 139.

35. Jeanine Basinger, *Silent Stars* (New York: Knopf, 1999), 65.

What Did You Do in the War, Daddy? (pp. 109–118)

36. Stuart Byron, "Blake Edwards."

37. John Wakeman, ed., *World Film Directors*, vol. 2 (New York: HW Wilson Co., 1988).

38. Myron Meisel, "Blake Edwards (1922)," p. 124.

39. Dave Kehr, "New DVDs: An Antiwar Farce and a Vintage Paramount Collection," *New York Times*, June 3, 2008.

40. Andrew Sarris, "The Bitter Essence of Blake Edwards," *Village Voice*, May 5, 1987.

41. Peter Stamelman, "In the Lair of the Pink Panther," 72.

42. Army Archerd, "Just for Variety," *Variety*, September 13, 1965.

43. Ibid.

44. Myron Meisel, "Blake Edwards (1922)," 125.

45. Jeanine Basinger, *The World War II Combat Film* (Middletown, CT: Wesleyan University Press, 2003), 232.

46. Myron Meisel, "Blake Edwards (1922)," 120.

47. Jeanine Basinger, *Silent Stars*, 233.

48. Raffaele Caputo, "Topping the Topper: Blake Edwards Interview," *Cinema Papers* no. 85 (November 1991): 25.

49. *What Did You Do in the War, Daddy?* film review, *Variety*, June 28, 1966.

50. Brendan Gill, *New Yorker*, October 10, 1966.

51. " 'What Did You Do in the War, Daddy?' Hilarious Comedy, Strong B.O. Entry," *Hollywood Reporter*, June 29, 1966.

52. Walter Mirisch, *I Thought We Were Making Movies, Not History*, 239.

Gunn (pp. 121–128)

53. Henry Mancini with Gene Lees, *Did They Mention the Music?*, 87.

54. "Edwards' Trio," A. H. Weiler, *New York Times*, April 17, 1966.

55. "Blake Edwards to Make 4 Pix for Paramount," *Variety*, March 24, 1966.

56. Anthony Cook, "Survival Is the Best Revenge," 323.

57. Peter Lehman and William Luhr, *Blake Edwards* (Athens: Ohio University Press: 1981), 122.

58. Charles Champlin, " 'Gunn' Presented in Film Version," *Los Angeles Times*, August 30, 1967.

59. John Mahoney, " 'Gunn' Should Blast Salvo at Box Office," *Hollywood Reporter*, June 9, 1967.

60. Pauline Kael, "Movies—Consumer Guidance," *New Republic*, July 15, 1967.

The Party (pp. 129–142)

61. Michael Starr, *Peter Sellers*, 233.

62. Peter Lehman and William Luhr, *Blake Edwards*, 163.

63. R.S.V.P. draft of April 12, 1967, Script Database, AMPAS Margaret Herrick Library, Los Angeles.

64. Ed Sikov, *Mr. Strangelove: A Biography of Peter Sellers* (New York: Hyperion Books, 2003), 268.

65. Roger Lewis, *The Life and Death of Peter Sellers* (New York: Applause Books, 2000), 266.

66. *The Party* film review, *Variety*, March 19, 1968.

4. BLAKE BURNS

Darling Lili (pp. 146–157)

1. Abe Greenberg, "Julie Andrews Signs with Blake Edwards and Paramount," *Citizen News*, March 9, 1967.

2. "Julie Andrews to Star as 'Darling Lil' for Par," *Film Daily*, March 10, 1967.

3. *Darling Lili* Publicity Files, Los Angeles.

4. Tom Gray, "On the Set of Darling Lili," *Motion Picture Herald*, March 20, 1968.

5. Hank Grant, "Rambling Reporter," *Hollywood Reporter*, July 8, 1969.

6. Bill Ornstein, "Lili $3–4 Mil Over Budget; Foreign Locales Be-Witched," *Hollywood Reporter*, October 15, 1968.

7. "Sec Over-Slick Rap; Bluhdorn to Fight," *Variety*, November 28, 1979.

8. Robert Evans, *The Kid Stays in the Picture* (New York: Hyperion Books, 1994), 167–68.

9. Peter Lehman and William Luhr, *Blake Edwards*, 222.

10. Stuart Byron, "Darling Lili," *On Film* 1, 34.

11. James Powers, "Para's Darling Lili WWI Spy Romance with Music," *Hollywood Reporter*, June 23, 1970.

12. *Darling Lili* film review, *Variety*, June 23, 1970.

13. Arthur Knight, "How Darling Was My Lili," *Saturday Review*, July 18, 1970.

14. Charles Champlin, "Darling Lili Has World War I Setting," *Los Angeles Times*, June 24, 1970.

15. Mike Prokosch, "UnHollywooden Musical," *Boston After Dark*, July 10, 1970.

16. Peter Stamelman, "In the Lair of the Pink Panther," 73.

Wild Rovers / The Carey Treatment (pp. 159–167)

17. Peter Stamelman, "In the Lair of the Pink Panther," 74.

18. Herb A. Lightman, "Wild Rovers: Case History of a Film," *American Cinematographer* 52, no. 7 (July 1971).

19. Ibid.

20. Ibid.

21. "The Cobra Strikes Back," *Newsweek*, April 2, 1973.

22. Jodi Lawrence, "Jungle Jim and the MGM Acid Test, An Exclusive Interview with Jim Aubrey," *Today's Filmmaker*, February 1972.

23. Paul Gardner, "Directors Protest Studio Film Cuts," *New York Times*, April 19, 1972.

24. Herb Lightman, *American Cinematographer*.

25. Peter Stamelman, "In the Lair of the Pink Panther," 74.

26. *Wild Rovers* film review, *Variety*, January 1, 1971.

27. Peter Stamelman, "In the Lair of the Pink Panther," 74.

28. "Uprising at MGM," *Time*, December 27, 1971.

29. *Filmfacts* 15 (1972), 8.

30. *Variety*, March 27, 1972.

31. Richard Cuskelly, " 'The Carey Treatment': A Who-Dun-It Mystery," *Los Angeles Herald-Examiner*, April 7, 1972.

32. Julian Fox, *The Carey Treatment* review, *Films and Filming*, July 1972.

33. Richard Cuskelly, "Blake and Julie: Hollywood Exiles," *Los Angeles Herald-Examiner*, January 5, 1975.

34. "The Lion and the Cobra," *Time Magazine*, November 12, 1973.

The Tamarind Seed (pp. 168–171)

35. *Playboy* Interview: Julie Andrews and Blake Edwards, December 1982, 90.

36. Ibid.

37. Judith Crist, "New Voyagers," *New York*, July 15, 1974.

38. Richard Schickel, *Time*, August 5, 1974.

39. Frank Rich, *New Times*, August 23, 1974.

5. PANTHER PICTURES (Blake Banks)

Sellers Lives (pp. 175–183)

1. Michael Starr, *Peter Sellers*, 236.

2. Jean-François Hauduroy, "Sophisticated Naturalism," 24.

3. "*Panther* Returning but It's Never Been Away (Via Tie-Ups)," *Variety*, November 26, 1974.

4. *New Yorker*, June 2, 1975, 90–92.

5. Michael Starr, *Peter Sellers*, 235.

6. Bart Mills, "Pink Panther Still in the Pink," *Los Angeles Times*, July 11, 1976, S1.

7. Michael Starr, *Peter Sellers*, 237.

8. Ed Sikov, *Mr. Strangelove*, 344.

9. Michael Starr, *Peter Sellers*, 237.

10. Roderick Mann, "Blake Bleak in a Sellers Market," *Los Angeles Times*, March 9, 1978.

11. Interview in *American Cinematographer*, July 1978, 657.

Sellers Lives On (pp. 186–198)

12. Michael Starr, *Peter Sellers*, 243–44.

13. Peter Lehman and William Luhr, *Returning to the Scene: Blake Edwards Volume 2* (Athens: Ohio University Press, 1989), 166.

14. Ed Sikov, *Mr. Strangelove*, 383.

15. Michael Starr, *Peter Sellers*, 242.

16. Ibid.

17. Ibid.

18. Kevin Thomas, "A Melancholy, Recycled 'Pink Panther,' " *Los Angeles Times*, December 20, 1982.

19. Vincent Canby, "Recollections on 'Pink Panther Trail,' " *New York Times*, December 17, 2006.

20. "Sellers' Widow Sues MGM/UA, Edwards," *Variety*, February 27, 1985.

21. Nancy Mills, "No Pink Slip for Sellers in 'Panther,' " *Los Angeles Times*, April 25, 1982.

22. "Ted Wass: New Kid on the Block. Curse of the Pink Panther," *Curse of the Pink Panther* MGM press release, 1983.

23. Janet Maslin, "The Curse of the Pink Panther," *New York Times*, August 13, 1983.

24. Linda Gross, " 'Pink Panther' No Curse for Ted Wass," *Los Angeles Times*, August 13, 1983.

25. Arthur Knight, *Curse of the Pink Panther* film review, *Hollywood Reporter*, August 15, 1983.

26. "Edwards Files $180-Mil Suit vs. MGM-UA Over 'Panther' Campaign," *Variety*, October 5, 1983.

27. Ivor Davies and Sally Ogle Davis, "Hollywood's New Star Wars and the Missing Millions," London *Times*, October 24, 1984.

28. Dale Pollock, "The Pink Panther v. Leo the Lion," *Los Angeles Times*, August 5, 1984.

29. Emmanuel Levy, *Son of the Pink Panther* film review, *Variety*, September 6, 1993.

30. Peter Rainer, "A Bumbling, Fumbling 'Son of the Pink Panther,' " *Los Angeles Times*, August 28, 1993.

6. BLAKE BOOMS

10 (pp. 202–222)

1. Peter Lehman and William Luhr, " 'Too Much to Do, Not Enough Time to Do It,' " 52.

2. 10 Production files, Orion Pictures.

3. *Playboy* interview, 1982, 105.

4. Gregg Kilday, "Segal Withdraws from '10'," *Los Angeles Times*, October 2, 1978.

5. Dan Yakir, "Dudley Moore Gets Serious: An Interview with Dudley Moore." *Film Comment* 15, no. 6 (Nov–Dec 1979): 52–55.

6. "Julie Andrews and Blake Edwards: A Private Conversation," *Hollywood Reporter* 49th Anniversary Issue, 1979, 98–100.

7. Peter Lehman and William Luhr, " 'Too Much to Do, Not Enough Time to Do It,' " 52.

8. Ibid.

9. *Playboy* interview, 1982, 85–86.

10. 10 Publicity Files, Orion Pictures.

11. Kodak advertisement, "Edwards: The More Real the Picture, the More Believable the Action," *Hollywood Reporter*, February 28, 1979.

12. Andrew Sarris, "Films in Focus," *Village Voice*, October 15, 1979.

13. Jerry Roberts, "Pure Blake," *Hollywood Reporter*, October 22, 1993.

14. Peter Lehman and William Luhr, " 'Too Much to Do, Not Enough Time to Do It,' " 53.

S.O.B. (pp. 224–240)

15. Myron Meisel, "S.O.B.: Do They Mean the Movie or Blake Edwards?" *Rolling Stone* 349 (1981): 22.

16. "Orion Drops 'Ferret' and 'S.O.B.'; Blake Edwards Sees Rough Deal," *Weekly Variety*, July 11, 1979.

17. Harland Kennedy, "Blake Edwards: Life after 10," *American Film* 6, no. 9 (July–August 1981): 26.

18. Myron Meisel, "S.O.B.," 21.

19. Jack Ellis, *A History of Film* (Englewood Cliffs, NJ: Prentice-Hall, 1979), 414.

20. Myron Meisel, "S.O.B.," 21.

21. Ibid, 22.

22. Aljean Harmetz, "Blake Edwards in Tiff over S.O.B.,' " *New York Times*, June 25, 1981.

23. Army Archerd, "Just for Variety," *Variety*, July 1, 1981.

24. Vincent Canby, "Why 'S.O.B.' Deserves to Be S.R.O," *New York Times*, July 12, 1981.

Victor/Victoria (pp. 245–253)

25. Harland Kennedy, "Blake Edwards: Life after 10," 27.

26. Blake Edwards commentary *Victor/Victoria* DVD (Turner Home Entertainment, 2002).

27. Harland Kennedy, "Blake Edwards: Life after 10," 28.

28. Nolletti, Arthur, Jr., "Gay Trappings and Straight Truths: A Study of Blake Edwards' *Victor/Victoria*," *Film Criticism* 6, no. 3 (Spring 1982): 43.

29. Vincent Canby, "Movie: 'Victor/Victoria,' A Blake Edwards Farce," *New York Times*, March 19, 1982.

30. Stanley Kauffmann, "Stanley Kauffmann on Films: Fine Farce, Dreary Drama," *New Republic*, March 24, 1982.

31. *Victor/Victoria* film review, *Variety*, January 1, 1982.

32. Andrew Sarris, "Films in Focus: The Edwards Touch," *Village Voice*, March 23, 1982.

33. Vito Russo, *The Celluloid Closet* (New York: Harper and Row, 1987), 280–82.

34. Ed Sikov, "Victor/Victoria," *Film Quarterly* 36, no. 1 (Fall 1982), 49.

7. BLAKE BREAKS

The Man Who Loved Women | Micki + Maude | A Fine Mess (pp. 257–263)

1. Dick Selzer, *The Star Treatment* (Indianapolis/New York: Bobbs-Merrill Co., 1977), 147–57.

2. Patrick McGilligan, *Clint: The Life and Legend* (New York: St. Martin's Press, 1999), 368.

3. Richard Schickel, *Clint Eastwood: A Biography* (New York: Knopf, 1996), 396.

4. Burt Reynolds, *My Life* (New York: Hyperion Books, 1994), 266.

5. Anthony Cook, "Survival Is the Best Revenge," 325.

6. Pauline Kael, "Lovers and Fools," *New Yorker*, January 28, 1985.

7. Interview with author, November 27, 2006.

8. *Micki + Maude* film review, *Variety*, December 5, 1984.

9. Barbara Paskin, *Dudley Moore: The Authorized Biography* (London: Sidgwick and Jackson, 1997), 276.

10. *A Fine Mess* film review, *Variety*, July 9, 1986.

11. Andrew Sarris, film review of *A Fine Mess*, *Village Voice*, August 26, 1986.

That's Life! (pp. 264–269)

12. Leslie Y. Rabkin, *The Celluloid Couch* (Lanham, MD: Scarecrow Press, 1998), 549.

13. David Robb, "Union Woes Mount for Edwards," *Variety*, October 22, 1985.

14. *Thats Life!* press release, Columbia Pictures, 1986, p. 2.

15. Ibid, 3.

16. Janet Maslin, "*That's Life!* Has Fun with Mortality," *New York Times*, September 28, 1986.

Blind Date (pp. 270–276)

17. David T. Friendly, "Bum Date," *Los Angeles Times*, September 14, 1986.

18. Interview with author, December 4, 2006.

19. Anthony Cook, "Survival is the Best Revenge," 289.

20. "In Brief," *New Yorker*, April 20, 1987.

21. Janet Maslin, " 'Blind Date,' A Comedy by Blake Edwards," *New York Times*, March 27, 1987.

Sunset (pp. 281–283)

22. Paul Schrader, "Notes on Film Noir," *Film Comment*, Spring 1972.

23. Ron Magid, "Sunset—1920's Movieland Myth," *American Cinematographer*, January 1988.

24. Jeanine Basinger, *Silent Stars*, 190–91.

25. Ibid., p. 179.

26. Vincent Canby, "Tom Mix, in a Talkie in a Talkie," *New York Times*, April 29, 1988.

27. Michael Wilmington, " 'Sunset's' Glow Is Pretty Faint," *Los Angeles Times*, April 29, 1988.

28. Army Archerd, "Just for Variety," *Variety*, September 25, 1986.

29. Peter Lehman and William Luhr, *Returning to the Scene: Blake Edwards Volume 2*, 238.

8. BLAKE BOWS
Skin Deep (pp. 287–297)

1. Charles Champlin, "Blake Edwards is Up to His Movie Maverick Tricks Again," *Los Angeles Times*, July 26, 1988.

2. Andrew Sarris, "The Bitter Essence of Blake Edwards," *Village Voice*, May 5, 1987.

3. Peter Lehman and William Luhr, " 'Too Much to Do, Not Enough Time To Do It,' " 52.

4. Patrick McGilligan, *Backstory* 4, 94–95.

5. *Skin Deep* press release, Twentieth Century Fox, 1989.

6. Vincent Canby, "A Writer with a Block and a Bottle," *New York Times*, March 3, 1989.

7. Lawrence van Gelder, "At the Movies," *New York Times*, May 6, 1988.

8. *Skin Deep* press release, Twentieth Century Fox, 1989.

Switch (pp. 299–306)

9. Bruce Feld, "Master Director Blake Edwards' Battle of *Switch*-ed Sexes," *Drama-Logue*, April 18–24, 1991.

10. Ibid.

11. Ibid.

12. Samir Hachem, "Case Study: *Switch*," *Hollywood Reporter* Independent Producers Special Report, August 1990.

13. Samir Hachem, "Switcheroo," *Village Voice*, July 24, 1990.

14. Ernest Becker, *Denial of Death* (New York: Simon and Schuster, 1997), 31.

15. Ibid, p.119.

16. Jeanine Basinger, *Silent Stars*, 78–79.

17. Molly Haskell, *From Reverence to Rape: The Treatment of Women in the Movies* (Chicago: University of Chicago Press, 1987), 61–62.

18. David Denby, *New York Magazine*, May 20, 1991.

19. Film review, *Variety*, April 8, 1991.

20. Michael Wilmington, "Blake Edwards' 'Switch' Takes Comedy to the Edge," *Los Angeles Times*, May 10, 1991.

21. Patrick McGilligan, *Backstory* 4, 93.

EPILOGUE (pp. 308–310)

1. Preston Sturges Award ceremony, Directors' Guild of America, Los Angeles, October 24, 1993. Video recording at WGA Shavelson-Webb Library, Los Angeles.

2. Ibid.

RECOMMENDED READING

INTERVIEWS

Caputo, Raffaele. "Topping the Topper." *Cinema Papers* 85 (1991).

Cook, Anthony. "Survival Is the Best Revenge." *Gentleman's Quarterly*, April 1989.

Hauduroy, Jean-François. "Sophisticated Naturalism: Interview with Blake Edwards."

Cahiers du Cinéma in English 3 (1966): 21–26.

Lehman, Peter and Luhr, William. " 'Too Much to Do, Not Enough Time to Do It': An Interview with Blake Edwards." *Wide Angle* 3, no. 3 (1979): 48–56.

Garnett, Tay. "Blake Edwards." In *Directing: Learn from the Masters.* (Lanham, MD: Scarecrow Press, 1996).

Lightman, Herb. "Riding Herd on a Chinese Fire Drill." *American Cinematographer*, (July 1978): 654–55.

Linderman, Lawrence. "Playboy Interview: Julie Andrews and Blake Edwards." *Playboy* (December 1982).

McGilligan, Patrick. "Blake Edwards: Jumping Around." In *Backstory 4.* Berkeley: University of California Press, 2006.

Stamelman, Peter. "Blake Edwards Interview—In the Lair of the Pink Panther." *Millimeter* 5, no. 1(January 1977): 18–75.

Starr, Michael. "Interview with Blake Edwards." In *Peter Sellers: A Film History* (Jefferson, NC: McFarland & Company, 1991).

Stelzer, Dick. "Interview with Blake Edwards." In *The Star Treatment.* Indianapolis/New York: Bobbs-Merrill Co. (1977):147–57.

Zeitlin, David. "Interview with Blake Edwards." Special Collections, Margaret Herrick Library, Los Angeles.

ARTICLES

Byron, Stuart. "*Darling Lili*." On Film 1: 30–34.

Canby, Vincent. "Blake Edwards—Peerless Farceur." *New York Times*, April 4, 1982.

Falwell, John. "The Art of Digression: Blake Edwards' *Skin Deep*." *Literature/Film Quarterly* 24, no. 2 (1996): 177–82.

Garbarino, Steve. "The Silver Panther Strikes Again," *New York Times*, Fashions of the Times Magazine, August 10, 2001.

Haller, Robert. "Peter Gunn: The Private Eye of Blake Edwards." *Film Heritage* 3, no. 4 (Summer 1968): 21–27.

Kehr, Dave. "Anatomy of a Blake Edwards Splat." *New York Times*, February 15, 2004.

Kennedy, Harland. "Blake Edwards: Life after 10." *American Film* 6, no. 9 (July–August 1981): 24–28.

Lehman, Peter and William Luhr. "Blake Edwards' Engagement of the Slapstick Tradition in *Blind Date*." *Film Criticism* 13 (1988): 20–32.

Lehman, Peter and William Luhr. "What Business Does a Critic Have Asking If Blake Edwards Is Gay?" In *Headline Hollywood: A Century of Film Scandal*, ed. Adrienne McLean (New Brunswick, NJ: Rutgers University Press, 2001).

Lightman, Herb A. "Wild Rovers: Case History of a Film." *American Cinematographer* 52, no. 7 (July 1971): 654–724.

Maslin, Janet. "Blake Edwards: Laughs amid the Brickbats." *New York Sunday Times*, May 3, 1987.

Maslin, Janet. "It's Not Just a Man's World for Blake Edwards." *New York Times*, May 5, 1991.

Meisel, Myron. "S.O.B.: Do They Mean the Movie or Blake Edwards?" *Rolling Stone* 349 (1981): 20–23.

Nolletti, Arthur, Jr. "Gay Trappings and Straight Truths: A Study of Blake Edwards' *Victor/Victoria*." *Film Criticism* 6, no. 3 (Spring 1982): 41–52.

Pollack, Dale. "The Pink Panther vs. Leo the Lion." *Los Angeles Times* Calendar. August 5, 1984.

Roberts, Jerry. "Pure Blake." *Hollywood Reporter*, October 22, 1993.

Sansweet, Stephen J. "Victor/Loser." *Wall Street Journal*, July 21, 1893.

Sarris, Andrew. "The Bitter Essence of Blake Edwards." *Village Voice*, May 5, 1987.

Sikov, Ed. "*Victor/Victoria*." *Film Quarterly* 36, no. 1 (Fall 1982): 46–50.

"Lost in Gloss or *Cineaste Maudit*: The Strange Case of Blake Edwards." *Monthly Film Bulletin* 51 (1984): 224.

BOOKS

Basinger, Jeanine. *Silent Stars*. New York: Knopf, 1999.

Lehman, Peter, and William Luhr. *Blake Edwards*. Athens: Ohio University Press, 1981.

Lehman, Peter, and William Luhr. *Returning to the Scene: Blake Edwards Volume 2*. Athens: Ohio University Press, 1989.

Mancini, Henry, with Gene Lees. *Did They Mention the Music?* New York: Cooper Square Press, 2001.

Sikov, Ed. *Mr. Strangelove: A Biography of Peter Sellers*. New York: Hyperion, 2002.

Windeler, Robert. *Julie Andrews: A Life on Stage and Screen*. New Jersey: Citadel Press, 1998.

CAREER SURVEYS

Byron, Stuart. "Blake Edwards." In *The National Society of Film Critics on Movie Comedy*, ed. Stuart Byron and Elisabeth Weis, 92–95. New York: Viking Press, 1977.

Kehr, Dave. "Blake Edwards." In *International Dictionary of Films and Filmmakers*, 5th ed. Chicago: St. James Press, 1991, 257–59.

35. *The Great Race* (1965). The splurcher splurches Natalie Wood. Jack Lemmon—already splurched—looks on from behind the camera. (Warner Bros./Photofest)

Meisel, Myron. "Blake Edwards (1922)." In *American Directors*. Vol. 2, ed. Jean-Pierre Coursodon with Pierre Sauvage, 117–32. New York: McGraw-Hill, 1983.

Morris, George. "Blake Edwards Takes 10." *Film Comment* 15, no. 6 (November–December 1979): 50–52.

Sarris, Andrew. "Blake Edwards." In *The American Cinema: Directors and Directions 1929–1968*. New York: Dutton, 1968, 91–93.

Sinyard, Neil. "Blake Edwards." *Cinema Papers* (September–October 1981): 31–35.

INDEX

Page numbers in italics refer to photographs. Titles of Blake Edwards' films as director are in boldface type.

ABOUT THE AUTHOR

Sam Wasson is currently working on a book about *Breakfast at Tiffany's*, forthcoming in 2010, and a book on filmmaker Paul Mazursky, forthcoming from Wesleyan University Press. He lives in Los Angeles.